Charting the Bumpy Road of Coparenthood:

Understanding the Challenges of Family Life

BY JAMES P. MCHALE

Washington, DC

Published by

2000 M St., NW, Suite 200, Washington, DC 20036-3307
(202) 638-1144

Toll-free orders: (800) 899-4301, *Fax:* (202) 638-0851, *Web:* http://www.zerotothree.org

The mission of the ZERO TO THREE Press is to publish authoritative research, practical resources, and new ideas for those who work with and care about infants, toddlers, and their families. Books are selected for publication by an independent Editorial Board.
The views contained in this book are those of the authors and do not necessarily reflect those of ZERO TO THREE: National Center for Infants, Toddlers and Families, Inc.

Cover design: K Art and Design
Text design and composition: Black Dot

Library of Congress Cataloging-in-Publication Data

McHale, James P.
Charting the bumpy road of coparenthood : understanding the challenges of family life / by James P. McHale.
p. cm.
ISBN 978-1-934019-11-5
1. Parenting—Research. I. Title.
HQ755.8.M446 2007
306.874—dc22

2007013088

10 9 8 7 6 5 4 3 2 1
ISBN 978-1-934019-11-5
1-934019-11-9
Printed in the United States of America

Suggested citations:
Book citation: McHale, J. P. (2007). *Charting the bumpy road of coparenthood: Understanding the challenges of family life.* Washington, DC: ZERO TO THREE.
Chapter citation: McHale, J. P. (with Talbot, J., & Kazali, C.). Looking ahead: Imagining family life during pregnancy. In J. P. McHale, *Charting the bumpy road of coparenthood* (pp. 55–77). Washington, DC: ZERO TO THREE.

To my beloved Trang, Hailey, and Christopher
I love you with all my heart
Every day in every way
For ever and ever and ever

And to Emily
I and our field will never forget you

Table of Contents

Foreword

When expectant and new parents turn to bookstores or on-line sources, as they do in increasing numbers, they find a wide but confusing array of books offering advice. Some simply describe children's development from birth onward, as if knowledge about the average child somehow provides guidelines for raising one's own. Others, perhaps the majority, offer different theories of parenting—"scream-free parenting," "supernanny parenting," "effective parenting," "attachment parenting," "grace-based parenting"—designed sometimes for parents of the average child, but more often for parents whose children are already diagnosed with emotional disorders, or whose children who are "spirited," "different," "hyperactive," or "strong-willed." With very few exceptions, the systems proposed in these books lack systematic scientific evidence that they work. And, with very few exceptions, these books focus on what mothers ought to be doing with their child. Fathers are allotted a few mentions. The relationship between the parents is not discussed.

James McHale's new book, *Charting the Bumpy Road of Coparenthood,* allows fathers to share the stage with mothers, demonstrating not only that they are important to children but also that the alliance between the parents plays a central role in children's development and adaptation. In contrast with the current tendency by authors to hype their contributions, McHale is perhaps excessively modest in his acknowledgement that the main message of the book has already been known by clinicians—that children profited when their mothers and fathers were working together as parents, and that children struggled when the parents were not working well together. Yes, this is a long-held belief, but it is essential to show where the belief fits the facts and where it does not.

The book contains a beautifully written, accessible account of a longitudinal study, "Families Through Time," in which McHale and a number of colleagues met with expectant couples and then followed the families when the infants were 3 months, 1 year, and $2^{1}/_{2}$ years old. The focus of the study goes beyond what is now an extensive body of work on the transition to parenthood to look in depth at the transition to coparenting and the building of a productive alliance formed when partners are "communicating regularly with one another about child-related issues and decisions and supporting one another's parenting efforts [from Chapter 1]." The investigators use state-of-the-art methods to document the dynamics of life, including extensive interviews with both parents, questionnaires, and observations of the couple as they worked and played with their child.

The book does not present data-heavy accounts of statistical tests that attempt to establish correlations between variables. McHale is a sensitive and sympathetic clinician, as well as a sophisticated researcher, who builds a complex picture from information about what the parents believe, how they understand their infant and each other, and what they actually do when they are with their child. What the book reveals, in telling detail, goes far beyond the correlations among couple relationship quality, parenting quality, and children's outcomes to describe how these connections work. Reading this book, both parents and clinicians will learn more than they knew before about "micro-moments"—how, in the blink of an eye, very common disagreements and conflicts between partners can spill over into each of their relationships with their child in ways that can result in worrisome levels of anxiety and anger for the child before he or she is 3 years old. Equally important, McHale shows us a number of examples in families that don't follow the statistical "rule," that is, when the parents don't see eye to eye but nevertheless manage to build a positive parenting alliance to support their children's social and emotional competence.

In the later chapters of the book are important answers to the "so what?" questions that inevitably are raised by any study—"so what does it all mean?" McHale does an excellent job of describing how parents can take an active role in building a coparenting alliance. He doesn't make pronouncements or prescriptions, but he provides enough examples from the families in the study to help parents think differently about the priority of attending to the couple relationship while still focusing on the needs of the child. McHale also contributes to more differentiated thinking by clinicians and mental health agencies working with families in the early childrearing years. The data in this study, and in other studies that he summarizes, point to the necessity of including fathers in family services much more than we do now, and helping the parents build a strong and positive coparenting alliance. He also provides accounts of some emerging new programs that could provide guidelines for the kind of interventions he has in mind. McHale does not say this in the book, but his emphasis on the importance of fathers is not part of the social "hot button" argument that two heterosexual parents are necessary for optimal childrearing. His perspective is more consistent with the notion that if two parents, any two parents, are raising a child, the quality of the alliance between them affects the optimal development of their children.

This last point raises an issue that McHale does discuss in the concluding chapters of his book. As I write, there is a strong federal push toward creating programs to strengthen marriages, enhance couple relationships, and foster and maintain fathers' involvement, especially in low-income families. McHale provides a very useful review of what we do and do not know about these kinds of programs that serves as a useful guideline for what is likely to be a strong federal presence in the business of enhancing the future of children.

Charting the Bumpy Road of Coparenthood is an important book. It has much to teach parents about dealing with the inevitable relationship tensions that occur, even in well-functioning, advantaged families. It has important messages for mental health professionals whose concern for children's well-being too often stops at mothers' door, ignoring the father and the couple. And family researchers should look to this book for lessons in how to write up a study. The writing is extremely lucid and jargon-free. There are many quotes from the extensive interviews with parents both before and after the babies arrive. And yet, there is enough information about the design of the study, method, and results that researchers can admire the mind of a master investigator at work. In short, this is a terrific book for everyone interested in how family relationships affect the course of young children's development.

Philip A. Cowan
Professor of Psychology, Emeritus
University of California, Berkeley

Acknowledgments

This project, and prior investigations on which it was based, received funding support from National Institutes of Health grants MH54250, HD37172, HD42179, and HD050730. I am very grateful to the NIH for its ongoing support.

Work on the book was also supported by an Irving B. Harris Award of the ZERO TO THREE Press. I extend my heartfelt appreciation to the ZERO TO THREE board for their thoughtful review of the book proposal and endorsement of the clinical importance of the work.

Several chapters of this book bear the names of coauthors who contributed substantively to the phase of the work highlighted in the chapter. I have also taken pains to acknowledge throughout the text the intellectual contributions of many other students and colleagues. Here, though, I want to formally thank all those students and colleagues whose devoted efforts ensured the exceptional quality of the data the study generated. At the very start, the project was launched thanks to the seminal efforts of Jean Talbot, Christina Kazali, Allison Lauretti, Meg Parmley, and Holly DiMario. Talbot and Kazali sensitively handled every one of the early prenatal visits and laid the foundation for the work of those who followed them. Parmley and DiMario, soon joined by Amy Alberts, masterfully cultivated a rhythm for the exceptionally complex and demanding home visits at 3 months, and Lauretti, subsequently joined by Inna Khazan, single-handedly conducted all of the 12-month assessments during the project's initial months. When it came time to develop the toddler assessments, Wendy DeCourcey, Melanie McConnell, and Tamir Rotman came aboard, providing both scientific vision and clinical acumen, and this trio conducted all of the 30-month assessments during the project's earliest phases. These devoted teams of clinicians were later joined by a number of equally talented and dedicated team members, without whose expertise we could not have completed the visits with parents and children: Julia Berkman, Mary Alston Kerllenevich, Easter Dawn Vo-Jutabha, Valerie Bellas, Regina Kuersten-Hogan, Nina Olsen, Kate Fish, Oliver Hartman, Rebecca Lieberson, Eleanor Chaffe, Stephanie Giampa, Kathryn Kavanaugh, and Meaghan DiLallo.

This was a unique study in the extent to which we collaborated with researchers throughout the United States and Europe both to learn the technologies and assessment systems used in the evaluations we describe and to obtain from them many of the process data we relied upon. In particular, I want to offer special thanks to Elisabeth Fivaz-Depeursinge and Susan Dickstein not only for assisting with our evaluations of process data but also for their ground-breaking intellectual contributions to the infant–family mental health field. Without their pioneering efforts, this study could not have had the same substance and depth. I and our field owe them both a true debt of gratitude. I am also extremely grateful to June Sroufe, Ellen Moss, Alan Sroufe, Lynn Fainsilber-Katz, and Lynn Lagasse, who helped prepare our assessment team not only by providing training in technology but also by deepening their clinical appreciation for the core phenomena they were evaluating. Understanding as much as they did about the essence of the evaluations they were undertaking with parents and infants allowed our assessment team to work sensitively with the families and children to obtain exceptionally rich and ultimately very meaningful information. In this vein, I also wish to thank Philip and Carolyn Cowan, whose friendship and scholarly wisdom has been without parallel; and Kai Von Klitzing, Jay Belsky, Mary Main, Martha Cox, Linda Sagrastano, Suzanne Denham, Barry Lester, Mary Rothbart, Harrison Gough, Maureen Perry-Jenkins, France Frascarolo, and Wendy Grolnick for their generous and meaningful consultation and input at various points in the enterprise.

Once information has been gathered, of course, talented sets of eyes and ears are needed to divine the underlying and essential meaning behind that which families have shared. Besides Dickstein and Fivaz-Depeursinge, a great many perceptive collaborators contributed to these formal evaluations of our families' contributions: Talbot, Kazali, Olsen, Sandy Fulton, Karen Jacob, Naomi Gribneau, Ariz Rojas, and Maureen Below assisted with ratings and evaluations of prenatal data; Carleton, Rotman, Lieberson, Alberts, Berkman, Kavanaugh, Rheanne Koller, Ghysleane Berthonneau, Jessica

Thompson, Chris Scull, Donna Elliston, Evelyn Alvarez, Traci Landers, and Meredith Machler helped evaluate the 3-month data; McConnell, Vo-Jutabha, Kerllenevich, Fish, Igor Gershensen, Suzanne Gurland, David Shaw, Annie Matthew, Leo Waterston, Robert Babigian, Carrie Price, Christina Sauck, Rahael Kurrien, Lisa Zawistowski, Kim DesRochers, and Symphony Thomas evaluated the 12-month data; and DeCourcey, Kuersten-Hogan, DiLallo, Haskell, Julia Lacks, Krista Beiswenger, Aldjenatu Romero, Crystal Cummins, Kathleen Carr, Spiro Kotsios, Eric Nemic, Bruce Nash, Christine Gower, Dan Alongi, and Neringa Bruzgyte completed the 30-month coding projects.

To the dedicated families who stayed with us over extended periods of time, scheduling and rescheduling visits; entertaining reminder calls, letters, and e-mails; generously and good-naturedly pardoning us when equipment didn't work, air conditioning systems went on the fritz, or other goofs in our staff coordination introduced periodic snags in the process; often coming long distances, occasionally even in blizzards, to fulfill their commitments to the project; and most of all, speaking with us candidly, sharing their fears, concerns, and vulnerabilities, as well as their family's soaring high points: I cannot thank you enough. Throughout the project, I did what I could to continue assuring you that in the end, your generous contributions of time and effort would reap benefit for countless other families. I hope you find this book to deliver on some of that promise.

These acknowledgments would be altogether incomplete without deep, heartfelt thanks to my dear colleagues and friends at Clark University. In an era when so many universities struggle to maintain perspective on their central values and missions, Clark as an institution has remained unwavering in its vision. Clark partners with and serves its community and its community's families, cares for and nurtures Clark students, and genuinely values and celebrates its faculty. The fact that the important work of this project was conceived and completed at this university is no fluke; my colleagues in Clark's psychology department urged me from the very day I first showed up in 1994 to privilege the conceptual foundations of my work and to lay the necessary groundwork to fully cultivate my ideas. The encouragement and freedom to lay this careful foundation in a climate that valued and defended ideas, and supported germination of those ideas, is becoming an increasing rarity in a world where "numbers" have somehow become code for accountability. Moreover, Clark's humane values extend far beyond its university walls to the support of its neighborhood, nation, and planet. Honestly and straightforwardly "walking the walk" of community is the karma that draws faculty and students to come to Clark, and the spirit that made the decade I spent there the most complete, validating experience a university professor could ask for. I extend my gratitude both to my colleagues and friends in Clark's administrative offices—especially Jack Foley, Sharon Krefetz, John Bassett, Julie Wolfenden, Nancy Budwig, Jaan Valsiner, Jim Laird, Len Cirillo, Fred Greenaway, and David Angel—and to my valued colleagues in Clark's psychology department for having supported not only my research endeavors but *me*, as a person. I will never forget and will always be grateful for my wonderful, generative, and life-affirming years at Clark. I hope that this book, and the program of work from which it grew, provides testimony to the wisdom of valuing quality above quantity and of investing in faculty lives over the long haul.

Leaving Clark for Florida in December 2003 was unquestionably the most excruciating decision I've ever had to make. The decision to relocate has grown easier to accommodate each time I've witnessed our children Hailey and Chris cavorting with, embracing, and coming to know and love the Floridian grandparents, aunts, uncles, and cousins who otherwise would have been only a peripheral part of our family's lives had we remained in our beloved Massachusetts home. And easing the research project's transition was the support of the University of South Florida St. Petersburg's administrative team in creating a viable and parallel Family Study Center to Clark's Center to house my work, along with the dedication of many Clark colleagues who helped bridge the move from Clark's Family Study Center to USF's. In particular, I thank Tamir Rotman, who supervised management and processing of data for the "Families Through Time" study from the days when we began receiving the project's very first completed questionnaires from Worcester families many years ago, through the study's final phase at USF St. Petersburg. Rotman's systems background enabled both the creation of an effective data management system for the wealth of information contributed by families and the conceptualization of systemic analyses pursued with data gathered in the study proper. He created the final composite variables used in the study's major analyses, and also consulted generously with project staff members both in Massachusetts and Florida on their various analyses, conference reports, and publications over the many years of the study. I, my chapter coauthors, and the Families Through Time project all owe Tamir a special debt of gratitude. Besides Tamir, Wendy DeCourcey and Ollie Hartman also played a crucial role in database oversight and data entry. Both Wendy and Ollie also contributed their time and expertise after I'd moved to Florida in helping prepare Chris Scull to assume oversight of the project's day-to-day database operations at USF. Jess Thompson and Donna Elliston contributed untold hours establishing the project's filing and data tracking infrastructure at USF, and Patricia White-Butcher and Linda Kraus provided priceless support, advice, and effort in helping to navigate the project through a new university operating system. And throughout the changes, Regina Kuersten-Hogan held sway as the project's emissary at Clark right on through the study's conclusion.

Last, I want to acknowledge two other individuals without whom this book would not exist. The first is Emily Fenichel. All of us who care about children and families have been touched by the long reach of Emily and her legacy. There was never a more formidable force in shaping the face of today's infant–family mental health field. Emily was my friend and editor, and someone who believed wholeheartedly in the dynamic force of the family dynamics explored in this book. Emily and I exchanged extensive correspondence about this book for over a year, and she episodically shared loving and admiring anecdotes about the strong coparenting alliance her son and daughter-in-law were developing with their new baby. I sent Emily the final version of the final chapter of this book only 2 days before her tragic death in June 2006, and she e-mailed me back almost instantaneously, "we have reached the shore!" Emily's wit, clinical depth, encouragement, counsel, and incisive feedback played an indispensable role in focusing and strengthening the messages readers will find in every single one of this book's chapters. I suspect those who know her well will recognize many of her insights throughout this book, in which I've incorporated a great deal of what Emily viewed as important in and for families. As such, I believe that the reach of her wisdom and her impact now extends further still.

The final, most central person to whom I owe undying gratitude is my amazing partner, Trang Tran McHale. Any academic author with children and a family understands only too well that it is humanly impossible to simultaneously devote full attention both to a major book project and to one's family. There were many, many days when this project spirited my time away from Trang, Hailey, and Chris—and on those days, Trang unfailingly and calmly shouldered the many responsibilities that were mine to share. More than this, she took on nearly the full mantle of family steward—at times redirecting our son's and daughter's energies elsewhere when they began clamoring for the attention from me that they wanted and needed, at other times coaxing me away from the office and computer when she sensed that we all needed some time together. She did these things with graciousness and decency, despite the very real tests and difficulties that the recurring invisibility of her coparenting partner presented. Knowing Trang as I do, I am rather certain that her chief enthusiasm upon the release of this book will owe not to its publication, but to its symbolic marking of my full reorientation back to our family. Nonetheless, to the extent that readers find coherence in this book and its content, Trang deserves due credit. Without her selfless and unwavering support, not only would my thoughts have failed to jell, but I would not have come to appreciate as I truly now do the depth of self-sacrifice that parents everywhere display in sustaining their partners and their families.

What Is Coparenting, and Why Is It Important?

With Regina Kuersten-Hogan

"Did you ask your mommy? And what did mommy tell you?"

"Does she really have to eat every single carrot? It's just not that big of a deal."

"Daddy, did Holly show you the beautiful artwork she made at school today?"

"You've had it. I'm telling your daddy as soon as he gets home and he will be very mad."

"You can stay up a little longer just this one time, but we won't tell Mommy."

Remarks like these are made every day in countless homes around the world. They are the comments of parents evoking implicitly or explicitly the child's other parent as they make parenting judgments and interventions. These routine comments to children afford insights into a poorly understood but critically important ingredient of family health—an ingredient that researchers who study families have come to call the family's "coparenting alliance." Its critical importance is witnessed by the fact that, in families in which a strong and supportive alliance exists, both parents and children show fewer signs of stress. Marital relationships are also on more stable footing, and children experience greater success in their outside-the-family peer relationships.

But what exactly is a coparenting alliance? And is there a best way to establish one? It seems that with the infinite variety of challenges and conflicting demands that parents confront in the new millennium—being unable to rely upon extended family supports because of geographical or emotional distance, making difficult decisions about whether one or both parents will work, balancing the family income with the dollar and emotional costs of having their babies and toddlers in day care (and worrying whether their day care choices are helping or hindering their children's development), battling exhaustion in the evenings at precisely the times their children are intensifying their own bids for love and attention from them, trying to muster the energy to keep their own romantic relationship afloat—there isn't likely to be just one best way of working together as parents and establishing family patterns and routines.

The answer to the question of what makes a strong coparental alliance is both deceptively simple and remarkably complex. The simple answer is that there does appear to be a route toward positive coparenting alliances that yields good results; the key guideposts along this route are communicating regularly with one another about child-related issues and decisions and supporting one another's parenting efforts. The complexity, of course, is that whereas very few parents would question the wisdom of communicating regularly or supporting one another's efforts, doing so often proves incredibly difficult, even for the best meaning parents. Differences in opinion about how best to manage and raise children exist in every family, and parents often find themselves saying and doing things not only that go against their partners' wishes, but that they themselves recognize may not be in the child's best interests.

Why do so many well-meaning parents struggle in their efforts to create a positive and effective coparenting alliance? What distinguishes families who meet with greater success from those who have trouble finding their way? Do disagreements and frustrations during the early months after a new baby arrives set the tone for later problems, or are they short-lived and not of particular significance in the longer run? And what becomes of children who grow up in families in which there is greater divisiveness between parents, compared with those who grow up in families in which adults figure out ways to parent effectively as a team? These were the questions foremost on the minds of those of us who planned the "Families Through Time" study of the transition to new coparenthood—the study that serves as the basis for what follows in this book.

When we set out to examine these questions in the mid-1990s, we were forging relatively new terrain, because the particular issues we were concerned with had been examined only infrequently and usually indirectly in the past. However, there were a handful of new studies that had begun to directly examine early coparenting relationships in nuclear families, a more extensive knowledge base on the challenges of coparenting for divorced partners, and a wealth of knowledge about marriages, parenting, and families available from studies completed during the 1980s and early 1990s that helped set the stage for our project. Among our first challenges were (a) trying to define exactly what it was that we meant by "coparenting" and establishing some sensible ways of measuring the construct and then (b) designing a study that allowed us to chart both continuity and changes in coparenting dynamics in families across the first 2.5 years of new parenthood. So let's begin with the key question of this opening chapter: What *is* coparenting?

WHAT IS COPARENTING?

In 1974, the family therapist Salvador Minuchin published a landmark volume called *Families and Family Therapy*, in which he outlined several principles defining adaptive family functioning. Among the most important points developed by Minuchin was that families who adjust well to life's many challenges tend to be those in which there exists a supportive partnership between the adults who are responsible for guiding the socialization of the family's children. Minuchin emphasized that, in families in which there are two or more parents or parenting figures in charge of children's acculturation and development, as is the case in most nuclear, adoptive, step-, and extended family systems, it is important that a clear hierarchy be maintained wherein leadership and decision making are shouldered only by the adult members of the family's "executive subsystem." When this hierarchy breaks down, problems begin.

What kind of problems? Minuchin observed that, in families in which significant levels of conflict, animosity, and antagonism impair the collaborative abilities of the members of the executive subsystem, there can actually be a rather wide variety of problems that follow. Sometimes, one of the important adults abdicates virtually all responsibility to the coparenting partner and simply disengages from active parenting. At other times, each of the coparents remains involved in the parenting role, but works at cross-purposes with the other, failing to back up and support the other's work with the children. When this happens, even very young children can sometimes find themselves possessing far too much "power" in the family system, as the result of special privileges bestowed upon them by one of the parents. As Minuchin mused, "when a four-year-old is taller than her mother, perhaps she is sitting on the shoulders of her father" (Minuchin & Fishman, 1981, p. 148).

Although Minuchin never used the term *coparenting* in his writing, it is a concept that is the very essence of his theory of family structure. Unlike many modern family researchers who study "shared parenting" and have investigated the particulars of "who does what" in the family—the specific arrangements families work out to decide who is responsible for handling what chores and responsibilities with children—Minuchin was not especially concerned with these particulars. In some families, each parent shoulders somewhat different responsibilities, with mothers handling much of what has been called the "emotional work" in the family and fathers handling "instrumental tasks." More commonly, parents divide such responsibilities between them, although rarely on a 50/50 basis.

With respect to the distribution of labor, fathers in some families with infants and toddlers do a fair amount of diapering, clothes changing, handling of middle-of-the-night needs, and scheduling doctor's appointments. In other families, mothers handle these chores and fathers do few or none of them. As children get older, disciplining toddlers falls primarily to one parent in some families, whereas in others, discipline is shouldered more equitably. What was critical to Minuchin was not the particulars of who did what, but rather evidence that the two parents came to a mutual accord about and supported one another's handling of parenting responsibilities—in other words, evidence that they had forged a strong coparenting alliance with one another.

The use of the term *alliance* is a significant one, requiring further inspection. True allies are those who not only agree publicly upon a plan of action but who then go on to support that plan both when they are parenting together with the partner and when they are parenting alone. Reaching an agreement that it really is time to wean an 18-month-old from her bottle means nothing if one of the parents stands firm in the partner's presence in refusing to give in to the child's bottle demands, only to accede to the same demands when the coparent is absent. Parents can and do use "alone time" with their children either to fortify the child's sense that the coparents are an allied team parenting the child as one or to deconstruct the child's sense of their alliance by teaching the child that rules are arbitrary and that the child can have her way when the coparent is not present (McHale, 1997). Agreed-upon parenting plans are always open to negotiation, of course, but they are not routinely changed arbitrarily or set aside by either ally without thoughtful discussion.

This focus on support and affirmation of one another's efforts is not intended to minimize the fact that the details of how child care labor gets divided are very important in many, if not most, contemporary Western families. Indeed, as will become clear in the pages that follow, one of the major points of contention for new parents concerns child care work. In families in which one or both partners are very dissatisfied with the amount of work that has fallen to them, this discontent can creep into the overall spirit of teamwork and sense of mutual responsibility for the child's family experience. In other families, albeit a minority of them, discontent over who does what can stir negative feelings between spouses but not materially influence their sense of joint purpose and shared responsibility for co-creating a supportive and harmonious family environment. The point being made here is that it is important for readers to keep in mind throughout this volume that the definition of coparenting guiding the work of this project refers not narrowly to the division of child care labor and responsibilities but broadly to the coordination and support between adults responsible for the care and upbringing of children. It is an enterprise set upon by the coparenting partners, full of ups and downs and bumps along the way. Ultimately, however, it succeeds when the coparents are true allies and weather storms without losing sight of their mutually agreed-upon goals.

How parents attain such mutually agreed-upon goals is one of the major themes of this book. Some partners never strike such an accord. Others do in some realms but not in others. Some believe they are in agreement but later come to recognize that they were actually pursuing very different aims. Some work well as allies during the baby's infancy but lose their way as their child enters into the terrible twos. Some manage to battle through occasional disruptions and cracks in their unity, coming back together stronger than ever after periods of dissonance. There are a great many roads traveled, and no clear road map for any of them.

Major Facets of Coparenting

Research on the development of coparenting alliances in families really began to take off once researchers began clarifying exactly what it was they were trying to study. Although different research teams have sometimes spotlighted different aspects of coparenting, there is growing consensus that all coparenting alliances can be described along a few fundamental dimensions. Among these are the following: how much solidarity and support there is between the adults sharing responsibility for the family's children and their upbringing; how frequent and intense the disputatiousness and undoing of one another's efforts are between the coparenting adults; how the family parses major child care roles and divides child care labor; and the extent to which each of the different coparental adults actively engages in organizing and managing the daily lives of their children and the decisions affecting them.

Over the past 10 years, a significant amount of creative thinking has gone into research decisions that have been made about how best to gauge each of these dimensions. When clinicians and researchers try to estimate solidarity and support, it's hard to know whether we should rely on what we actually see happening between the parents as they interact together with their child or whether we should privilege what parents tell us about their coparenting relationship and dynamics. Both methods have their strong points and their flaws, of course. For example, when engaging together in parenting with observers present, family members are frequently on guard prompting them to be, as one of the parents in our study described it, "on our best behavior." Hence, a parent whom our observers noticed supporting and affirming his or her partner's decision-making processes during family interaction tasks in our lab may have failed to step in and help that same partner deal with a rambunctious child later that evening when everyone's nerves were frazzled and both parents were at wit's end.

Similar concerns can be raised about reliance on parental reports, of course. The same parent who regularly neglected to provide backup, support, or a willingness to take over from an exhausted partner to enforce mutually agreed-upon curfews or disciplinary violations may have described the partnership as problem-free when queried on one of our questionnaires or in an interview. Sometimes such glowing reports have been described as defensiveness on the part of the parent, and sometimes that is an accurate descriptor. However, other times, as our study taught us, it reflects a genuine unawareness on the part of the parent that something might be amiss in the family's coparenting alliance.

These problems noted, research efforts to date have generally supported the validity of both observational and self-report tools in assessing coparental functioning. Despite the demand characteristics that come with being observed either by a researcher's camera or through a family therapist's one-way mirror, family members do in fact disagree with and sometimes undermine one another, withhold support at times when the partner could use a hand, draw back and disengage from active interactions with the child, and fail to express warmth toward the child and/or toward one another. Research suggests that the expression of these different family dynamics is often linked to parents' reports of similar family processes, although the strength of the connections varies from study to study and is rarely eye-popping in magnitude. Still in all, a fair number of parents who appear to struggle in their coparenting roles while they are being observed also acknowledge experiencing coparental strain when someone asks them. Also, remarkably, many parents who say critical and disparaging things about their coparenting partner to the child in that parent's absence are willing to acknowledge this on self-reports, and self-reports of disparagement have been linked to other problems in family and child adjustment (McHale, 1997; McHale & Rasmussen, 1998).

It is important to recognize that neither the observational nor the self-report route to understanding coparenting is ever likely to be fully adequate. Unfortunately, though, the family research field has been a bit slow to recognize this. A reading of most published research reports on coparenting processes in nuclear families right up through the time of this writing in 2006 reveals that the overwhelming majority have relied principally or solely on just a single method, either self-report or observation, as a proxy for coparenting. These studies helped open the door for the major advances in theory and research evidence that we've seen over the past 10 years, and in virtually all cases the investigators who conducted the studies were careful to caution about the limits to which their findings could be generalized. Although we owe a debt of gratitude to this first generation of coparenting studies, in future studies of coparenting in families, researchers must spend enough time with families to be certain that they have approached the topic from multiple vantages and angles. It will still always be the case that for whatever reasons, both observational and self-report methods fail us for some families. However, our experience has been that, given sufficient time to ponder the issues about coparenting posed to them, families are quite forthcoming and game to reveal both their strengths and their struggles.

Let's now consider briefly each of the major coparenting constructs that have been studied by researchers over the past decade.

Solidarity

Solidarity encompasses a great many things, perhaps most notably a joint perspective shared by each of the coparenting partners that they are in fact a solid team. When conducting observational studies, researchers typically assess something they call "cooperation" between parents and are also on the lookout for indicators of warmth and connection, affirmation, and validation between the adults as they parent together. In different observational studies, warmth and cooperation have received a variety of labels including "cohesion," "harmony," and "positivity." In all cases, however, they have referred to the presence of a "one for all and all for one" attitude, buoyed by a spirit of positive regard and usually signaled in observational studies by laughter, playfulness, "knowing" glances, or humor; occasionally by a combination of all four; and sometimes, although rarely, even by affectionate touch. Studied by self-report methods, solidarity is measured by surveys that ask parents to report on the extent to which they approve of the partner's parenting and feel supported by the other parent (e.g., Abidin & Brunner, 1995) or that ask parents to indicate how frequently they themselves engage in behaviors promoting a sense of coparenting solidarity and family integrity (McHale, 1997). Few interview-based assessments of solidarity are currently in existence; later, we present evidence gathered in this study for the utility of a coparenting interview.

Antagonism

In a thoughtful conceptual paper on the effects of marital conflict on children, John Grych and Frank Fincham (1990) made the point that perhaps most destructive of all kinds of nonviolent family conflicts were disputes about the children. This idea has permeated research on coparenting far and wide. Researchers have made concerted efforts to disentangle general marital conflicts and disagreements from child-related conflicts, pursuing the notion that child-related conflicts (most pertinent to the coparenting construct) would be the ones most closely related to child adjustment and health (Bearss & Eyberg, 1998). Assessed observationally, antagonism can be broken down into a few key components: verbal sparring between the adults, competitiveness in guiding the child's attention and interests, and undermining of one another's dictates to the child. Although antagonism often runs high in clinical contacts with families, it is much more subtle in observational studies and sometimes takes the guise of "ribbing" between adults. This can create difficulties for researchers trying to infer underlying meaning, which is a good reason for observations to be augmented by self-reports of coparenting conflict. Many instruments assess such conflict directly, from an item on the O'Leary–Porter Scale (OPS; Porter & O'Leary, 1980), which has been in use for several decades, to instruments that directly inquire about child-related conflict.

Some researchers have used differences between the views of the two coparents concerning their own "Ideas About Parenting" as a proxy for coparenting antagonism, although this requires a significant inferential leap from reported belief differences to enactments of these differences in practice. Still, the notion that different beliefs translate into different practices with the children is an intriguing one—and the few studies that have used belief differences as an index of disharmony have sometimes found linkages with child behavior problems in the expected direction (Block, Block, & Morrison, 1981). Finally, although clandestine or covert conflict is often challenging to observe, it can be estimated by having parents report on the frequency with which they denigrate the child's coparent or interfere with their disciplinary efforts (McHale, 1997).

In statistical analyses, different indicators of coparenting conflict often hang together quite well in multimethod studies (McHale,

Kuersten-Hogan, Lauretti, & Rasmussen, 2000). Although studies seldom examine the issue directly, it would seem that frequency and intensity of child-related conflict from the parents' perspective would be a particularly important bit of information to have when assessing coparental antagonism, perhaps more so than observed conflict alone, although taken together the different indicators might be expected to provide the most robust index. Here too, interviews with parents in which the adults raise concerns about significant coparenting conflict might also be expected to provide particularly valuable data.

Division of Labor

Without question, the division of child care labor has received the most attention of any coparenting-related construct since the wave of "transition to new parenthood studies" of the 1980s. The consensus among most research studies is that, during the early months after babies arrive, and often for far longer than this, women report doing far more of the close-up child care labor than do men, whereas men believe that they do far more than their wives give them credit for. There is not a straightforward relationship between how much fathers do and how satisfied mothers are with fathers' participation. Some discontent exists in most families (very few parents indicate on ratings that they are "perfectly happy" with who does what); hence, what seems to be key for the coparenting partnership is whether fathers and mothers are in general agreement that the levels of work each of them are contributing sit well with them. Although it is generally the case that mothers are unhappy when fathers do less of the work than the mothers had expected before the baby arrived, there have been some intriguing reports that some women experience discontent when fathers take on more of an active role than the mothers had imagined they would (e.g., Goldberg & Perry-Jenkins, 2004; Hackel & Ruble, 1992).

Mutual Engagement

In some of Minuchin's writings about families (e.g., S. Minuchin & Nichols, 1993), he drew attention to problems that can occur in families showing "enmeshed" or "disengaged" dynamics. In enmeshed families, parents became intrusively involved with their children, often showing difficulties recognizing and responding sensitively to children's needs because of difficulties they were having managing their own emotional needs. Many looked to children for emotional support and comfort before looking to their partner and/or imbued children with inappropriate power and decision-making responsibilities (how late to stay up, when to ignore family rules, etc.). Doing so had the effect of undermining adult authority, promoting power struggles, and hindering the children's development of autonomous, mature, rule-governed behavior. In other families, family difficulties were reflected quite differently, signaled by the emotional withdrawal or disengagement of a parent. Although a withdrawing parent could have had any number of reasons for disengaging, many did so after disagreements with the other partner's handling of the child. Withdrawal typically begat criticism, prompting further withdrawal, with the cycle often culminating in the disengaged parent's not responding to child and family problems even when clearly needed. Disengagement and enmeshment can and often do coexist in some families, whereas in others, one or the other dynamic may be especially prominent.

A criticism that has sometimes been levied toward Minuchin's characterization of these problematic family dynamics is that a straightforward application of his ideas can lead to a blaming of mothers for their activities as parents. Most prominently, Deborah Leupnitz (1988) has cogently articulated from a feminist perspective how the "enmeshed mother/disengaged father" syndrome (S. Minuchin & Nichols, 1993) is problematic insofar as it pathologizes a family arrangement that is actually sanctioned by many cultures, both currently and historically. Leupnitz's analysis is a scholarly one, and her points about blaming either parent for the family's struggles are very well taken. Historical family analyses (e.g., Harrell, 1997; see also McHale et al., 2002) indicate that mothers around the world and through time have always drawn emotional support from their children. Moreover, coparenting and family difficulties are seldom, if ever, premeditated or arrived at intentionally, and family dynamics are always co-constructed by each of the family members involved, as Wille's (1995) work suggests.

Equally, however, within the sociohistorical context in which current family practice and research are embedded and studied by Western scholars, significant skew in parental engagement without some teamwork, structure, and mutual collaboration by parents often does signal imminent difficulties for parents and children. The recognition by coparenting researchers that mild to moderate withdrawal by one of the parents during family exchanges can sometimes signify early gravitation toward later emotional disengagement prompted some investigators to focus in on imbalances in parental engagement during observations of the family group. The same level of detail as outlined above for solidarity and conflict has not yet gone into developing self-report assessments of mutual engagement/disengagement by coparents, although individual questions on several instruments asking about the respondent's satisfaction with the partner's participation in family decision making or level of engagement with the children (apart from their satisfaction with the partner's participation in child care work, per se) do begin to get at the notion of teamwork and shared oversight of the coparenting enterprise.

In summary, then, coparenting alliances can be described along a number of dimensions simultaneously, and consideration of all of these dimensions is needed to develop a thorough understanding of the family and its developing coparenting dynamic. In the pages that follow, we outline how we set out to capture these different dimensions of the coparenting alliance in our study of the transition to new coparenthood.

Before concluding this introductory chapter, we provide a brief overview of a different network of research findings that captures the central importance of early coparenting in families. Indeed, some of these findings provided the main impetus for the study to be described in this book. Much of this work, which focused explicitly on coparenting and family group dynamics, was completed during the early 1990s and was published first in a volume edited by McHale and Cowan (1996). Among the major discoveries from the studies summarized in that volume, and from earlier and subsequent work on coparenting, have been that coparenting and family-level dynamics show a fair degree of stability across time, can be linked to both individual and dyadic functioning in other family subsystems, cannot be estimated reliably from information about parent–child relationship dynamics, and uniquely predict important aspects of toddler and child adjustment. The final section of this chapter summarizes some of these linkages and sets the stage for this study and the questions we set out to pursue.

The Importance of Early Coparenting: Evidence From Preliminary Studies

The very first observationally based studies of early coparenting dynamics in nuclear families were published in the mid-1990s, although there had been rumblings for several years prior that something new and distinctive in our understanding of early social environments in families was coming down the pike. Elsewhere, we have described some of the major historical impetuses for a focus on joint or shared parenting (McHale et al., 2002; McHale & Kuersten-Hogan, 2004). These included, perhaps most prominently, major changes in family life attendant to the North American Women's Movement of the 1970s and attention by mental health professionals to the skyrocketing divorce rates of the 1970s and to the needs for parents to coordinate their efforts across multiple households.

Looking further back still, from a theoretical vantage point, the implications of severe coparenting conflict and disruptions had been attended to in the family therapy literature since the 1950s, culminating in Salvador Minuchin's 1974 volume articulating most clearly the ramifications of fragmented coparental alliances. A further spark was provided in 1985, when Patricia Minuchin took developmental psychologists to task for their myopic focus on parent–child relationships. She drove home the sensible but almost always overlooked point that the full family unit, rather than any individual dyadic relationship within the family, became the child's significant reality after infancy.

These scholarly contributions, together with well-articulated papers by Weissman and Cohen (Cohen & Weissman, 1984; Weissman & Cohen, 1985), Frank, Jacobson, Hole, Justkowski, and Huych (1986), and Floyd and Zmich (1991) distinguishing marital from coparenting alliances helped provide the broad outlines for the more focused work in studying coparenting alliances that was to follow. Indeed, Weissman and Cohen's (1985) proposition that parents can make headway in strengthening their coparenting alliance as long as each parent was invested in the child, valued the other parent's involvement with the child, respected the judgments of the other parent, and desired to communicate with the other still echoes true today. A set of articles by Sarah Gable, Jay Belsky, and Keith Crnic (1992, 1995), further clarifying the value of conceptualizing coparenting as a family construct related to but also separable from other forms of marital conflict and distress, solidified the terrain upon which subsequent empirical studies began to take root.

Reports by both Belsky and his colleagues in 1996 and McHale in 1995 concurred that coparenting difficulties during infancy and toddlerhood were more frequent when there were signs of distress in the marriage, a finding that has since been replicated many times by subsequent coparenting studies. This is, in and of itself, not particularly surprising; if parents are struggling in their marital partnership, they are likely to have a more difficult time forging a strong working alliance as coparents. However, the relationship between marital distress and coparenting problems is not as straightforward as it may seem. McHale's (1995) report indicated that the kinds of coparenting problems seen in families in which the couple was distressed in their marriage differed depending on whether their baby was a boy or a girl. In families with sons, mutual parenting engagement by parents was clearly in evidence, but it was frequently marked by antagonistic and competitive exchanges. By contrast, in families with daughters, this hostile–competitive dynamic was less often in evidence; rather, coparenting problems were signified instead by greater imbalances in levels of parental engagement.

Subsequent research by Sarah Schoppe-Sullivan, Sarah Mangelsdorf, and their colleagues has provided even more intriguing evidence on the relationship between marital and coparental adjustment. On the basis of their longitudinal look at both marital and coparenting systems over time, Schoppe-Sullivan, Mangelsdorf, Frosch, and McHale (2004) found that, when the predictive capability of their measures of coparenting behavior at infant age 6 months was contrasted with the predictive capability of marital behavior at infant age 6 months in accounting for later coparenting and marital behavior when children were 3 years old, early coparenting predicted later marital behavior—but not vice versa! They also found evidence for stability of coparenting behavior over time, a theme that has also been pursued in other studies.

The first report to document short-term stability in coparenting processes was a report by Gable et al. (1995), in which they detected moderate stability in coparenting interactions over a 6-month period between infant ages 15 months and 21 months. In 1998, McHale and Rasmussen found that early signs of coparenting distress observed in the triad predicted parental reports of coparenting difficulties 3 years later. Also, in perhaps the most careful and elegant research on the stability of early family dynamics detected during infancy, Elisabeth Fivaz-Depeursinge and her colleagues (Fivaz-Depeursinge & Corboz-Warnery, 1999; Fivaz-Depeursinge, Frascarlo, & Corboz-Warnery, 1996) at the Centre d'Etude de la Famille (CEF) in Lausanne, Switzerland have charted marked coherence in family alliance types across periods ranging from 3 to 18 months postpartum. The CEF's contributions are especially worthy of note here; they are discussed again in the chapters that follow.

Fivaz-Depeursinge's work is remarkably intricate and thorough, evaluating family alliances on the basis of subtle body postures and affect signaling and sharing. Researchers at the CEF are unique among those pursuing observational studies of early coparenting and family dynamics in that they take into consideration not only coordination between the coparenting partners but also integration of the baby into the family dynamic. Also, their data resonate with those reported by other family researchers, indicating that children from alliances marked by either antagonism and collusion (a dynamic that shares similarities with the hostile–competitive pattern noted in Belsky's, McHale's, and Schoppe-Sullivan's work) or by distress and disconnection (a pattern also detected and corroborated in McHale's studies) are more likely to manifest clinically significant symptomatology by the time they reach preschool age (Fivaz-Depeursinge et al., 1996).

In addition to the CEF findings on linkages between family alliances and child adjustment, Belsky, McHale, and Mangelsdorf have also documented linkages between early coparenting dynamics during infancy/toddlerhood and later measures of child adjustment. In McHale and Rasmussen's work, coparenting difficulties detected from family interactions during infant age 8–11 months predicted greater aggression and anxiety among preschool children 3 years later. Similarly, Belsky, Putnam, and Crnic (1996) reported that, in families in which there was greater animosity and undercutting between coparents, children gravitated toward showing greater disinhibition over time. The nature of the finding was such that children from families showing coparenting conflict were much less inhibited by age 2 than their temperaments at age 1 would ordinarily have led researchers to suspect. Also, Mangelsdorf and colleagues (Frosch, Mangelsdorf, & McHale, 2000) found that coparental hostility during family play at infant age 6 months predicted less secure preschooler–mother attachment at age 3.

These emerging, compelling findings concerning stability and predictive power of very early coparenting dynamics have been of great interest to us as we navigated our own longitudinal study of families. The unwavering importance of coparenting throughout childhood was underscored still further by several studies documenting linkages that tied coparenting dynamics to the adjustment of older children. In a 1999 report, McHale, Johnson, and Sinclair described a study in which they spent the better part of an entire preschool year tracking the social interactions of 4-year-olds with their peers on the preschool playground. What they found was quite remarkable: Children who showed more peer difficulties were those whose parents had demonstrated more problematic coparenting dynamics during family assessments completed earlier in the year—but there was a twist.

Although McHale and colleagues found some direct linkages between observed coparenting dynamics and children's playground behavior, in other cases coparenting could be connected to peer adjustment only among those children who showed evidence of having developed a negative view of family dynamics. The researchers had asked the children to tell stories about happy, sad, mad, and worried families and to answer questions about family conflict posed by a set of puppets, and they had evaluated the nature of children's responses and family representations. Their findings revealed that the children whose responses to the family tasks conveyed signs of distress and anxiety were principally those also showing difficulties with peers. That is, children's views mediated between observed family dynamics and observed peer behavior.

Other researchers, too, have documented linkages tying troubled coparenting dynamics to the adjustment of preschool- and elementary school-aged children (Brody & Flor, 1996; Katz & Gottman, 1996; Katz & Low, 2004; Leary & Katz, 2004; Lindahl & Malik, 1999; McConnell & Kerig, 2002; Schoppe, Mangelsdorf, & Frosch, 2001; Stright & Neitzel, 2003). Lynn Katz's work, in particular, has been instructive on many fronts. It has helped to disentangle relations between child-related and coparenting predictors of peer adjustment and it has also helped to clarify the nature of interrelationships between marital violence, coparenting, and child adjustment.

In what may be the most compelling of all the reports Katz and her colleagues have published, a 2004 paper by Katz and Low determined that hostile–withdrawn coparenting is important insofar as it mediates the relationship between marital violence and children's anxiety and depression. That is, children in families in which there exists a history of marital violence are at greatest risk when the marital problems spill over into the family's coparenting dynamic. When the coparenting process is kept clear of the effects of marital aggression, children do not suffer quite as dramatically. This report clarifies perhaps better than any before it that there is reason to look separately at marital and coparenting processes and not treat them interchangeably. Katz and Low's analyses also revealed, as have other reports that assessed marital and coparenting indicators separately, that marital violence, coparenting, and family-level processes each functioned independently in predicting child outcomes.

For a great many years, family therapists have positioned that the family "whole" is distinct from the different subsystems that constitute it. That is, it is very difficult to know, on the basis of information gathered about the mother–child or the father–child dyadic relationship, what the family group dynamic will look like. Katz's work and that of others (e.g., Bearss & Eyberg, 1998; McHale & Rasmussen, 1998) clarifies this distinction some. It does seem to follow that the coparenting and family dynamics of couples experiencing marital distress are at greater risk for problems. Equally, however, problems between husband and wife in the marital dyad do not inevitably translate into problems between the two as coparents in the family triad.

Similar principles can be demonstrated when studying the dynamics of families as collective entities, rather than conceiving of family functioning simply as a "product" of each of the two parent–child relationship systems studied individually. For example, in a particularly revealing study, McHale et al. (2000) asked parents to complete McHale's (1997) Coparenting Scale and describe their own coparenting conduct on dimensions capturing promotion of solidarity, engagement in conflict, and joint management of the child's behavior. They also observed the parents and their toddler-aged children interacting together as a family, as well as parents and children playing together independently (without the other parent there).

Using ratings of how the parents behaved independently (when they were alone with the child), the researchers created a score reflecting (a) the discrepancy in how engaged each parent was when playing with the toddler alone and (b) the total degree of limit setting observed within the two dyadic settings considered individually. They then also calculated the same two scores on the basis of the parents' behavior within the family triad. What they found was quite telling: Parents' reports of their coparenting conduct were associated only with the indicators created from observations of behavior in the family triad. They were altogether unrelated to indicators describing the family that were constructed from dyad-based data. In short, parents were attuned to the dynamics of their joint coparenting relationship, and their perceptions resonated with what observers saw in the triad. They did not echo impressions of the family formed by combining dyad-based data. The whole indeed seemed different from the sum of its parts.

Where We've Been, and Where We're Going

The point of belaboring these sometimes overly complicated research findings is to highlight one simple but critically important fact: Careful empirical studies of family group dynamics over the past 10 years have almost uniformly supported the clinical observations of Salvador Minuchin and the many other family theorists and therapists whose work progressed quite outside the mainstream of developmental psychology's research on socialization for so many decades. Parents co-create relationships as architects and heads of the family. Coparenting dynamics are related to, but also distinct from, dynamics of other relationship systems in the family. On the basis of the limited evidence available, coparental solidarity appears to be stable over the relatively short (1–2 months to 1–2 years) time periods over which they have been studied, and problems in coparental solidarity beget problems in child adjustment.

Piecing together these various strands of research begins to paint a rather compelling portrait of family life, but something remains missing—an understanding of the evolution and development of coparenting alliances through time. So often, research studies by necessity lump the world into "good" and "bad" categories. It's difficult to read research reports and not come away with black-and-white conclusions such as "parents who wean their babies on time are good, and those who indulge them for too long are bad," or "parents who lose their tempers with kids are bad, and those who don't are good." After all, linkages are often found between overindulgence or negative emotion and indicators of child adjustment. However, few parents, if any, ever start out family life intending to spoil or yell at their children. Most have clear ideas about what they would and would not want to happen, even though these prebaby ideas about family life have rarely been studied by researchers. Also, precious little is known about whether or how parents' prebaby ideas about family life eventually get translated into practice or about what happens when the pre- and postbaby ideas of the two parents diverge (as they nearly always do, to at least some extent, in virtually every family). That's where our study comes in.

In the pages that follow, we outline a study of the transition to coparenthood and of stability and changes in coparenting from infancy to the toddler years. We aim both to portray the big picture concerning major themes encountered by the families who worked with us over time and to describe some of the individual journeys traveled by particular couples and families in our project. We end with a consideration of major lessons learned from the project, but we caution that we found no single blueprint or set of blueprints about how best to chart the course. We think that most families will see much of themselves in this book, and we hope that some of the considerations that we highlight along the way will be of use in helping others to navigate the bumpy road of coparenthood.

References

Abidin, R. R., & Brunner, J. F. (1995). Development of a parenting alliance inventory. *Journal of Clinical Child Psychology, 24*, 31–40.

Bearss, K., & Eyberg, S. M. (1998). A test of the parenting alliance theory. *Early Education and Development, 9*, 179–185.

Belsky, J., Putnam, S., & Crnic, K. (1996). Coparenting, parenting, and early emotional development. In J. McHale & P. Cowan (Eds.), *Understanding how family-level dynamics affect children's development: Studies of two-parent families* (pp. 45–56). San Francisco: Jossey-Bass.

Block, J. H., Block, J., & Morrison, A. (1981). Parental agreement-disagreement on child-rearing orientations and gender-related personality correlates in children. *Child Development, 52,* 965–974.

Brody, G. H., & Flor, D. L. (1996). Coparenting, family interactions, and competence among African American youths. *New Directions for Child Development, 74,* 77–91.

Cohen, N. E., & Weissman, S. (1984). The parenting alliance. In R. Cohen, B. Cohler, & S. Weissman (Eds.), *Parenthood: A psychodynamic perspective* (pp. 33–49). New York: Guilford Press.

Fivaz-Depeursinge, E., & Corboz-Warnery, A. (1999). *The primary triangle: A developmental systems view of mothers, fathers, and infants.* New York: Basic Books.

Fivaz-Depeursinge, E., Frascarolo, F., & Corboz-Warnery, A. (1996). Assessing the triadic alliance between fathers, mothers, and infants at play. In J. McHale & P. Cowan (Eds.), *Understanding how family level dynamics affect children's development: Studies of two-parent families* (pp. 27–44). San Francisco: Jossey-Bass.

Floyd, F. J., & Zmich, D. E. (1991). Marriage and the parenting partnership: Perceptions and interactions of parents with mentally retarded and typically developing children. *Child Development, 62,* 1434–1448.

Frank, S., Jacobson, S., Hole, C. B., Justkowski, R., & Huych, M. (1986). Psychological predictors of parents' sense of confidence and control and self- versus child-focused gratifications. *Developmental Psychology, 22,* 348–355.

Frosch, C. A., Mangelsdorf, S. C., & McHale, J. L. (2000). Marital behavior and the security of preschooler–parent attachment relationships. *Journal of Family Psychology, 14,* 144–161.

Gable, S., Belsky, J., & Crnic, K. (1992). Marriage, parenting, and child development. *Journal of Family Psychology, 5,* 276–294.

Gable, S., Belsky, J., & Crnic, K. (1995). Coparenting during the child's 2nd year: A descriptive account. *Journal of Marriage and the Family, 57,* 609–616.

Goldberg, A. E., & Perry-Jenkins, M. (2004). The division of labor and working-class women's well-being across the transition to parenthood. *Journal of Family Psychology, 18,* 225–236.

Grych, J. H., & Fincham, F. D. (1990). Marital conflict and children's adjustment: A cognitive-contextual framework. *Psychological Bulletin, 108,* 267–290.

Hackel, L. S., & Ruble, D. N. (1992, June). Changes in the marital relationship after the first baby is born: Predicting the impact of expectancy disconfirmation. *Journal of Personality and Social Psychology, 62*, 944–957.

Harrell, S. (1997). *Human families*. Boulder, CO: Westview Press.

Katz, L. F., & Gottman, J. M. (1996). Spillover effects of marital conflict: In search of parenting and coparenting mechanisms. *New Directions for Child Development, 74*, 57–76.

Katz, L. F., & Low, S. M. (2004). Marital violence, co-parenting, and family-level processes in relation to children's adjustment. *Journal of Family Psychology, 18*, 372–382.

Leary, A., & Katz, L. F. (2004). Coparenting, family-level processes, and peer outcomes: The moderating role of vagal tone. *Development and Psychopathology, 16*, 593–608.

Lindahl, K. M., & Malik, N. M. (1999). Marital conflict, family processes, and boys' externalizing behavior in Hispanic American and European American families. *Journal of Clinical Child Psychology, 28*, 12–24.

Luepnitz, D. A. (1988). *The family interpreted: Feminist theory in clinical practice*. New York: Basic Books.

McConnell, M. C., & Kerig, P. K. (2002). Assessing coparenting in families of school-age children: Validation of the coparenting and family rating system. *Canadian Journal of Behavioural Science, 34*, 56–70.

McHale, J. P. (1995). Coparenting and triadic interactions during infancy: The roles of marital distress and child gender. *Developmental Psychology, 31*, 985–996.

McHale, J. P. (1997). Overt and covert coparenting processes in the family. *Family Process, 36*, 183–201.

McHale, J. P., & Cowan, P. A. (1996). *Understanding how family-level dynamics affect children's development: Studies of two-parent families*. San Francisco: Jossey-Bass.

McHale, J. P., Johnson, D., & Sinclair, R. (1999). Family dynamics, preschoolers' family representations, and preschool peer relationships. *Early Education and Development, 10*, 373–401.

McHale, J., Khazan, I., Erera, P., Rotman, T., DeCourcey, W., & McConnell, M. (2002). Coparenting in diverse family systems. In M. H. Bornstein (Ed.), *Handbook of parenting: Being and becoming a parent* (2nd ed., pp. 75–107). Mahwah, NJ: Erlbaum.

McHale, J. P., & Kuersten-Hogan, R. (2004). The dynamics of raising children together. *Journal of Adult Development, 11*, 163–164.

McHale, J. P., Kuersten-Hogan, R., Lauretti, A., & Rasmussen, J. L. (2000). Parental reports of coparenting and observed coparenting behavior during the toddler period. *Journal of Family Psychology, 14,* 220–236.

McHale, J. P., & Rasmussen, J. L. (1998). Coparental and family group-level dynamics during infancy: Early family precursors of child and family functioning during preschool. *Development and Psychopathology, 10*, 39–59.

Minuchin, P. (1985). Families and individual development: Provocations from the field of family therapy. *Child Development, 56*, 289–302.

Minuchin, S. (1974). *Families and family therapy*. Cambridge, MA: Harvard University Press.

Minuchin, S., & Fishman, H. C., (1981). *Family therapy techniques.* Cambridge, MA: Harvard University Press.

Minuchin, S., & Nichols, M. P. (1993). *Family healing: Strategies for hope and understanding*. New York: Free Press.

Porter, B., & O'Leary K. D. (1980). Marital discord and childhood behavior problems. *Journal of Abnormal Child Psychology, 8*, 287–295.

Schoppe, S. J., Mangelsdorf, S. C., & Frosch, C. A. (2001). Coparenting, family process, and family structure: Implications for preschoolers' externalizing behavior problems. *Journal of Family Psychology, 15*, 526–545.

Schoppe-Sullivan, S. J., Mangelsdorf, S. C., Frosch, C. A., & McHale, J. L. (2004). Associations between coparenting and marital behavior from infancy to the preschool years. *Journal of Family Psychology, 18*, 194–207.

Stright, A. D., & Neitzel, C. (2003). Beyond parenting: Coparenting and children's classroom adjustment. *International Journal of Behavioral Development, 27*, 31–39.

Weissman, H. S., & Cohen, S. R. (1985). The parenting alliance and adolescence. *Adolescent Psychiatry, 12*, 24–45.

Wille, D. E. (1995). The 1990s: Gender differences in parenting roles. *Sex Roles, 33,* 803–817.

Our Study of Coparenting From Pregnancy Through Toddlerhood

With Jean Talbot, Allison Lauretti, and Christina Kazali

Embarking on the study of a relatively new and not very well understood topic can be a daunting task. We found this to be the case as the four of us met to chart the course of the Families Through Time project. In the fall of 1997, we met weekly and worked both from our own areas of clinical and research expertise and interest, and from the existing literature on families that we outlined in chapter 1, to sketch the outlines of the project. Our goals as we met to design the study were (a) deciding which particular point in the family's development represented the best times to find out about the progress of the developing coparenting process; (b) pulling together the very best of what was currently known about coparenting and family dynamics to make sure we conducted thorough evaluations of marriages, parenting, and coparenting processes each and every time we met with families; (c) supplementing these tried and true assessments with new evaluations when no existing measure fit our needs; (d) determining what we thought would be the best bets for predicting which families would find early successes as coparents and which might struggle; and (e) specifying what aspects of children's development we thought would be most closely tied to coparental adjustment at each time point and why. The literature previously reviewed gave us some helpful prompts toward reaching decisions in many of these realms, but in other areas we relied primarily on the clinical experience and wisdom of the members of our group and that of a number of family clinicians and researchers throughout the United States and Europe whom we consulted during the planning stages of our study.

This chapter provides the broad outlines of our project. We begin with a discussion of why we decided to visit families at the four points in development that we chose, and then we outline the specifics of the different evaluations that we completed at each time point to assess the family domains of major interest to us. We conclude with a summary of the major research questions and hypotheses pursued in the project and addressed in the remaining chapters of this volume.

Joining Families at Times That Matter to Them: When We Conducted Assessments and Why

Most parents of 2- to 3-year-olds have had the experience of running across photographs or videos of their family that they took shortly after their children were born and feeling a rush of nostalgia, delight—and sadness, at times gone past so quickly and so seemingly long ago. The changes babies undergo as they develop from earliest infancy through the toddler years are so dramatic, and occur so rapidly, that they are in many ways unparalleled by changes at other stages in development. For the better part of a century now, theorists have written about these changes and about the accommodations they necessitate for parents as the children mature. Many, if not most, of these accounts of infants' psychological and emotional development through the first 2 years have emphasized the salience of the mother's role—from her provision of an early "holding environment" (Winnicott, 1958, 1986) that helps the baby develop regular rhythms and a capacity for effective signaling and for self-soothing (Sander, 1964; Stern, 1985; Tronick, 2003) to her availability and support in promoting the infant's emotional security and attachment (Ainsworth, Blehar, Waters, & Wall, 1978; Bowlby, 1988; Sroufe, 1985).

Discussions of fathering of infants had never been particularly central to the writings of these influential theorists; indeed, the role of fathers during infancy was only "discovered" by family researchers about 30 years ago (Lamb, 1975; Parke & Sawin, 1976). In the late 1970s and early 1980s, researchers labored to show in a number of conceptual papers and research that fathers could be as competent as mothers and that fathers often did contribute in unique ways to their children's social and emotional development (e.g., Chiland, 1982; Field, 1978, 1979; Golinkoff & Ames, 1979; Lamb, 1977, 1979; Langlois & Downs, 1980; Power & Parke, 1986; Yogman, 1981; although, for an interesting contrast to these reports, see Osborn & Morris, 1982). It is also not fully accurate to say that fathers had been altogether absent in the theoretical and research literature on child socialization prior to that time; for example, in many psychodynamic theories, fathers were brought clearly into the center ring as important social agents as children got older; required closer monitoring, disciplinary activity, and sex role socialization; and needed support in managing their ambivalent feelings toward mothers (e.g., Greenspan, 1981; Henderson, 1980; Siegal, 1987).

Today, we stand at a very interesting and mildly perplexing juncture in the development of ideas about fathers and families. On the one hand, the understanding of fathering has unquestionably progressed markedly since the late 1970s. On the other hand, despite the now-extensive knowledge about roles that fathers can and do play in the baby's emotional world, there remains to this day a dominant bias in the "infant mental health" world to see early infant development as unfolding principally within the matrix of mother–baby relations. Reasons for this bias have been discussed at some length elsewhere (see, e.g., McHale, 2007; McHale & Fivaz-Depeursinge, 1999), but there are several interesting quandaries that this bias provokes. Primarily, it is consistent with the mental health field's propensity (commented on by, e.g., Leupnitz, 1988; Rich, 1976; and Singh, 2004) to hold mothers responsible for children's ills (Caplan & Caplan, 1994; Kindlon & Thompson, 2000; Sax, 1997). Perhaps as a counterreaction to these tendencies, the pendulum shifted for a while during the 1990s when the term *deadbeat dads* became a part of the cultural rhetoric in the United States, and scrutiny came upon fathers as major culprits in children's woes (Blankenhorn, 1996; Booth & Crouter, 1998; Earle & Letherby, 2003; Marks & Palkovitz, 2004; Schwartz, 2001). Indeed, the notion of blame has been almost impossible to escape in writings about families—when children struggle, somebody has to be at fault. If it isn't mothers or fathers, then it must be the children themselves—so much so that many parents have looked for and found solace in writings about childhood disorders indicating that some youngsters are just "born different" (Singh, 2004).

The blame that parents already feel and place upon themselves for their children's struggles served as a sobering backdrop for the discussions we had about risk factors, family dynamics, and points of development at which to assess infants and families. We knew, of course, that we did need to do our best to assess traditional prenatal risk indicators (e.g., parental depression, struggles with impulse control, and serious marital distress), as well as evaluate early temperamental difficulties shown by the infants themselves. Equally, however, we did so with the full understanding as clinicians and scientists, and as parents ourselves, that the notion of risk needs to be seen through a completely different lens than the notion of blame. Virtually every person is at some form of risk for specific medical and mental health issues simply by virtue of their sharing the same bloodlines as their ancestors and kin. It is also possible in many cases to reduce (although not eliminate) risks through sensitive, supportive interventions at critical points in development. It does not follow, however, that individuals should be blamed for breast cancer, diabetes, and other health problems that ultimately surface over the course of their lives. We want to make this point clear here at the outset: Our study is about the factors that increase the likelihood that couples will encounter later successes or difficulties as coparents, as a step toward heightening parents' awareness of these factors and toward increasing health providers' attentiveness to and capacity for providing relevant supports for coparents both before and after babies arrive on the scene.

Which returns us to the focal question of interest here: When are the appropriate times to take stock of the adjustments parents are making? Our first assessment was relatively easy because we wanted to begin our inquiry before parents even welcomed their baby into the family. On the basis of prior conceptual work by S. Minuchin (1974) and others, as well as on prior studies of families making the transition to new parenthood (Cowan & Cowan, 1992; Lewis, 1989), we knew that it would be important to learn as much as we could during the pregnancy about how well the parents-to-be were faring in their marriage. We also knew that it would be important to assess parents' well-being and their personality characteristics as individuals. Also, we knew from a fascinating, emerging literature on parents' prenatal states of mind with respect to attachment that it would be important to gauge the representations that each parent had about close intimate relationships. We will discuss marital quality, personality characteristics and well-being, and states of mind with respect to attachment in greater detail shortly. Although each of these factors seemed to be sensible choices as potential foreshadows of later adaptation in the early postpartum months, we also recognized that something important was missing and anticipated that the missing ingredient may be most important of all in predicting later coparenting adjustment. The missing element was parents' perspectives on what family life ought to be like and what they hoped to create individually and together with their partner in the new family.

At what point, however, should we talk with parents during the pregnancy? Prior writings on the transition to new parenthood had portrayed the cognitive and emotional shifts that take place during pregnancy as a gradual, slowly unfolding process for parents-to-be (Raphael-Leff, 1991). Hence, we did not anticipate that parents would actually have given a great deal of thought to the impending family process prior to the final months of the pregnancy. For this reason, we targeted the beginning of the third trimester as our point of entry for families, although we often registered parents for the study much earlier than this. As it sometimes turned out, we danced back and forth with families for several weeks before we could find mutually agreeable times for interviews, and some parents ended up having their babies earlier than expected and thus couldn't participate even though they had expressed interest in our project. Among those parents we did see, babies also often came early—we actually saw a handful of couples just a week or less before the unexpectedly early arrival of their baby. The commonality among all our interviews is that everyone spoke to us at some point between the 7th and 9th month of the pregnancy.

The first real major challenge we faced was agreeing upon a relevant starting point for our initial postbaby family assessments. Although families had occasionally been assessed by researchers even during the very first hours of the baby's life (Belsky, 1985), most prior research studies that had been published at the time we began planning this study had investigated and observed coparenting interactions only toward the end of the baby's first year of life or even later still. There are certainly a great many good reasons to visit families near the end of the first year. By this point, the declines in marital dissatisfaction documented by many researchers have leveled out for some families (although they continued declining further in others). By this point, it is also possible to accurately assess the quality of the infant's attachment to each of her parents. And by 12 months, the infant's capacities for mobility and social referencing permit assessments of their active contributions during triadic family interactions (Dickstein & Parke, 1988; Hirshberg, 1990).

One year certainly seemed an ideal time to assess families, and we made a decision that we too would complete evaluations at 12 months, but we also believed that there would be value in seeing families much earlier than this. We knew that, relative to the family routines of later infancy which have had a great deal of time to crystallize, family patterns in earlier infancy would be in greater flux. However, this very fact made early assessments seem a worthwhile enterprise. In making a decision about how early, we relied heavily on what we had learned from conference reports and consultations with scientists at the Centre d'Etude de la Famille (CEF) in Lausanne, Switzerland. At the World Association for Infant Mental Health in 2000, three researchers from the CEF—Elisabeth Fivaz-Depeursinge, France Frascarolo, and Antoinette Corboz-Warnery—described microanalyses of family interactions that they had completed at 3, 9, and 18 months postpartum, in which they had carefully evaluated the positioning of each family member's pelvis and torso, gaze, and affective connection as the mother, father, and baby interacted together in a play setting. The researchers found that families showed much greater miscoordination in their interactions at 3 months postpartum than they had either earlier during the pregnancy or during later infancy. Yet at the very same time, the CEF team also discovered higher order patterns signifying four distinctive "family alliance" types that remained stable over this 15-month period in over 80% of cases studied (Fivaz-Depeursinge & Corboz-Warnery, 1999). Hence, despite the upheaval of the early postpartum period, by 3 months postpartum, important relationship dynamics that signaled something salient and enduring about the developing family dynamic appeared to be already crystallizing. We were probably most taken by reports from the CEF team that two of the four alliance types they discovered (collusive and disordered alliances) were quite common both among families who sought clinical help for themselves or their children and among preschool children who exhibited clinically significant behavior problems. By contrast, two other types (stressed and cooperative alliances) were more common among children and families who had not found their way into the mental health system (Fivaz-Depeursinge, Frascorolo, & Corboz-Warnery, 1996).

There were other reasons why we thought 3 months would be an ideal starting point for our study. Initially, studies of the transition to parenthood that had charted stability and change in how well the marital relationship was doing suggested that there was a continuing downward decline in marital satisfaction through at least 12 months, and often through 18 months postpartum. However, as studies began to include earlier postpartum time points, it became clear that the low watermark for marital satisfaction was at 3 months postpartum. For example, Belsky, Spanier, and Rovine (1983) found that the most dramatic declines in marital satisfaction had occurred at 3 months postpartum, with modest improvements over 3-month levels reported at 9 months—and the wives' reports of marital adjustment were most closely linked to other facets of the marital partnership (see also Lewis, 1988). It is also important to say that it probably isn't just that mothers feel generally miserable at 3 months, as some of the recent media coverage of postpartum depression might suggest. For example, although it is true that 86% of mothers who were interviewed in a study by Fleming and colleagues in 1990 offered some negative remarks about their infants, over 90% of these same women spontaneously indicated feeling close to their babies and enjoying caring for them. Indeed, Fleming and colleagues actually found a steady postpartum growth in positive statements about the baby from 1 to 3 months postpartum. By contrast, mothers in Fleming's investigation experienced the least positive feelings about their spouse during the third postpartum month.

A subsequent study by Terry, McHugh, and Noller (1991) further clarified this finding; although women's affectional expressions toward their partners did decline from the last trimester of the pregnancy to 3 months postpartum in their study, this decline was evident only for women who were dissatisfied with their partners' contribution to household tasks. In this study by Terry et al., women's perceptions that men were contributing fairly to household tasks were actually associated with an increase in reported marital quality across the transition to parenthood. We find these results interesting and important, because a study by Tomlinson and Irvin in 1993 indicated that negative perceptions of the marriage as early as 4 months postbirth forecast later adjustment problems for the family. Given this finding, along with the other work we have discussed that links marital quality to family process at later ages, it seems quite conceivable that individual variability in negative feelings about the spouse and marriage, even as early as 3 months postpartum, may already be giving rise to a less-than-collaborative coparenting and family dynamic that could itself remain stable over time.

Finally, beyond these intriguing husband–wife and family group patterns, we also had reason to believe that the child herself may already be making a far greater impact on the developing family system by the 3-month mark than had previously been appreciated. First, consider for a moment the potential influence of babies' early regulatory and self-soothing abilities. Studies indicate that infant colic peaks between 1 and 3 months of age. By definition, colic lasts for at least 3 weeks running. Hence, colic can create a tremendous deal of stress for even the best prepared parents. When colic is combined with infant problems in other realms significant to parents (e.g., sleeping and eating), or with a difficult temperament, the challenges faced by parenting partners during the first few months can seem monumental. Fortunately, and thankfully, available research evidence suggests that temperamental difficulty and colic appear to be unrelated. Still, we thought it important to know whether early coparenting processes are sensitive to these infant characteristics. If they were, this would be very important information for those who work with young families. Second, after beginning our study, we learned of a remarkable new set of findings based on microanalytic data that were gathered both by Fivaz-Depeursinge (1998) and by Nadel and Tremblay-Leveau (1999) in separate studies. These data revealed that infant capacities to coordinate their attention and to share affect with multiple partners simultaneously may already be firmly operative by 3 months postpartum! More specifically, babies who demonstrate a greater triangular propensity to coordinate attention and affect with both parents during triadic family play are more likely to belong to stressed or cooperative, rather than to collusive or disordered, alliances. Hence, the family system has already begun to incorporate, and to take cues from, the infant in remarkable ways within the first 100 days after the baby's birth.

To summarize, we found the lack of attention that had been given in the child health literature to early emerging coparenting processes rather puzzling. In their 1992 volume on becoming a family, Philip and Carolyn Cowan had challenged sociologists' characterizations of the early postpartum months as a "honeymoon" period, reporting that many of the couples in their study felt unprepared for the changes in lifestyle and major adjustments they had to make during the first 3 months after the birth of their first child (1992, pp. 76–77). To us, for the many reasons outlined above, the 3-month mark stood out as an important point in which to chart early directions that had already been taken by the coparenting partners and to ascertain the extent to which these directions could have been forecast from information about the parenting partners prior to the baby's arrival. Hence, 3 months represents Time 2 in our longitudinal project.

As infants continue developing through the first year, their capacity for sharing their subjective experiences and for empathic-like intimacy with others (intersubjective relatedness in Stern's [1985] terms) begins blossoming, and they become thoroughly embedded within the emotional environment of their families. They have become aware of and have begun to respond to interadult conflict and dissonance by these latter months of the first year (DeJonghe, Bogat, & Levendosky, 2005; Hirshberg, 1990), reliably seek joint attention in games and share actions and intentions about objects (Stern, 1985), and have cultivated person-specific attachments (Ainsworth et al., 1978). Given these important developments, the emotional significance of the child's first birthday for most families and the availability of prior empirical studies concerning coparenting interactions and infants' attachment security at the end of the baby's first year (attachment has traditionally been assessed by family researchers in the Ainsworth Strange Situation at 12 months of age), we identified the 1-year mark as the next salient point for assessing family adjustment.

The final point at which we assessed families was midway through the child's third year. Much has been written about the "terrible twos" and the demands that maturing children place on their parents once they begin saying "no." Toileting becomes an issue for families during the child's third year, and families almost universally find that they need to cocreate rules, standards, and routines to support the child and provide the requisite degree of structure the child needs to master new challenges. We suspected that for many families, the demands of the active 2-year-old would draw parents into new (for them) conversations and negotiations about jointly managing the child's behavior, even if they had never previously had such conversations when the child wasn't "pulling" as strongly or regularly for rules and guidelines. In other words, we imagined that the pressures placed on the coparental unit by 2.5-year-olds would likely be very different than the demands placed on the unit by 1-year-olds. We believed that reconnecting with families at 30 months postpartum would provide an opportunity for us to assess both continuity and change in coparenting over time; hence, we selected this time point for the final set of evaluations we completed with families.

With the points of entry determined, we then set out to develop assessments for each time point that would be as comprehensive as possible in sampling that which was of importance to families across multiple realms—the individual adjustment of each family member (mother, father, and child), the quality of adjustment within each of the family's different dyadic relationship systems (i.e., mother–child, father–child, and husband–wife), and the adaptations that had been made by the coparenting team. We also planned to systematically include in our study's design a subset of families in which the baby had a preschool-aged brother or sister, so that we might systematically compare the coparenting and family dynamics of one- and two-child families. The assessments we developed are outlined next, followed by our identification of the sample of families recruited for the project and the final set of research questions that guided our work.

Our Evaluation Process During the Pregnancy

As discussed earlier, our aims during the pregnancy contacts with families were to learn as much as we could about the individual adaptation of both parents, about their bond as husband and wife, and about their "representational world," the belief systems they had constructed about relationships past and future. We thought we could best do so by spending time talking with parents one on one, by asking them to engage together in a problem-solving discussion that allowed us to learn something about their interpersonal and problem-solving process, and by having them report privately on such matters as how flexible, tolerant, and self-restrained they perceived themselves to be, their recent experience of depressive symptoms, their happiness in the marriage, their own ideas about parenting, and the like.

During the third trimester of the pregnancy, parents visited the Family Study Center at Clark University. After receiving a brief overview of the study and its focus, parents adjourned to separate rooms, where interviewers completed Main and Goldwyn's Adult Attachment Interview (AAI; in press). The AAI has been around for about 25 years, and it is firmly rooted in Bowlby's (1969, 1973) attachment theory. For those unfamiliar with Bowlby's writings on internalized representations, among his most generative contributions was his proposition that the early relationship experiences infants and toddlers have with primary caregivers lead them to actively construct generalized expectancies about safety and danger, about the availability and responsiveness of others, and ultimately about both self and others in relationships. These expectancies ultimately coalesce into an organized pattern of internal representations that includes both cognitive and emotional components and that often functions outside of conscious awareness—a pattern often referred to as a "working model" of self and others (Bretherton, 1985; Main, Kaplan, & Cassidy, 1985). One of the primary functions of this working model is to organize attachment-related percepts so as to guide interpersonal behavior in new situations. Although such models begin developing rather early on, they are sometimes revised on the basis of later attachment-related experiences during childhood and adolescence (Bowlby, 1973; Bretherton, 1990; Oppenheim & Waters, 1995; Waters, Hamilton, & Weinfeld, 2000).

As attachment theory and research flourished during the 1980s, the AAI was developed by Main and her colleagues to capture adults' generalized representations of attachment. The interview asks about both childhood attachment relationships and the meaning that individuals give to these relationships. It has been an extremely important tool for attachment theorists over the past 20 years, emphasizing the person's ability to provide cohesive, integrated, and believable accounts of their experiences and their meaning; how parents use language and discourse during the interview is thought to reflect the person's state of mind with respect to attachment. Details of the interview and its scoring system are discussed further in chapter 3. Here, we highlight our expectation that those parents-to-be already anticipating reliability in interpersonal relationships would be drawing upon a base more likely to support their ability to work through challenges to collaboratively co-construct a cohesive three-person family process and a mutually supportive coparental alliance during the early postpartum months.

After parents completed AAIs, we sought to learn more about the second domain that we expected would be related to the capacity for mutuality, coordination, and intimacy—the dynamics of their marital partnership. Here, we expected (on the basis of both theory and past empirical research) that adults who had cultivated more respectful and supportive relationships with their mates would also have an easier time than those who struggled in their marriages to find a path toward mutuality as coparents. We asked parents to come together to discuss two topic areas in their marriage on which they did not see eye to eye. One topic selected was one that the husband identified as a problem but the wife did not; the second was a topic that the wife identified as a problem but the husband did not. Among the marital processes that these discussions are known to evoke include individual differences in the presence of warmth and of intimacy of communication, egalitarianism in shared power or dominance by one partner, ability of each person to present an autonomous voice or perspective, success in problem-solving together, and presence of overt unresolved conflict. At the completion of each of the two problem-solving discussions, partners independently completed checklists summarizing their own reactions to the discussion and how they judged their partner's role in the discussion. Later, they were also asked to provide self-ratings of marital satisfaction on the Marital Adjustment Test (MAT; Locke & Wallace, 1959), which was included in the surveys discussed below.

Although we expected that our assessments of adults' states of mind with respect to attachment and their marital relationship dynamics would help us to predict with a fair degree of accuracy which coparenting partnerships would find the most success during the early postpartum, we also recognized that there was something missing from these assessments. The AAI allows determination of whether an adult possesses a secure or insecure state of mind with respect to attachment, but its focus is largely a dyadic one. That is, it focuses on a single state of mind with respect to attachment, emphasizing past dyadic experiences with caregivers and predicting to the individual's ability to "give security" to her or his own infant. We believed that, in addition to forming working models of self and others in relationships, individuals also develop working models of coparenting, families, and family-level dynamics. Such models might be expected to show some relationship to attachment security, in the sense that expectancies of more cohesive family functioning might be more likely in adults who had secure attachment representations. However, we thought it equally plausible that many individuals who had experienced significant disruptions in their origin family's coparental relationship, including antagonism and undermining, disengagement, and high-conflict divorces, might nonetheless have had positive relationships with each parent individually and, hence, have cultivated secure states of mind with respect to attachment. We hypothesized that parents from origin families high in coparental distress may be at greater risk for early coparenting difficulties themselves, even when they had secure states of mind with respect to attachment, if their experiences heightened their concerns that they may encounter coparenting difficulties with their partners. To pursue the possibility that negative prenatal expectancies about future coparenting could potentially affect early coparenting efforts, we conducted one-on-one interviews with each parent asking about coparenting in their origin and future families. A focus of these interviews was on the person's propensity to think in terms of family as well as dyadic solidarity and on the nature of their expectancies. They are described in greater detail in chapter 3.

We examined parents' prenatal expectancies in other ways as well. Also included in our evaluation was an assessment of each parent's "Ideas About Parenting" (Heming, Cowan, & Cowan, 2001), in which parents-to-be rated both their own ideas about different parenting beliefs and practices (e.g., too much cuddling spoils a child) and their partner's beliefs. We then calculated scores representing the difference in perspective between mothers-to-be and fathers-to-be as one indicator of the degree of difference in what they envisioned. We also asked partners to independently complete a prenatal version of Cowan and Cowan's Who Does What inventory of child-care activities (bathing, diapering, bedtimes, middle-of-night needs, etc.) by signifying how they expected the couple would divide each responsibility after the baby's arrival and how they ideally wished it would be. This allowed us to calculate the discrepancy between imagined and ideal child care expectations, so that smaller scores indicated that the anticipated reality was more closely in line with the respondent's wishes.

Finally, beyond states of mind with respect to attachment, coparenting expectancies, and marital dynamics, we imagined that adults who were more self-controlled and resilient would be better able to manage the expectable ups and downs of becoming new parents than those who were more sensitive, hot-tempered, or rigid in their ideas about how best to handle things. We anticipated that more flexible and tolerant parents might be better able to cultivate collaborative, rather than antagonistic or distant, coparenting partnerships. To assess mothers' and fathers' personality and adaptive resources, we asked them to complete survey booklets on their own. Among the surveys they completed was one that provided information about their adaptive psychological resources (the California Psychological Inventory, or CPI; Gough, 1987). The CPI is a 472-item report measuring adaptive psychological and interpersonal functioning, including self-control and ego resilience (Klohnen, 1996). A second survey completed, not just during the pregnancy but at subsequent time points as well, was the Center for Epidemiological Studies Depression Scale (CES-D; Radloff, 1977), which indexes overall level of depression.

Our Evaluation Process at 3 Months

At 3 months postpartum, we wanted to get a first hand look at how parents were adapting to family life, so we asked for permission to visit families at their homes. Families were almost uniformly relieved not to have to trundle their babies to the university, especially during the chilly winter months in Massachusetts; hence, we were met with resounding welcomes. During our visits, we sought to do three things: assess how well parents were faring individually and in the marriage; evaluate the nature of the early coparental alliance that had begun to develop; and learn a bit about the baby—whether she had been showing signs of an easy or a more challenging temperament and whether she had posed any significant difficulties with self-regulation, including eating, sleeping, and crying.

To assess maternal and paternal adaptation, we again had parents complete the CES-D. To assess marital adjustment, we again asked them to complete the MAT. Parents completed these surveys at the end of their visits with us, along with ratings of the baby's temperament. First, however, they participated in the coparenting assessments designed for the study. The assessments themselves will be described in more detail in chapter 4; here, we provide just a brief summary to capture the overall flow of the visits.

Upon arrival at families' homes, we brought with us a specially designed infant seat created by Jean-Pierre Thouveny, a well-respected orthopedic designer from Lesquin, France. Thouveny's seat, which was first created for Elisabeth Fivaz-Depeursinge and her team at the CEF in Switzerland, supports babies of all different shapes and sizes by allowing them to sit comfortably in a small chair that swivels and supports their head and back. The seat allows babies to be active partners in three-person family interactions and was used for both the Lausanne Trilogue Play (LTP), which began the visit, and for an assessment of the babies' and parents' adaptation to a "still-face" challenge, which occurred later in the session. Between the LTP and still-face assessments, parents (a) took part in a joint interview during which they discussed the day that their baby was born and (b) completed the same "Who Does What" instruments they had completed during the pregnancy and then shared their responses with one another and worked to try to come to consensus on how things actually had gone in the home. From these various tasks, which were videotaped, raters worked to evaluate the degree of collaboration, oppositionality, and disconnection between the coparenting partners. Parents also provided ratings of the degree to which they had felt supported by the coparenting partner on Abidin and Brunner's (1995) Parenting Alliance Inventory.

At the completion of the family assessments, researchers determined whether they could complete a temperament evaluation with the baby. Sometimes doing so was no problem, as the babies had slept or had been fed during the coparenting discussions their parents had been having. Other times, babies had fallen asleep and not reawakened or had gotten too fatigued from the earlier excitement, and so temperament assessments were completed on a separate day. Whenever babies were seen for the assessments, the research team administered Garcia Coll and colleagues' (Garcia

Coll, Halpern, Vohr, & Seifer, 1992) tasks, a series of 15 successive challenges that included such activities as having a hat placed on the baby's head; wiping the baby's nose; picking the baby up and cuddling her; and presenting a noisy bell, a loud electronic toy, and a human mask. Babies' reactions to these various presentations were recorded and later rated by trained coders. Parents also rated the babies' temperament themselves on the Infant Behavior Questionnaire (IBQ; Rothbart, 1986).

Our Evaluation Process at 12 Months

At 1 year of age, our aims were largely the same as before: We wanted to learn how each of the parents was doing individually, what the baby's temperamental profile was looking like, and how the marriage was faring. We also wanted to know how each of the parent–child relationships were progressing and, most importantly, how the coparental relationship was faring. Our study design also called for 50 new families, each with a 12-month-old baby and a preschool-aged brother or sister, to join us at this time point so that we might compare coparenting of 12-month-olds in one- versus two-child families. For these families, we assessed both coparenting during triadic (mother–father–infant) interactions, as well as coparenting during tetradic (mother–father–infant–sibling) interactions. The tetradic interactions also allowed us to examine sibling relationships.

Families came to the Family Study Center on three separate occasions at 12 months. On one of the visits, the couple came alone without the baby, and the session progressed much as did the prenatal assessment. Parents completed interviews about their coparenting relationship; took part in two marital discussions; and completed questionnaires addressing their own personalities and adjustment (the CPI and CES-D again), the marriage (the MAT), and the baby's temperament (IBQ). During a second visit, just one parent attended with the baby, and during a third visit, both parents attended with the baby (and with the sibling, if there was one). During the second and third visits, we began with Ainsworth et al.'s (1978) separation–reunion assessment to assess the quality of the baby's attachment; after a break, families completed a parent–child play and teaching task, during which the parent attempted to teach the baby to do some mildly challenging things (e.g., building with blocks, completing a puzzle). We counterbalanced these sessions so that in half the cases, the mother completed the separation–reunion and play tasks on the second visit and in the other half, the father completed them on the second visit.

In the second visit, after the separation–reunion and teaching tasks, researchers completed an assessment of the baby's temperament, on the basis of a paradigm outlined by Park et al. (1997). The temperament task included two successive exchanges in which first the parent, and then a stranger, approached the baby from a series of premarked places on the carpet and attempted to make the baby laugh; the approach gradually brought the approaching person closer and closer to a high chair in which the baby was seated. Next, the researchers brought out a pair of brightly colored Sesame Street puppets and enacted a puppet show in front of the baby's high chair. Finally, the parent played with the baby for 1 minute, with a colorful electronic game that made a variety of engaging cartoon sounds. After playing for 1 minute, the parent withheld the toy from the baby for 1 minute while posing a motionless face; then he or she returned the toy to the baby but maintained the emotionless facial pose for 1 minute; finally, the parent re-engaged with the baby. Sessions were taped and later coded, which was similar to the process for assessments of 3-month temperament.

During the third session, after the separation–reunion and play/teaching episodes, the family engaged together in a series of play and teaching tasks similar to those each parent had engaged in individually but with new toys and challenges (e.g., snapping a series of plastic beads together, completing a different, more complicated puzzle). After the teaching tasks, the researchers brought in some new toys, including a plastic ride-on helicopter and a large beach ball, and the family was afforded floor time to play together as they saw fit. For families in which there were two children, the sessions were altered just slightly: Visit 2 included both parents, and the triadic family interaction just described was scheduled after a break and before the temperament assessment. Visit 3, which included the sibling, was conducted in the same manner as the procedure described above, except that the sibling was brought into the family interaction with the parents and baby.

Our Evaluation Process at 30 Months

Our final assessment point was at 30 months, and in many ways the assessment mirrored those of earlier time periods. We examined how each of the parents was doing individually, how the marriage was faring, how each of the parent–child relationships was progressing, and above all, how the coparental relationship was faring. At this final assessment point, we also were very interested in understanding a bit more about the family's emotional life and about whether and how the coparenting and family indicators we had been tracking could be linked to indices of the toddler's adjustment.

As at 12 months, families came to the Family Study Center on three separate occasions at 30 months. On one visit, the couple came alone without the baby. That session included an interview about the coparenting relationship, the two marital discussions, and time to complete the CES-D and MAT. Also during this session, parents were interviewed one on one to assess their philosophies about and socialization practices concerning the child's emotions. Researchers administered Gottman, Katz, and Hooven's (1997) Meta-Emotion Interview, and trained coders later evaluated the interviews to assess the extent to which parents reported encouraging and coaching children's expression of different emotions, including joy, sadness, and anger. As always, we were interested in potential effects of differences between the two parents in their emotion-coaching practices. The notion of emotion coaching has been an influential one in recent years, with evidence suggesting that parents who are good coaches facilitate their children's understanding of emotional experience and of emotional expression.

During a second visit, just one parent attended with the toddler, and during a third visit, both parents attended with the child (and with any siblings). During the second and third visits, we began with brief separation–reunion and parent–child teaching tasks (e.g., identifying colors and shapes on a computer game; trying to reason through a series of Piagetian conservation tasks). Afterward, researchers completed an assessment of the toddler's ability to regulate his or her behavior and emotions during a waiting task

(Grolnick, Bridges, & Connell, 1996). Toddlers were shown an attractively wrapped present or were given a taste of goldfish crackers and then watched as the item was placed out of reach for 6 minutes. During the wait period, parents were kept busy completing questionnaires and interacted with the children only minimally. We were interested in the regulatory strategies toddlers used while waiting, especially the extent to which they were able to rely on their own devices, rather than interrupting their parents, as they waited.

We also assessed children's receptive language skills on the Peabody Picture Vocabulary Test (or PPVT); their understanding of emotions (using a task introduced by Denham, 1986, in which they interacted with and answered questions about a set of faces to signify their understanding of the emotions happy, sad, and mad); and the comfort they showed while navigating a separate task involving happy, sad, and mad feelings within a pretend bear family. In a prior pilot study for the Families Through Time investigation that had been funded by the National Institute of Mental Health, Allison Lauretti and her colleagues (1999) had discovered that it was toddlers' comfort level, reflected in the quality of their participation in the task, rather than the manifest content of their story responses per se that was most closely related to family dynamics at age 30 months.

During the third session, after separation–reunion and teaching tasks, the entire family (mother, father, toddler, and siblings, if any) engaged together in play and teaching tasks. This session included the competitive block-building game Jenga, a game of horseshoes, enactment of a pretend family meal, and exploration of a toy box containing a variety of gender-stereotypical (e.g., Barbie dolls, action figures, and guns) and gender-neutral toys (e.g., musical instruments, Viewmaster). Parents also completed two sets of ratings of the child's behavioral adjustment—Achenbach and Rescorla's (2000) Child Behavior Checklist 1.5-5, which focuses principally on internalizing (sadness, shyness, anxiety) and externalizing (defiance, aggression, hyperactivity) behavior problems, and Cowan and Cowan's (1992) Child Adaptive Behavior Inventory (CABI), which focuses equally on behavioral difficulties and on competencies in adaptive behavior (including social and academic competence). Parents were also asked to have children's day care or preschool center teachers complete the CABI as well. In this manner, we had both observational (self-regulation of emotions during a frustration task) and informant reports of the toddler's behavior, and information on children's language (PPVT) and socioemotional competencies (understanding of emotions, comfort with emotions portrayed during the bear task). We then sought to link these various child outcomes to the indicators of coparenting and related family processes that we had gathered through time. We outline the major hypotheses guiding our project shortly; first, we briefly summarize the various cohorts of families seen at various time points through the study.

The Families Through Time Cohort: Characteristics of the Families Who Participated in the Various Subphases of the Overall Project

The design of our study was a complicated one. We sought to learn several things in the project and were fortunate enough to receive the support of the National Institutes of Health (NIH) to pursue different questions in different investigations. Overall, there were two distinct NIH-funded projects that provided the infrastructure of the Families Through Time study. One was an investigation of 120 families making the transition to new parenthood. In this study, which coincided with the birth to 3-month phases of our study, 137 families expecting a first child took part in the prenatal and 3-month postpartum visits. Among these families, 116 fathers were of European American descent, 4 were African American, 2 were Hispanic, 6 were Asian American, 4 were of mixed descent, and 5 chose not to disclose their ethnicities. Among the mothers, 120 were European American, 5 were African American, 3 were Hispanic, 3 were Asian American, 1 was Native American, and 5 chose not to disclose their ethnicities. The average age was 31 years for mothers (range = 22–47) and 33 for fathers (range = 21–52). Average family income was $70,000, although the range was from <$20,000 to >$100,000. Eighty-nine percent of fathers and 6% of mothers were working full-time before their babies were born, and 24% of mothers were working part-time. Sixty-eight of the 137 mothers seen during the pregnancy gave birth to sons, and 69 gave birth to daughters.

Fifty of these families contracted with us to continue on for follow-up assessments at 12 and at 30 months, and 46 of these 50 families stayed with us through both assessments. These 46 families and their stories are centrally featured throughout this book; our data analyses indicated that there were no significant differences between the 46 families who remained with us through all time points and those who had contracted with us at the outset to complete only prenatal and 3-month assessments. The second investigation, which was a study of continuity and change in family dynamics from infancy through toddlerhood, coincided with the 12- and 30-month phases of the overall project. In addition to the families who continued forth with us from pregnancy forward, another 114 families (62 with a first-born 12-month-old and 52 with a second-born) joined us at the 12-month mark. Of these 114 families, 96 fathers were of European American descent, 7 were African American, 1 was Hispanic, 1 was Asian American, 3 were of mixed descent, and 6 were of undisclosed ethnicity. Among the mothers, 102 were European American, 4 were African American, 3 were Hispanic, 4 were Asian American, and 1 was of undisclosed ethnicity. The average age of mothers was 32 (range = 20–44) and of fathers, 34 (range = 20–50). Average family income was $70,000, with a range from $20,000 to >$100,000. Ninety-two percent of fathers and 15% of mothers were working full-time at 12 months, and 48% of mothers were working part-time. Sixty-one of the 114 families who joined us at 12 months had sons, and 53 had daughters. Half of the families with two children had firstborn boys and half had firstborn girls.

In the chapters that follow, we focus on links between coparenting dynamics and other child and family factors within each time frame, as well as on cross-time linkages between earlier and later coparenting dynamics. The cross-time analyses linking prenatal functioning to 3-month functioning (chapter 4), and linking 12-month to 30-month functioning (chapter 6) hence involve significantly larger numbers of families than the analyses linking prenatal and 3-month functioning to 12- and 30-month functioning. However, as we discuss later, even within the smaller cohort who participated at all time points, marked stability in coparental solidarity was evinced through time.

Our Guiding Research Questions and Hypotheses

The major hypotheses guiding our investigation had to do with the degree of continuity in coparental adjustment through time and the relationship between coparental and child adjustment. We anticipated, first, that couples showing less evidence of risk during the pregnancy would show greater coparenting solidarity (relative to other families in the study) at 3 months and that such solidarity would set a stage for more solid alliances at 12 and 30 months. Conversely, we expected that there would be several kinds of prenatal risk, such as pessimistic outlooks that would foreshadow difficulties for the coparental partnership through time. We expected that mild coparenting distress would be normative at 3 months, as parents struggled to try to figure out how to parent together; that more stable patterns (for good or ill) would be in evidence by 12 months, as parents settled into well-worn patterns and routines; and that we would learn of new adjustment struggles at the 30-month toddler assessment, as children would be posing new comanagement challenges for parents.

Hence, the following are the major questions asked and answered in the pages that follow:

1. Do stronger marriages and/or more coherent states of mind with respect to attachment lead expectant parents to think more positively and less negatively about their own future families?
2. Do men's and women's outlooks and expectations about their future families during the pregnancy come to shape the nature of early coparenting dynamics?
3. Are early emerging coparenting dynamics meaningful and prognostic of later coparental adjustment?
4. Is solidarity in the coparenting alliance linked to children's social and emotional adjustment as early as the toddler years?

Beyond these organizing questions, a variety of other issues are raised and examined in the chapters that follow. The next five chapters contain the main new findings from our investigation. In chapter 3, we detail findings from the first of the four assessment periods we chose: the family's "prebaby expectancy" stage. Chapters 4 through 6 then detail findings from each successive stage of development, and chapter 7 provides a look at the two-child families who constituted the comparison group in our project. As we and the study's various co-collaborators proceed in detailing major findings these chapters, we will keep an eye both on group findings that captured patterns detected across the group as a whole and on the unique stories of individual families as they navigated their way down the bumpy road of coparenthood.

References

Abidin, R. R., & Brunner, J. F. (1995). Development of a parenting alliance inventory. *Journal of Clinical Child Psychology, 24*, 31–40.

Achenbach, T., & Rescorla, L. (2000). *Manual for the ASEBA preschool forms and profiles.* Burlington: University of Vermont, Department of Psychiatry.

Ainsworth, M., Blehar, M., Waters, E., & Wall, S. (1978). *Patterns of attachment.* Hillsdale, NJ: Erlbaum.

Belsky, J. (1985). Experimenting with the family in the newborn period. *Child Development, 56*, 407–414.

Belsky, J., Spanier, G. B., & Rovine, M. (1983). Stability and change in marriage across the transition to parenthood. *Journal of Marriage and Family, 45*, 567–577.

Blankenhorn, D. (1996). *Fatherless America: Confronting our most urgent social problem.* New York: Harper Perennial.

Booth, A., & Crouter, A. C. (1998). *Men in families: When do they get involved? What difference does it make?* Mahwah, NJ: Erlbaum.

Bowlby, J. (1969). Disruption of affectional bonds and its effects on behavior. *Canada's Mental Health Supplement, 59*, 12.

Bowlby, J. (1973). *Separation: Anxiety and anger.* New York: Basic Books.

Bowlby, J. (1988). *A secure base: Parent–child attachment and healthy human development.* New York: Basic Books.

Bretherton, I. (1985). Attachment theory: Retrospect and prospect. *Monographs of the Society for Research in Child Development, 50*, 3–35.

Bretherton, I. (1990). Communication patterns, internal working models, and the intergenerational transmission of attachment relationships. *Infant Mental Health Journal, 11*, 237–252.

Caplan, P. J., & Caplan, J. B. (1994). *Thinking critically about research on sex and gender*. New York: HarperCollins.

Chiland, C. (1982). A new look at fathers. *Psychoanalytic Study of the Child, 37*, 367–379.

Cowan, C. P., & Cowan, P. A. (1992). *When partners become parents: The big life change for couples*. New York: Basic Books.

DeJonghe, E. S., Bogat, G. A., & Levendosky, A. A. (2005). Infant exposure to domestic violence predicts heightened sensitivity to adult verbal conflict. *Infant Mental Health Journal, 26,* 268–281.

Denham, S. A. (1986). Social cognition, prosocial behavior, and emotion in preschoolers: Contextual validation. *Child Development, 57*, 194–201.

Dickstein, S., & Parke, R. D. (1988). Social referencing in infancy: A glance at fathers and marriage. *Child Development, 59*, 506–511.

Earle, S., & Letherby, G. (2003). *Gender, identity and reproduction: Social perspectives*. London: Palgrave.

Field, T. (1978). Interaction behaviors of primary versus secondary caretaker fathers. *Developmental Psychology, 14*, 183–184.

Field, T. M. (1979). Games parents play with normal and high-risk infants. *Child Psychiatry & Human Development, 10*, 41–48.

Fivaz-Depeursinge, E. (1998). Infants' triangulation strategies: A new issue in development. *The Signal, 6,* 1–6.

Fivaz-Depeursinge, E., Frascarolo, F., & Corboz-Warnery, A. (1996). Assessing the triadic alliance between fathers, mothers, and infants at play. In J. McHale & P. Cowan (Eds.), *Understanding how family level dynamics affect children's development: Studies of two-parent families* (pp. 27–43). San Francisco: Jossey-Bass.

Fivaz-Depeursinge, E., & Corboz-Warnery, A. (1999). *The primary triangle: A developmental systems view of mothers, fathers, and infants.* New York: Basic Books.

Fleming, A. S., Ruble, D. N., Flett, G. L., & Van Wagner, V. (1990). Adjustment in first-time mothers: Changes in mood and mood content during the early postpartum months. *Developmental Psychology*, *26*, 137–143.

Garcia Coll, C. T., Halpern, L. F., Vohr, B. R., & Seifer, R. (1992). Stability and correlates of change of early temperament in preterm and full-term infants. *Infant Behavior & Development, 15*, 137–153.

Golinkoff, R. M., & Ames, G. J. (1979). A comparison of fathers' and mothers' speech with their young children. *Child Development, 50*, 28–32.

Gottman, J. M., Katz, L. F., & Hooven, C. (1997). *Meta-emotion: How families communicate emotionally*. Hillsdale, NJ: Erlbaum.

Gough, H. (1987). *CPI administrator's guide*. Palo Alto, CA: Consulting Psychologists Press.

Greenspan, S. I. (1981). *Psychopathology and adaptation in infancy and early childhood: Principles of clinical diagnosis and preventive intervention.* New York: International Universities Press.

Grolnick, W. S., Bridges, L. J., & Connell, J. P. (1996). Emotion regulation in two-year-olds: Strategies and emotional expression in four contexts. *Child Development, 67*, 928–941.

Heming, G., Cowan, P., & Cowan, C. (2001). Ideas about parenting. In J. Touliatos, B. F. Perlmutter, & M. Straus (Eds.), *Handbook of family measurement techniques* (Vol. 1, p. 178). Thousand Oaks, CA: Sage.

Henderson, J. (1980). On fathering: The nature and functions of the father role: II. Conceptualization of fathering. *Canadian Journal of Psychiatry, 25*, 413–431.

Hirshberg, L. M. (1990). When infants look to their parents: II. Twelve-month-olds' response to conflicting parental emotional signals. *Child Development, 61*, 1187–1191.

Kindlon, D., & Thompson, M. (2000). *Raising Cain: Protecting the emotional life of boys*. New York: Ballantine Books.

Klohnen, E. C. (1996). Conceptual analysis and measurement of the construct of ego-resiliency. *Journal of Personality and Social Psychology, 70*, 1067–1079.

Lamb, M. E. (1975). Fathers: Forgotten contributors to child development. *Human Development, 18*, 245–266.

Lamb, M. E. (1977). The development of mother-infant attachments in the second year of life. *Developmental Psychology, 13*, 637–648.

Lamb, M. E. (1979). Paternal influences and the father's role: A personal perspective. *American Psychologist, 34*, 938–943.

Langlois, J. H., & Downs, A. C. (1980). Mothers, fathers, and peers as socialization agents of sex-typed play behaviors in young children. *Child Development, 51*, 1237–1247.

Lauretti, A., Hill, A., Connell, A., & McHale, J. (1999, April). *Links between toddlers' nonverbal responses during doll play and family relationships.* Paper presented at Society for Research in Child Development, Albuquerque, NM.

Lewis, J. M. (1988). The transition to parenthood: II. Stability and change in marital structure. *Family Process, 27*, 273–283.

Lewis, J. M. (1989). *The birth of the family: An empirical inquiry*. Philadelphia: Brunner/Mazel.

Locke, H. J., & Wallace, K. M. (1959). Short marital-adjustment and prediction tests: Their reliability and validity. *Marriage & Family Living, 21*, 251–255.

Luepnitz, D. A. (1988). *The family interpreted: Feminist theory in clinical practice*. New York: Basic Books.

Main, M., & Goldwyn, R. (in press). Adult attachment rating and classification systems. In M. Main (Ed.), *A typology of human attachment organization assessed in discourse, drawing and interviews* (working title). New York: Cambridge University Press.

Main, M., Kaplan, N., & Cassidy, J. (1985). Security in infancy, childhood, and adulthood: A move to the level of representation. *Monographs of the Society for Research in Child Development, 50*, 66–104.

Marks, L. D., & Palkovitz, R. (2004). American fatherhood types: The good, the bad, and the uninterested. *Fathering, 2*, 113–129.

McHale, J. (2007). When infants grow up in multiperson relationship systems. *Infant Mental Health Journal, 28*(4).

McHale, J. P., & Fivaz-Depeursinge, E. (1999). Understanding triadic and family group interactions during infancy and toddlerhood. *Clinical Child and Family Psychology Review, 2*, 107–127.

Minuchin, S. (1974). *Families and family therapy*. Cambridge, MA: Harvard University Press.

Nadel, J., & Tremblay-Leveau, H. (1999). Early perception of social contingencies and interpersonal intentionality: Dyadic and triadic paradigms. In P. Rochat (Ed.), *Early social cognition: Understanding others in the first months of life* (pp. 189–212). Mahwah, NJ: Erlbaum.

Oppenheim, D., & Waters, H. S. (1995). Narrative processes and attachment representations: Issues of development and assessment. *Monographs of the Society for Research in Child Development, 60*, 197–215.

Osborn, A. F., & Morris, A. C. (1982). Fathers and child care. *Early Child Development and Care, 8*, 279–307.

Park, S., Belsky, J., Putnam, S., & Crnic, K. (1997). Infant emotionality, parenting, and 3-year inhibition: Exploring stability and lawful discontinuity in a male sample. *Developmental Psychology, 33*, 218–227.

Parke, R. D., & Sawin, D. B. (1976). The father's role in infancy: A reevaluation. *Family Coordinator, 25*, 365–371.

Power, T. G., & Parke, R. D. (1986). Patterns of early socialization: Mother– and father–infant interaction in the home. *International Journal of Behavioral Development, 9*, 331–341.

Radloff, L. S. (1977). The CES-D scale: A self-report depression scale for research in the general population. *Applied Psychological Measurement, 1*, 385–401.

Raphael-Leff, J. (1991). *Psychological processes of childbearing*. Boca Raton, FL: Chapman & Hall/CRC.

Rich, A. (1976). *Of women born: Motherhood as experience and institution*. New York: Norton.

Rothbart, M. K. (1986). A psychobiological approach to the study of temperament. In G. A. Kohnstamm (Ed.), *Temperament discussed: Temperament and development in infancy and childhood* (pp. 63–72). Lisse, the Netherlands: Swets & Zeitlinger.

Sander, L. (1964). Adaptive relationships in early mother–child interaction. *Journal of the American Academy of Child Psychiatry, 3*, 231–264.

Sax, P. (1997). Narrative therapy and family support: Strengthening the mother's voice in working with families with infants and toddlers. In C. Smith & D. Nylund (Eds.), *Narrative therapies with children and adolescents* (pp. 111–146). New York: Guilford Press.

Schwartz, H. S. (2001). *The revolt of the primitive: An inquiry into the roots of political correctness*. Westport, CT: Praeger Publishers.

Siegal, M. (1987). Are sons and daughters treated more differently by fathers than by mothers? *Developmental Review, 7*, 183–209.

Singh, I. (2004). Doing their jobs: Mothering with Ritalin in a culture of mother-blame. *Social Science & Medicine, 59*, 1193–1205.

Sroufe, L. A. (1985). Attachment classification from the perspective of infant–caregiver relationships and infant temperament. *Child Development, 56*, 1–14.

Stern, D. N. (1985). *Interpersonal world of the infant: A view from psychoanalysis and developmental psychology*. New York: Basic Books.

Terry, D. J., McHugh, T. A., & Noller, P. (1991). Role dissatisfaction and the decline in marital quality across the transition to parenthood. *Australian Journal of Psychology, 43*, 129–132.

Tomlinson, P. S., & Irvin, B. (1993). Qualitative study of women's reports of family adaptation pattern four years following transition to parenthood. *Issues in Mental Health Nursing, 14*, 119–138.

Tronick, E. Z. (2003). "Of course all relationships are unique": How co-creative processes generate unique mother–infant and patient–therapist relationships and change other relationships. *Psychoanalytic Inquiry, 23*, 473–491.

Waters, E., Hamilton, C. E., & Weinfield, N. S. (2000). The stability of attachment security from infancy to adolescence and early adulthood: General introduction. *Child Development, 71*, 678–683.

Winnicott, D. (1958). *Collected papers: Through paediatrics to psycho-analysis.* London: Tavistock.

Winnicott, D. (1986). *Home is where we start from: Essays by a psychoanalyst.* New York: Norton.

Yogman, M. W. (1981). Games fathers and mothers play with their infants. *Infant Mental Health Journal, 2*, 241–248.

Looking Ahead: Imagining Family Life During Pregnancy

With Jean Talbot and Christina Kazali

"What am I concerned about? That life will be over! Let's see . . . I'm concerned that I won't be able to stay as active as I always have been and that we'll get on one another's nerves because we'll all be home together more . . . but she'll handle most of the child care responsibilities—she's going to be a stay-at-home mom, and I'm hoping she'll change all the diapers."

"I'll be the primary caregiver during the day, but when he gets home, he'll take over. I want to be able to get out a bit so I won't go insane . . . I think he'll be a very involved dad because his father wasn't. . . . I want us to be really together and involved as a group so the baby will respond to both of us."

These comments were among those shared by expecting parents as they spoke with us during the pregnancy's closing months about their hopes, their concerns, and their expectancies of family life after the baby arrived. They were not chosen as being prototypical of the views expressed by all fathers or all mothers, but they do provide a beginning sense about the very different expectancies that parents-to-be can hold.

There's also one other point worth noting about the two sets of comments above. They were shared with us by Ron and by Candice, a father- and mother-to-be—who were married to one another! In our interview with Ron, besides sharing his concerns and expectations about life after the baby's arrival, he confided that he also did have some concrete ideas about what he hoped to carry forward from the family he grew up in:

"A sense of family—I want to recreate a sense of family. I'd like us to have Sunday dinners together, to take family trips together."

Despite this positively cast memory and wish, he was also clear that there were things that he absolutely did not want to carry forward:

> "They argued about us kids a lot. I don't want us to recreate the kinds of arguments that I always used to experience between my parents."

In contrast to the vivid illustrations of what he hoped for, Ron hedged much more as he mused about what he expected his own family life would bring. What struck us most was that Ron indicated that he and Candice had begun talking about life after the baby "at least once a week," yet we saw many significant differences between the ideas and expectancies he had about future family life and the wishes expressed by Candice.

In our interview with Candice, she too expressed many vivid illustrations of what it was that she did and didn't want to see happen:

> "My family always had 'family days' on Sundays—we went to church together, to parks, to baseball games. I want us to be doing these things too, as a family . . . but I want to avoid the chauvinism I experienced with my parents—the woman at home, barefoot, pregnant."

The interviews are most interesting when considered side by side. On the one hand, it is easy to see some considerable overlap in Ron and Candice's hopes—that their family would share meaningful bonding times together as a family, that their weekends (or at least their Sunday nights) would be privileged as special times, and that the specific kinds of negativity they remembered encountering in their own origin families would be avoided. From there, however, the couple's expectancies seemed to depart radically. We noted a variety of subtle but important differences in expectations about who would do what, about the balance and nature of their future together and alone time, and about the baby's impact on their personal space and lives. Ron's half-joking comment about his life being over, more openly stated than that of many fathers with similar worries, connoted some pessimism of outlook we expected may hold meaning. Although Ron and Candice seemed unaware of their differences, we wondered whether they might serve as flash points for the two of them as they began their journey together into coparenthood.

We've begun chapter 3 with this vignette to highlight the powerful role that men's and women's expectancies about shared parenting and family dynamics could have, at least potentially, in shaping their early adaptation as coparents. Just weeks before his baby's arrival, Ron found himself worrying, as do many fathers and mothers, about losing a central part of himself after the baby arrived ("life is over"). He imagined, or at least fantasized, that the transition would not be as jarring as it could be because of his hope that Candice would be stepping up to shoulder the yeoman's portion of the caregiving responsibilities ("she will change all the diapers"). Equally, however, recognizing that the baby would demand the couple's being home together more than they had ever been accustomed to, he worried that he and Candice might not create as cohesive a unit as they might want to because they could begin getting on one another's nerves.

Although it is possible that Candice entertained the very same concerns, they were certainly not featured as prominently in her narrative. Rather, her dominant focus was on finding ways to carry forward to her new family the sense of love and belonging she'd felt in her origin family while righting past wrongs, including what she'd seen as a troublesome gender bias in her origin family. Ron played an important part in her plans, because Candice fully expected him to be a more invested father than hers was, someone who would take over in the evenings and afford her the freedom to continue pursuit of her own interests so she wouldn't "go insane." During other times, when she and Ron *were* home together with the baby, Candice had a clear idea that she and Ron would be doing a great many things together, living life as a tight-knit family. She seemed as unaware of Ron's worries that he would have no time for himself as Ron was unaware of hers, and the major concern Ron had expressed about the couple spending too much time together was never touched upon in Candice's narrative.

Perhaps these differences in expectancies and outlook were just minor differences in emphasis. Perhaps they were indications that the couple was poised to encounter significant difficulties during the early postpartum months because each partner anticipated something rather different than did the other. We had no way of knowing, of course, until we followed Ron and Candice, and many other families, to examine the extent to which their prenatal expectancies foreshadowed their postnatal adjustment. In this chapter, we summarize our study of parents' prenatal expectancies and trace linkages between their expectancies and other indicators of risk that we estimated during our prenatal visits with them. We begin by providing a general overview of how the couples in our study told us they were faring as they drew ever closer to the moment of their baby's arrival, by describing their reported symptoms of depression and of marital satisfaction and dissatisfaction. We then outline what we learned from the prenatal coparenting interviews and how these coparenting narratives varied as a function of parents' states of mind with respect to attachment. Finally, we provide a summary of different risk profiles we detected during the pregnancy. As we show later, in many families we saw little evidence of any significant risk. In others, risk seemed minimal, aside from some mild pessimism expressed in parents' coparenting interviews. In others still, there was a more extensive pattern of risk that was evinced not only in the interviews but in other domains as well.

How Couples Were Faring During the Third Trimester: General Findings From the CES-D and the MAT

Whenever researchers complete studies of families, one question outsiders have from the outset is "how representative was the sample?" For us, the answer to this question rests on what is meant by "representative." In some ways, we clearly did not see a subgroup of families representing the face of America or even of the community in Massachusetts where our families lived. Our sample was relatively well educated and was largely of middle- and upper-middle-class means. Fewer than 15% of the families we saw had parents of color, and we focused principally on nuclear family systems and so did not systematically study the many other kinds of families into which babies are born. However, in other important ways, our sample did capture much of the important variability that attends the transition to new parenthood. As will be seen, families reported a wide variety of experiences in their origin families, from abandonment by one parent to high-conflict divorce, to chronic coparental strife and antagonism, to relatively benign and supportive family environments. Although ours was not a study that targeted families in clinical distress, we found a wide range of patterns of individual adjustment among the mothers- and fathers-to-be in the sample.

As a first step toward "taking the pulse" of how the families in our study were adjusting, we looked at mothers' and fathers' scores on two measures: the Center for Epidemiological Studies Depression Scale (CES-D; Radloff, 1977) and the Marital Adjustment Test (Locke & Wallace, 1959). Each of these measures offers the benefit of providing agreed-upon threshold or cutoff scores that clinicians and researchers can use to establish whether the respondent is experiencing a level of distress that would be considered clinically meaningful. For the 20-item CES-D, on which parents rate items along a scale ranging from 0 (*rarely or none of the time; less than one day*) to 3 (*most or all of the time; 5–7 days*), the cutoff point is scores of 16 or higher. Items on the CES-D, all of which begin "During the past week:" include "I felt that I could not shake off the blues, even with help from family and friends," "I felt that everything I did was an effort," and "I had crying spells."

For the MAT, the cutoff point is scores below 100 (Christensen & Heavey, 1999; Gottman, 1994). There are 16 items on the MAT, each of which is weighted somewhat differently. Eight items ask partners to rate the degree of agreement or disagreement between themselves and their partners on topics such as handling family finances and sex relations; scores in the direction of "always disagree" receive very few points, and scores in the direction of "always agree" receive higher points. Couples are also asked to rate how happy they are in the marriage, from *very unhappy* (receiving 0 points) to *perfectly happy* (35 points), and to answer additional questions including "Do you ever wish you had not gotten together with your partner?" and "If you had your life to live over again, would you choose the same or a different partner (or not be involved in a long-term relationship at all)?"

The average CES-D depression score for expectant mothers in this community sample was 14.2, and the average depression score for fathers was 10.7. On the depression index, we found that 4 in 10 expectant mothers in our sample (40%) and 22% of expectant fathers reported clinically noteworthy levels of symptomatology even before the baby ever arrived. Among the women, in particular, our sample included several individuals reporting depression scores of noteworthy concern; 12 pregnant mothers (9% of the overall sample) had depression scores of 25 or higher on the CES-D index. This seemed extraordinarily high to us, but after much scrutiny and discussion we came to suspect that, for many parents, the CES-D index may actually have been serving as a general index of overall anxiety about the pregnancy and impending parenthood, rather than as an index of clinically significant depression. Our basis for this hunch is that very few parents actually endorsed items signifying feelings of worthlessness or extensive crying spells; more commonly chosen were items signifying difficulties concentrating, sleeping, and the like.

At minimum, a great many parents in our sample were experiencing jitters. Quite often these were significant levels of jitters, and many experienced much more than that. By contrast, the story with marital satisfaction was not quite as dire; the average Locke–Wallace marital satisfaction score for mothers was 124.1, and for fathers it was 123.6. Very few families (only about 5% of mothers and 7% of fathers) were as yet reporting clinically significant levels of marital distress. This said, there was still a rather wide range of satisfaction scores for both men and women, with mothers' marital satisfaction scores ranging from 75 to 156, and fathers' scores ranging from 68 to 157. All told, when we asked how many families there were in our sample in which at least one partner reported struggling to a significant degree on the CES-D or MAT, we determined that this figure was an astonishing 50.7%. That is, half of the participant families in our study contained at least one parent who reported a CES-D score of 16 or higher, and/or a MAT score below 100.

Furthermore, 17% of the families in our sample showed multiple indications of risk on the CES-D and MAT (i.e., scores exceeding the established thresholds on two or more of these four risk indicators). Also, when we included the number of cases in which one or both parents were rated as high in negativity on the future family coparenting interview (i.e., receiving scores of 5, 6, or 7 on the Negativity scale), the number of families with two or more risk indicators increased to 36%. Hence, despite the fact that our sample solely comprised couples who had decided to take part in our study after hearing a brief informational presentation in their prenatal classes, placing absolutely no emphasis on individual or family distress, we found that a significant proportion of our participants reported experiencing anxiety and adjustment difficulties, with more than one in every three families conveying worries in multiple realms.

Given the sheer number of families who reported prenatal struggles with depression or marital dissatisfaction, a key question is whether such difficulties were problematic for families as they approached new parenthood. We examine this issue in greater detail in chapter 4. Our expectation was that these risk factors could be problematic if they served to undermine the family's coparenting alliance. Conversely, if in the face of depression or marital dissatisfaction, couples found a way to forge a strong coparenting alliance nonetheless, then the family would be starting out on stronger footing. To create a strong early alliance, however, parents would need to talk to, understand, and support one another during the early postpartum months. They would also need to monitor and tend to their own stress levels and to mutually accommodate any especially strong proclivities that diverged markedly from one another—propensities potentially borne of different child-rearing philosophies. For example, they would need to be able to talk about and resolve differences in whether and when to bring the baby to their bed, whether to let the baby cry, who would calm an inconsolable child at 4 a.m., and the like.

Recognizing the importance of parents' adaptability is why we focused on the specific personality features that we chose during the pregnancy: parents' self-restraint and their flexibility (which we operationalized as ego resilience). As discussed later, these personality traits proved to be relevant as predictors of certain of the 3-month outcomes we examined. It was also what led us to assess in some detail the individual representations or working models of family-level dynamics and of future family life that the partners' held before their baby arrived. Our reasoning was that one basic factor underpinning parents' capacity to work together in a coordinated way was whether they had developed any shared ideas about how they thought they would care for and tend to their child. To have begun developing such shared philosophies, parents had to have spoken together about their hopes and ideals.

However, did they actually begin doing so before the baby was born? We didn't know, and so we drew upon the assessments outlined in chapter 2 to investigate expectant parents' dawning representational models of coparenting. Piggybacking on studies that found problems when women's prenatal expectancies about the division of child care responsibilities are violated, we asked parents to indicate whether they anticipated that the division of labor between them was or wasn't going to be what they were hoping for. Anticipating that significant difference in mothers' and fathers' views about parenting may be a harbinger of problems to come, we asked them to indicate how similar or different their own ideas about parenting were from those of their partner. Working with the premise that each of them had already begun to develop, consciously or unconsciously, explicit and powerful beliefs and ideas about how they would ideally want family life to proceed, we interviewed them at length about what they imagined and hoped coparenting would be like in their own future family. These assessments, and what we learned from them, are described next.

Expectancies for the Future Family

As we've indicated already, the strongest leg that we had to stand on as we began our work on coparenting was the robust set of findings in the literature concerning parents' prenatal expectations about the division of child care labor. Studies that chart expectancies during the pregnancy and follow families after babies arrive find that both women and men expect men to do more than they actually end up doing (Cowan & Cowan, 1992), and when the extent of violated expectancies is quite large, women in particular adapt less well to new parenthood and become very disenchanted with the marriage.

Although we found these findings fascinating, we were interested in a slightly different question: Are there differences in the extent to which women anticipate being let down by their partners, even before babies ever arrive? We were interested in this expectation of inequity in the future division of child care labor principally as a potential indicator of a negative "cast" or outlook. Although such outlooks can be described as "pessimistic," we acknowledge that pessimism is not an ideal term, as many parents holding negative outlooks turn out simply to have had a realistic view of what was to come. Nonetheless, the outlook seemed important to us, and so we asked each parent to complete a prebirth version of Cowan and Cowan's (1988) Who Does What scale (WDW). The WDW is a 44-item self-report questionnaire assessing each partner's perceptions of the partners' division of roles for family and household responsibilities along three sets of tasks. These include household and family tasks (e.g., cooking, paying bills), family decision-making (e.g., handling finances, planning vacations), and tasks involved in the care and rearing of children (e.g., diapering, responding to distress, middle-of-the-night needs, scheduling medical appointments). On each item, parents indicate who does what on a 9-point scale ranging from 1 (*she does it all*) through 5 (*we do this about equally*) to 9 (*he does it all*).

Because of our interest in coparenting, only the instrument's 20 child care-related items were used to form the summary index for this construct. Following Cowan and Cowan (1988), both spouses indicated how they expected the task to be divided once the baby had arrived and then how they wished this task could be divided ideally. The discrepancy between "How it will be" and "How I'd like it to be" was calculated for each item and then summed to arrive at an index reflecting the magnitude of difference between anticipated and wished-for realities or future family labor concerns. Although absolute difference scores were used, it turned out never to be the case in this sample that parents expected fathers to do more of the work than mothers on any of the child-care items.

To assess perceived discrepancies in parenting ideologies, parents completed Heming, Cowan, and Cowan's (1991) Ideas About Parenting survey (IAP). This questionnaire, comprising items from scales by Baumrind (1971), Block (1971), and Cohler, Grunebaum, Weiss, and Moran (1971), asks parents to specify their own opinions on a scale ranging from 1 (*strongly agree*) to 9 (*strongly disagree*) about each of 46 different parenting beliefs and then to indicate what they perceive their partner's opinion about that item to be. Absolute difference scores were calculated between the respondents' stated opinions, and what they perceived their partners' opinions to be, for each of the 46 items. These difference scores were then summed to form an index indicating perceived degree of difference in child-rearing philosophies. Higher IAP difference scores, as with higher scores on the WDW, indicated greater dissonance (a bigger self–partner difference in parenting ideology, a wider gap between expected and ideal circumstances involving the baby's care).

These measures were gathered to augment our interview-based evaluations of optimism and pessimism in parents' future family outlooks. The interviews permitted us to evaluate much more directly how parents imagined family life might go. From the time they are very small, girls and boys fantasize about their futures, including their future families. In fact, we discovered several years ago in a study of Clark undergraduate students that college students are more likely to have chosen the names for their future children—even before they are ever even in a relationship—when they grew up in families marred by coparenting conflict (McHale, Loding, Blaisdell, & Lovell, 1996). So we had a rather firm basis for anticipating that parents-to-be would also have hopes and fears about future family life. These are the attributes we hoped to assess in our interviews: How rosy, or how bleak, are expectant parents' views of family?

When we designed this study, and our interview, there were few established guideposts to rely upon, except for one. The work of Kai von Klitzing, Dieter Bürgin, and their colleagues in Basel, Switzerland, a research team that had launched its own study of parents' prenatal fantasies, had great appeal to us. The Basel group had devised an assessment of expectant parents' "triadic capacities" (von Klitzing, Simoni, Amsler, & Bürgin, 1999), or propensity to call upon triadic rather than dyadic imagery during an interview about family processes (including that of their own future family). The Basel group's interview had been developed as a couple's interview rather than an individual interview, however, and they probed for wider ranging content than we were in a position to gather. Also, at the time of our study's inception, von Klitzing's system and protocol were still evolving and not yet ready for dissemination. Nonetheless, our contacts and correspondence with the Basel group were of great value as we conceptualized our own instrument.

Our primary aim was to create an interview that would allow a valid assessment of the explicit coloring of the parent-to-be's outlook on the future family. Because we were also interested in whether parents' anticipated futures could be linked to their experienced pasts, we also scripted questions asking about coparenting in the family of origin (see McHale et al., 2004). Questions covered themes including how the person's parents worked together as a team to raise them; what they hoped to carry forward, and not carry forward, from their own family and from their partner's family; how often they'd found themselves thinking about what it would be like for the three of them to be a family; what those fantasies were like; and what their and their partner's strong points as parents would be, and what concerned them about themselves and about their partner. Interviews were transcribed, and we developed an evaluation system through standard methods of narrative inquiry. To establish whether different raters could successfully evaluate the transcripts using the same criteria, 30 interviews were double coded by this chapter's coauthors. Interrater reliability agreement was quite acceptable, with intraclass correlations ranging from .76 to .87.

In the scoring system we developed, we evaluated the parents' triadic propensity, the extent of their positive outlook, and the extent of their negative outlook. The latter was of greatest interest to us, and we anticipated finding linkages between negativity and the other future family measures (the IAP difference score and the WDW real–ideal discrepancy score). In evaluating triadic propensity, we examined the extent to which the interviewee included considerations of both themselves and their partner in discussing life after the baby came. Parents receiving high scores were those who mentioned the coparent frequently and with no probing from the interviewer. It did not matter whether the parent did so portraying common interests or differences in emphasis; the key was whether the narrative was about "the three of us" more than being about "me and my baby." Parents who scored low on triadic propensity were those who spoke of themselves and the baby, often at length, but never mentioned the partner unless explicitly probed by the interviewer. In evaluating positive outlook, high scores were given to parents who described vivid and specific images of intimate or joy-filled family moments—cuddling the baby in a rocking chair, singing songs together, going as a family to dance recitals or community events. Low scores were given when imagery lacked detail and events were portrayed in only the most perfunctory terms with no expansion or embellishment.

Negativity scores were assigned to both the origin family and future family segments of the interview. As on the previous two scales, scores of 7 were the highest, and were assigned only to transcripts of respondents who presented numerous negative characterizations. The contents of these negative characterizations could be (and certainly were!) quite wide ranging. The most negative characterizations of both origin and future family coparenting were those in which coparents were portrayed as having been (in the origin family), or as expected to be (in the future family), actively and intentionally nonsupportive, competitive, and undermining of one another, or alternatively, overly disinterested, disengaged, and/or quietly hostile. When discussing origin families, many parents remembered pointed instances of their parents arguing about the children and what was best for them or speaking disparagingly about one another to the respondent. Indeed, such recollections of interparental animosity were relatively commonplace among parents' recollections of their origin family process; 46% of mothers and 42% of fathers received the most extreme negativity scores of 5, 6, or 7 on this index.

Extreme worry about hostility in parents' expectations about their future families was much less common. Nonetheless, we did not find it unusual for parents to be worried about negative interactions and relationships with their coparenting partner, and these concerns led to high future-family negativity scores. Take, for example, Sylvia's concerns about her partner's response to parenthood:

> "I'm afraid he may be withdrawn both physically and emotionally; babyhood scares him, and that's how he responds to anxiety."

Not surprisingly, Sylvia entertained other significant concerns about the couple's coparenting relationship, as well, and some of these were quite explicit:

> "I'm worried that he won't support me, or back me up, or that he will encourage our child to deceive me."

This latter comment indicates far more than a concern that her partner might withdraw; it connotes a fear that he may attempt to gain an "in" with the child and use his father–child bond to sabotage Sylvia's relationship with their child. Many of the men and women we interviewed reflected on how disruptive parent–child alliances of this sort had been in their own origin families, but Sylvia was one of the rare few we found who was already expressing explicit concern even before the baby was born that such a dynamic might materialize again in her own family.

A more common worry among mothers was the concern, often couched within commentaries of how loving and engaged they expected their partners to be, that the baby's father would not prioritize fatherhood and family life. Take for example Millie's comment:

> "He's going to be good with reading and at fantasizing with our child . . . but I'm worried that he's going to get too involved in work. I'm also concerned about how much patience he'll have, especially at the end of a long day."

It seems likely that many parent concerns were rooted not only in recalled origin-family experiences but also in what they had been experiencing already during the pregnancy. For example, Davis told us the following:

> "Honestly, I rarely think about the baby coming, though I think she thinks about it a lot. We haven't really talked about the baby or what our life will be like much. I think that's probably because of me. We have just been too busy to sit down and talk . . . haven't discussed division of responsibilities or anything like that."

Rita, his wife, concurred.

> "We really haven't spoken at all. We need to. We did decide though that discipline is going to come from both of us. That's going to be important."

Other parents were attuned to possible intergenerational effects being carried over from the partner's family to the new family. Take, for instance, Sol's comment:

> "She had to grow up fast, and she became in some ways her family's 'de facto' mom. Part of her agenda is to come through where her mother wasn't able to."

On the one hand, Sol's comment indicated sensitivity to his partner's desire (a desire expressed by many of the parents we spoke with) to create a more positive and secure family atmosphere for their child than she had herself experienced. On the other hand, his reference to her desire as an "agenda" rather than as a wish or a hope suggested that he might be somewhat wary about the agenda.

Sol's prenatal interview was among those receiving a high negativity rating. It was not simply the skeptical glance Sol cast toward his partner's motivations; his interview also indicated his ambivalence about his own impending transition to new parenthood. Besides his worries about his partner, Sol (and many other parents we interviewed) was unsure about his own response to impending parent and coparenthood. Recall Ron's worries at the beginning of this chapter that the baby was going to necessitate changes that he was not yet prepared to make. This was a common theme across many interviews and was a concern that was communicated explicitly by Sol:

> "This is really her project . . . I was ambivalent to the idea of children to begin with. . . . It's going to be crowded, and I'm worried about the noise. We'll need a bigger house so that I can move to the other end of it and not hear things."

Our impression in talking to Sol was that the coparenting risk in his future family might move more in the direction of disconnection than of competition or undermining.

These kinds of concerns were very different from those expressed by parents who were rated low on the Negativity scale.

Parents receiving low family of origin Negativity scores provided few or no examples of negative memories or untoward events having affected the family in negative ways. For example, when asked about the most distressing family memory from childhood, Chris recalled a storm affecting his town and how his parents responded, remembering:

> "I remember it being pretty scary. My parents did their best to assure us kids, but you could tell that they were worried too."

Parents receiving low future-family Negativity scores expressed neither explicit nor implicit concerns about problematic family dynamics per se. Rather, our question about their future family concerns was more likely to elicit worries about logistical matters, such as day-to-day needs of the baby or sleep deprivation. Cindy, for example, mused:

> "The only thing I'm really worried about is that we're both heavy sleepers—what if we don't hear the baby crying?"

For individual parents such as Sylvia (who worried about an undermining father–child alliance developing in her future family), origin-family experiences sometimes fueled negative future-family expectancies. However, there was little evidence of a direct one-to-one correspondence between origin-family recollections and future-family imaginings: far from it, in fact. Although we had expected to find considerable overlap between negativity in depictions of origin- and future-families, we were surprised to discover that this association was only modest for fathers ($r = .29$, $p < .05$) and was not present for mothers ($r = .18$, *ns*). This interesting finding suggested that there wasn't simply a pessimistic "cast" in family narratives that colored every story parents told—past and future families were thought about differently. Also of relevance in this regard, negativity about the future-family process was not greater among parents who reported more depressive symptoms on the CES-D. This was true both for mothers ($r = .12$, *ns*) and for fathers ($r = .08$, *ns*).

We did, however, find some very interesting associations between parents' future-family outlooks and their states of mind with respect to attachment, as captured by the Adult Attachment Interview (AAI). These linkages are described next.

How Family Stories Varied as a Function of States of Mind With Respect to Attachment

In the 1990s, adult attachment theory revolutionized the field's understanding of the intergenerational transmission of attachment patterns. Quality of attachment develops from interactions shaped by parents' organization of attachment-related percepts and memories. Secure states of mind with respect to attachment allow parents to respond sensitively and contingently to their own infants' needs, or in Main's terms, to "give security" to their own baby. Insecure states of mind are more likely to lead to misattunements and misreadings of infant signals, giving rise to insecure infant attachments.

Earlier, we hypothesized that, in addition to promoting secure attachments, expectations of trust and security in relationships are also important for expectant parents who are in the process of co-constructing parenting alliances. When expectant parents' belief systems include expectations that others can be trusted to provide support and affirmation, the challenge of "sharing a parenting space" is made somewhat easier, although it seldom comes without at least some trepidation. To test the idea that secure states of mind with respect to attachment would support expectant parents' tendencies to represent the future family in positive and triadic terms, we posed the following questions:

1. Do parents who report more rejection, who derogate attachment or insist on lack of recall, or who show poor coherence of mind on the AAI demonstrate less of a propensity to envision the future family in triadic terms?
2. What can be said about these parents' expectancies concerning their future coparenting relationship?

To address these questions, a subgroup of 40 couples was selected from the larger sample, and transcripts were produced for both their AAI and coparenting interviews. In the AAIs, we assessed both attachment-related content and parents' efforts to distance from attachment-related memories. Four major AAI indicators were of primary interest:

Rejection in the Origin Family

The AAI's Rejection scale measures the probable extent to which each of the interviewee's parents rejected the child's attachment-seeking behavior. Interviewees who portrayed their parents as minimizing, ridiculing, criticizing, or punishing their expressions of distress, need, or attachment-related affects received high ratings on this scale.

Derogation of Attachment

This is a "process" measure, and it reflects the extent to which the expectant parent engaged in the derogating dismissal of attachment figures and experiences during the interview. High scores were given when the expectant parent spoke contemptuously of attachment-related topics, implied that such topics were not worthy of attention, or offered only brief disparaging comments before abruptly moving on to other material.

Lack of Memory

High scores on this index were given when the expectant parent insisted that he or she could not recall childhood, to the point of blocking further inquiries by the interviewer.

Coherence

The coherence measure is the index most closely associated with overall attachment security. Interviewees scoring high on coherence described attachment experiences in a coherent and collaborative fashion, no matter what the emotional valence of the material they discussed. Unlike those who received low coherence scores, they also provided convincing anecdotal evidence that supported the generalizations they made about their attachment histories. By contrast, the discourse patterns of those whose narratives were rated as less coherent were marked by multiple contradictions, distortions, irrelevant digressions, and confusion.

Let's first look at coparenting narratives of men and women who reported high rejection in the origin family. We had anticipated that the experience of rejection might heighten parents' desires to protect their own children from similar experiences and bias them to be on the lookout for similar insults in their own future family. What we found was largely in line with this expectation. Expectant mothers reporting greater rejection from their own mothers showed a lower triadic propensity (speaking principally of themselves and the baby and excluding the father-to-be from their narratives) while also expressing less positive outlooks concerning their future family dynamics. Men reporting greater rejection by their own mothers also showed a lower triadic propensity and a less positive outlook concerning their future family. Also, expectant parents, both men and women, who reported greater rejection from their own fathers tended to have very negative future-family outlooks. In fact, high paternal rejection appeared to be especially relevant in the prediction of negative coparenting expectancies.

Next, we examined the two process-related measures: Derogation of Attachment and Lack of Recall. Past research with the AAI has indicated that these two indicators are usually high among parents who show active attempts to distance themselves from attachment-related percepts. Given this tendency to distance from emotional contents relevant to the family of origin, what do future-family narratives look like? Our results were quite interesting.

Expectant mothers who derogate attachment, perhaps not surprisingly, show less triadic propensity in talking about families, but they also show a less negative future family outlook. In other words, they are less likely than other pregnant women to engage any negative thoughts about the future. Expectant mothers who insist on lack of recall show a somewhat different pattern. They express less positive (but not more negative) future-family outlooks. That is, they are less likely than other women to share substantive positive imagery about the future family. Expectant fathers who insist on lack of recall show a lower triadic propensity, express a less positive future-family outlook, and tend to also show a less negative future-family outlook. Although these findings may seem a little puzzling at first blush, we see a trend: Expectant parents who distance from attachment-related percepts on the AAI are less likely than other parents to think of the future-family in triadic terms and are also less likely to engage any emotionally laden anticipatory imagery, positive or negative.

Finally, we found that women whose AAIs indicated greater coherence of mind did not, as we had anticipated, show any greater triadic propensity than other women. More coherent women did, however, express a more positive outlook when discussing the future family. Men showing greater coherence of mind with respect to attachment did, as predicted, show both a greater triadic propensity than did men with less coherence of mind and, like women, related narratives laden with more positive anticipatory imagery. These findings seem rather consistent: Expectant parents who have "gotten in front" of origin-family difficulties, who engage their memories and experiences fully, and who have come to a balanced understanding of their own histories anticipate the future family more openly, robustly, and positively.

In this chapter's final section, we consider the various risk factors we examined—significant depressive symptomatology, self-reports of poor self-restraint or low ego resilience, indications of marital distress, insecure states of mind with respect to attachment, and negative future-family outlooks.

Looking Across Risk Factors: Varying Profiles Among the Couples in Our Study

We were interested in determining whether there might have been different subgroups of families represented in our study, each containing families similar to one another in one or more ways. To examine this question, we conducted a series of cluster analyses using the CES-D, MAT, and coparenting interview Negativity scores as indicators of risk. These analyses allowed us to determine ways in which the families in the study were similar to one another and ways in which they differed. The results of the analyses suggested three relatively small and interesting subgroups and a fourth larger group that comprises a great many different family patterns. Because of the relatively small numbers of families in each of the first three groups and the considerable heterogeneity of the fourth group, the clusters did not prove particularly helpful in and of themselves as predictors of postpartum family adjustment. However, we did find the patterns to be of interest for their commonsense value, and so we present them here.

The smallest group of families was one in which fathers, but not mothers, appeared to be having a significant personal struggle with the transition to new parenthood. Men in this group expressed significant concerns about their future families in the coparenting interview (average Negativity score: 5.7 out of 7, compared with a sample mean of 3.6 for fathers) and also reported significant symptomatology on the CES-D (average CES-D score: 23.7), but they did not report high levels of marital distress (average MAT score: 116). Their wives were a mixed lot, some showing no risk, others showing risk on either the MAT or the coparenting interview.

The second (also small) group of families was one in which both mothers and fathers were struggling on multiple fronts, both individually and as a couple. Families in this group showed risk on both indicators of depression (mean scores of 21.2 and 26.6 for mothers and fathers, respectively; clinical threshold = 16 or greater) and marital dissatisfaction (mean scores of 91.6 and 92.0, respectively; clinical threshold = below 100). Future-family negativity scores were not, however, significantly different from the sample average.

The third group of families contained mothers who were struggling in their transitions, as were fathers in the first group. They reported, on average, clinically significant levels of symptomatology on the CES-D ($M = 20.0$), and as a group had the highest future-family negativity scores ($M = 4.7$, with 70% of mothers in the group scoring 5 or higher, compared with a sample mean of 3.8 for mothers). Their partners were also a mixed lot, with several having elevated CES-D scores (for fathers in this group, $M = 15.0$) but others showing no risk signs.

The last group of families was a very mixed bag. They could be considered a low-risk group only in the sense that, on average, they did not score (as a group) in the clinical risk range on any particular variable. However, among the diverse families in this group, 8 of the 90 showed risk on two or three indicators. Included among these 8 were 4 families in which both mothers' and fathers' coparenting narratives were high in negativity, 2 families in which high coparenting negativity scores by fathers were accompanied by high maternal depression scores, and 2 families in which the parent reporting high coparenting negativity scores also reported significant marital distress. This group also contained 18 families for whom the only sign of risk was a prenatal interview that was high in negativity (10 of the negative interviews were with mothers, and 8 with fathers). In all, high coparenting negativity was present among 28 of the 90 families.

The remaining families in this group showed either no risk (42 families), maternal depression only (18 families), paternal depression only (1 family), or marital dissatisfaction reported by one parent only (one mother, two fathers).

What this suggested to us as we prepared to begin our postpartum visits was that a very large number of expectant parents look ahead to life after their baby arrives with some anxiety. For some, it is little more than anxiety about the unknown. For others, it is anxiety more explicitly colored by worries about how well they and their partners will fare together as coparents for their new baby. For many families, concerns about coparenting co-occurred with other signs of risk whereas in others, they were the only indications we had of any concerns within the family. In some families, the absence of coparenting negativity seemed to signify a relatively positive and problem-free preparation for new parenthood. In others, however, problems in other areas (e.g., depression, marital distress) did surface even though parental outlooks on coparenting were not especially negative.

What this told us was that there was value in looking separately at parents' future family outlooks and not simply presuming that negative outlooks accompanied other signs of distress. In some cases they did, but in as many cases they did not. In the next chapter, we trace links between the different prenatal predictors we assessed and the indicators of early coparenting and family functioning that we sought at 3 months postpartum. As shown later, different prenatal predictors proved to be helpful in forecasting certain, but not other, postnatal outcomes.

References

Baumrind, D. (1971). Current patterns of parental authority. *Developmental Psychology, 4*, 1–103.

Block, J. (1971). *Lives through time*. Berkeley, CA: Bancroft.

Christensen, A., & Heavey, C. L. (1999). Interventions for couples. *Annual Review of Psychology, 50*, 165–190.

Cohler, B. J., Grunebaum, H. U., Weiss, J. L., & Moran, D. L. (1971). The childcare attitudes of two generations of mothers. *Merrill-Palmer Quarterly, 17*, 3–17.

Cowan, C. P., & Cowan, P. A. (1988). Who does what when partners become parents: Implications for men, women, and marriage. *Marriage and Family Review, 12*, 105–131.

Cowan, C. P., & Cowan, P. A. (1992). *When partners become parents: The big life change for couples*. New York: Basic Books.

Gottman, J. M. (1994). *What predicts divorce? The relationship between marital processes and marital outcomes*. Hillsdale, NJ: Erlbaum.

Heming, T., Cowan, P., & Cowan, C. (1991). Ideas about parenting. In M. Touliatos & M. Perlmutter (Eds.), *Handbook of family measurement techniques* (Vol. 1, p. 178). Newbury Park, CA: Sage.

Locke, H. J., & Wallace, K. M. (1959). Short marital-adjustment and prediction tests: Their reliability and validity. *Marriage and Family Living, 21*, 251–255.

McHale, J. P., Kazali, C., Rotman, T., Talbot, J., Carleton, M., & Lieberson, R. (2004). The transition to coparenthood: Parents' prebirth expectations and early coparental adjustment at 3 months postpartum. *Development and Psychopathology, 16*, 711–733.

McHale, J. P., Loding, B., Blaisdell, B., & Lovell, S. (1996, August). *Conceptions of parenting and coparenting among college-aged students*. Paper presented at the meetings of the American Psychological Association, Toronto, Canada.

Radloff, L. S. (1977). The CES-D scale: A self-report depression scale for research in the general population. *Applied Psychological Measurement, 1*, 385–401.

von Klitzing, K., Simoni, H., Amsler, F., & Bürgin, D. (1999). The role of the father in early family interactions. *Infant Mental Health Journal, 20*, 222–237.

Early Adjustment: The Coparental Alliance at 3 Months

With Meagan Parmley, Amy Alberts, and Julia Berkman

During the 1980s and early 1990s, several important books and articles concerned with the transition to new parenthood began popping up in scientific journals and in bookstores around the country, describing the major adjustments that couples faced as they welcomed their first new baby to the family (Cowan & Cowan, 1992; Entwisle & Doehring, 1981; Lewis, 1989). One of the eye-opening lessons learned from these research reports was that in many families, both men and women reported experiencing unexpected declines in their contentment with the marriage—at the very same time as they reported experiencing many joys of having become parents. Furthermore, many reports indicated that a significant proportion of first-time mothers also reported experiencing levels of postpartum blues that, although falling short of postpartum depression, were nonetheless a significant, foreign, and unsettling experience for them. The exact point at which these individual and relationship changes began surfacing varied somewhat from report to report, but in at least some investigations, researchers documented that major dips could be seen as early as the third month after the baby's arrival. Indeed, as we outlined earlier, several reports concluded that 3 months postpartum was the very lowest ebb in marital satisfaction for first-time mothers!

Of all the reports we read on the transition to new parenthood, we were probably the most intrigued by these compelling findings. It was, as we noted in chapter 2, a big part of the reason we chose 3 months postpartum as our initial postnatal port of entry into the new, three-person family system. Given previous reports that both individual and marital distress are common by the time babies reach 3 months of age, it seemed important to know whether these early distress signals had anything to do with the nature of the family's evolving coparenting alliance. We had a hunch that they might, on the basis of previous studies indicating that marital dissatisfaction and depression were amplified among women whose prenatal expectations concerning the division of child care responsibilities had been seriously violated during the early postpartum months. So we wondered whether such disillusionment was simply in the annoyance that new mothers expressed when they felt that fathers weren't shouldering their fair share of diaper changing, middle-of-the-night needs, or other caregiving duties or whether the nature of the problem was more insidious and reflected in the very foundations of the coparenting alliance that the two parents had begun forming together.

We also felt that 3 months was about the earliest we would want to connect with families to study coparenting because we believed that an assessment any earlier than this might simply have been too soon to find significant predictability or routinization in the families' patterns. As most parents know, the first days and weeks after their first baby comes home can be a time of tremendous upheaval and worry. New parents become concerned when their infants (as they are wont to do) lose significant amounts of their birth body weight, eliminate too little or in the wrong color, show breathing patterns that seem unusual, have trouble developing any sort of cohesive sleep pattern, and so forth. Calls to hospital nurseries can become regular occurrences, especially when there are no extended kin or other seasoned support system members around to help out and provide perspective. Stable routines, therefore, can take weeks to evolve, especially when babies are born jaundiced or face other medical challenges. Hence, although families' early adaptive efforts are themselves extremely interesting and important (and in our view, worthy of study in their own right!), attempting to measure coparenting at the height of family disequilibrium is unlikely to be the best way to access stable, enduring patterns of interaction. In contrast, by the time families had been together for 3 months—approximately 100 days into new coparenthood—we anticipated that they would have come to establish their own unique coparenting patterns and styles of commerce, marked to greater or lesser degrees by cooperation, coordination, and solidarity between the parenting partners.

The major challenge we faced as we planned our first visits was in designing a strategy that would allow us to meaningfully capture these core features of coparenting support and collaboration, as well as (on the flip side) coparenting disagreement, miscoordination, and detachment. Despite all we had learned from the scientists and helping professionals who had studied new parenthood during the prior decade, we were venturing into relatively uncharted territory when it came to assessing the nascent coparental alliance. Assessing depressive symptomatology, marital dissatisfaction, and the division of child care labor were of less concern to us, as we followed in the footsteps of our colleagues who had successfully used self-report instruments such as the Center for Epidemiological Studies Depression Scale (CES-D; Radloff, 1977), the Locke–Wallace Marital Adjustment Test (MAT; Locke & Wallace, 1959), and the Who Does What measure (WDW; Cowan & Cowan, 1992) to assess these important markers of individual and family functioning. Capturing the essence of the emerging coparental dynamic was indeed a new frontier.

Our solution was to turn to our colleagues at other institutions who had developed interview, survey, and observationally based assessment techniques and paradigms that in our view accessed relevant information about the inner workings of the early coparental alliance. We also adjusted the methodology of a respected paradigm that had been used extensively by infancy researchers to study early parent–infant interactions, in order to study coparent–infant exchanges. As we assembled these different assessment tools and planned our approach, we were guided by an expectation that a common underlying theme (similar to what John Byng-Hall, 1996, has conceptualized as a family "script") and a deep, foundational structure (akin to that described by Salvador Minuchin, 1974, in his structural family theory) would underpin and guide parents' reactions to the various tests we chose to showcase coparenting collaboration and support. To the extent that this was the case, we expected to find significant coherence across the impressions left by the different interview, questionnaire, and family interaction tasks.

Assessing Coparental Support and Solidarity: "Insiders'" and "Outsiders'" Perspectives

In chapter 1, we outlined how the strongest coparenting alliances are those characterized by cooperation, support, and solidarity between the adults providing the care and upbringing of children for whom they share responsibility. We also made the argument that what is most important about coparenting is not the particular way in which partners divvy up different child-care tasks but the sense of joint purpose, shared goals, trust in the coparenting partner as a parent, and instantiation of this felt solidarity in supportive and coordinated action. It was this conceptualization that guided our efforts to devise a meaningful strategy for assessing the family's coparenting system.

A debate occasionally raised by family researchers is whether the most relevant information about family functioning comes from family members themselves, in that their perspectives are informed by their own extensive experiences in the family, or from outsiders who may be more objective in picking up on distress signals unnoticed or unreported by family members. Commenting on this debate, Philip Cowan (e.g., Cowan, 1999) has frequently pointed out the futility of worrying about which view was "more accurate," because insiders and outsiders each offer unique perspectives that collectively provide a much more complete picture of the family than ever possible from insider or outsider reports alone. Concurring fully with Cowan's perspective, we used multiple instruments and observers to evaluate each family's coparenting system.

As we sought a self-report index to capture the parents' own views on the strength of the coparental relationship they were developing with their partner, we discovered a unique and very relevant survey instrument developed by Richard Abidin at the University of Virginia. Abidin's Parenting Alliance measure (PAM; Abidin & Brunner, 1995) was specifically designed to assess the degree to which men and women felt supported and validated by their coparenting partners. The PAM contains 20 different statements such as "My baby's other parent and I communicate well about our baby," "My baby's other parent believes I am a good parent," and "I feel good about my baby's other parent's judgment about what is right for our baby." Parents are asked to provide their first reactions to each of these statements, using a scale that ranges from 1 (*strongly disagree*) to 5 (*strongly agree*). Hence, the higher the total score, the greater the amount of solidarity the respondent perceives within the coparental alliance they share with their partner. Although the PAM had never before been used with families of infants less than 12 months old, we felt that its items and content were quite relevant in assessing the strength of the early coparental alliance from the parents' perspectives.

As a second indicator, one that capitalized both on the insiders' working models of their family and on outsiders' takes on the degree of support and solidarity between them, we analyzed couples' interactions with one another as they told us their stories about the day their baby was born and about life since the baby's arrival. At the time we designed our study, Susan Dickstein at Brown University, Barbara Fiese at Syracuse University, and several of their collaborators working together in a cross-site consortium had just developed an innovative new approach to evaluating co-constructed narratives by and about families. Dickstein's paradigm, in particular, was especially relevant to understanding the nature of coparental collaboration and support. On the basis of the give and take between partners as they work collaboratively to recount their family's birth experience, researchers evaluate (a) the coherence of the narrative (how organized and internally coherent it is); (b) the narrative interaction style of the couple (how well they coordinate with and how often they provide confirmation or disconfirmation to one another); and (c) beliefs expressed about the marriage, the infant, and the family's social world. Of these various indicators, the ratings of coordination, confirmation, and disconfirmation seemed to us especially relevant for assessing coparental support and solidarity, so we chose them as a second index of the developing coparental alliance.

Studying coparenting behavior is much more complex than asking parents to complete a survey or to grant an interview. Although research studies from our own lab (McHale, 1995; Talbot & McHale, 2004) and from the lab of Sarah Mangelsdorf and her colleagues (Frosch, Mangelsdorf, & McHale, 2000; Schoppe-Sullivan, Mangelsdorf, Frosch, & McHale, 2004) had validated the use of brief family play and teaching tasks to assess coparenting dynamics in families with infants aged 6–12 months, there had been no studies using observationally based methods to study coparenting in families with children as young as 3 months old. However, at the time we were planning this project, results of the prospective, longitudinal study of families conducted at the Centre d'Etude de la Famille (CEF) in Lausanne, Switzerland (see chapters 1 and 2) using the Lausanne Trilogue Play (LTP; Fivaz-Depeursinge & Corboz-Warnery, 1999) had begun making the scholarly circuit. They caught our immediate attention. As we described previously, Fivaz-Depeursinge and colleagues were taking an unusually careful and descriptive approach to cataloguing the body orientations of mothers, fathers, and infants at play together. From these remarkably intricate data on body formations, they made a brilliant conceptual leap to illustrate how the forms of physical and affective contact that were reflected in their microanalytic data characterized distinctive family alliance types. Even more remarkably, their study of the same families over time substantiated that there was significant stability in the type of family alliance from 3 months forward.

The LTP paradigm is a deceptively simple one. Family members are seated facing one another in a triangle, with the two adults each facing the baby but also easily able to turn to face one another. Parents are instructed to take turns interacting with the infant; first, one parent interacts with the child with the second parent present, then the second parent takes a turn with the first parent moving into the role of third party. Next, the three family members all interact together, and finally, the parents engage with one another, placing the infant into the third-party role. No toys and props are used, and parents handle the interactions and transitions as make the most sense to them. Hence, all possible family configurations (the three different "2 plus 1s" and the 3 together) are represented in the LTP assessment.

It was through poring over Fivaz-Depeursinge's data (e.g., Fivaz-Depeursinge & Corboz-Warnery, 1999) that we realized how many of the features of family interaction that caught their eye paralleled the ones that had captured our attention in our studies of older infants. Families were seen as functioning more effectively when the coparents participated together but did not intrude upon one another's initiatives or interventions with the baby. They were seen as most cohesive when the adults took turns and gave one another the space or room to interact with the baby and when the adults built upon one another's efforts to co-create a coordinated and relatively seamless experience for the baby rather than a disjointed one. Also, they were judged particularly effective when all family members maintained genuine and warm affective contact with one another during the interactions. Family members who participated fully, shared their orientation, and kept in affective contact with one another were said to have achieved cooperative alliances; those showing problems along one or more of these dimensions were judged to have stressed, collusive, or disengaged alliances. What was most unique to this system and what set it apart from our assessments of coparenting was that the infant's contributions to the interaction and the alliance were weighted just as markedly as were those of the coparenting adults, making the alliance type a true "family" index.

For these reasons, the LTP seemed ideally suited as a means to assess coparental cooperation, competition, and engagement among the families in our study. We reasoned that, in families in which a stronger coparental alliance was blossoming, the coparental partners would engage in better attuned and coordinated interactions with their baby and with one another, participating fully and enthusiastically but not domineering or intruding upon one another's efforts with the baby. In contrast, we anticipated that, in families still finding their way to an effectively functioning coparental alliance, there would be either a press for one or both partners to be critical of, interfere with, or otherwise disqualify one another's efforts with the child and/or for the partners to distance themselves affectively from the triad at all times except for when (and sometimes even when) they were themselves engaged with the baby. To estimate these various parameters, we adapted McHale, Kuersten-Hogan, and Lauretti's (2000) Coparenting and Family Rating System (CFRS). Our adaptation included several new microanalytic codes (e.g., flirting with or distracting the baby when he or she was engaged with the other parent, extending an invitation to the unengaged partner to join their interaction with the baby). Trained coders provided both these micro-analytic ratings and the more traditional global ratings of cooperation, competition, warmth, and engagement.

Although we expected that these measures would provide a well-rounded view of the coparental alliance from both the parents' and the clinician's perspective, we were concerned that the observational measure missed out on one very important facet of coparental functioning: how well the adults worked as a team under more stressful conditions. Certainly, the LTP is itself an unusual and challenging task and induces a fair modicum of stress for many families, but we also thought it apt to take a page from Salvador Minuchin's book to intensify the focused spotlight we placed on coparenting alliances as problem-solving units. Minuchin (1974) had observed that core family patterns and dynamics are particularly likely to emerge in circumstances in which explicit family processes are evoked and families must work to solve circumscribed dilemmas. We chose two such dilemmas relevant to coparenting for families to try to resolve at 3 months. The first was direct confrontation of the difference between the two of them in their perspectives about child rearing. The second was how to jointly comfort an acutely distressed baby. To evoke each of these two dilemmas, we needed to create two new paradigms. To create the new, we borrowed liberally from the old.

The Cowans had outlined in great detail in their 1992 book *When Partners Become Parents: The Big Life Change for Couples* how even minor decisions in perceptions about who does what can stir major feelings of anger, hurt, and lack of appreciation. Parents almost never see fully eye to eye on the division of labor, and in many cases, both partners end up feeling underappreciated for that which they do contribute. During the couples' groups that the Cowans led as one facet of their "Becoming A Family" study, they had asked couples to compare their own perceptions on the WDW instrument described in chapter 2 along a number of different dimensions. We saw the potential diagnostic value in formalizing this process and so built upon the Cowans' observations and made use of a procedure introduced by Schoppe-Sullivan and colleagues (2004). During our home visit, we first asked partners to independently complete the WDW as we readied our cameras for another task. When they finished, we gave them a third blank WDW sheet. We asked them to share their just-completed survey responses with one another and to work toward consensus in completing the third WDW jointly. Couples were free to go about this task in any way they wished. While we were interested in the outcome of the negotiation, our real focus was on the process. Specifically, we rated different behavioral patterns demonstrated by the couple as they worked together and the extent to which their jointly reached consensus had truly been collaborative. We anticipated that, in some families, the process would involve sharing of viewpoints and decisions respecting both parents' perspectives, whereas in others the process would be colored by negative emotion and criticism, by affective withdrawal, or by both.

We also thought there was value in devising a second stressful paradigm that involved the baby. Our rationale was that many situations demanding coordinated coparental effort during the early months require joint decisions about how to handle infant needs. Parents must develop coordinated plans of action for everything from how to handle regulatory and feeding problems to whether infants should sleep independently or sleep with the parents. Sometimes decisions are made planfully and with careful deliberation, but often there is little time for such deliberation when immediate action is needed. To date, there have been no assessments of coparenting, at least in families with infants and/or toddlers, that have capitalized on the use of mild stressors to evaluate coparental coordination in the moment. Some researchers have argued that asking parents to teach their babies how to perform a developmentally challenging task a bit too advanced for the baby affords such challenge. However, although such tasks may tax certain adults who are accustomed to showing off how clever their babies are, it is not clear whether they are stressful to the babies. Much more relevant would be an assessment in which the coparental partners would need to work together to soothe a genuinely distressed infant.

This was, of course, the genius of Mary Ainsworth's Strange Situation paradigm (Ainsworth, Blehar, Waters, & Wall, 1978). In this assessment, patterns of infant–caregiver attachment became apparent precisely because the caregiver–child system was placed under stress, allowing the underlying deep structure of the parent–child relationship to come into view. There is as yet no parallel indicator for encouraging the show of the coparental system's deep structure, but we thought it worthwhile to experiment with a paradigm that had been designed to induce stress in parent–infant pairs with infants as early as 3 months of age. Tronick's still-face paradigm (Tronick, Als, Adamson, Wise, & Brazelton, 1978) has been widely used to instigate distress among infants and to permit researchers to evaluate the sensitivity of parents as they strive to re-engage their baby and restore calm and equilibrium. It occurred to us that we could adapt this procedure to evaluate how well the coparental partners coordinated with one another. That is, we created an opportunity for observing parents working jointly to soothe their infant immediately after the period of emotional disconnect and distress caused by their having been nonresponsive to the baby for an extended period. Trained raters then evaluated both the behavior of mothers and fathers individually (on dimensions including sensitivity, warmth, verbalization, and use of touch) and the quality of coordination between the coparenting adults (cooperation, joint expression of positive affect, competitiveness, verbal disagreement).

Having settled upon this array of measures to estimate coparental cooperation and solidarity (summarized in Table 4.1) and on the other key indicators of individual and family functioning (total depressive symptoms, total marital satisfaction, perceived

TABLE 4.1. 3-MONTH MEASURES OF COPARENTAL SOLIDARITY AND SUPPORT

From Parents' Self-Reports:
Perceived support and solidarity (Parenting Alliance Measure; Abidin & Brunner, 1995)
From Co-Constructed Birth Narratives:
Couple coordination
Confirmation/disconfirmation (by father of mother)
Confirmation/disconfirmation (by mother of father)
From "Who Does What" Discussions
Coparental collaboration
Mother withdrawal
Father withdrawal
From Still-Face Interactions:
Coparental cooperation
Coparental warmth
Coparental competition
From Lausanne Trilogue Play Interactions:
Coparental cooperation
Coparental warmth
Coparental competition
Disengagement by one or both parents

satisfaction with the who-does-what of child-care labor), we recontacted the families who had taken part in the prenatal assessments. All but two consented to take part in the 3-month follow-up. Details of our visits with these families are described next.

Visiting Families at Home: Challenges and Lessons Learned

Scheduling and coordinating hundreds of trips into the community to visit with families in their homes can be a daunting task, made no easier by the bevy of props we needed to trundle along with us on the visits to help standardize the assessments we undertook. However, there was also a collective sense that we were really engaging with families on their own turf and visiting them at times when both the parents and their babies were ready to receive us. We also had to come to terms with and accept the scores of last-minute cancellations stemming from parents or babies being sick, sleeping, or otherwise feeling that they were not quite prepared for an assessment. Members of our research team learned to be flexible in contouring our availability to the rhythms of the families who took part in our study, and we believe that the quality of our 3-month data are all the better for it.

Most families were visited at least twice. This is because we sought to obtain both observational, interview, and self-report measures of coparenting and an evaluation of infant temperament and behavior (the latter gleaned both from parent report and through observation). As detailed earlier, parents completed Rothbart's (1986) Infant Behavior Questionnaire, and we utilized the behavioral assessment of temperament developed and validated by Garcia Coll, Halpern, Vohl, and Seifer (1992). As described in chapter 2, the assessment evaluated infants' behavioral reactions to a variety of increasingly intrusive interventions, from relatively mild stressors like wiping the baby's nose and putting a hat on her head to more noxious stimulation such as presenting a human mask, an overwhelming robot toy, and a human scream. For completion of the assessment, infants needed to be at their best, and because the family assessments described above often ran well over an hour, return visits were often the order of the day to gather the temperament data.

Whenever possible, our visiting team included at least one person who had been involved with the family since their entry into the study. All visitors were trained in the various methodologies of the study, and several team members visited Dickstein's lab and Garcia Coll's lab in Providence, Rhode Island, and Fivaz-Depeursinge's center in Switzerland to hone their skills in conducting the assessments. The observational assessments were conducted first, followed by the birth narrative assessment and finally questionnaire completion. Some families requested waiting until the follow-up temperament assessment to complete their surveys, and of course they were accommodated.

We found families to show much of the same diversity at 3 months as we had seen during the pregnancy assessments. Some parents offered team members the red carpet treatment, inviting them to share coffee and even occasionally a meal and taking the opportunity to ask questions, share stories and anecdotes, bring out photo albums, and in other ways provide extended glimpses into their lives. Parents breastfed and bottle fed their babies during the visits, changed their diapers, took breaks to make their babies comfortable when they nodded off during extended birth narrative assessments, answered phones, and let dogs go outside when they requested to do so. Some parents shed tears during the birth narratives or held hands at tender moments. Others proceeded confidently, systematically, and methodically through the assessments, wrapping things up in record time. Disputes over facts during the birth narrative and during the WDW discussions were commonplace, and more than one parent commented, "Can there be anything else that you don't know about us yet?!"

Overall, our sense was that parents appreciated and valued the follow-up contact, and many parents shared with us that they had been looking forward to seeing us again. We also felt that parents' openness to sharing what one parent called "our flabby underbellies" increased over time. Although most families' enthusiasm for follow-up visits dissipated somewhat the longer they stayed with us in the study, the commitment and loyalty of study participants as they stayed with the enterprise over time was a validating and positive experience for long-time members of the research team.

How Families Were Faring at 3 Months: General Findings From the CES-D and MAT

To begin addressing the question of how families were faring at 3 months, we examined the same CES-D and Locke–Wallace MAT scores that we had used to take families' pulses during the pregnancy. The average CES-D depression score for new mothers in this community sample was actually substantially lower than it had been during the pregnancy, though a substantial number of women and men continued reporting symptoms in the clinical range. At 3 months postpartum, the average CES-D score for new mothers was 9.2 (compared with 14.2 during the pregnancy), and the average score for fathers was 9.9 (compared with 10.7). However, there continued to be a very wide spread of scores for both men and women; for mothers, CES-D scores ranged from 0 to 32, and for fathers, scores ranged from 0 to 33. Moreover, on the depression index, we found that 24% (nearly one in four) of the mothers in our sample, as well as 13% of the fathers who took part, reported clinically significant levels of depressive symptomatology at 3 months postpartum. Among the women, in particular, several individuals continued to report depression scores of noteworthy concern. Ten new mothers had depression scores of 25 or higher on the CES-D index.

Marital satisfaction also, somewhat surprisingly, remained relatively stable for the group as a whole. Average declines in marital satisfaction among couples in our study were not nearly as pronounced as the 10- to 15-point decline reported in Belsky and Rovine's (1990) community sample, although we saw some subtle changes from prenatal assessments. The average Locke–Wallace marital satisfaction score of mothers (124.5) was essentially identical to the prenatal mean of 124.1, although among fathers it had declined slightly to 119.6 (down from 123.6). However, both mothers' and fathers' marital satisfaction scores ranged widely (29–157 for women and 65–153 for men), and whereas only 5% of mothers and 7% of fathers had reported clinically significant marital dissatisfaction during the pregnancy, these figures had jumped to 10% and 20%, respectively, by 3 months postpartum. That is, in challenging portrayals of the early months of new coparenthood as a "honeymoon" period, we found that the number of martially distressed mothers doubled and the number of martially distressed fathers almost tripled, only 3 months into new parenthood. Taking our depression and marital satisfaction scores together, the proportion of families in which someone was struggling to a significant degree was 33%. That is, one of every three participant families in our study contained at least one parent who reported a 3-month CES-D score of 16 or higher and/or a MAT score below 100.

We found the very low marital satisfaction scores reported by many fathers to be an especially poignant finding, given that so many men are reluctant to reveal signs of their relationship vulnerability to outsiders. Perhaps the most pertinent statistic concerning early family adjustment was the number of families for whom there were multiple (two or more) indicators of distress. We found that in 18% of the families in our sample (up from 16% during the pregnancy), there were scores exceeding the established thresholds on two or more of the four risk indicators.

Indicators of Strength and Strain in the Early Coparenting Alliance

How burdensome was this individual- and couple-level distress for parents working to co-create a strong coparenting alliance? We shall see. Before addressing this question, we first needed to ascertain the story told by our various measures of coparenting. As we have outlined, we focused on five primary indicators: the experience of solidarity and support as reported by parents on Abidin and Brunner's PAM; the extent to which couples accommodated one another's perspectives in a coordinated way, and voiced confirmation of (or alternatively, discomfirmed) one another during the jointly constructed birth narratives; the pair's propensity to engage cooperatively and warmly (or conversely, in a competitive or detached fashion) during the face-to-face LTP play interaction; the extent of collaboration in evidence as they worked to find consensus in WDW; and the quality of coordination as they worked together to soothe their infant after the concentrated stress induced by the brief still-face challenge (Table 4.1). To the extent that these different indices were capturing common, underlying coparenting themes or structures, we expected to find statistically significant connections among related measures of solidarity and support.

Table 4.2 summarizes the nature of the relationships among these various indicators. While the pattern of significant associations is selective, rather than "across the board," several things stand out from this matrix. The first is that there were indeed a number of significant associations, in the predicted directions, linking related self-report, interview-based, and observational measures. This is significant, in that none of these indicators had ever been used before to estimate coparental functioning in families of infants quite so young, and yet all appear to have revealed something of significance

TABLE 4.2. INTERCORRELATIONS AMONG MEASURES OF COPARENTAL SOLIDARITY AND SUPPORT AT 3 MONTHS

	PAM		Birth Narrative			WDW		Still-Face Reunion		
	Mom	Dad	Coord	ConfM	ConfD	Collab	WthdrD	Coop	Warm	Comp
Birth Narrative										
Coordination	No			Same		See			See	
Confirmation-Mom	Significant			Paradigm		Below			Below	
Confirmation-Dad	Correlation									
Who Does What										
Collaboration			+		+	Same			See	
Withdrawal-Dad		–				Paradigm			Below	
Still Face										
Cooperation	+	+		+		No			Same	
Warmth				+		Significant			Paradigm	
Competition					+	Correlation				
LTP										
Cooperation	No				+			+		
Warmth	Significant					+		+	+	
Competition	Correlation									
Disengagement			–				+	–		

PAM = Abidin & Brunner's Parenting Alliance Measure; WDW = Elliston & colleagues "Who Does What" consensus discussion; LTP = Fivaz-Depeursinge & Corboz-Warnery's Lausanne Trilogue Play.

about the degree of struggle or success the coparental partners had been having. Also striking is that for both mothers and fathers, scores on the self-report PAM (which gauged the parent's private experience of support from and solidarity with the co-parent) were elevated in families that demonstrated greater coparenting cooperation during the still-face assessment. For fathers, scores on the PAM were also higher in families where fathers stayed engaged and refrained from withdrawal during the WDW interactions. We found these correlations of special interest because in psychology studies, measures that are based on the same source (e.g., several different paper-and-pencil reports all provided by the same person or several observations of the same person's behavior) are usually more closely interrelated than are measures based on different sources (as happens when personal reports are linked to independent measures of behavior). This has been referred to as a problem of "shared method variance." It is noteworthy, then, that in the data from this study, links were found not just among the different behavioral measures but also between both maternal and paternal self-reports on the PAM and observed behavior in two different observational assessments. On the basis of this pattern of associations, we believe that the various strategies we chose to estimate the underlying coparental alliance in families had a fair measure of success.

Another thing standing out in Table 4.2 is the number of significant intercorrelations involving the measure of coparental cooperation during the emotionally charged still-face interaction. Three of the four indicator sets—the PAM scores of both mothers and fathers, the birth narrative ratings indexing mothers' confirmation of fathers, and the LTP measures of high coparental cooperation, high warmth, and low disengagement—were all associated with how well mothers and fathers accommodated one another's inclinations and worked together during the still face. Said differently, in families in which the coparental partners showed more effective cooperation in soothing their distressed babies, there was parallel evidence of more cooperative and effective interaction in the LTP and birth narrative assessments and a sense by both parents that they were members of a supportive coparenting team. As such, our hunch that the family's base coparental structure might best be revealed during moments of emotional stress appears to have been borne out. Parents who can work effectively together even when they are confronting emotional strain appear to be able to do so because they have a strong and supportive coparental base upon which to stand.

Although the pattern of associations between LTP behavior and the other self-report and observational indicators was not as extensive as was the pattern of associations linking still-face cooperation to these indicators, one LTP linkage in particular stood out to us: Disengagement observed during the LTP correlated with fathers' withdrawal during the often affectively charged WDW conversations. This was of interest to us because meaningful disengagement patterns are notoriously difficult to evaluate during routine family interactions. Yet in our sample of non-referred families, early indicators of disconnection, just like early indicators of solidarity and warmth, did coalesce across multiple coparenting assessments at 3 months

Data in Table 4.2 further indicate that what our research team learned from parents' behavior during the LTP provided a useful but somewhat incomplete read on the strength of the coparental alliance. The five sets of measures considered together, however, afforded a very formidable evaluation of coparental solidarity and support. That is, in families in which a strong coparental alliance was developing, parents worked effectively together whether jointly playing with their baby, portraying the birth of their child and their family to a curious outsider, collaborating to resolve differences in perspective on their division of child care labor, or helping the baby attain a regulated state after she had been perturbed, and they each experienced a sense of support and validation from their partner. Conversely, in families in which the alliance was not on equally strong footing, parents often stepped on each other's toes or withdrew during those same play, narrative, problem-solving, and co-soothing assessments and reported feeling less support and validation from their coparent.

Not every measure we pursued showed equal promise as coparenting indicators. For example, one of the still-face ratings we initially piloted was called "inclusion of the other parent." We designed this rating on the basis of some prior research suggesting that mothers sometimes serve a gate-keeping function within families (either integrating fathers into a coparenting role or keeping their involvement with children to a minimum). We wondered whether mothers' welcoming inclusion of fathers into family interactions could be taken as a signal of comfort in their sharing of the coparent role. However, after rating inclusion during the still-face interactions, we found no association whatsoever between this index and any other measure of coparenting.

A more complicated issue concerns the trustworthiness of our evaluations of coparental miscoordination and interference. In 1995, when the first observational studies of coparenting were published by our lab and by Jay Belsky and his colleagues, one conclusion drawn by both investigative teams was that observational methodologies could be used to validly assess themes of competitiveness, opposition, and undermining in families of infants and toddlers. Although this central finding has since been replicated by other researchers in their studies of early family dynamics, it is not entirely clear to us whether we were as successful in estimating early coparental competition or antagonism from our 3-month coparenting indicators. To be sure, there were some coparenting partners who showed signs of disqualification and disconfirmation during the birth narrative recountings, who disrupted one another's interactions with the baby during the LTP, and who worked at cross-purposes when trying to soothe their baby after the still face. However, the degree of interrelatedness among these different indicators was not what we had imagined it would be, indicating that these indicators were not tapping equally effectively into underlying family themes of opposition and competitiveness in the coparental relationship. As we discuss in later chapters, it was the indicators of high or low cohesiveness in the coparental relationship (signified by cooperation and warmth) that proved to be the most stable over time, and the overall best predictors of later toddler adjustment. This said, evidence also indicated that the indicators of opposition assessed at 3 months and especially at 12 months were not inconsequential.

The Interrelatedness Between Individual and Marital Adjustment and Coparenting Solidarity

Given the numbers of parents in the study who were reporting significant depressive symptomatology and/or significant dissatisfaction in the marriage, we anticipated finding significant ties between individual and coparental adjustment. We were therefore surprised to find that very few such associations actually materialized. Table 4.3 summarizes the associations between depression and marital satisfaction, and the different indicators of coparenting.

As shown in Table 4.3, parents who were more depressed and less satisfied with their marriages also reported less cohesive coparental

TABLE 4.3. INTERCORRELATIONS BETWEEN DEPRESSION AND MARITAL SATISFACTION, AND COPARENTING INDICATORS

	MCESD	DCESD	MLW	DLW
PAM				
Mom	–		+	+
Dad	–	–	+	+
Birth Narr				
Coord				
Conf-Mom	–			+
Conf-Dad				
WDW				
Collab				
Withd-Mom				
Withd-Dad				
Still Face				
SF Coop				
SF Warm				
SF Comp				
LTP				
LTP Coop				
LTP Warm				
LTP Comp				
LTP Diseng				

- + signifies a positive and significant correlation between the two variables ($p < .05$)
- – signifies a negative and significant correlation between the two variables ($p < .05$)

PAM = Abidin & Brunner's Parenting Alliance Measure; Birth Narr = Dickstein and colleagues' Birth Narrative; WDW = Elliston & colleagues' "Who Does What" consensus discussion; LTP = Fivaz-Depeursinge & Corboz-Warnery's Lausanne Trilogue Play; MCESD, DCESD = mothers and fathers' reports of depression on the Center for Epidemiological Studies Depression Scale; MLW, DLW = mothers' and fathers' reports on the Locke-Wallace Marital Adjustment Test.

alliances. Although this finding was not an unexpected one, given the shared method variance issue described above, it is nevertheless quite important. Parents' perceptions of coparental solidarity may not only reflect, but also have the potential to color, family interactions over time. And as children grow older, parental perceptions of coparental solidarity are linked to their perceptions of child behavior problems. In one pertinent study, Bearss and Eyberg (1998) established that parents' perceptions of coparental solidarity on the PAM were significantly associated with reports of child adjustment problems and that the link between coparenting and child adjustment was stronger than the link between marital adjustment and child adjustment. In other words, although marital stress may be a risk indicator in families, the family's problems in coparenting appear to be the channel through which marital distress affects children.

This distinction between risk indicators and risk mechanisms, first elucidated by Michael Rutter, was also pursued in a 2001 study by Gayla Margolin and her colleagues. Paralleling Bearss and Eyberg, Margolin et al. (2001) documented that problems in coparenting are also more closely related to parenting problems than is marital distress. Hence, the fact that perceptions of coparenting are already closely tied to depressive symptomatology and marital dissatisfaction just 3 months after the baby's arrival indicates that these early risk indicators, sometimes downplayed as normative responses to new parenthood, must not be taken lightly.

Beyond the interrelatedness of depression, marital dissatisfaction, and perceptions of a less cohesive coparental alliance, however, none of the other coparenting indicators consistently reflected parents' current adjustment levels. The assessment that echoed parental adjustment most clearly was the birth narrative, during which mothers who were reporting greater depressive symptomatology showed less inclination to confirm their partners' perspectives. This finding was elucidated further in analyses of variance (ANOVAs) comparing women whose CES-D scores were above the clinical threshold with those below; clinically depressed mothers showed significantly lower levels of partner confirmation than did nondepressed women (Soyka, DePalma, Dickstein, & McHale, 2005). Perhaps relatedly, fathers in families where mothers were more disconfirming reported greater marital dissatisfaction. So in this narrative task, mothers' endorsement of fathers (but not fathers' endorsement of mothers) could be traced to current levels of individual adaptation by both individuals. ANOVAs also revealed trends approaching significance for cooperation during the still-face interactions to be lower, and competitive behavior higher, in families where mothers' CES-D scores were above clinical threshold. Across the remainder of the assessments, however, there were no compelling associations between self-reported depression or marital dissatisfaction by either partner, and concurrent indicators of coparenting process. It is hence even more noteworthy that self-reported perceptions of coparenting on the PAM were associated with early coparenting behavior.

Seek and Ye Shall Find: How Parents' Prenatal Expectations Foreshadowed Coparental Solidarity

In chapter 2, we described a new prenatal interview that we developed to assess parents' portrayals of coparenting in their family of origin and their expectations concerning coparenting in their new family of procreation. In chapter 3, we reported that many parents had been entertaining mild to serious concerns about how well they and their partner were going to mesh as parents for their child. Parents expressing a greater degree of negativity about their future coparenting alliance tended, not surprisingly, to be those from marriages that were on somewhat shakier footing during the pregnancy, but did these parents actually have cause for concern? Were parents' prenatal expectations about problems with coparental solidarity borne out in their postnatal coparenting dynamics at 3 months?

To address this question, we identified three indicators of coparenting process at 3 months. First, we combined indicators of cooperation and warmth (self-reported coparenting support, coordination during the birth narrative, warmth and cooperation during the still face, and warmth and cooperation during the triadic play) to form an overall index of coparental cohesion. Second, we created a parallel index of coparental conflict by combining the relevant scores capturing dissonance during the birth narrative, still face, and triadic play interaction. And third, we focused on withdrawal during the WDW interactions separately (rather than combining it with the conflict measures), since disconnection and detachment represents a different form of adaptation than shows of opposition. We then asked whether the degree of negativity and pessimism about future coparenting that had been expressed by mothers and by fathers during the pregnancy predicted, prospectively, low levels of observed solidarity and support, high levels of observed conflict, or tendencies toward withdrawal at 3 months postpartum.

What we discovered was that parents who were already holding more negative expectations about the coparental process during the pregnancy did, in fact, exhibit lower levels of cohesiveness during their coparenting efforts at 3 months. We also found that the negative expectations of mothers, but not of fathers, predicted fathers' later withdrawal during the 3-month Who Does What assessments. We did not, however, find any significant association between negativity by mothers or by fathers during the pregnancy and coparenting conflict in the postpartum. That is, men and women who had expressed a greater number of concerns about how well they and their partners would work together as coparents during the postpartum were not any more likely to be behaving in an undercutting or disqualifying manner with their partners during coparenting exchanges.

We found this pattern of findings quite intriguing. It appeared that parents' worries that they might have difficulties forming a strong coparental alliance were realized in the difficulties they seemed to be having striking upon a supportive, positive connection with one another as they parented their baby together. Keep in mind that parents with low scores on our summary index of 3-month coparenting cohesion just weren't clicking quite as well in the various assessment settings. They failed to show the same level of teamwork in the birth narrative context and the same level of collaborativeness and complementarity during the still-face and play interactions, as couples with higher scores on the index of solidarity and support. It was this relative absence of a well-coordinated affirming alliance that was foreshadowed by pessimism during the pregnancy.

It was also quite fascinating that women's pessimism about coparenting solidarity during the pregnancy, but not men's pessimism, foreshadowed greater disconnection by men during 3-month coparenting negotiations. Recall that some of the women in our study had shared concerns during the pregnancy about whether they'd be able to count on their partners to "be there" for the family as dynamically as the women had hoped. Although earlier we surmised that partners' prenatal concerns about future coparenting stem in large part from their experiences with coparenting distress in their own families of origin, this finding underscores the possibility that at least some parents may also, or instead, have been basing their misgivings on the couple's own relationship history. A significant association found between greater levels of strain in the marriage and greater pessimism and negativity in future family expectations was certainly consistent with this interpretation, and could help explain the prescience of women's prenatal pessimism in predicting their partner's behavior during the WDW negotiations. Even so, we would reiterate here that a negative cast by one or both partners can itself contribute to the early amplification and perpetuation of existing relationship patterns and structures.

So what should we make of the finding that prenatal pessimism did not predict greater coparenting conflict at 3 months? One possibility already noted is that our coparenting assessments simply did not have adequate "pop" for detecting meaningful forms of conflict in the coparental alliance. But let's suppose for the moment that we did do a reasonable job of estimating early coparental conflict. In this case, the absence of a connection between prenatal pessimism and 3-month conflict might be important. It was clear from our data that in families where one or both parents were already entertaining prenatal misgivings about their capacity to collaborate effectively as coparenting partners, the couple was in fact struggling to find ways to work effectively and collaboratively together. This was apparent from our observations of low cohesion in their coparenting process. Suppose, however, that this very same heightened sensitivity to their difficulties in working collaboratively kept couples at arm's length and prevented them from developing an antagonistic and combative coparental relationship with one another. In other words, while parents' prenatal concerns about coparenting solidarity did come to be realized in their difficulties forging a supportive and cohesive coparental alliance in the first 3 months, they did not forewarn or touch off early coparenting battles.

Although this interpretation is consistent with the "prenatal expectancies" data, we offer this interpretation with caution because as it turned out, early coparental conflict actually was foretold by one prenatal factor: The coherence of mothers' states of mind with respect to attachment on Main and Goldwyn's (in press) Adult Attachment Interview (AAI). Talbot, Elliston, Thompson, Scull, Lieberson, and McHale (2006) examined both mothers' and fathers' prenatal coherence scores (which readers may recall from chapter 3 are important determinants of whether parents have developed secure states of mind with respect to attachment), and found that greater incoherence among women during their pregnancies begat greater coparenting conflict at 3 months. Talbot and colleagues' (2006) analyses also hinted that somewhat counterintuitively, early coparental dissonance may not be reduced, but may actually even be slightly elevated (at least during the early postpartum months), when mothers with less coherent states of mind are married to men with more coherent states of mind! Although the subset of families that showed this latter pattern was too small for statistically valid conclusions to be drawn with confidence, the pattern of findings in our data did underscore that maternal insecurity may be worth considering carefully during clinical contacts with families transitioning to new parenthood as a potential risk factor not just for insecure attachments, but also for early emerging coparental conflict.

What can be said about incoherent states of mind with respect to attachment among fathers? Talbot and colleagues (2006) found that men displaying less coherent states of mind with respect to attachment during the pregnancy, though no more likely to be involved in conflictual coparenting alliances, were more likely to exhibit withdrawal behavior at 3 months. Specifically, men but not women with less coherent prenatal AAI scores showed a greater propensity to check out emotionally during WDW negotiations, while more coherent men were more likely to remain connected with their partners even under duress. Hence the coparenting correlates of coherence and insecurity may differ for men and women—women's incoherence fueling greater early coparental conflict, and men's fueling greater disconnection, at least as exemplified by paternal withdrawal from conflict exchanges.

Because we did not have the benefit of visiting recurrently with families during the 100 days leading up to our postpartum assessments at 3 months, we cannot disentangle how and why a lack of coherence in mothers' states of mind with respect to attachment came to be so closely interconnected with early coparental conflict. There is any number of possible explanations. For example, in some cases, fathers who stepped in to shoulder care for the baby may have overstepped the amount of assistance desired by mothers and threatened the mother–baby bond, with the longer term outcome being heightened competitiveness during both routine and stressed interactions. Alternatively, highly engaged fathers may have prompted feelings of low efficacy and/or resentment in wary, at-risk mothers. If such mothers responded by resisting or opposing their partners' efforts with the baby, and especially if their partners remained highly engaged and did not back away at all, the stage would be set for opposition and dissonance in the early coparental process.

These interpretations are highly speculative and are neither exhaustive nor mutually exclusive. We offer them primarily to underscore the fact that, in those families in which coparental conflict appeared to have been brewing as early as 3 months postpartum, this dynamic appears to have been foreseeable from greater maternal incoherence, if not insecurity, during the latter stages of the pregnancy.

And Then You Add a Touch of Spice: How Babies' Temperaments Entered Into the Equation

Most parents who have had two or more children are more than willing to provide testimony to the power of infant temperament. Babies can vary dramatically with respect to what they bring to the table from the outset. Some infants are more placid, take more readily to routines, and are prone to long periods of quiet concentration. In contrast, other babies are more demanding, take longer to quiet, and resist limitations.

As we planned our study, we spent many hours discussing the ways in which we thought that infant characteristics might shape the early coparenting and family process. We speculated, for example, that difficulties experienced during the birth process or high levels of perinatal risk might be factors that would bond the coparenting partners and lead to greater coparental solidarity, support, and cohesion. In contrast, we speculated that a "difficult" baby who had greater problems with self-regulation might stir greater disagreements between partners about how best to handle the baby's needs, leading to less coparental solidarity and possibly also to higher coparental conflict.

As it turned out, the story is not quite so simple. Although there were a number of families in our study who encountered birth complications and some degree of perinatal risk, just a handful had faced severe, imminently life-threatening circumstances. Also, we found no statistically significant differences in overall levels of solidarity and support between the families who had confronted milder or more severe forms of perinatal risk and the families who had not. Similarly, we found no main effects of infant temperament when comparing the family processes of babies with easy and difficult temperaments. That is, as a group, families of infants who showed less distress to novelty and to limitations on the different temperament indicators that we described earlier were no more likely to show high levels of solidarity and support, or low levels of conflict, than were families of babies judged to have more difficult temperaments.

A somewhat different question, however, is what happens when a difficult or less difficult baby joins a family system that may already be at risk for developing coparenting difficulties. As we have described, families with higher levels of prenatal marital strain, and in which parents hold more negative expectations concerning their future family process, are at such risk. That is, in families with stressed marriages and in which parents are less optimistic about their abilities to forge a strong coparental alliance, there is an increased chance that the early coparental process will be characterized by low levels of coparental solidarity and support. So we went back and asked: Is this trajectory from prenatal risk to postpartum coparenting difficulties affected in any way by the new baby's temperament? We addressed this question by examining the interaction between levels of prenatal risk and degree of difficulty of infant temperament.

What we discovered was that the baby's temperament did, indeed, play a very important role. In families in which high prenatal risk (high marital strain, high maternal pessimism, high paternal pessimism) was present and in which the parents were joined by a baby who had a difficult temperament, there was a very high likelihood that the prenatal risk would translate into coparenting problems (McHale et al., 2004). However, among higher risk families in which the parents were joined by a less difficult child, the relationship between prenatal risk and low solidarity and support in the postpartum failed to materialize. That is, among study families with an easy baby, we found no relationship between degree of prenatal risk and observed solidarity and support in the postpartum. This suggests that any interventions developed to support families and strengthen coparental solidarity at the transition to new parenthood need to take into consideration the additional strains that a temperamentally difficult baby introduces into a system already at risk for other reasons.

Summing Up: The Coparental Alliance at 3 Months

In summary, our maiden voyage into families' homes to study the developing coparental alliance at 3 months postpartum proved to be a very meaningful and fruitful one. Rather than finding an underdeveloped and unformed system, we uncovered evidence that families had already begun developing signature alliances that could be accessed by self-report, by interview, and by observation. Parents shared with us the experience of bringing their baby into the world; of surviving the early minutes, hours, and days after their baby's arrival; and of establishing a family routine in the weeks and months since. They shared with us their perceptions of how supported they felt by their partner and how effective a parent they thought their partner to be. They also showed us something of how they shared their parenting space, both during a face-to-face play interaction with their partner and their baby and during the emotionally charged moments after they had perturbed their baby by failing to respond to bids during a still-face challenge. Remarkably, we found patterns of coherence across this variety of disparate indicators, suggesting that parents had been having varying degrees of success in forging a strong coparental alliance characterized by solidarity and support.

Our data also indicated that couples who had been struggling in their marriages before the baby's birth and who had expressed concerns about their ability to co-construct a positive coparenting relationship with their partners did indeed show lower levels of cohesion and support for one another during the assessments we completed in their home. Further, low levels of coherence in parents' states of mind with respect to attachment also predicted early coparenting outcomes. When mothers' states of mind during the pregnancy were less coherent, the coparenting dynamic was at greater risk for showing early signs of conflict and discord. When fathers' states of mind during the pregnancy were less coherent, early coparenting patterns were characterized by greater likelihood of paternal withdrawal.

What might these distinctive family dynamics portend for later child and family adjustment? Is the dissonance seen in some families at 3 months a passing phase, or does dissonance continue or even mount by the end of the first year? We consider these questions next in chapter 5.

References

Abidin, R. R., & Brunner, J. F. (1995). Development of a parenting alliance inventory. *Journal of Clinical Child Psychology, 24,* 31–40.

Ainsworth, M. S., Blehar, M. C., Waters, E., & Wall, S. (1978). *Patterns of attachment.* Hillsdale, NJ: Erlbaum.

Bearss, K., & Eyberg, S. M. (1998). A test of the parenting alliance theory. *Early Education and Development, 9,* 179–185.

Belsky, J., & Rovine, M. (1990). Patterns of marital change across the transition to parenthood: Pregnancy to three years postpartum. *Journal of Marriage and the Family, 52,* 5–19.

Byng-Hall, J. (1996). *Rewriting family scripts.* London: Guilford Press.

Cowan, C. P., & Cowan, P. A. (1992). *When partners become parents: The big life change for couples.* New York: Basic Books.

Cowan, P. (1999). What we talk about when we talk about families. *Monographs of the Society for Research in Child Development, 64,* 163–176.

Entwisle, D., & Doering, S. (1981). *The first birth: A turning point.* Baltimore: Johns Hopkins University Press.

Fivaz-Depeursinge, E., & Corboz-Warnery, A. (1999). *The primary triangle: A developmental systems view of mothers, fathers, and infants.* New York: Basic Books.

Frosch, C. A., Mangelsdorf, S. C., & McHale, J. L. (2000). Marital behavior and the security of preschooler–parent attachment relationships. *Journal of Family Psychology, 14,* 144–161.

Garcia Coll, C. T., Halpern, L. F., Vohr, B. R., & Seifer, R. (1992). Stability and correlates of change of early temperament in preterm and full-term infants. *Infant Behavior and Development, 15,* 137–153.

Lewis, J. (1989). *The birth of the family: An empirical inquiry.* New York: Brunner/Mazel.

Locke, H. J., & Wallace, K. M. (1959). Short marital-adjustment and prediction tests: Their reliability and validity. *Marriage and Family Living, 21,* 251–255.

Main, M., & Goldwyn, R. (in press). Adult attachment rating and classification systems. In M. Main (Ed.), *A typology of human attachment organization assessed in discourse, drawing and interviews* (working title). New York: Cambridge University Press.

Margolin, G., Gordis, E. B., & John, R. S. (2001). Coparenting: A link between marital conflict and parenting in two-parent families. *Journal of Family Psychology, 15,* 3–21.

McHale, J. P. (1995). Coparenting and triadic interactions during infancy: The roles of marital distress and child gender. *Developmental Psychology, 31,* 985–996.

McHale, J., Kazali, C., Rotman, T., Talbot, J., Carleton, M., & Lieberson, R. (2004). The transition to co-parenthood: Parents' pre-birth expectations and early coparental adjustment at three months post-partum. *Development and Psychopathology, 16,* 711–733.

McHale, J. P., Kuersten-Hogan, R., & Lauretti, A. (2000). Evaluating coparenting and family-level dynamics during infancy and early childhood: The Coparenting and Family Rating System. In P. Kerig & K. Lindahl (Eds.), *Family observational coding systems: Resources for systemic research* (pp. 151–170). Hillsdale, NJ: Erlbaum.

Minuchin, S. (1974). *Families and family therapy.* Cambridge, MA: Harvard University Press.

Radloff, L. S. (1977). The CES-D scale: A self-report depression scale for research in the general population. *Applied Psychological Measurement, 1,* 385–401.

Rothbart, M. (1986). Longitudinal observation of infant temperament. *Development Psychology, 22,* 356–365.

Schoppe-Sullivan, S. J., Mangelsdorf, S. C., Frosch, C. A., & McHale, J. L. (2004). Associations between coparenting and marital behavior from infancy to the preschool years. *Journal of Family Psychology, 18,* 194–207.

Soyka, A., DePalma, K., Dickstein, S., & McHale, J. (2005, April) *Family adjustment correlates of birth narratives told by new parents.* Paper presented at the Southeastern Psychological Association, Nashville, TN.

Talbot, J., Elliston, D., Thompson, J., Scull, C., Lieberson, R., & McHale, J. (2006). Do early coparenting dynamics benefit from coherent states of mind with respect to attachment? *Infant Mental Health Journal, 27*(3), No. 43.

Talbot, J. A., & McHale, J. P. (2004). Individual parental adjustment moderates the relationship between marital and coparenting quality. *Journal of Adult Development, 11,* 191–205.

Tronick, E., Als, H., Adamson, L. B., Wise, S., & Brazelton, T. B. (1978). The infant's response to entrapment between contradictory messages in face-to-face interaction. *Journal of the American Academy of Child Psychiatry, 17,* 1–13.

A Year in the Making: Coparenting Patterns at 12 Months

With Inna Khazan

"We're always rushing. Randy always makes us wait when it's time to leave for services, and so we're usually late. Week after week it's the same. But somehow when we have to go somewhere he wants, it's a different story."

"We co-sleep. We have since he was born, and we wonder sometimes how long it will go on. But for now we're both really used to it and don't talk about it much."

"We have to figure out a way to get her together with other kids. Like, we take her to the play area at the mall, but that's always different kids and she never gets to see the same people twice or develop relationships."

"Sometimes it feels like I just can't get her off of me. She just can't always be with me. It'd be nice if he stepped in sometimes . . . but he doesn't see it that way. We're still fighting over it, but I am going to get some help from him."

The indoctrination of babies into a family process through the rhythms of teamwork and coordination that color three-person family outings. The quest for ways to help babies begin establishing peer skills. Dealing with sleeping and, for many families, transitioning from co-sleeping. Finding ways to help children turn equally to either parent rather than consistently seeking out one. Parents described a rather different set of coparenting and family issues than we saw at 3 months, although many of the same themes surfaced, too. In this chapter, we provide a window into some of the most pertinent coparenting challenges described by parents of 1-year-olds and offer some insights into how different patterns came to be embedded in the family contexts we have described thus far in the book.

For our research team, the days and weeks between our 3- and 12-month visits with families rocketed by like a flash. Parents too, although usually in retrospect, asked themselves where time had gone so quickly. For babies, however, that same time span was a lifetime. The transformation from an as-yet immobile infant looking quizzically at her parents as they buckled her into our unusual Lausanne Trilogue Play (LTP; Fivaz-Depeursinge & Corboz-Warnery, 1999) seat, to a fully mobile, curious, and playful baby navigating a toy-filled laboratory playroom at the university's Family Study Center, was truly utterly astonishing. During families' 12-month visits with our research team, babies protested mightily when their parents stepped out of the room for a few minutes, leaving them alone with a student researcher, and settled—sometimes sooner, sometimes quite a bit later—after their parents returned. They took their seats in a high chair and worked to solve simple puzzles, stack blocks, and snap and unsnap beads together. They effectively signaled their likes and dislikes to their parents, who regularly seemed to anticipate the babies' next moves well before we did. They wriggled with delight in their highchair seats as their mothers stood initially at a distance and then began inching closer and ever closer, attempting to elicit smiles, but they then grew much more pensive moments later when an examiner tried the same ruse.

Later, they watched with some bemusement and some consternation as yet another new set of researchers animated a puppet show in front of them. They enthusiastically embraced an electronic toy that broadcasted cartoon sounds and then struggled as best they could moments later to manage their emotions as their mothers took the toy from them and posed a "still face" for a spell. Later released from the constraints of the high chair in which they'd been confined, they frolicked with a plastic ball almost as big as they were, climbed aboard a helicopter rocking toy, munched goldfish crackers, explored every nook and cranny of the playroom, and altogether won the hearts of the graduate students who coordinated the families' visits with us. Our research staffers were no longer fleeting curiosities to the babies, as we had been during our 3-month visits to their homes. Rather, we became very central and salient figures—shied away from at the beginning when the families arrived for their first return visits in 9 months but greeted enthusiastically and often flirted with openly by the time families bid us good-bye for another 18 months after completing their final 12-month visit.

Babies weren't the only ones who had changed. Coparenting teams, too, looked quite different to us. The families we had seen in their homes at 3 months, almost all of whom had still been working to find a comfortable stride those 9 months ago, now seemed to have co-created a much more stable family pattern and routine. For some of them, the pattern suited them fairly well, and they felt comfortable with it (although we didn't see a single family in which the parents didn't tell us about things they wanted to improve). For other families, the pattern they had fallen into wasn't sitting especially well with one or both parents, and some significant change was desired. Indeed, now quite familiar with our repartee of questions about how things were going, the families we had seen at 3 months didn't hesitate to open up to us about their happiest moments, their biggest frustrations, and their most fervent hopes for change.

Families who newly joined the study at 12 months were, not unexpectedly, a little less forthcoming as a group, at least at the outset. Before long, however, probably because of the many complexities of managing family life with a 1-year-old, our "new" families too were sharing their stories with us. Although being a continuing family in the study did help the more veteran study participants avoid initial opening night jitters as they sat down again with our interviewers, the content of what the continuing and new families shared with us was quite similar—so much so, in fact, that analyses comparing the key indicators of coparenting solidarity that we gathered at 12 months postpartum did not reveal any significant differences for new and continuing families. Perhaps the greatest change we saw from 3 to 12 months was the confidence with which parents engaged their children. Whereas many parents at 3 months were exquisitely sensitive and respectful, and even sometimes (in our view) a bit cautious when engaging their 3-month-olds in the LTP, parents' handling of their 12-month-olds—although still quite sensitive—belied a confidence and a quiet knowing that was relatively rare in our earlier assessments.

Despite these dramatic shifts in babies and in the coparenting teams themselves, however, there was also substantial continuity; families who had hit the ground running in the early months after their babies arrived continued, by and large, to adjust relatively well to the new challenges of the mobile, passionate, 12-month-old. Families who had found the early months more of a challenge often continued to struggle at 12 months. Some families, of course, turned things around dramatically, and others began encountering difficulties where none had existed earlier, but as a rule, we found continuity in coparental adjustment to be noteworthy, through the myriad developmental changes in children and families. We detail these connections from 3 to 12 months a bit later in this chapter. To begin, however, we share in the parents' own words some of the major changes and challenges they told us they were facing at the time of their baby's first birthday.

Our Interviews With Parents at 12 Months: What We Asked and What Parents Said

As already indicated at many points in this book, our principal aim in this study was developing a thorough understanding of how and how well parents were working together to coparent their children at the various time points at which we visited them. As we set out to develop this evaluation at 12 months, we had the benefit of prior work on coparenting interactions completed at the University of California at Berkeley during the late 1980s and early 1990s (McHale, 1995). However, no one had yet sought to systematically assess coparenting solidarity through the use of interview methodologies. So we were once again charting new terrain: What kinds of questions might help us cut to the chase to get at the heart of parents' views of the coparenting alliance that had begun developing in their family?

We decided on two sets of queries. In our direct set of questions, we simply asked what parents saw as their own and their partners' strongest points as parents and what they thought they and their partners needed to work on as parents. We also asked them to tell us about times when they had worked well together as a team and about times when they had not done so and about what they wanted to change in their families. Finally, we asked them to tell us how they rated themselves as a coparenting team. As a more indirect window into parents' conceptualizations of family life and dynamics, we asked parents to tell us about a typical time when their family was all together as a threesome or foursome, as well as about the best and worst moments in their families. In listening to these responses, we were interested in such things as the ease or difficulty with which parents came up with a best and worst time, as well as the details of the depictions themselves.

In a series of conference papers, our colleagues Leo Waterston and Bob Babigian (who developed a scoring system for the best and worst times segments of the interview which they dubbed the NAS-TBW, or Narrative Assessment Scale of Typical, Best, and Worst Times) outlined both the overall landscape of the data and some interesting associations linking aspects of parents' stories and their current levels of adaptation in the family (Babigian, Waterston, & McHale, 2002; Pellegrini, Liebling, Waterston, & McHale, 2007; Waterston, Babigian, & McHale, 2001, 2002). Overall, most parents' recollections were balanced and even-handed; they tended to paint neither an unusually rosy picture or an unusually bleak one. For example, ratings of overall positive and negative tone in the fathers' stories indicated that relatively few fathers (16%) told stories ranked highly (scores of 2 through 4) on the negative tone scale. Although fathers' stories did cast something more of a positive hue, fully 41% of fathers received the lowest score of 1 on the positive tone scale, with another 33% receiving a score of 2. Overall, fathers' depictions of family life with a 1-year-old were conveyed in matter-of-fact fashion, summarizing highs and lows in a convincing but moderate tone.

Families' worst moments were actually much easier for fathers to remember than typical or best times. Ratings of the degree of difficulty with which fathers came up with each of the stories indicated that 60% of fathers showed no difficulty, delay, or hesitation in relating a story of a typical time when the family was all together. Portraying the family at its best was most difficult for fathers, as only 41% conveyed that story without significant pondering or delay. In contrast, describing the family at its worst was not a chore for fathers; 84% of the fathers studied were primed to describe the family's worst moments at a moment's notice! We do not interpret this finding to mean that fathers' most readily accessible imagery concerning their families is negative; the worst-moment question was the last one asked, so fathers could have had some reason to anticipate this question on the basis of the previous two. Equally, however, we were struck by how many fathers offered unsolicited remarks along the lines of "That one's easy," or "No problem!" when asked about the family at its worst. Family life with a 1-year-old presents many challenges, and fathers were at the ready to share some of those with us; yet despite the ease with which fathers shared stories of infant irritability, coparental disagreement, and family disarray, only 11% of the story sets offered by fathers were judged by the coders to have conveyed a sense that the father felt overwhelmed.

What about mothers? We found a similar patterning to mothers' stories, with a few differences worthy of note. A slightly higher percentage of mothers than fathers (70%, compared with 60%) had no difficulty relaying a story of a typical time when the family was all together, and 60% of mothers (compared with 41% of fathers) readily came up with a story of the family at its best. Like fathers, however, mothers too had the easiest time portraying the family at its worst (76% of all mothers recounted this vignette with ease, akin to the 84% of fathers who did the same). So, like fathers, mothers had no difficulty recalling and describing in some detail family flops. Given the percentages, we anticipate that most readers will readily resonate with these findings. Although most families aspire to co-create positive and supportive coparenting alliances from the time they are pregnant with their firstborn, by the end of their baby's first year they have collected a great many war stories to tell, and most share them readily and with little hesitation.

Overall, the tone of mothers' stories was also similar to that of fathers. As noted above, three in four fathers (74%) received scores of 1 (41%) or 2 (33%) on the positive tone scale. The percentage was almost identical for mothers; 77% received scores of 1 (35%) or 2 (42%). With respect to negative tone, a similar proportion of mothers (20%, compared with 16% of fathers) told stories that cast a negative hue. A slightly larger difference was seen in the "conveys a sense of feeling overwhelmed" rating, for which nearly a third of mothers (31%, compared with 11% of fathers) communicated or conveyed a sense that the family burden had felt insurmountable at times.

It's not entirely clear to us how much to read into this latter finding. A number of researchers and theorists (e.g., Bauer, Stennes, & Haight, 2003; Chance & Fiese, 1999; Fivush, Brotman, Buckner, & Goodman, 2000; Ruth & Vilkko, 1996; Saarni, 1999; Tannen, 1990) have described in detail the different ways in which emotions are expressed and regulated in men and women's dialogues about emotionally laden content. Men, in particular, often respond adversely to implications that they are feeling overwhelmed, even (and perhaps especially) when they *are* feeling overwhelmed. Hence, judgments about whether fathers are or not feeling overwhelmed may be more difficult to come by from analyses of their narratives than parallel judgments about mothers. As our colleague Roger Bibace at Clark University has pointed out (e.g., Valsiner, Bibace, & LaPushin, 2005), interview data reflect public discourse about private relationships and should be accorded their due with this consideration always firmly in mind. This said, however, the finding that approximately one third of the mothers in our sample conveyed a sense of feeling overwhelmed as they recounted their family's typical, best, and worst moments strikes us as significant and reconciles well with other data reported throughout this book. The facility with which most mothers and fathers recollected times when their family had been at its worst speaks to the routine challenges of parenting a young infant. However, we also underscore our finding that, overall, stories tended to be more positively than negatively hued. This finding helps ground and balance these otherwise sobering statistics: Coparenthood brings with it high highs and low lows.

Waterston and Babigian's reports also examined linkages between the content of parents' family stories and other markers of family adjustment at the 12-month mark. Perhaps the clearest finding to emerge from these analyses was that mothers who characterized their families less positively and more negatively reported higher levels of depression on the CES-D than did other mothers. Furthermore, a substantial proportion of these women exceeded the threshold for clinically significant levels of depression (i.e., scores of 16 or higher). Mothers whose stories were less positive and more negative also reported greater dissatisfaction with their marriages on the Locke–Wallace MAT. Perhaps most intriguingly, fathers' marital satisfaction was higher in families in which mothers told stories more positive in tone. Hence, the evidence was good that mothers' family stories could be linked to both their own and their partners' reports of adjustment in other realms.

The fact that depressed mothers told fewer positive and more negative stories, although noteworthy, isn't a brand new contribution to the literature. Susan Dickstein and her colleagues reported similar findings in their analysis of parents' birth narratives (Fiese et al., 1999). What is new and of interest were linkages between the tone of mothers' typical, best, and worst stories and other assessments of coparenting at 12 months. For example, when mothers told stories more positive in tone, they reported significantly less coparental conflict on McHale's (1997) Coparenting Scale. Scores from their partners concurred; fathers in these families also reported less conflict and said they spoke disparagingly about mother to baby less frequently than other fathers. In contrast, mothers who told family stories that were negative in tone reported more coparental conflict on the Coparenting Scale. Independent judges documented a greater discrepancy between their and their partner's level of engagement with the baby during triadic family interactions (see below). This is significant, because McHale and Rasmussen (1998) found such discrepancies to be indicators of emotional disconnection that are predictive of children's later adjustment to preschool.

We did not find this same pattern of results for fathers. In fact, there were no linkages between men's stories and their own or their partners' depressive symptomatology or marital dissatisfaction, nor did fathers' stories correlate significantly with any of the concurrent self-report or observational indicators of coparenting. Indeed, at first glance, it seemed that men's family stories at 12 months were little more than idiosyncratic portrayals of their personal phenomenologies but not of any deeper family realities, until, that is, we checked cross-time ties between our measures of coparenting at 3 months and fathers' stories at 12 months. When we did so, we discovered a trend approaching significance for greater coparenting negativity at 3 months to predict negative tone in fathers' stories at 12 months. Hence, some of the seeds of paternal negativity in family representations at 12 months appeared to have already taken root in the coparental partnership by the time of our earlier 3-month assessments.

What were the main themes that parents raised at 12 months when asked what they hoped might improve in their coparental partner? Our colleagues Jessica Thompson and Symphony Thomas, examining parents' responses to interview queries about coparenting strengths and areas in need of improvement (Thomas, Elliston, Waterston, Thompson, & McHale, 2005), detected a number of common themes in these reports. In response to our question "What would you most want to change about your partner?" three sets of themes predominated: less intensity, greater involvement, and greater structure and rule-setting. Perhaps not surprisingly, these themes were underscored somewhat differently by mothers and fathers. Men were most likely to want their partners to be less intense in their expectations, relax more, be less reactive, or work on being more patient. Almost half of the father narratives analyzed by Thomas et al. (46%) included such themes, exemplified by comments such as "she tends to fluster quickly" and "she's not as patient as I am." At the other extreme, 13% of the fathers we interviewed were unable to come up with any specific area in need of partner improvement, claiming to be "perfectly content" with their partner's parenting.

Unfortunately, none of the mothers whose replies were analyzed by Thomas et al. likewise indicated perfect contentment! In contrast with men's wishes that their partners show less intensity, women were much more concerned with the regularity of fathers' engagement with and caregiving of the baby. Some mothers were looking for greater help of any kind, exemplified by Trisha's wish that Phil "would just say to himself, 'okay, I'm going to change her diaper' without my having to say 'can you go change her diaper?'" Stepping in to provide care without being asked was mothers' most common wish at 12 months, although a significant number went further to say that they wanted fathers to give higher priority to the child and family.

Although the "what would you want to change about your partner" question provided the most direct window into the major coparenting concerns that men and women had at 12 months, we also learned a great deal from parents' answers to the question "What would need to change in your family for things to be going as well as you'd wish when next we visit you at 30 months?" Although parents' responses to this question were much broader in range, they frequently highlighted what parents wished could be different in their shared parenting of the baby. Among fathers, the most common concerns had to do with the day-to-day home environment. "Challenging/stimulating the baby intellectually," "organizing and structuring the baby's day better," and "arranging play time for peers" were among the more common categories of response among fathers, with nearly 25% offering comments such as "I'd like her to provide more of a learning environment." It was sometimes unclear whether fathers were commenting that they and their partners as a coparental team needed to change the baby's routines or whether this was a wish for change in the partner. Not all comments were along the lines of the previous comment, "I'd like her to do this." Many were couched in more general terms, such as "she [the baby] really has to start spending time with other kids," or "he [the baby] just doesn't have a real routine right now, and he needs to."

Fathers' focus on the baby's home environment rather surprised us and prompted us to take a closer look at our sample. The families in our study contained a somewhat higher proportion of stay-at-home mothers than recently reported national statistics, and we wondered whether fathers in single-earner families were more focused on quality of mothers' parenting than were fathers in dual-earner families. Our analyses did not provide a clear answer; among fathers who expressed wishes for changes in the daily home environment, three in five were sole-earner fathers and two in five were dual-earner fathers. As we see later, however, clearer evidence of some potentially important distinctions between the coparental adjustments of single- and dual-earner families did surface in our analyses of coparenting interaction data. These findings are discussed later in this chapter.

Fathers also expressed other concerns, including the amount of time the family spent together as a family, and maternal work outside the home. Many fathers lamented the demands of their own jobs and noted that time was lapsing quickly without their getting to know their babies. Most felt helpless to change this situation, describing sacrifices and accommodations they had already made within the constraints of their jobs. Very few fathers felt that the time they had been able to spend with their family was fully adequate. With respect to maternal work, fathers were quite unsettled about this issue. Many commented on the family's reliance on income contributed by mothers (when the mothers had returned to work) or their need for such a contribution (when mothers were at home full time) but also expressed the parallel desire that their babies be raised principally by their mothers rather than by other caregivers. Bob, for example, sighed "Things would be much better if she was home 75% of the time."

In contrast to fathers' concerns, mothers' focus was seldom on the caliber of the learning environment that was being provided for the child or on the need to titrate current work commitments. Rather, mothers' comments embellished their wishes for more substantive caregiving by fathers and that their family come first, with the baby given top priority. Indeed, the two most common subthemes identified by women when asked what they felt needed to change in their family were more time together as a family and more time dedicated to the child. Mothers' comments, like fathers, were most often offered indirectly. They sometimes belied personal guilt over not having enough time for the baby and at other times communicated discontent with the amount of time their partners had to give. Examples of such comments were Miriam's remark that "to function better as a family is to create more time together," and Connie's comment that "your time needs to be spent with your child and not worrying about trying to get all the other stuff done."

Overall, these data revealed both commonalities and distinctions between men and women as we directed them to focus on their family's coparenting environment. Fathers of 1-year-olds attended most often to the tenor of the overall coparenting climate that they perceived in the home, noting stylistic differences and especially wishing that their partners could be less concerned with precisely how things got done. A smaller, but significant, subgroup of fathers also expressed wishes for more structured daily routines for the baby, in the service of acculturating habits and intellectual curiosity. Mothers were more apt to express concerns about the lack of parenting support they often felt, their frustrations over being delegated the role of field marshal, and the sheer amount of time and psychic energy that fathers had to give.

From these data, it appears that one coparenting dynamic that takes shape in many families of 1-year-olds is one in which fathers look to mothers and in some cases, hold them largely responsible for the early work of shaping the child's personality, only to weigh in with concerns when they perceive mothers to be establishing a socialization climate that they see as either too demanding (or too lax). Mothers in many of these families, by contrast, are looking for greater father participation in the parenting process itself, and rarely is either parent fully satisfied with the family climate they are co-creating for their baby. In discussing what most needed to change, the most dominant theme was the prioritizing of time for the family. Virtually all mothers and more than half of all fathers believed that their families were not currently being prioritized with the little discretionary time they had to allocate.

This is a sobering statistic, one that is likely to hit home with most readers. Parents' struggles with the competing demands of this period were ubiquitous, in evidence throughout their interviews. With respect to mothers' widespread desires for greater father engagement in coparenting, Hilda pointedly summarized the sentiments of this subgroup of mothers when she commented:

> "It'd be good for *both* of them, and for the family, if they spent more time together. I am happy to see that she's attached to him, though."

Mothers weren't alone in these sentiments; in families in which mothers raised father engagement as an issue, fathers largely concurred. For example, Hilda's husband Phil, commenting separately in his individual interview with our team, echoed Hilda's observations:

> "I definitely think she's closer with my wife than with me. We have our little special moments, but in general I think she bonds more closely with my wife."

Representing one of the even greater extremes, Harry shared with us that in his family, most of the intimacy had slipped away from the relationship he shared with Christine and come to be concentrated in the relationship between Christine and their children:

> "I have my own bed in there (laughs), she nurses her and goes to sleep with them. I think that physically they are definitely more intimate."

We have been describing the concerns of parents in families in which fathers are still struggling to find their place coparenting side by side with their partners. Lest we paint an inaccurate portrayal of a sample dominated by devoted mothers and disconnected fathers, it is important to assert that many of the fathers in our study were actually very closely attuned to the importance of developing emotional ties with their babies and working diligently to forge such connections. Sheldon exemplified the perspectives of this cadre of fathers as he mused:

> "I want to spend as much time with her as I can now, because she's only going to be one for a little while."

Father involvement, as we discovered, was often a very complex issue in the evolving coparental alliance at 12 months. Consider, for example, the comments of Cindy. Cindy was one of the mothers in our study who parented full time at home. She offered a somewhat different perspective, one that was voiced by a great many of the other mothers in the study as well:

> "It's frustrating sometimes—the kids are more receptive to him when he comes home, even thought it's been me who's been home all day with them."

Cindy's honest ambivalence about what she saw as her children's infatuation with their father was actually quite commonplace among the mothers in our sample. Almost to a person, women clearly valued the roles their partners played in their children's lives, and expressed frustrations when they felt their partners' work lives were taking them away from the family. As we've summarized, nearly all mothers yearned for more time together as a family, and called for more active paternal involvement in the work of caregiving. However, the paradox was that although a majority of the mothers did often talk about the positive bond existing or emerging between their partners and their children, they nonetheless felt a sense of unfairness, and sometimes even indignation, when they saw their partners reaping benefits of close father–infant ties without putting in the same effort (e.g., diaper changings, nail clippings, soothings and calmings, feedings, bathings) that they themselves had devoted.

Some fathers were aware of these sentiments by mothers, but others were not. Even among those who were, finding solutions that felt equitable to both partners didn't come easily. Many mothers reported still searching for options that would help to even the playing field. Mary, for example, stayed at home with her two children Billy (12 months) and Ellie (43 months). She reported that she did nearly all of the routine child care work from Monday through Friday. Although Vic shouldered some of the caregiving duties on the weekend, freeing Mary to do some things for herself, Mary was still yearning for more. She told us, almost apologetically,

> "I really need more time for myself—I sometimes feel like I'm just buying time until he finally takes them on the weekend."

This was an interesting contrast between our 3- and 12-month assessments. At 3 months, many mothers were beginning to reveal frustrations that they had been doing more of the child care work than the couple had planned during the pregnancy. Their views surfaced most often during the "Who Does What" conversation, often catching their partners quite, quite unaware. By 12 months, however, the division of labor had become an ingrained pattern in the family, for better or worse. Mothers were typically very open about their frustrations, about desiring more time for themselves, and about feeling frustrated when they saw their partners playing the role of hero for their receptive babies while contributing little to the work of child care.

Also by 12 months, many fathers spontaneously expressed an awareness that they needed to do more, yet surprisingly few felt they had sufficiently stepped up to the plate. The most common metaphor was that of "helping out" rather than sitting side by side with their partners to take hold of the reins. An exemplary comment came from Tim, who had been talking about having a second child with his wife Corinne. Tim told us:

> "You know, spending 10 hours a day with him, and hopefully with another little one, is tough, and I know she's going to need a break."

Other fathers were even less attuned to their partners' needs than this, focusing more squarely on their own frustrations. Many fathers felt that they were doing as much as they could and that their partners were not acknowledging the stresses they encountered at the workplace. For example, Richard opined:

> "It's like she thinks I just go out and play all day. Then I come home and she wants to hand the baby to me immediately. My job is work, not play. I'm 100% responsible for our bills right now because she's not working. And sometimes we barely make ends meet—we've bounced half a dozen checks this year. She doesn't seem to feel that pressure, but I do. I need a little time to unwind at the end of the day. And I never have a second for myself. If I sit down for a minute to watch the news or something on TV, she gets upset. It feels really unfair sometimes"

Richard's comments embody the frustrations many parents were beginning to feel by 12 months—too many responsibilities, not enough time. Work–family issues were not an explicit focus of our study, but workplace and financial issues contributed to many of the strains couples were experiencing in their coparenting relationship. Whether mothers worked or did not, the stresses were still there. In Peter and Lily's family, Lily had returned to work full time. Peter expressed the ambivalence felt by many fathers whose partners were back at work by 12 months:

> "To be honest, I wish she could just stay home—I'd prefer working and I'd prefer her to be home with him."

In Lily's interview, she provides a perspective voiced by many working mothers:

> "I wish it was feasible for me to cut my work hours, even just a bit. If I was able to do that, then maybe when I was with the baby I wouldn't feel like I was putting so much pressure on myself when I have to put him in the playpen for 10 minutes."

Alice, also back at work full time, summed up several different perspectives in commenting:

> "I want to give more to my family and less to work. I'd also wish—and I admit that this is really pressure I'm feeling coming from my husband—that we'd be able to find the time to enjoy each other more."

Readers may be wondering whether there was any linkage between what parents imagined life would be like in their future family during the pregnancy and what they were telling us in their coparenting interviews at 12 months. The answer is both yes and no. Very few parents accurately predicted what family life would be like after the baby's arrival, and this is something we've known for a very long time. The Cowans elegantly portrayed the widespread surprises of new parenthood in their 1992 volume on becoming a family. For many families, however, there was something important and even prescient about how parents imagined what life would be like in their future family.

In chapter 4, we described how pessimism during the prenatal interviews predicted low coparenting cohesion at 3 months. By 12 months, the links we began seeing related more to differences in how the two parents had envisioned their future families before the baby's arrival. Recall, for example, the disparities in the perspectives of Ron and Candice that opened chapter 4. Ron and Candice had expressed what in our view looked to be diametrically opposed expectancies about family life after the baby's arrival. At 12 months, we could pinpoint how the disparities already in evidence during the pregnancy had come to trigger clear coparenting discontent. The evolution from prenatal differences to 12-month discontent was clearest in Candice's interview when she told us softly:

> "I just feel like a single mom right now . . . If we yell loud enough, the baby gets upset, and we stop. Overall, I'd have to say I'm pretty miserable. Ron needs to be more involved, more often, for longer periods. Our styles *would* work well together—if he did more. As it is, I do 98%. We both have a kid. That's the deal."

Despite Candice's conciliatory comment that Ron's and her styles would mesh well together, she later goes on to reveal that it really isn't just that she wants Ron doing more, although that's certainly a major contributor to her unhappiness. Rather, Candice also cites more palpable dissonance and lack of support for her efforts:

> "Like, I'll yell at her 'get off the table,' and instead of backing me up, he says 'you yell too much.'"

The lack of solidarity is, of course, most directly pertinent to the case we are developing for the critical importance of supportive coparental alliances in acculturating infants, toddlers, and young children. Divisiveness between partners initially confuses and disorganizes children and later comes to fuel the kinds of parent–child coalitions that S. Minuchin documented as being especially destructive in families. Here, we note that Ron and Candice's situation was not a unique one, but it illustrates well both the importance of the expectations that men and women bring with them to new parenthood and the importance of having developed channels of communication for working through differences and impasses. As a couple, Ron and Candice had been faring relatively well before the baby's arrival, having built large segments of personal time into their lives. This arrangement worked well for them, as it did for many couples in our study; they felt invigorated by their alone time, which generally allowed them to connect meaningfully rather than to feel disconnected or alienated when they did spend time together as a couple. Neither, however, had quite been prepared for the demands of new parenthood. Candice looked to share the load equitably with Ron so that she might keep her vibrant selfhood alive, whereas Ron anticipated that Candice would handle the bulk of the caregiving. These differences in perspective might not have become so overwhelming had the couple been able to talk regularly about their differences, yet such discussions had not been a commonplace feature of their relationship before the baby's arrival, and this circumstance did not change after her arrival. In the next section, we examine in some detail the strong connection between marital and coparental functioning in evidence at 12 months, as at other points in our study, with a special look at the microprocesses by which marital distress comes to affect coparenting behavior.

Marital–Coparenting Linkages

As we discussed in chapter 1, one of the most reliable findings in all of the coparenting research thus far has been the strong linkage between marital and coparenting adjustment. In families in which partners are struggling in their marriage, coordination of coparenting often suffers. Coparenting interactions of maritally distressed parents are low in warmth, cooperation, and positive affect and/or high in disputatiousness or disconnection and lack of engagement by one or both partners. Although the specific nature of these linkages varies from family to family and may differ depending on whether the child is a boy or a girl (McHale, 1995), it is not uncommon to see spillover from marital discontent into coparenting processes. To date, much of what we've learned about marital–coparenting connections has come from studies like ours, in which marital adjustment is assessed in one pass, through observational and self-report measures, and coparenting dynamics are assessed separately either during family interactions or by parental self-report. Although these kinds of studies have permitted us to establish the requisite statistical support for the existence of marital–coparenting linkages, they have fallen short of providing glimpses into how such dynamics actually play out in families.

Our study provided many illustrations of the dynamic nature of this process in ways that could probably never be captured by the kinds of observational studies researchers typically conduct. Take for example an illustration provided by Jay, whose comments about co-sleeping opened this chapter, as he discussed a marital–coparenting episode in his family:

"She usually puts him down, but some nights I do. There was one evening when we were visiting my parents and sleeping in the living room. We'd had a royal fight about money just before his bedtime. I think she left it to me to put him to sleep because she was so mad. So I was sitting with him on the sofa bed, singing and patting him, but every time he'd almost get to sleep she'd come into the kitchen and turn the light on and leave it on when she left. The kitchen was right next to the living room, so it would wake him up. So I'd go turn it off and try to get him to sleep, and then she'd come in again 10 minutes later and do the same thing, and he'd startle again. It happened like four times. I was boiling mad but I didn't say anything because I didn't want to start another fight. Finally after more than an hour he fell asleep."

This example is illustrative for a number of reasons. First, the silent anger that the couple was experiencing after their spat is probably something to which many, if not most, couples can relate. Second, the link between the couple's marital distress and their coparenting miscoordination is clear—owing in part to the anger stirred by their marital dispute, there was a failure to coordinate properly in the task of soothing the baby—or to communicate about the miscoordination. Third, we see some of the challenge that theorists and researchers have often encountered in attempting to distinguish parenting from coparenting. Jay's efforts to put baby Victor to sleep are rightly considered an example of parenting behavior; at the same time, it is easy to see how the "putting baby to sleep" ritual reflects a coparenting endeavor, one that, this night, went awry. Fourth, we can see clearly at work here the mediational model that has been proposed by several coparenting researchers. In such a model, marital distress is held to have its primary effects on child development through its impact on coparenting quality. In this example, marital distress disrupts the baby's regulation by virtue of the problematic coparental dynamic. Had either partner interrupted the negative sequence of events that emanated from their marital spat, it is likely that they would have much more successfully negotiated their shared parenting responsibility of putting their son to sleep.

Several of these points are deserving of further comment. First, this example illustrates why marital strain and coparenting problems are often inextricably linked. Many couples in the throes of a marital dispute unconsciously or (perhaps more often) consciously act out in subtle ways to drive their point across to their partner. Feeling criticized one time too often, one partner may turn the tables and criticize the partner to convey how it feels. Ditto with feeling neglected and ignored; a spouse who feels unseen or invalidated often elects to give his or her partner the cold shoulder, so that the spouse ends up in the parallel position of finding no one "at home" when he or she comes in search of affirmation, support, or emotional contact. However when partners allow criticism, withdrawal, or other conflict tactics to enter into the mix at a time when they need to be pulling together and supporting one another's parenting efforts, they are effectively unable to coparent.

On the conceptual issue of distinguishing parenting from coparenting, we have always seen this as something of an artificial designation advocated principally by research-oriented scholars seeking often-elusive precision in the operationalization and measurement of family constructs. The answer to the question of what distinguishes parenting from coparenting is really a very simple one, explicated by Patricia Minuchin (1985) many years ago: It is the level of analysis undertaken. This example elegantly illustrates that, at the same moment, it is possible to conceive of Jay's efforts to soothe Victor as reflective of his parenting style, skills, and propensities and to view this episode as one indicator of the couple's longer term collaborative effort to help Victor develop effective internal regulation and rhythms.

Which leads to a third point: In research studies of coparenting–child linkages to date, investigators (ourselves included) have evaluated coparenting in one or more of the ways detailed in this book. They have also assessed child adjustment via informant reports, by laboratory-based measurements (Belsky, Putnam, & Crnic, 1996) or, rarely, by actual playground observations of peer interactions (McHale, Johnson, & Sinclair, 1999). Then they have traced links between coparenting and child adjustment scores. We take that tack in this book as well. But usually missing from these accounts is consideration of the "micro-events" by which coparenting dynamics actually come to influence children's developing skill sets. In this example, we see one such micro-event. A lack of coordination between Victor's coparents disrupts his efforts to effectively attain the comfortable rhythm of his personal sleep cycle. Were this episode to play out only very rarely, chances are good that the coparenting rift would not play a formative role in shaping Victor's capacities for self-soothing. If the coparenting dynamic were to occur more regularly or intensively (such that it created alarm or dysregulation), there could very well be longer term ramifications for the baby's developing competencies.

It is easy to view this example and indict Hannah as the culprit in the failed coparenting effort. Indeed, just as our research studies try to tease out marital from coparenting constructs, or parenting from coparenting constructs, so too do we try to isolate individual traits or symptoms (as a feature of the mother or father apart from any relationship dynamics) and assess the impact of these individual traits or symptoms on the coparenting dynamic. This is exemplified in our study by our measurement of depressive symptomatology and by our assessments of self-restraint and resilience. However, there is another way to think of Hannah's behavior that is much more systemic and much more relevant to the grander conceptualization of coparenting. Some of the interview snippets we provided earlier hint at this conceptualization.

Amy Carmola Hauf and Lynne Bond at the University of Vermont drew our attention to interesting differences in how men and women think about paternal roles in coparenting. Men often portray their role as being one of a steadying influence, stepping in to maintain family equilibrium when mothers are at the end of their ropes and losing patience with children. By filling in emotionally when needed, fathers view themselves as helping to assure greater overall sensitivity and continuity of measured, supportive parenting for the child. Mothers often describe things a little differently. Although not disputing the fact that their partners do often step in at just the right moment to take over a parenting intervention when their nerves have become frazzled, they point out that they would probably never have reached the point of "frazzlement" had their partners been doing more of the parenting work from the beginning. Therefore, they experience not gratitude but frustration when their husbands ride in on white horses to save the day, in part because children then come to see fathers as the more patient, reasonable parent. From the father's perspective, he is baffled and agitated that his wife did not appreciate his effort. For some, such as Richard, whose earlier comments about long days fighting battles at work conveyed the same need for time to rejuvenate as that needed by his wife, the anger and lack of appreciation from partners can stir further animosity.

The exchanges that follow the moments at which these critical "handoffs" from mother to father occur represent some of the genuine moments of truth in coparental partnerships. These semi-regular episodes can serve as an impetus for discussions about why tempers flared, about needs, and about the big picture of how things have been going, or they can just go unrequited, with silence settling in and a level of relative comfort eventually returning. However, the comfort comes at the cost of another opportunity having been missed, and one or both partners banking another example of having felt underappreciated and misunderstood.

In some families, such episodes occur occasionally but are largely blips on a background otherwise characterized by solidarity, support, and understanding. A key in such families is that these disputes are routinely discussed by the partners soon after they occur. In many other families, however, they are seldom discussed and crystallize into an ongoing theme that is a latent constant for the family, always below the surface and never openly addressed. For the remainder of families, the situation falls somewhere in between these two extremes. Couples generally let child-rearing disagreements go, occasionally erupting when at their wit's end, otherwise suffering in silence, until finally a particularly worrisome spat prompts them to talk about their differences. They then gain some perspective, make the necessary adjustments, and show greater sensitivity to one another's sensibilities for a spell but then return to their status quo until another big coparenting conflict encountered in the road ahead sets them to talking once more.

The regularity of coparenting disputes isn't news to most parents. Nearly all of the families in our study acknowledged at least occasional coparenting disagreements about their 1-year-olds, and most believed that the babies were affected by disagreements between the two of them. As Sally put it,

> "When my husband and I are having troubles, she feels it, and she knows it."

Coparenting and Family Interactions

The work on coparenting described in this book traces its origins to McHale's study of 50 Berkeley, CA, families coparenting infant sons and daughters during the late 1980s. In that work, a system for evaluating coparenting during triadic family interactions was designed and later refined at Clark University during the mid-1990s. The Coparenting and Family Rating System, or CFRS as it later came to be called (McHale, Kuersten-Hogan, & Lauretti, 2000), represented a preliminary effort to capture key coparenting dynamics as they transpired between coparents and children at play together. Its premise was really a very simple one—in families in which there was greater solidarity in the coparenting partnership, the coparents (whoever they may be) might be expected to show more pleasure and enjoyment; greater evidence of cooperation, support, affirmation, and working together; and less evidence of disputatiousness or disengagement by one or both partners. It is only one of many systems, and there is nothing particularly magical about it. Other researchers have used related observational systems of their own design that likewise effectively capture similar constructs. The key to the system is its careful focus on what transpires between the parents as they help the child navigate challenging developmental tasks, share play time together with the child, and help the child manage emotions when play time has come to a close.

To date, we have never introduced any particularly difficult challenges to families during the late infancy period, akin to the stressful still-face procedure we piloted at 3 months. This is relevant because it is quite possible that in many families in which there is a significant degree of coparental distress, the adults are able to put aside differences and effectively engage the baby during the brief (usually 10–15 minutes) family interactions we conduct. In other families, in which the coparental alliance is generally on fairly stable footing, there is always the possibility that the baby may be having a particularly difficult day at the hour of our evaluation, presenting the parents with a greater coparenting challenge than other families face with better modulated babies. In such circumstances, we may find evidence of greater miscoordination between the parents, documenting mild perturbations in coparental process where otherwise we may not have found any. Such are the vagaries of brief observations, one of the primary reasons we have moved in the direction of advocating multimethod assessments of coparental functioning whenever feasible (McHale, Kuersten-Hogan, & Rao, 2004; McHale & Rotman, 2007).

Despite these challenges, however, we have generally found that ratings of the family's coparental process using the CFRS provide interesting and useful descriptive data about coparental functioning. Family therapists who use brief observations of family process to establish strengths and weaknesses in the family process are quite familiar with the level of analysis we are describing here. During the patterning of family interaction, we are on the lookout for evidence of cohesion between the coparenting partners (building upon one another's initiatives with the baby, mirroring of the partner's physical or vocal intonations and directives in helping to simplify a learning environment for the child, inviting back into the interaction a partner who had taken a back seat in deference to the active parent's efforts, sharing a genuine laugh or knowing glance with one another). We also take note of instances of discord (interruptions, redirections of the baby's efforts away from the other parent, dual sets of competing stimulation being offered to the baby without either parent drawing back, sarcastic comments either to oneself or to the baby about the partner's actions—often uttered almost indecipherably in what Kuersten-Hogan, Haskell, & McHale 2005, affectionately dubbed the "coparenting mumble"). We systematically evaluate overall levels of engagement by mother and by father and calculate a score reflecting the discrepancy in levels of parental involvement. Higher scores, by definition, hence signify either mild disengagement by one parent, mild overinvolvement by the other parent, or both.

Rating scales for the various scales (cooperation, warmth, competition, verbal sparring) have been described in some detail in other publications (McHale, 1995; McHale, Kuersten-Hogan, & Lauretti, 2000), and we will not reiterate them here. In general, lower scores reflect little evidence of the particular coparenting or family process during the session, and higher scores reflect multiple, regular, and/or convincing evidence of the processes at work. For the Families Through Time study, our colleagues Melanie McConnell and Suzanne Gurland also developed two new codes. The first captured the overall levels of affirmation (from none to regular) each partner provided for the other's efforts during the interaction. The second was an overall rating of the quality of verbal sparring. McConnell and Gurland found this helped them to distinguish families in which there were multiple ribs and put-downs made at one another's expense, but in an atmosphere of connection and esprit de corps, from families where there were similarly multiple jabs made but within an atmosphere of quiet hostility that concerned the raters.

Here, we provide an overview of how families worked together during the triadic play sessions at 12 months. A wide range of adaptations were made by our study families, and our sense was that families soon forgot they were on camera as they worked diligently to help their babies learn how to stack blocks, complete puzzles, interlock plastic beads together, and the like. It was not at all uncommon to see interruptions and overriding of one another's efforts—in only 27 of the 139 families coded by McConnell and Gurland (less than one in five) did they discern no instances of at least mildly competitive or contrarian behavior between the parents. In 18 of the families, or about 13%, the competitive behavior they discerned was judged to be intense. In the remaining 94 families, there were from one to several instances of intrusiveness, interruption, or conflicting messages sent to the baby but with some efforts to keep such behavior in check.

We are sometimes asked whether our ratings of competitive behavior are truly indicative of a *coparenting* dynamic, or whether they are actually just a reflection of only the more competitive parent's personality style. In some ways, we see this question as off point; for competitive behavior to recur in families, both partners must contribute to the dynamic. Even when one parent is more interfering, the other parent is in a position to alter or sustain the miscoordination dynamic by calling it (or not calling it) to the partner's attention so that the two of them might work together toward providing greater clarity, communication, and organization in joint dealings with the child. When such mutual accommodations do not take place, the competitiveness can become more of a trademark feature of the interparental and family dynamic. Nonetheless, we see value in assessing whether one or the other parent shows more competitive inclinations, and so in this study for the first time examined the proportion of families for whom greater competitiveness could be ascribed to one or the other partner. We found that, in 24% of families in which competitiveness was detected, mothers were the more competitive of the two; that in 32% of the families, fathers were more competitive; and that in the remaining 44% of families, the parents were judged to be equally competitive. There were no clear trends linking parent competitiveness to baby gender; in the 36 families where fathers were more competitive, half of the babies were boys and half were girls. In the 27 families in which mothers were more competitive, 13 were boys and 10 were girls. In families in which parents were equally competitive, 26 were boys and 21 were girls.

Families were less likely to engage in overt verbal sparring (although we can't be certain McConnell and Gurland heard every one of the many mumbles!). In approximately one third of the families (35%), ribbing and criticism were readily detected and in 13 of those 48 families (27%), the verbal sparring was judged to be extensive. The new "sparring quality" indicator that was piloted in this study indicated that the coders saw 8 of these 12 families, on the basis of the interaction data alone, to be on a potentially problematic path. Unlike the competitiveness data, there was a clear gender difference in who sparred more; in 62% of the cases, mothers were the more critical partners. Fathers were more critical in 26% of these families, and the partners were equally critical in 11%. With respect to baby gender, however, no clear trends were in evidence. Although there was a somewhat greater likelihood that parents would engage in verbal sparring with sons (25 families) than daughters (20 families), neither gender was safeguarded from verbal sparring in families prone to disagree during coparenting interactions. In 61% of the 28 families in which mothers were more critical, children were boys and in 39% girls; among the 12 families in which fathers were more critical, the figures were 58% boys and 42% girls. In the remaining five families, one baby was a boy and four were girls.

Verbal sparring during family interactions looked to be a meaningful variable, despite the artificiality of the laboratory setting. Our data at 12 months indicated that both mothers' and fathers' self-reports of the frequency of conflict episodes in front of the baby correlated significantly with the observational ratings of verbal sparring. It is interesting that observed verbal sparring was also significantly associated with a greater discrepancy between mothers' reports of how things were and how they would ideally wish them to be, on the child-care segment of the Cowans' Who Does What instrument. Father's self-report of the frequency with which he made disparaging remarks to the baby about the mother also correlated significantly with observed conflict. Maternal reports of disparagement did not so correlate. We found this interesting because it is often maternal reports of father disparagement, rather than paternal reports of mother disparagement, that correlate with child adjustment outside the home (e.g., McHale & Rasmussen, 1998). We have had the sense in our research studies through the years that for fathers, conflict is conflict is conflict—if coparental conflict is salient to men, its manifestation cuts across settings and contexts. With mothers, however, criticism of the father can selectively occur privately, in public, or in both contexts; data hint that mothers may be more selective than fathers about when and where they criticize partners to children.

Similar variability was found for rating variables capturing coparental cohesiveness. The most common rating given to families on the active cooperation variable was a low one (31% of the 139 families judged), in which parents showed no real evidence of facilitating or augmentation of the partner's behavior (this variable is not the opposite of competition; we judged the two completely separately and found there to be no statistically significant association between high competition and low cooperation or high cooperation and low competition). The next most common rating (26%) was one in which families benignly acknowledged one another's efforts (by signaling that they were giving room) but again not building or embellishing. In fact, in only 17% of the families rated did the judges see multiple clear instances of facilitative behavior. This proportion reconciles well with our observations from past studies of other samples (e.g., McHale, 1995; McHale, Johnson, & Sinclair, 1999; McHale, Kuersten-Hogan, Lauretti, & Rasmussen, 2000); coparenting partners who really make efforts to work collaboratively constitute a relative minority of the families we see. Most families simply allow one another to do their thing during the lab sessions without ever shifting into a coordinated joint teaching or play surround for their babies, even occasionally.

Family warmth (a composite of mother–baby, father–baby, and mother–father warmth) also varied widely among families in this study, as it has in every study we have conducted. This phenomenon has become a major point of interest for us, because in all samples studied from our lab, as well as many other samples in studies published by others (including multi-ethnic samples studied intensively by Kristen Lindahl and Gene Brody), ratings of family warmth factor significantly into overall evaluations of coparental and family harmony. And—here's the key point—harmony is often the best family-level predictor of child adjustment. In our research, high family warmth scores can only be attained when there are significant levels of warmth and connection within all legs of the family triad: mother–baby, father–baby, and mother–father. An absence of warmth in any one leg, even in the presence of warmth in one or two of the others, affords families a midrange warmth score at best. Families in which there is low warmth throughout the system typically receive the lowest scores on this variable. As in prior research studies, cooperation and family warmth were highly associated with one another and served as the bedrock observational indicators of coparental cohesion at 12 months.

Finally, we once again found a relatively large spread with respect to the balance in levels of engagement demonstrated by the two parents during the family interactions. In over half the families (52%), one parent was somewhat or significantly more engaged in the family interaction than the other. As the imbalance in levels of parental engagement grew larger, so too did the likelihood that there would be other negative features of the family interaction. Larger discrepancies in levels of engagement by the two parents were significantly correlated with lower levels of cooperation, higher levels of verbal sparring (including more worrisome quality of sparring), and less affirmation of fathers by mothers and of mothers by fathers.

These are overall portraits of the families' adaptation to the family play sessions. One of our colleagues, Kate Fish, became interested in the question of whether family process differences would be seen in single- versus dual-earner families, or in families where babies were and were not in day care. In a series of reports, Fish and colleagues (e.g., Fish, DeCourcey, McConnell, & McHale, 2002; Fish & McHale, 2001) took a systematic look at coparenting dynamics as a function of work and day care status. What they found may surprise you.

Family Group Processes in Single- and Dual-Earner Families

Since the publication of Hochschild and Machung's (1989) *The Second Shift*, families have come to appreciate the challenges in child rearing in families in which both parents are working. Although some researchers, such as Chase-Lansdale and Owen (1987) find more insecure attachments to fathers in families where mothers work, others such as Scarr, Phillips, and McCartney (1989) have found more beneficial effects. For example, Scarr and colleagues suggest that maternal work actually enhances teamwork, such that fathers with working wives know more about their children's whereabouts, school activities, and friends than do other fathers (e.g., Crouter, Helms-Erikkson & Updegraff 1999), and show more involvement with child care than fathers whose wives do not work (Crouter, Perry-Jenkins, Huston, & McHale, 1987). Some researchers have suggested that maternal work intensifies maternal involvement with young children when mother and child do reconnect at day's end—potentially to the detriment of more mutual coparental engagement as mothers seek more quality time with their children (Zaslow, Pedersen, Suwalsky, & Rabinovich, 1986, 1989). Yet very few studies have ever directly examined the coparenting process of families with lives organized by different work schedules. Fish and McHale did just this in a 2001 report, in which they asked whether there was evidence for greater coparenting support, or less, among dual earner families when compared with families where mothers stayed at home.

At the time of our 12-month assessment, fathers were working an average of 48.3 hours per week (with a range from 30 to over 80 hours!). Mothers were averaging 16.8 hours, although this figure is deceptive because there were three distinct subgroups—mothers not working at all, mothers working part time, or mothers working full time. Overall, both parents worked full time in 23% of the families examined by Fish and McHale, whereas in 35% of the families mothers did not work at all. In the remaining 42% of families, fathers worked full time and mothers worked part time. In multivariate analyses of variance, Fish and McHale examined the CFRS ratings provided by McConnell and Gurland, in search of coparenting and family dynamics that distinguished among the different families in the study grouped by work schedules.

Results indicated several dimensions on which the different kinds of families differed during the family interactions we observed. First, fathers were more likely to endorse mothers' parenting efforts in families in which mothers worked, and this was so whether mothers worked full or part time. Second, mothers were more likely to endorse fathers' parenting in families in which mothers worked full time than in families in which mothers did not work. Finally, families in which both parents worked were more likely to engage cooperatively than families in which mothers remained at home, but in this case, only when the baby was a girl. No effects of work status were found for the coparental conflict variables (competition or verbal sparring), indicating that the impact of maternal work status was felt most prominently on levels of support rather than on propensities to engage in an oppositional or antagonistic manner. Hence, in contrast to some of the common media portrayals of dual-earner families as chaotic and stressed, our observational data indicated that there appear to be more substantial efforts made by parents in such families to offer affirmation and support for one another's efforts with the baby. A similar set of findings emerged when Fish and her colleagues (2002) examined family interactions as a function of day care status; these findings are discussed next.

Family Group Processes in High and Low Day Care Families

Most readers are likely to be familiar with the often heated controversies surrounding infant day care during the past 2 decades. Although some consensus has been reached on this topic, thanks to the National Institute of Child Health and Human Development's consortium efforts, many questions still remain for family researchers. One that was of particular interest to us was whether coparenting and family group dynamics vary as a function of infants' day care experiences during their first year. Kate Fish again took the helm on this study and uncovered some rather interesting findings.

On average, babies in our study spent about 100 hours (100.7 to be exact) in nonparental care during their first year, although this figure is again quite deceptive because the range varied dramatically, from 0 to 493 hours. Most parents indicated being relatively happy with the quality of care their baby received, averaging 4.2 on a 5-point scale, on which 4 was *very good* and 5 was *absolutely superb*. Families used a wide array of day care options, including center-based care, family day care in a home, babysitters or nannies, and care by family members. High and low day care groups were formed by conducting a median split of the total number of hours babies spent in other-than-parent care during the first year. In the high day care group, infants spent an average of 210 hours in day care their first year, whereas in the low day care group (which included 40 infants who spent no time in day care at all), the average was 15.7 hours.

Multivariate analyses of variance indicated a significant effect for time in day care, and univariate analyses were then conducted to elucidate the nature of day care effects. These analyses indicated that mother–child investment and the discrepancy between mother and father involvement with the baby were greater in low day care families. Additionally, both fathers' endorsement of mothers' parenting and the index of total family warmth were significantly higher in high day care families. Mirroring the maternal work findings, analyses further indicated that these effects may be particularly pronounced in families with baby *girls* in day care.

These findings, in our view, significantly qualify the patterns we discerned earlier in this chapter and contribute significantly to ongoing controversies about infant day care. Contrary to the general dearth of findings indicating positive correlates of day care in both the academic and popular literatures, these analyses indicated that high day care families may be providing more coordinated and supportive coparenting environments for infants, especially infant daughters. Perhaps as a function of their utilization of day care and the time spent away from their infants, families make an extra effort to come together at the day's end and make the most of their time together as a family, hence promoting family warmth and coparental endorsement. Fathers, in particular, appear to be stepping in more and supporting their wives in high day care families, perhaps sensitive to the fact that mothers may be experiencing guilt in leaving their infants in day care for several hours per week, as reported by Roopnarine, Church, and Levy in 1990.

Recall that a significant subgroup of fathers in our sample seemed to be on the outside looking in, expressing criticisms about the home environment that mothers were providing for babies. Mothers, for their part, were critical about the contributions they received from fathers. We wondered whether patterns such as these were more common among the subgroup of families in which mothers had not returned to work. Fish and her colleagues' analyses of day care data indicated that mothers in low day care families did show significantly higher overinvolvement with their infants than other mothers and that the magnitude of involvement discrepancies between the two parents was higher in these families (again with mothers more invested than fathers). Might it be that mothers who are with their infants more often throughout the day develop very well-worn routines with the infant, unmatched by fathers, explaining in part the observed discrepancies we saw in parents' involvement during family interactions? It seems plausible that stay-at-home mothers may actually be more, rather than less, likely to undertake a gate-keeping role of the sort described by DeLuccie (1995), wittingly or unwittingly shutting fathers out of family commerce. These data raise the possibility that the extra amounts of time spent with the infant may have translated into overinvolvement and imbalance during family group processes.

The finding about infant girls reaping greater coparenting benefits than boys is also intriguing. Might it be that parents felt more protective of baby girls and possibly even more guilty about leaving their daughters in day care compared with their sons? It was striking that parents with infant daughters in frequent day care made an exceptional effort to foster positive family harmony when the whole family was together, a finding that mirrored our maternal work findings. In a society that has become increasingly reliant on infant day care, Fish's analyses provide some heartening news for dual-earner families who do rely on high-quality day care for infants. More work is clearly needed, but these data, which take a family-level approach to understanding the complex dynamic of care in contemporary American families, plot an important direction for further studies.

Marital-Coparenting Connections Revisited: What Prevents Spillover?

We now return to several other intrafamily dynamics and patterns of interest at 12 months, beginning with another look at the robust connection between marital and coparental adjustment that has been found in virtually all prior studies of coparenting in families. Our study, not surprisingly, was no different. Using a composite index of marital adjustment that we formed by combining our observational measures of the marital interactions engaged in by mothers and fathers (see chapter 2) and both mothers' and fathers' overall appraisals of the marital interaction after it had ended (on items such as "After we stopped the discussion, I felt understood by my partner"; "During the discussion, I was critical and blaming"; and "During the discussion, I avoided talk about the issue"), we established that significant associations did indeed exist between overall marital quality and composite indicators of both coparenting harmony and coparenting negativity (see below) in our families as well (Talbot & McHale, 2004).

Although this finding came as no surprise, it caused us to wonder whether some of the parents in marital distress had been able to beat the odds by finding ways to put aside the differences between them so as to forge effective coparenting relationships. Although we had little to go on from studies reported in the extant literature, we were struck by some relatively unheralded findings that had emanated from a major study of marital–family linkages conducted about 25 years earlier by Jerry Lewis (Lewis, Beavers, Gossett, & Phillips, 1976; Lewis & Looney, 1983). Lewis reported that among a subgroup of the families in his study, the typically seen overlap between marital and coparenting quality did not hold. That is, couples in certain families were experiencing appreciable levels of marital distress, yet their coparenting did not exhibit the markers of risk that have since been linked to adverse child outcomes. Lewis described such families as "Competent but Pained."

In describing these families, Lewis chronicled problems in intimacy and closeness that had come to characterize the marital partnership, often accompanied by detachment, unresolved anger, and sometimes also disparities in the distribution of power. In the whole-family context, however, the story was different. The two members of the couple maintained comparable levels of engagement with their children and cooperated efficiently when task performance was called for. They refrained from engaging in competitive interactions and shows of hostility in the presence of their children. Although neither the spouses nor their children displayed the high degree of warmth or affective spontaneity characteristic of Lewis's

"Highly Competent" or optimally functioning families, family members did maintain a tone of matter-of-fact politeness. They were attentive to one another and generally clear in their communications of their own views. Most important was Lewis's finding that the teenaged sons and daughters of the Competent but Pained families benefited from their parents' success in maintaining a supportive coparental alliance and showed high levels of psychological health. Although less emotionally open than teenagers in Highly Competent families, they were free of the adjustment problems that often beset adolescents from family environments rated dysfunctional in Lewis's research samples.

Lewis's findings, along with evidence discussed by McHale (1995) in his sample of families with infants, raise the possibility that in some families, protective factors operate to mitigate negative effects of marital problems on partners' ability to function as a coparenting team. But what sets families such as the Competent but Pained ones apart from others in which both marital and coparenting subsystems show disturbance? In reflecting on individual interviews that had been conducted with participating parents in his study, Lewis commented that Competent but Pained partners, unlike adults in more distressed families, emphasized a willingness to make personal sacrifices as a means of promoting their children's well-being. For the sake of their children, they sought to maintain cohesive family relationships and suppress their resentment against their spouses to promote whole-family functioning.

Another distinguishing characteristic of Competent but Pained partners was their capacity for objectivity in their appraisals of family dynamics. In particular, they seemed able to distinguish between feelings about one another as spouses and feelings about one another as parents. Although clearly dissatisfied with their marriages, they were able to acknowledge one another's child-rearing strengths. Furthermore, they made efforts to view family dynamics through the eyes of their children, showing respect for the children's attachment to the other parent, and they were able to read children's responses to their coparenting efforts, recognizing that coparenting cooperation enhanced their children's sense of security, whereas coparenting conflict prompted their children's feelings of distress and fear.

Lewis's observations suggested to us that some parents may possess key psychological strengths that could help attenuate the relationship between marital quality and coparenting quality and, thus, limit the damage done to coparenting by distressed marital functioning. In particular, his findings suggested that maritally distressed parents who approach family interactions with an attitude of altruistically motivated self-control may be able to minimize hostility and reactivity toward partners and cooperate during family interactions. It also seemed that coparenting quality was partially protected from the impact of marital conflict when parents showed cognitive flexibility in thinking about family dynamics. When maritally dissatisfied parents consider their children's perspectives on family relationships and try to be objective in making judgments about their partners' parenting, they are more likely to appreciate the importance of their partners in their children's emotional lives. In so doing, they may be motivated both to inhibit expressions of resentment toward their partners in front of children and to collaborate more effectively in coparenting.

Talbot and McHale (2004) pursued this possibility by considering whether linkages between marital quality and coparenting differed in our sample of families depending on the degree of self-control or flexibility reported by parents. They tested the hypothesis that better developed flexibility and self-control not only would be associated with more harmonious and less dissonant coparental dynamics during family interactions, but also would alter the expected relationship between marital processes and coparenting dynamics. High flexibility, in particular, was seen as a potential aid to parents. Flexible parents were thought to be better positioned to attain insight into the impact of overt conflict on children and thereby to curb verbal expressions of hostility during family interactions—limiting the extent to which coparenting negativity would escalate in the face of declining marital quality. Among parents who had reported higher flexibility and self-control on the CPI (see chapter 2), marital strain was expected to have eroded coparenting harmony less substantially than it had in families in which parents did not possess these same attributes. High self-control or flexibility was also expected to limit the escalation in coparenting negativity that generally accompanies declines in marital quality.

Findings from this study did indeed indicate that paternal flexibility moderated the association between marital quality and coparenting negativity in the manner predicted. Specifically, coparenting negativity did not vary significantly with changes in marital functioning among those families in which fathers were highly flexible. In other words, among this subgroup of families, deterioration in partners' marriages did not predict significant increases in the extent to which partners engaged in negative, sarcastic verbal exchanges in the coparenting context. In contrast, when fathers were less able to adopt other points of view and less skilled in adjusting their behavior to accommodate changes in the interpersonal context, decrements in marital quality were linked with increases in coparenting negativity. Said more simply, when men were able to "take a hit" without retaliating, the coparental alliance benefited.

Among mothers, findings were much more complex and, in some ways, counterintuitive. Among mothers, greater flexibility and self-control actually made it more likely that the women would divest energies from the coparental partnership and instead invest them in the baby (Talbot & McHale, 2004). One possible explanation offered for these findings is that highly flexible women may be more likely to cater to signals they are receiving from their partners, signifying the partners' preferences for mothers to take the lead. At this point, it's too early to draw definitive conclusions about maternal traits that help prevent spillover from marital into coparenting systems, but Talbot and McHale's analyses have provided some interesting leads and starting points in this search.

Parent-Child Attachment and Coparenting Processes

Thus far in this chapter, we have emphasized dynamic linkages between marital and coparenting systems in the family, but we have not made much mention of potential linkages between parent–child and coparenting systems. There is a wealth of evidence that marital distress compromises parent–child relationships (see Erel & Burman, 1995, for a comprehensive review), but relationships between parenting and coparenting in families is less well understood. In many of the writings about coparenting that have appeared in the published literature, the emphasis has been on how the nature and dynamics of the family's coparenting partnership can diverge markedly from seemingly related features of dyadic parent–child relational systems such as warmth, sensitivity, and engagement (Frosch, Mangelsdorf, & McHale, 2000; Lauretti & McHale, 1997; McHale et al., 2000). In fact, what little data there are on this topic suggest that it is difficult to predict properties of the coparental process (such as relative levels of parental engagement during family interaction) from properties of dyadic, parent–child commerce (such as each parent's engagement level during dyadic play; e.g., McHale et al., 2000). Such findings lend support to P. Minuchin's contention that the coparent–child triad should be seen as a distinctive family unit, one that is not readily reducible to comprising parent–child dyadic systems. At the same time, there is also limited evidence indicating that some features of parent–child commerce (such as fathers' warmth and playfulness) do predict certain aspects of the coparental dynamic (such as greater coparenting cohesion; e.g., McHale, Lauretti, Talbot, & Pouquette, 2002).

One of the questions we tackled in this study was whether parent–infant attachment quality might be one of the features of parent–child dyadic relationship systems that could be dynamically linked to coparental dynamics in families. We debated whether the nature of this link might be a straightforward one, such that secure attachments would be more common in families with supportive coparenting systems (e.g., Frosch et al., 2000), or one more complex than this. Our reason for expecting more complex linkages was our reading of Chase-Lansdale and Owen's (1987) study, in which they reported that infants were more likely to be insecurely attached to fathers in families where mothers worked (although rates of insecurity were not higher with the working mothers in those same families). We wondered whether Chase-Lansdale and Owen had been indirectly tapping into something about coparenting alliances in families but, of course, could not know from their data. As we've indicated, our data in this study actually hinted at better coordinated coparenting in dual-earner families. Surprisingly, aside from the Frosch et al. study we cited earlier, which had linked coparenting during infancy to later toddler attachment security, we knew of no studies linking attachment security to coparenting or family-level processes at the same point in developmental time.

Our colleagues Dawn Vo-Jutabha and Mary Alston Kerllenevich (Vo-Jutabha, Kerllenevich, McConnell, & McHale, 2005) took a look at this issue in our study families, asking whether infants who were insecurely attached to mothers or to fathers belonged to family systems in which there were either symmetrical or compensatory processes operating at the level of the triadic or family group dynamic. On the basis of past theory and research, they focused particularly on signs of cohesion and discord between coparents, and on heightened levels of engagement shown by the other parent within the family group dynamic.

Vo-Jutabha and Kerllenevich examined families in which videotaped records were available for both parents and infants navigating Ainsworth, Blehar, Waters, and Wall's standard (1978) Strange Situation and rated security of parent–child attachment using the avoidant (A), secure (B), and resistant (C) nomenclature. Eighty-nine of the families had codeable records for both mother and father. Table 5.1 summarizes the number of infants with avoidant, secure, and resistant attachment to their mothers and fathers. These rates were consistent with rates of secure and insecure attachment reported elsewhere in the literature.

Analyses of variance comparing parents' behavior during triadic interactions with the baby in families in which infants were and were not securely attached to fathers did not identify any dimension on which the two groups differed. However, the same analyses comparing families in which babies were or were not securely attached with mothers did indicate one dimension on which the two sets of families differed: father investment (or level of engagement with the baby). The direction of effects was such that in families in which infants were insecurely attached with mothers, fathers were more invested or engaged with the baby during the family group interaction.

In follow-up analyses, we established that this relationship system was driven by families in which infants had developed an

TABLE 5.1. RATES OF PARENT–INFANT ATTACHMENT

Attachment	Avoidant	Secure	Resistant
With father	18	60	11
With mother	15	54	15

Figure 5.1. Mean Differences in Coparental Behaviors for Avoidantly Attached and Nonavoidantly Attached Mother–Infant Dyads

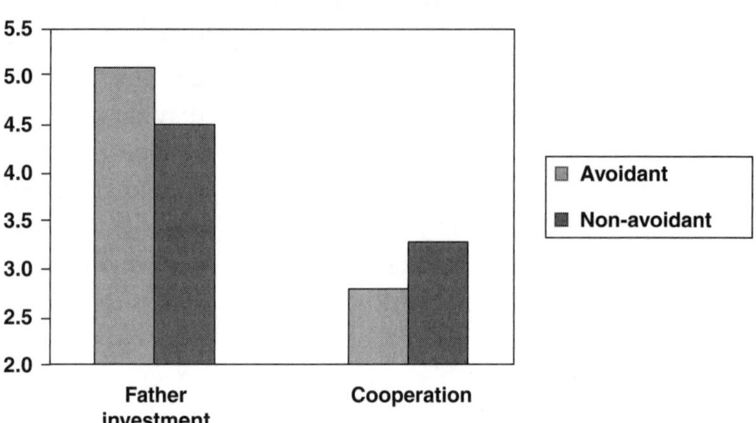

avoidant attachment with mothers. In such families, McConnell and Gurland (blind to the attachment data) had rated fathers as being significantly more engaged and invested with their babies during triadic interactions (see Figure 5.1). In comparing infants with avoidant and nonavoidant attachments with mothers, there was also a trend approaching significance ($p < .10$) for there to be less overall coparental cooperation during triadic interactions in the avoidant group (Figure 5.1).

In an attempt to ascertain why this pattern appeared in our data, we looked at a number of different possibilities, but none of the explanations we pursued accounted for why it was that fathers of babies who were avoidantly attached with their mothers were themselves more invested during family group interaction. First, pursuing compensatory or buffering hypotheses, we wondered whether fathers whose children were avoidantly attached with mothers came from unhappier marriages or had wives who were more depressed. However, neither of these hypotheses was supported. Neither marital dissatisfaction (on the MAT) nor maternal depression (on the CES-D) distinguished paternal engagement in families with avoidant mother–infant dyads from paternal engagement in families in which babies were not avoidantly attached.

Taking an individual personality perspective, we also pursued the hypothesis that fathers of infants who were avoidantly attached with mothers themselves might have possessed certain personality characteristics (e.g., greater dominance, empathy, responsibility, or even narcissism) that might have helped to explain their greater investment with the child during family interactions. However, our data indicated that none of these personality characteristics (as measured by the California Psychological Inventory) helped to account for the greater investment of fathers whose children were avoidantly attached with their mothers.

What to make of these intriguing findings? We appear to have found evidence for a true systemic process, wherein there is a balancing effect at the level of the full family system in families in which babies have cultivated insecure attachments with mothers. In such families, coparental cooperation is also low and fathers appear to be filling in gaps by virtue of their greater investment with babies. We could not pinpoint a person-based trigger for this cross-contextual linkage or evidence of marital dissatisfaction on the part of either parent in such families. We acknowledge that it is certainly possible that the relatively small size of the mother-avoidant group in this study (15 of 88 families) may have been insufficient to detect small to moderate-sized effects for the personality or marital indicators examined or that other unexamined factors may have helped to account for the between-group differences in family process that we detected.

The bigger picture, for us, is that even though we did find some modest support for lawful associations between this particular patterning of coparental and parent–child attachment dynamics, the overall landscape of our data did not suggest major linkages between attachment and coparenting quality. This finding is consistent with P. Minuchin's (1985) contention that dyadic relationships (parent–child, marital) are not always consonant with coparent–child triadic dynamics. By and large, properties of the coparenting and family group dynamic do not follow in straightforward ways from properties of dyadic, parent–child commerce, including security of attachment to each parent. Do they, however, as Ross Parke suggested in 1986, perhaps follow their own unique trajectories as a distinctive system in its own right through time? That is the thesis of our study, and as we outline in this chapter's concluding section, Parke appears to have been right.

Could We Have Forecast Quality of Coparental Adjustment From What We Knew Earlier?

To determine whether families adapting more successfully at 12 months had been those with more positive profiles during either the pregnancy or at 3 months, we first needed to create summary scores reflecting overall levels of cohesion and conflict in the coparenting alliance at 1-year postpartum. To do so, we combined the various indicators of coparental cohesion and of coparental conflict in a manner identical to the one we used to create composites at 3 months. At 12 months, the composite score for coparenting cohesion was created by combining (a) CFRS ratings of coparenting warmth, cooperation, maternal endorsement of fathers, paternal endorsement of mothers, and child-centeredness of the coparenting interactions we observed; (b) maternal and paternal reports of family harmony promoting behavior on McHale's (1997) self-report Coparenting Scale to assess the frequency with which parents showed affection to, were inclusive of, and spoke affirmatively about their parenting partner during interactions involving the child; and (c) Waterston, Babigian, and McHale's (2001, 2002) NAS-TBW ratings of the overall positive tone of parents' coparenting interviews as they described their work together as a coparenting team and their family's best and worst moments. Summary variables for each indicator outlined above were standardized and then summed to form a single index of 12-month coparenting cohesion. The internal consistency of this measure suggested that it was an acceptable summary index for the construct measured ($\alpha = .77$).

To establish a summary score for 12-month coparenting conflict, we used (a) CFRS scores reflecting competition, amount of verbal sparring, quality of verbal sparring, and degree of discrepancy between the parents' engagement with the baby during the family interaction; (b) Coparenting Scale indicators of conflict and disparagement as reported by mothers and by fathers; (c) negative tone ratings of parents' coparenting interviews; and (d) overall perceived difference scores between parents' reports of their own ideas about parenting and what they perceived their partners' ideas to be on the Ideas About Parenting Scale. Higher scores on this last variable indicated that the respondents saw themselves and their partners as more distant from one another in their parenting views. The spread of these particular discrepancy scores was quite marked, ranging from a low of 8 to a high of 132! Hence, as we did with the coparenting cohesion composite, we used standardized scores for each individual measure to form the coparenting conflict composite. Like the cohesion composite, the composited conflict score had acceptable internal consistency (α = .72).

We then went one step further and also calculated an overall solidarity score by subtracting the standardized coparental conflict score from the standardized coparental cohesion score. In so doing, we ensured that families with the highest solidarity scores would be those showing both high coparenting cohesion and low coparenting conflict. Likewise, families with the lowest scores were those whose relationships were marked by both low cohesion and high conflict. The remaining families took places in between these two extreme profiles.

Could we have guessed how coparenting alliances would look at 12 months on the basis of what we had learned from families earlier? In large measure, we did find noteworthy consistency through time. Let's start first with the aftereffects of women's pessimism during the third trimester of the pregnancy. Recall from chapter 4 that we had struck upon a set of measures that coalesced very well during the pregnancy in suggesting that some mothers were already entertaining a more negative outlook on what family life would be like after the baby arrived. These indicators of pessimism about coparenting in the future family during the pregnancy had predicted lower levels of coparenting cohesion 3 months after the baby's arrival, but not higher levels of conflict. At 12 months, however, higher prenatal pessimism did predict overall coparental solidarity, and this was largely because greater prenatal pessimism was now linked with higher levels of coparental conflict. It is interesting that the link with lower coparenting cohesion was no longer in strong evidence at 12 months, falling short of statistical significance. In other words, in families where mothers had maintained more pessimistic outlooks about future coparental solidarity during the pregnancy, we found marked evidence of greater conflict in the coparental alliance at the time of the baby's first birthday, over a year down the road!

The aftereffects of negative prenatal future-family outlooks among men were similar; men who had expressed more negative future-family outlooks during the pregnancy later belonged to coparenting alliances marked by less overall coparental solidarity. We also identified a cross-time link between an objective (arithmetical) calculation of the degree of difference between the partners' individually rated ideas about parenting (an IAP discrepancy score) during the pregnancy and our index of coparental solidarity at 12 months. Parents who had been more "*un-alike*" in their parenting views before the baby was born were now showing less overall solidarity by the time of the baby's first birthday. And our analyses confirmed that the cross-time link was being driven largely by a statistically significant association with *high coparental conflict*, rather than with low coparental cohesion.

Finally, we also found evidence that coparental solidarity itself was indeed stable across time. The association between coparental solidarity assessed at 3 months and coparental solidarity assessed at 12 months was also statistically significant, suggesting continuity in adjustment across the developmental changes that took place between the early postpartum months and the baby's first birthday. Hence, despite the marked shifts in family emphasis that we have chronicled throughout this chapter, early patterns of adjustment laid the foundation for subsequent adjustment.

Conclusions

The big picture emerging from the wealth of information families shared with us at 12 months is that life was good but that the challenges to the coparental partnership were many. Parents were working hard to juggle competing demands of work and family, to find ways to stay connected as a threesome or foursome (chapter 7 spotlights our two-child families in greater detail), and to reconcile their differing perspectives on how best to acculturate their babies. Struggles in the marriage made coparental coordination and compromises more difficult, although some distressed families were able to at least partially prevent marital stress from spilling over into their coparental partnership. The quality of parent–child attachments and the success of the coparental partnership were largely unrelated to one another, although some compensatory father engagement was found among a subgroup of families in which babies had developed insecure attachments with mothers. Also, coparental adjustment at 12 months was predicted, to a significant degree, by parents' prenatal outlooks and by the early successes or difficulties they had had as a coparental team at the time of our earlier (3-month) assessments.

Was coparental functioning at 12 months a harbinger of things to come? In chapter 6, we turn our attention to how our families were faring during the terrible twos, examine cross-time linkages between earlier and 30-month coparental functioning, and report on the linkages we found between 30-month coparental adjustment and toddler adaptation.

References

Ainsworth, M., Blehar, M., Waters, E., & Wall, S. (1978). *Patterns of attachment: A psychological study of the Strange Situation*. Hillsdale, NJ: Erlbaum.

Babigian, R., Waterston, L., & McHale, J. (2002, April). *Family life with a one-year-old: What parents' stories tell us*. Paper presented at the International Conference on Infant Studies, Toronto, Ontario, Canada.

Bauer, P. J., Stennes, L., & Haight, J. C. (2003). Representation of the inner self in autobiography: Women's and men's use of internal states language in personal narratives. *Memory, 11*, 27–42.

Belsky, J., Putnam, S., & Crnic, K. (1996). Coparenting, parenting, and early emotional development. *New Directions for Child Development, 74*, 45–55.

Chance, C., & Fiese, B. H. (1999). Gender-streotyped lessons about emotion in family narratives. *Narrative Inquiry, 9*, 243–255.

Chase-Lansdale, P. L., & Owen, M. T. (1987). Maternal employment in a family context: Effects on infant–mother and infant–father attachments. *Child Development, 58*, 1505–1512.

Cowan, C. P., & Cowan, P. A. (1992). *When partners become parents: The big life change for couples*. New York: Basic Books.

Crouter, A., Helms-Erickson, H., & Updegraff, K. (1999). Conditions underlying parents' knowledge about children's daily lives in middle childhood: Between- and within-family comparisons. *Child Development, 70*, 246–259.

Crouter, A. C., Perry-Jenkins, M., Huston, T. L., & McHale, S. M. (1987). Processes underlying father involvement in dual-earner and single-earner families. *Developmental Psychology, 23*, 431–440.

DeLuccie, M. F. (1995). Mothers as gatekeepers: A model of maternal mediators of father involvement. *Journal of Genetic Psychology, 152,* 225–238.

Erel, O., & Burman, B. (1995). Interrelatedness of marital relations and parent–child relations: A meta-analytic review. *Psychological Bulletin, 118*, 108–132.

Fiese, B. H., Sameroff, A. J., Grotevant, H. D., Wamboldt, F. S., Dickstein, S., & Fravel, D. L. (1999). The stories that families tell: Narrative coherence, narrative interaction, and relationship beliefs. *Monographs of the Society for Research in Child Development, 64*, 1–162.

Fish, K., DeCourcey, W., McConnell, M., & McHale, J. (2002, July). *An examination of family group processes in high and low day care families.* Paper presented at the Eighth World Congress of the World Association for Infant Mental Health, Amsterdam, the Netherlands.

Fish, K., & McHale, J. (2001, April). *Parental employment, coparenting, and family interaction at one year.* Paper presented at the Society for Research in Child Development, Minneapolis, MN.

Fivaz-Depeursinge, E., & Corboz-Warnery, A. (1999). *The Primary triangle: A developmental systems view of mothers, fathers, and infants.* New York: Basic Books.

Fivush, R., Brotman, M. A., Buckner, J. P., & Goodman, S. H. (2000). Gender differences in parent–child emotion narratives. *Sex Roles, 42*, 233–253.

Frosch, C. A., Mangelsdorf, S. C., & McHale, J. L. (2000). Marital behavior and the security of preschooler-parent attachment relationships. *Journal of Family Psychology, 14*, 144–161.

Hochschild, A., & Machung, A. (1989). *The second shift: Working parents and the revolution at home*. New York: Viking-Penguin.

Kuersten-Hogan, R., Haskell, V., & McHale, J. (2005, April). Beyond the lab: Coparenting dynamics during mealtimes of preschool-aged children. In J. McHale, R. Kuersten-Hogan, & D. Elliston (Eds.), *Coparenting from pregnancy through preschool: Expansion and validation of a construct.* Symposium presented at the Society for Research in Child Development, Atlanta, GA.

Lauretti, A., & McHale, J. (1997, April). Shifting patterns of parenting styles between dyadic and family settings: The role of marital quality. In J. McHale & R. Kuersten (Eds.), *Conceptions of family: Views from inside and out*. Symposium presented at the Society for Research in Child Development, Washington, DC.

Lewis, J. M., Beavers, W. R., Gossett, J. T., & Phillips, V. A. (1976). *No single thread: Psychological health in family systems*. New York: Brunner/Mazel.

Lewis, J. M., & Looney, J. (1983). *The long struggle: Well-functioning working class Black families.* New York: Brunner/Mazel.

McHale, J. P. (1995). Coparenting and triadic interactions during infancy: The roles of marital distress and child gender. *Developmental Psychology, 31*, 985–996.

McHale, J. P. (1997). Overt and covert coparenting processes in the family. *Family Process, 36*, 183–201.

McHale, J. P., Johnson, D., & Sinclair, R. (1999). Family dynamics, preschoolers' family representations, and preschool peer relationships. *Early Education and Development, 10*, 373–401.

McHale, J., Kuersten-Hogan, R., & Lauretti, A. (2000). Evaluating coparenting and family-level dynamics during infancy and early childhood: The Coparenting and Family Rating System. In P. Kerig & K. Lindahl (Eds.), *Family observational coding systems: Resources for systemic research,* (pp. 151–170). New Jersey: Erlbaum.

McHale, J. P., Kuersten-Hogan, R., Lauretti, A., & Rasmussen, J. L. (2000). Parental reports of coparenting and observed coparenting behavior during the toddler period. *Journal of Family Psychology, 14*, 220–236.

McHale, J. P., Kuersten-Hogan, R., & Rao, N. (2004). Growing points for coparenting theory and research. *Journal of Adult Development, 11*, 221–234.

McHale, J. P., Lauretti, A., Talbot, J., & Pouquette, C. (2002). Retrospect and prospect in the psychological study of coparenting and family group process. In J. P. McHale & W. S. Grolnick (Eds.), *Retrospect and prospect in the psychological study of families* (pp. 127–165). Mahwah, NJ: Erlbaum.

McHale, J. P., & Rasmussen, J. L. (1998). Coparental and family group-level dynamics during infancy: Early family precursors of child and family functioning during preschool. *Development and Psychopathology, 10*, 39–59.

McHale, J., & Rotman, T. (2007). Expectant parents' outlooks on coparenting and later coparenting solidarity. *Infant Behavior & Development, 30*, 63–81.

Minuchin, P. (1985). Families and individual development: Provocations from the field of family therapy. *Child Development, 56*, 289–302.

Parke, R. (1986). Fathers: An intrafamilial perspective. In M. Yogman & T. Brazelton (Eds.), *In support of families* (pp. 59–68). Cambridge, MA: Harvard University Press.

Pellegrini, T., Liebling, C., Waterston, L., & McHale, J. (2007, February). *Who's at fault? How parents of infants characterize family mishaps.* Paper presented at the Southeastern Psychological Association, New Orleans, LA.

Roopnarine, J. L., Church, C. C., & Levy, G. D. (1990). Day care children's play behaviors: Relationship to their mothers' and fathers' assessments of their parenting behaviors, marital stress, and marital companionship. *Early Childhood Research Quarterly, 5*, 335–346.

Ruth, J., & Vilkko, A. (1996). Emotion in the construction of autobiography. In C. Magai & S. H. McFadden (Eds.), *Handbook of emotion, adult development, and aging* (pp. 167–181). New York: Academic Press.

Saarni, C. (1999). *The development of emotional competence*. New York: Guilford Press.

Scarr, S., Phillips, D., & McCartney, K. (1989). Working mothers and their families. *American Psychologist, 44*, 1402–1409.

Talbot, J. A., & McHale, J. P. (2004). Individual parental adjustment moderates the relationship between marital and coparenting quality. *Journal of Adult Development, 11*, 191–205.

Tannen, D. (1990). Gender differences in conversational coherence: Physical alignment and topical cohesion. In B. Dorval (Ed.), *Conversational organization and its development* (pp. 167–206). Westport, CT: Ablex.

Thomas, S., Elliston, D., Waterston, L., Thompson, J., & McHale, J. (2005, April). *What would you want to change? Parents' views of co-parenting*. Paper presented at the Southeastern Psychological Association, Nashville, TN.

Valsiner, J., Bibace, R., & LaPushin, T. (2005). What happens when a researcher asks a question? In R. Bibace, J. D. Laird, K. L. Noller, & J. Valsiner (Eds.), *Science and medicine in dialogue: Thinking through particulars and universals* (pp. 275–288). Westport, CT: Praeger/Greenwood.

Vo-Jutabha, E. D., Kerllenevich, M. A., McConnell, M. C., & McHale, J. P. (2005, April). *Quality of attachment and coparenting dynamics at twelve months post-partum*. Presentation at the Biennial Meeting of the Society for Research in Child Development, Atlanta, GA.

Waterston, L., Babigian, R., & McHale, J. (2001, April). *Representations of family among parents with one and two young children*. Paper presented at the Eastern Psychological Association, Washington, DC.

Waterston, L., Babigian, R., & McHale, J. (2002, July). *Parents' stories about their families reflect individual and family functioning at infant age 12 months*. Paper presented at the Eighth World Congress of the World Association for Infant Mental Health, Amsterdam, the Netherlands.

Zaslow, M. J., Pedersen, F. A., Suwalsky, J. T., & Rabinovich, B. (1986). Fathering during the infancy period: Implications of the mother's employment role. *Infant Mental Health Journal, 7*, 225–234.

Zaslow, M. J., Pedersen, F. A., Suwalsky, J. T., & Rabinovich, B. A. (1989). Maternal employment and parent–infant interaction at one year. *Early Childhood Research Quarterly, 4*, 459–478.

CHAPTER 6

Coparenting Dynamics and Toddler Adjustment

With Wendy DeCourcey and Valerie Bellas

Anyone who has ever parented a 2-year-old has marveled over the child's boundless energy, inquisitiveness, alternating capacities for sweetness and mischief, and dawning awareness of the world of emotions. Two-year-olds can switch effortlessly between having incredibly moving, intimate "conversations" with adults despite their relatively limited verbal repertoires and engaging in naughty escapades that push their parents' tolerance to its very limits. They can protest about even the smallest issue and be reduced to tears at a moment's notice when tired or frustrated, amaze and enchant parents with the wealth of new learning they engage in spontaneously every day, and often leave parents shaking their heads in wonder over their sheer complexity, fire, and thirst for life.

Having once again changed dramatically from their personas during infancy, 30-month-olds have somehow become both calmer and more untamed, all at once. The richness of their daily experience is often mirrored in their parents' inner experience. Adults discuss both their own sense of inner coherence in now knowing well their child and his or her propensities and sensibilities and their puzzlement that they themselves have suddenly become more emotional creatures themselves, sometimes given to occasional moments of frustration and yelling that seem not so different from their toddler's outbursts.

At those moments, alluded to in chapter 5, having a coparenting partner to turn to and say "you handle this" can be of greatest value. Many of the parents we spoke with described their partner's important role in helping keep things copasetic at home. However, as parents often told us, many of their own worst moments in handling toddlers occurred at moments when their annoyance with their partner's handling, mishandling, or ignoring of the toddler's antics had boiled over. Coparenting at 30 months, once again, can and should be conceptualized as a joint enterprise, but it remains an enterprise guided and exemplified by the variety of formative moments that we examined in this study.

The New Demands of a 2-Year-Old

Boundless energy. Banging pots and pans. Writing on walls. Emptying bookshelves. Demanding sweets. Protesting bedtimes. Undressing and bolting naked through the house.

Expressing an awareness of but ambivalence about toileting. Wrestling with the urge to give a sibling a good swat. Disintegrating from fatigue in shopping malls. Hiding keys and TV remote controls. Strewing blocks, modeling clay, crayons, and assorted other small objects throughout the house. But also, singing. Dancing. Giggling. Glowing with pride over mastery of numbers, letters, shapes, colors, and creation of simple designs and figures on paper. Snuggling. Hugging. Trying to get dressed alone. Leafing through story books alone. Learning traditions. Mimicking the habits of parents and grandparents. Melting parents' anger with broad ear-to-ear grins.

With the exception of certain phases of adolescence, there is no other point in the child's life that parallels the rollercoaster experience that is toddlerhood. For coparents, the child's endless, daily frolics through creativity, discovery, and, occasionally, mayhem demand ever-increasing efforts to communicate and coordinate. Coordination is required at a "meta-level," determining how the week's activities are prioritized and managed, and at a microlevel, making a quick judgment about how to intervene with a distraught toddler who has just lashed out at an older sibling upon feeling victimized; establishing which fatigued parent handles the latest lipstick artwork incident, fumbling for how to reconcile, at a moment's notice, a clear interparental disagreement that has suddenly arisen during a valuable teaching moment. Although coparents by this point in our study were primed to tell us of times they had worked well together as a team, virtually every one we spoke with also had vivid examples of coparenting gaffes and disputes, and many were struggling actively even to find their way onto the same page in working with their 2-year-old. As we detail later in this chapter, those who found greater success in creating an effective alliance at 30 months were those who had set the stage for such success during the child's infancy.

When helping professionals point out the importance of maintaining consistency, parents often find themselves thinking, "Have these people ever *been* parents themselves?!" Consistent management of toddlers takes tireless work, considerable energy, and fortitude. Even when an individual parent has been gifted with these admirable attributes, consistency can still be quite difficult to sustain. However, when the consistency needed is consistency *between* parents, the magnitude of the challenge increases exponentially. Consider a few comments from families in our study as they discussed the challenges of coparenting their toddler:

"I think Janine and I do disagree on certain things. Like when Kelly takes a bath, she likes to run around naked. Janine wants Kelly to go get dressed right away and this makes Kelly laugh and so she ends up running around in circles. Me, I don't see the big deal—let her run off a little steam. But it drives Janine crazy."

"I think we need to work on discipline a lot. Jim and I need to work more as a team and we need to find ways to deal with her a little better. I think kids need disciplining, and it's not healthy for them not to have it. And it's not healthy for me to always hand it off to Jim especially since I'm the one who spends the most time with them—if on a daily basis I'm not disciplining her it's not healthy. She won't know her limits and I don't want a child who's not well behaved."

"She needs to work on discipline, but she is working on it. I want everyone in a consistent routine where the kids go to sleep on time. If they could sleep from 8 at night til 8 in the morning, that'd be fantastic and it would give us some quality time together. Right now, we get just an hour here or there but then it's not quality time. It's more like, 'Thank God we got a minute for ourselves, we're just so exhausted.'"

"He pawns discipline off on me. Which I understand. He'd rather be the hugger than the hitter—we've been fighting over this since he was born. Like with the baby not sleeping in our bed, Tom would let him come in with us and say, 'Oh, but it's not going to hurt him,' and then *I'd* have to fight twice as hard to get him back into his own bed. Then he'd cry for 20 minutes in fits in his crib, and once again I was the one who had to deal with it to finally get him to sleep. And *then* one afternoon after he'd gotten the habit, Tom brought him back to our bed, and—boom—it started all over again. He'll say, 'I just can't stand to see him cry, how can you stand it?' I'll say 'It's good for his lungs, every baby cries, he'll get over it.'"

There were as many comments of this nature as there were parents in our study, although for some parents, the differences between them and their partners were an overwhelming, constant reality, whereas for others, they were occasional annoyances. Differences between parents were most frustrating when parents maintained really different perspectives on what was best for the child. Consider for a moment Jay's recollection of an incident that occurred on the way home from a niece's soccer game:

> "He'd gone over with his cousin to a blanket where the people had a collie. He asked if he could pet it, and they said yes and he did. When Mary saw that, she called him back to where we were sitting and told him never to pet strange dogs. Then all the way home in the car, Mary would say 'Never pet dogs,' and I'd say 'Yes, Mommy's right. Always ask the person before you pet their dog,' and she'd say 'No. Don't ever pet dogs,' and I'd say 'Mama's right, if it's a real big dog, maybe you should just look and don't touch.' But the she'd say 'No, any dogs.' And our son was getting real confused, like he'd say 'Can I pet a little dog, Daddy?' And I'd say, 'Only if you ask his owner,' at the same time as Mary said 'No, you can't.' Finally, he yelled, 'Yes I *can*, Mommy,' and I said, 'Don't talk to your mommy like that,' and he started to cry. We put him in a position he couldn't resolve. I know Mary was just wanting to be protective, but she'd already made him afraid of bugs and I didn't want to create a fear of dogs in him."

Balancing responsible levels of protectiveness and developmentally appropriate autonomy encouragement is a universal challenge for parents and one that often places coparents at odds. What seems like commonsense care and concern to one parent may be seen by the other as a stifling overprotectiveness. What seems encouragement of autonomy to one parent can appear a reckless lack of monitoring to the other. Regularly during the toddler years, parents look for teachable moments during which to help inculcate good habits and healthy attitudes in their toddler, but when disagreements occur about what *is* good and healthy, parents are faced with a true test. The more they hammer home differing messages, the more confused their toddler becomes. Most toddlers find ways to integrate or ignore occasional contradictory messages from parents, though even then they often look quizzical or point out the inconsistency. However, when the interparental disagreements are not reconciled and become a family theme, toddlers truly struggle. They can become inhibited, if not paralyzed, during moments of high emotion. They can tune out and become disorganized behaviorally and emotionally, or they can learn that their safest strategy is to behave one way with one parent and a different way with the other. The latter adaptation may seem a sound strategy (and every child probably develops such "customized personas" to a greater or lesser degree), but over time the regular need for shifting accommodations may lead the child to become more secretive and waylay the child's moral development. We develop this line of reasoning further in chapter 8.

It may have occurred to readers that the dispute highlighted above between Jay and Mary was prompted by differing emotional histories of the two parents. We were not in a position to check this hunch out with them, but it would not surprise us in the least if this were so. Parents always draw upon their own knowledge base to teach in a way that they think will maximally strengthen and protect their child, and few parents bring exactly the same emotional histories to their new family. Many parents commented on this explicitly during the prenatal interviews, noting how different their origin family had been from that of their partners. Hers was more expressive, his kept emotions in check. Hers denied the expression of angry feelings, his allowed anger to escalate out of control. Parents linked these differences to current coparental issues in their families. For example, Jane told us:

> "In his family they tried to avoid conflict at all costs—with our daughter, he just takes his time and coddles her so she won't get upset. I'm different. Like recently, she went through a phase where getting dressed in the morning was a major issue. So I'd just dress her myself, regardless of how much she yelled or squirmed. But he goes to too much to an extreme the other way. Like on the weekend he'll spend half an hour coaxing her into getting dressed so she doesn't start crying. If I had to rely on him to get her dressed, we'd never get anywhere."

Commenting on differences between herself and her husband Bill, Carrie told us:

> "He does discipline him, but not enough. It's hard because we grew up in such different environments. I want him to be more stern—not yell, but be more stern. Like instead of saying 'Please sit down,' I want him to say 'Sit down now,' so Ty realizes this is not a game. I don't want Bill to beg him, I want him to say 'Here's the way it is,' and I want Ty to listen to him and respect what his father is saying. I think his discipline definitely needs some tweaking, and he knows it."

We anticipated that the toddler years would challenge many coparents to reckon with differences between them concerning how best to help their child to navigate the world of emotions. The next section provides a window into what our data told us.

Helping Toddlers Manage Emotions: Parents' Perspectives

Few parents spontaneously told us that helping the toddler to express and manage emotions was an area in which they were struggling, but upon reflection many acknowledged that such emotion socialization was a centrally important task in their day-to-day lives. We made the decision to ask parents systematically about their experiences with and attitudes toward emotional expression by administering Gottman, Katz, and Hooven's (1997) Meta-Emotion Interview. In this hour-long interview, parents first spent time recalling their own childhoods and the emotional propensities of their own parents or caregivers. They reminisced about how their families expressed and handled anger, sadness, and affection and how each family member responded to their feelings as a child. They then examined their own current propensities for expressing and managing emotions and using emotions instrumentally within social relationships. They attempted to identify specific recent events during which they had felt anger, sadness, or affection and to discuss the process of expression, management, and regulation. Finally, they turned their attention to their toddlers. They described specific emotional events, distinguishing events evoking sadness from those evoking anger, and attempted to provide a play-by-play of particular emotional episodes with their children. As it turned out, this was a surprisingly difficult and occasionally a thoroughly impossible exercise for a number of parents, particularly fathers. Indeed, a substantial number of fathers believed that their toddlers were only beginning to experience emotions and to develop real feelings. Not surprisingly, distinguishing sadness and anger proved particularly difficult for parents who held this perspective.

The final question of the very long interview asked parents, "If you could sum it all up, what would you say you are trying to teach your child about the world of feelings?" Kerllenevich and DeCourcey (2005) transcribed parents' responses to this question and examined responses in search of organizing themes about emotions and emotion socialization. Their analyses suggested four major groupings of respondents. One group of parents was adamant that they were not trying to teach their child anything about emotions. "Emotions are emotions," they told us, organic intrinsic reactions that occurred and developed without any need for parental intervention or scaffolding. A second subset of parents was focused largely on the importance of developing emotional controls and actively striving to limit expressiveness. Although some of these parents viewed emotions positively, they nonetheless felt that effective emotion containment was necessary for satisfying social relations. Other parents who emphasized emotional control, by contrast, had the view that emotional extremes were dangerous. They wanted their children to learn to restrain their expressiveness to avoid discharging their anger in destructive ways, hurting others' feelings, and squandering time enmeshed in emotional dramas.

The third and fourth groups explicitly spoke of their roles as teachers and models for their children in navigating the world of emotions but described the role they played in rather different voices. One subset of parents concentrated on how their own emotional experiences acculturated the child, emphasizing their efforts to be available for the child as an active guide and support. Will remembered his young son once advising him to "go for a run" when Will was upset, recognizing "I teach him every day just by how I do things." Sue was acutely aware of the intensity with which her son experienced various emotions, commenting "I don't want him to think he is alone; he can always come to me." A final group also discussed their roles in socializing their children into the world of emotions but explicitly told us they were trying to avoid cross-generational transmission. This group expressed regret about ways in which their manner of managing emotions had interfered with personal goals and relationships. They sought to teach their child to approach emotions differently, through freer expression or by reigning in the extremes.

Clearly, parents varied widely in what they sought to teach their children about emotions. Many parents wished for their child to feel comfort experiencing the entire spectrum of emotions and talking about their feelings rather than closing them off. Some of these parents spoke explicitly of encouraging the child not to be ashamed or afraid of emotional experiences, discussing their desire to overcome personally stultifying experiences with emotions. Many told us that anger had been taboo in their families and that they did not want their children similarly uncomfortable when normal feelings of frustration and anger surfaced. Other parents had well-developed narratives about how emotions were tools within social relationships, assisting in developing and maintaining connectedness with others, defining personal goals, and motivating for change. Such parents saw themselves as playing a particularly active role in encouraging emotions, helping to shape children's reactions when emotional, and explicitly teaching them about emotions. Also, there stood the significant subgroup of parents who wanted their toddlers to contain emotions and avoid the damaging and crippling potential within emotional situations (Kerllenevich & DeCourcey, 2005). Of particular interest to us in this study of coparental coordination and solidarity were, of course, those families in which the two parents had different views about what they were trying to accomplish with their toddler.

We used a set of coding schemes developed by Gottman et al. (1997) to evaluate parents' responses to the longer subset of questions about specific emotions for evidence of (a) acceptance of different emotions and (b) coaching attitudes. Following Gottman et al.'s nomenclature, high acceptance parents were those who reported more respectful responses to their child's emotional experiences, and high coaching parents were those who reported more discussions and problem solving around emotion expression. For example, Haley recalled responding to Kimmie's question about why a child was crying in the park by sitting Kimmie down on a bench and discussing why the child might be feeling sad and how she could be soothed and calmed. Wayne described sitting his toddler and his older son down to talk to the two of them about sharing toys and the feelings that surfaced when the sibling didn't share. Lower scoring parents were sometimes also accepting of their child's emotional experience but portrayed themselves as much less involved or available when toddlers wrestled with emotions, affording the child greater independence in their emotional experiences. Mark described how he and Ina allowed their tenacious toddler to vent alone for long periods of time, so that she now simply stomped away to be on her own for a while when she was angry. Other parents who reported little emotion-coaching behavior seemed less aware of their child's emotional experience, had trouble giving detailed examples of emotional interactions, or openly admitted that emotional discussion and expressiveness were not regular features of their family environment.

As we pored over our data concerning interparent differences in emotion philosophies and emotion coaching, we discovered that the issue was much more complex than we'd imagined initially. We had begun with the rather straightforward expectation that when parents were on different pages about what they were trying to do, toddlers would be confused about what was acceptable and, therefore, would have greater difficulty in managing their own feelings and behavior. Substantial differences in parental attitudes did indeed exist in many families, especially with respect to the acceptance and coaching of the negative emotions, sadness and anger.

What we failed to anticipate, however, was the sheer variety of different situations in families that color and complicate any search for straightforward linkages between different parental meta-emotion philosophies and concurrent toddler adjustment patterns. In certain families, mothers and fathers did indeed appear to be coming from very different places. For example, Jill and Ralph in their individual interviews with our research staff provided a prototypical coparental mismatch. Discussing anger, Jill said:

> "She has this bad habit of yelling and crying when she doesn't get her way. I've gotten to where I just try to ignore her when she raises her voice. It isn't that often, but sometimes I do get just so annoyed with her that I tell her to go to her room to calm down."

Addressing the same issue, Ralph told us:

> "I've been trying to help her talk about it when she is angry. Jill thinks I baby her, but I want her to be able to tell us why she's mad so she doesn't take it out on her toys or on her brother."

In their family, however, their child Alise did not strike us as showing any particular indication of emotional or behavioral adjustment problems. Despite Jill's occasional annoyance with Alise, both she and Ralph rated their daughter within normal bounds on behavior reports. Alise's performance during the emotion-regulation waiting task was unremarkable (she spent most of her time with mother playing quietly and most of her time with father playing quietly and occasionally peering up at the brightly wrapped box), and she demonstrated a mature understanding of emotions (notching 11 out of 12 points on Denham's puppet task). Clearly in this family, the differing perspectives between the parents about dealing with Alise's expressions of anger did not appear to be having an adverse impact on the child's adaptive skills or competencies.

In other families, such as Rick and Millie's, however, we did see the expected linkage. Rick told us:

> "When she goes off on these dramatic crying and whining bouts, it really gets to me. She plays on each of us. Millie gives in but I won't. She'll say 'that's OK,' and indulge her."

Meanwhile, Millie told us:

> "It's just so hard for me to cut her off when she's sad. I'm with her all day and she relies on me. He always says to me 'you let her do this' and 'you let her do that.' I think daughters look to their mothers to be understanding and if *I'm* not, who will be?"

Our assessment of their daughter Polly indicated that she was rated by both her father and her teacher (but not her mother) as showing some difficulties with internalizing symptomatology (shyness, social isolation). During the wait task, Polly showed more passive time (sitting quietly without engaging with objects or parents) than did any of the other children we saw, and while in the family, Polly was compliant but also rated as showing low levels of happiness and warmth. Hence, in this family, the differing views about emotions were connected with some concerning symptoms, although they were symptoms of underexpression and internalizing rather than symptoms of behavioral dysregulation and acting-out behavior.

Two comments are in order. First, it occurred to us that in Alise's family, the differing perspectives by her two parents may have been reflecting the couple's propensity to be very vocal about their differences. Ralph's comment, "Jill thinks I baby her" reflects his awareness of his partner's perspective, and evidence from other points in the study substantiated this: The couple indicated high levels of conflict on the Coparenting Scale, were seen as engaging in moderate levels of verbal sparring in the family interactions, and were in the top 10% of families on their Ideas about Parenting difference score. At the same time, however, raters also judged the couple high on coparenting warmth and cooperation during family interactions. We also noted that Elise had enjoyed a secure attachment with both parents at 12 months and that the couple's marital satisfaction was neither exceptionally high nor very low. In other words, Elise's was an expressive family (perhaps kindred to the subgroup of coparenting families identified by McHale, 1997, and dubbed "Passionate"), but one in which there existed a background context of support and openness between the parents.

By contrast, in Polly's family, similar indicators of conflict and distress were in evidence, but were not counterbalanced by indicators of cohesion. Family interactions were rated as low in warmth and in coparental cooperation, Millie reported significant levels of coparenting conflict on the Coparenting Scale and of depressive symptmatology on the Center for Epidemiological Studies Depression Scale (CES-D; Radloff, 1977), and Rick's report of marital satisfaction fell in the clinical range of distress. Hence, the family context of Millie and Rick's differences about emotion management and regulation amplified the likelihood that Polly might develop some difficulties.

What did our data tell us about the link between differences in parents' emotion coaching propensities and toddler adjustment? As we hinted above, we actually found relatively few univariate connections in evidence. According to our analyses, toddlers from families in which parents reported more disparate stances toward anger and sadness were not more likely to be rated as showing behavior problems, nor were they more prone to show negativity during the emotion regulation task described in chapter 2. The only indication that coparenting differences in this realm may be important was a finding at the trend level ($p < .10$) that toddlers from families in which parents reported more disparate emotion socialization stances did more poorly in identifying specific emotions on Denham's emotion understanding task. Although this finding is of interest and consistent with our expectations concerning interparental differences, it was but a small-sized effect.

What did turn up, however, was evidence of a rather different nature suggesting the value in taking stock of both parents' emotion-coaching attitudes and behavior. In examining links between emotion coaching and toddlers' negativity during the waiting task described in greater detail below, DeCourcey (2005) determined that fathers' coaching of negative emotions came most strongly into play in families where mothers did not engage in much coaching themselves. More specifically, in families where mothers did little coaching, children tended to show higher levels of negative expressiveness when waiting with mothers—but only when fathers too did less emotion coaching (DeCourcey, 2005). By contrast, in families where fathers reported engaging in frequent coaching activities, toddlers' tendencies were to express fewer negative emotions with their low-coaching mothers (see Figure 6.1). This puts a rather different spin on the "like/unalike" dichotomy suggested earlier. Maintaining similar parenting approaches is not always ideal, and we believe this is a fact that has sometimes been overlooked in coparenting theory and research to date.

We also caution that it would be premature, and probably mistaken, to conclude that differences in emotion-coaching philosophies are inconsequential. Our index was based solely on what parents told us during interviews without their children or partners present. These interviews have proven to be a valid indicator in prior studies from Katz's lab, and they do appear to be good

Figure 6.1. Negative Expressiveness While Waiting With Mother

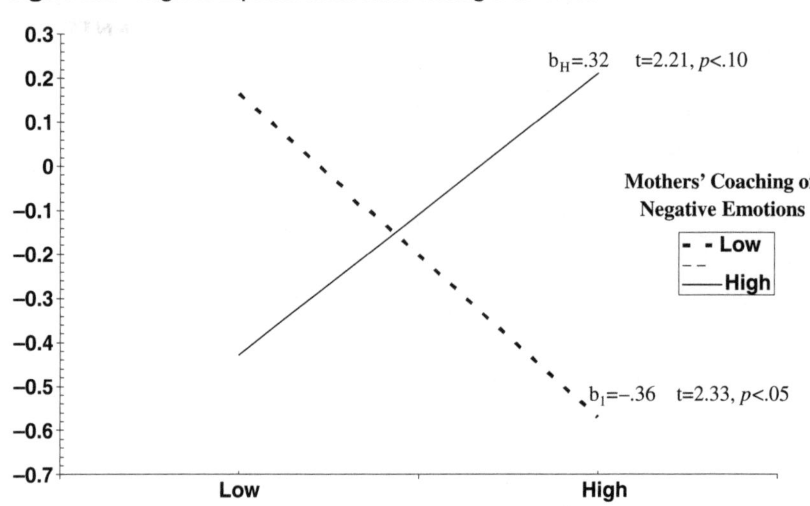

reflections of parents' actual practices with children (Gottman et al., 1997; Katz, Wilson, & Gottman, 1999; Katz & Windecker-Nelson, 2004). What we would add here is that the differences in philosophy need to be understood within the broader context of how the adults are functioning as coparents. When parents see emotions differently but have cultivated a better joint appreciation for their work as coparenting partners, they may be able to prevent their differences from catching their toddler in the middle. When parents have not yet developed this capacity, differences may indeed create problems.

What Parents Would Most Want to Change

The focus of the last section—emotion socialization of children—was a primary interest of ours. From parents' perspectives, however, teaching children about emotions was relatively far down on the list as they told us about the things in their families they felt were most in need of change. Having said this, we found it interesting that attainment of better control of *adult* emotional expression was atop many parents' lists when they were asked what they would like to change in their families (see

TABLE 6.1. WHAT PARENTS OF TODDLERS WOULD MOST LIKE TO CHANGE ABOUT THEIR COPARENTS AND IN THEIR FAMILIES

Disciplining more effectively (usually being firmer, but occasionally being less firm)
Getting a better handle on control of (adult) temper and emotional outbursts
Remaining patient and calm rather than getting flustered
Letting hair down, not being so concerned with exactly how things get done
Spending more one-on-one time with the toddler
Spending more time together as a family
Re-channeling the child's energies to more worthwhile activities
Becoming better attuned to the child's developmental needs
Doing a better job of organizing and structuring the child's day
Making more developmentally appropriate maturity demands
Creating more opportunities for the child to play together with peers
Combating the impulse to disengage
Shedding feelings of guilt for doing things the wrong way
Not letting factors outside of the home affect parenting
Prioritizing greater consistency with the other parent
Spending more time together as a couple
Combating overprotectiveness
Talking about and/or expressing emotions in front of the child
Cultivating emotional openness and expression
Stimulating the child's creativity and providing greater intellectual stimulation
Learning to multitask and manage time better
Taking time off for oneself
Feeling greater confidence in parenting decisions
(In bilingual families) Working harder to use the partner's native language with the child

Table 6.1). Recall that we asked partners what they would most want to change about their own parenting and their partners' parenting and what would most need to change in their families for them to feel they had created the kind of family environment they had most hoped to cultivate as coparents. Table 6.1 summarizes parents' responses to the latter two questions in order of the frequency mentioned.

Perhaps not surprisingly, some of these comments were made more often by mothers about fathers than by fathers about mothers, whereas the reverse was also true; some categories were more often fathers' wishes but not topics mentioned much by mothers. For example, mothers but not fathers identified among their wishes that their partners spend more one-on-one time with the toddler and feel greater confidence in their parenting decisions. Fathers but not mothers wished their partners would let their hair down more without worrying as much about precisely how things got done, shed feelings of guilt for not parenting properly, and take time off for themselves.

We had been prepared to hear a lot about discipline. During the toddler years, children take the word "mobility" to a new level: They are prone to climb up on countertops; empty out the contents of cabinets under kitchen and bathroom sinks; somersault off of furniture; race at breakneck speeds through the house; and hide in out-of-the-way places and elect not to respond when parents call them, initially in a matter-of-fact voice and subsequently a bit more frantically. They sometimes have no hesitation opposing or ignoring parents' directives to clean up, come for a bath, eat their meal, and come get ready for bed. They ask one parent for something and immediately turn to the other when the first parent says "no." They stomp, whine, tantrum, yell, cry, and sometimes turn their anger and frustration toward objects. Oversight, structuring, and discipline are 24–7 activities for parents, and we have yet to meet a parent who has had 24–7 energy; so we weren't at all surprised when an overwhelming preponderance of our families told us that some changes in disciplinary efforts were needed at home.

What we were less prepared for, although not taken aback by, was the large number of parents who told us that they, their partner, or the both of them needed to work on controlling their temper, cutting down on emotional outbursts, and remaining patient and calm. This was a major area of focus and guilt for almost two thirds of the families with whom we worked. In some families, parents described just a few outbursts occurring within an overall context of positive, responsive parenting. Jake, for example, remembered:

> "We were in his bedroom near bedtime and I was really exhausted, and he was really hyper, kind of delirious, which he gets sometimes on days when he doesn't nap. He was just laughing and rolling all

over me, wanting me to pick him up or swing him around, which I was just too tired to do. So he started just jumping onto me. I'd tighten my stomach so it didn't hurt too much. Then he stopped and I relaxed for a minute. What I didn't know was he climbed on his bed and leaped off it onto my stomach, and I doubled over. I got really mad and grabbed his shoulders and looked right at him and said 'Don't ever do that again.' I really scared him and immediately I felt awful. I'm usually really patient with him and he hasn't seen me like that, and I know it frightened him. I apologized and held him for a while and kissed his head and he fell asleep a few minutes later. But I feel awful that I lost it like that and scared him."

For other parents, it wasn't a single instance but rather a more consistent pattern of losing patience that frustrated them the most. Miriam told us:

"I need to stop yelling, I have these kids a neurotic mess. I'm incredibly demanding—I recognize it but don't quite know how to change it. Some of what Cheri does is lie to me—I know children do, but hers is from fear and not just going through a phase. I see she's so afraid to disappoint me and I've instilled that in her—I've done that trying to do what's best for her. I need to be a little less harsh and not so anal."

Frustrations can run high in families with toddlers, and parents have different ways of handling the frustrations. As we discussed in chapter 5, family work plays a huge role in many families and can affect both parenting sensitivity and coparenting coordination and solidarity. Demanding work schedules keep parents away from their families, leading to almost across-the-board frustrations. Overwhelmingly, working parents lamented how work schedules and demands ate into quality family time, although in some cases, parents also confided that work sometimes served as a means for delimiting family frustrations. Jerry, for example, mused:

"I do wish I had a little more patience . . . I have to confess that I really don't look forward to the weekends. During the week, I have the pressures of work, but there I'm not around screaming kids all day."

Indeed, in some families, parents left for work early in the morning before family members awoke and came home late in the evenings (and even when home, checked on e-mail and other work brought home). In such families, coparenting partners (in all but one or two cases, mothers) often felt underappreciated, and the change they most yearned for was a change in their partner's family investment. It was among such families, in particular, that mothers discussed the need for fathers to prioritize their parenting roles and spend more one-on-one time with their toddlers. Amy told us:

> "He needs to take more of a role now. I did all the work when Trisha was an infant, but she's more work now and I don't think Bob sees that. Sometimes I'd just like to leave the house for an entire day and write down all the things I do, and maybe then he'd see why I'm so tired and so irritable at the end of the day."

Kim told us:

> "I don't want him working so many nights. I want him there more for dinnertime. We've got to have at least one meal a week when we're all physically present."

Fearing fathers were not participating meaningfully enough in their rapidly growing toddlers' lives, a few mothers teetered on the border of having lost faith in their partners' parenting competencies altogether. Kelly told us, only half jokingly:

> "I'm not even sure if I left them home with John for an entire day what Tina would be fed."

Family lives were also challenged in dual-career families. Despite the generally greater teamwork of dual-career families during infancy, discussed in chapter 5, many families were struggling during the toddler years. Addressing what most needed to change in their family, Jim told us:

> "I think her work situation definitely has to change, because right now it doesn't provide her with enough time that she's satisfied. I think there's a lot of guilt there. She wants to be with Crystal, but she doesn't have enough time. A lot of our problems stem from lack of time and communication with one another."

Ron's focus was more on how Fran's work schedule affected the couple's relationship:

> "I think just the two of us having alone time together is what we need most. We haven't gone out in 6 months, and it does make a difference. Her job situation has to change or we're going to snap."

Still other parents discussed links between their differing views over work schedules and their toddlers' adjustment. Sid told us:

> "It's been really stressful shuffling him through different day cares. I kept telling her, 'Quit your job,' and she didn't want to do that. I was really worrying and hoping that the situations we were having at day care with his temper weren't going to affect him later in life."

The effects of work exhaustion were often quite pervasive. In many families, even when parents did find rare moments of time together without toddlers underfoot, they often avoided discussing their frustrations. As noted above, a change that many fathers wanted to see was that their partners recognize that household and child care work did not need to subsume every free moment or be done "just so." Indeed, a significant number of fathers' counterpoints to partners' wishes that they do more were parallel wishes that mothers' would do less or at least let their hair down a bit. They described wishes that mothers not worry if children sometimes refused to drink their juice, got sidetracked in fantasy while getting ready for an outing, or otherwise didn't meet up to what fathers sometimes saw as too demanding of standards. Rick said,

> "One thing we've talked about is her lightening up when the kids are not cooperating. Like when the kids don't just come out of house to the car and climb right in and buckle their seatbelts, I need to remind her 'Hey, this is how things are going to be at this age.'"

Some fathers believed that mothers silently telegraphed their frustrations with them about their perceived lack of engagement with household and child care work by working feverishly in the father's presence, even and sometimes especially once children had gone down for naps or for the night. Some fathers took this as their cue to get up and help, but others like Vincent described their frustrations at such moments when they and their wives missed opportunities to connect:

> "Evening time will come and we'll have a little quiet time but we can never just sit down and talk or whatever. She's got to be cleaning up the kitchen, doing the laundry, putting away the toys. She could let some of it go and do some of the other things that are interesting and important to her."

We have provided these glimpses into family life with a toddler to highlight many of the most commonly discussed challenges to effective coparenting coordination and communication. Many parents do recognize when they are not working well together and do what they can to persuade their partners to do things differently. Some even take steps to show symbolically that they are aware of the other's preferences and needs and that they are trying to make some changes themselves, but most find such conversations difficult, wearying, and potentially conflict-escalating. The path of least resistance is to let something go, particularly when the child is not in any imminent jeopardy by the parent's intervention. Even then, parents secretly wish their partners would do things differently. As Jerry's wife Sue told us:

> "There are some times when Jerry says things or puts things a certain way and I'm thinking 'That's not quite the message we want to be sending to them.'"

Unfortunately, keeping sentiments to oneself does little to change the status quo. Conversations are what are needed. We did find some families in which partners' descriptions of changes sought in their families did seem to reflect discussions having been had. For example, in the Turner family, Shelly told us:

> "Norman needs to understand more about Chris' outbursts so he can just walk away from them, totally ignore them, not give them any credence. He just needs to let Chris do them and not worry. He'll come back when he's done and join back into the fold."

Norm echoed Shelly's take on what he wanted to be working on:

> "I need to internalize some of what Shelly understands intuitively. I guess I just need more experience with emotions, and more awareness of where he's at to help him learn the skills he needs."

Effective coparenting alliances were rarely "done deals" at 30 months. They were almost always works still substantially in progress. An important realization that we came to after working with over 100 families with toddler-aged children was that among the more telling evidence for effectively functioning alliances were indications in the one-on-one interviews that partners had been talking to one another! When interviews at least indicated that the partners were aware of one another's perspectives on what they needed to work on—even if they did not necessarily share these perspectives fully—we had the sense that the coparents were moving in the right direction.

Let's now move from the revealing windows afforded by our interview-based data to what we learned from our observations of families at play with their 30-month olds.

What Did Family Interactions Look Like at 30 Months?

As we watched the Henson family through the one-way mirror, we had a sense that there were some things that had shifted a bit from 12 months, though other aspects of the family interaction had a ring of familiarity. During the 12-month family interaction session, Marjorie had been the one introducing toys to Caleb and determining when it was time to put away one task and bring out the next. At 30 months, she seemed more comfortable letting Steve orient Caleb to Jenga, the tower-building game that the family played together to start the session. She couldn't help but offer a couple of suggestions for how to approach the task when Caleb took his turn. For all intents and purposes, however, it looked to us as though she and Steve were participating equally in the game and sharing the responsibility for helping Caleb contain his impulse to dive into the game in his typically exuberant manner, which in this game would almost certainly have toppled the creation. Marjorie took more of a leadership role in the next game, a pretend family picnic, instructing Caleb which plates to set out and what she and Daddy would like to have for lunch. Steve played along, pretending to munch his hot dog and commenting how good it was but generally took more of the role we'd seen during infancy, allowing Marjorie to call the shots. Marjorie decided when it was time to clean up the picnic table, but all the family members pitched in, singing "Clean up, clean up" (a children's song introduced, to many parents' appreciation, by the children's program icon Barney the Dinosaur).

Steve next showed Caleb a horseshoe game that had been set up in a more spacious area of the room and demonstrated how to play. After a couple of errant tosses, Caleb quickly decided he would sit right next to the stake and drop the horseshoes on. Steve tried to correct him but Marjorie gently chided him to let Caleb play his way. Steve grew noticeably less active and allowed Caleb to play his way until Marjorie called him over to the toy box, which contained both gender-neutral (Viewmasters, musical instruments) and gender-specific (Barbie dolls, G.I. Joe action figures). Steve was the last to join, and he and Marjorie sat selecting different toys, manipulating them themselves, and offering them to Caleb, who was doing his own selecting and manipulating, then discarding toys. In this last task, family members seemed much more disjointed to us, each playing separately without coordinating with one another. Caleb's play was not at a very deep level; although he explored many items, he did not initiate extended play sequences with any, and there were no protracted dyadic or triadic interactions of any significance during this last task. After a couple of minutes, Steve's play also became notably less animated. Marjorie became very interested in a set of Aladdin and Jasmine dolls at one point, but her play interaction did not interest Caleb. At clean-up time, Marjorie again began singing "Clean up." Steve did not sing along this time but did help clean up the toys. Caleb did not help, escalating the intensity of his play efforts as he examined then discarded object after object.

The Hensons' patterning and pacing through the various teaching and play tasks was not an unusual one. Seldom did we find families in which one parent orchestrated the entire session with the other following along, as many mothers (and a handful of fathers) had done at 12 months. Parents did divvy up roles, often along the lines we saw during this interaction: father orienting the family to the building and sporting task; mothers to the eating, toy box exploration, and cleanup activities. There was every possible permutation, of course, and the team that coded the 30-month family interactions took note of both the structure of the visit and the management of transitions, as well as the interpersonal process among family members during the visit. They evaluated the same coparenting and family dimensions that their colleagues had rated at 12 months: overall presence and quality of cooperative exchanges and support between coparents; overall levels of warmth among all three members of the family triad; overall presence of affirmation and validation of mother by father, and of father by mother; flow of the session (guided principally by child's preferences and initiatives, by adults' preferences and initiatives, or equally by both); frequency and quality (benign to worrisome) of the disagreements and disqualifications (and other forms of verbal sparring) seen between adults; behavioral competition (parental propensities to overturn, one-up, or seek ascendance in guiding the toddler through the play sessions). Coders also evaluated both parents' overall levels of engagement, and we calculated (as we had earlier) a score reflecting disparity in levels of engagement by the two parents.

In the Hensons' case, the early cooperation we saw during the Jenga task persuaded raters to give the family a mid-range score in cooperation, despite the fact that the team spirit had clearly soured by session's end. Low-end scores were assigned only to families we saw in which the same level of spirited family engagement and cooperative effort was absent from any of the interactions. Most notable for us in this family interaction were the relatively low levels of family warmth and the low scores in affirmation and validation. With respect to warmth, coders began the session quite taken by the spirit of the interaction and the zeal Caleb showed, and at that point warmth too would have been highly rated, but as with cooperation, warm exchanges ebbed as the family interaction session progressed. Coders also saw little evidence of the partners' openly supporting one another's efforts with Caleb, although it could be argued that there may have been implied support in Steve's silent acceptance of Marjorie's structuring of the picnic and in the general lack of interference, aside from the horseshoe game exchange, in one another's teaching efforts. Marjorie's request of Steve to let Caleb do things his way during the horseshoe game gave the couple a mid-range, though not high, score on the negative coparenting ratings (higher scores went to families for whom we saw multiple critical exchanges; such exchanges were almost inevitably low key and often mumbled, as we indicated in chapter 5). This family received a high-end score on relative levels of parental engagement; there were some parents who were more engaged than Marjorie and many who were less engaged than Steve, but in contrasting the two parents' relative levels of engagement, coders documented a significant imbalance between the two.

On the overall rating scales, the Hensons were among the families who were in the lower tier of study families, although they were far from the most distressed. Marjorie's leadership and Steve's propensity to sit back and let his wife guide the show took on significance for us principally because of the lack of warmth, support, and affirmation that accompanied the discrepancy in engagement. In other families, in which one or the other parent also had the clear role of "play-master," the less active parent seemed more comfortable with and accepting of the partner's role, participating actively in each task, joking with the coparent and the child, occasionally proposing a novel twist on the activities (welcomed and amplified by the usually more active partner), and helping make the bond between the two adults more vibrant and palpable. Similarly, in another family, Marjorie's "correction" of Steve's efforts to teach Caleb proper gamesmanship in the horseshoe activity may have been met by either a laugh and a smile of agreement or by a forthright response that the child was already really good at dropping, so it was time to try something trickier because the child might just be able to do it. The passive, silent response, followed by some disengagement, was one that surfaced more often and colored subsequent family process principally in our more distressed families. Indeed, it was the Henson family's gravitation toward disconnection that concerned us the most, and the pattern of ratings bore out this concern.

We emphasize here that we were very aware of and respectful of the limits of observational data throughout our study. This was one of the primary reasons that our observational ratings are augmented by interview-based and self-report data at every time point. In the Hensons' case, data from the coparenting interviews (especially Marjorie's) and from the parent self-reports on McHale's (1997) Coparenting Scale (on which Marjorie weighed in highly on the conflict and disparagement items and Steve weighed low on the Family Harmony Promotion scale) were in line with our observations. In other families, however, Marjorie's high level of engagement and oversight of the visit and Steve's movement toward disconnection during the visit may have reflected little more than Marjorie's sensitive overcompensation for Steve's fatigue owing to a late night the evening before (many family sessions were held on weekday mornings), to a minor spat the couple had in the car on the way over, or to any number of more transient factors that may have led the session to misrepresent the prototypical pattern of family commerce. Caleb too was an important player in the overall family dynamic on this day. Our emphasis in this book has been largely on ways in which coparenting might help shape child adjustment patterns, but children themselves ultimately become equal partners in the evolution and consolidation of family group dynamics. Had Caleb been having an unusually difficult or "off" day, his provocations in the family group process may have catalyzed a different reaction pattern from one or both adults that could have led to a different set of conclusions.

Given our training as family therapists, we likely often erred in the direction of amplifying seemingly trivial glances, muttered comments, response chains and event sequences, creating meaning where perhaps none existed. Equally, however, such subtle indicators are the stuff family interactions are made of at 30 months. Our extended play interaction sessions were somewhat limited in that they had no parallels to the stressful still-face task of our 3-month visits or the separation–reunion challenges of the 12-month assessments to introduce significant strain into the dyadic or family system. Thirty months was a bit too early to have families sit down together to discuss child misbehavior or other stressful topics, as researchers sometimes do with families of older children. Therefore, we relied on having families do what they typically do together during the toddler years: engage together in play and clean-ups. Overall, this strategy did prove a fruitful one, as we outline further below. Before doing so, however, we take a parallel look at how the children themselves were adjusting at 30 months.

How the "Families Through Time" Toddlers Were Faring at 30 Months

Our emphasis through most of the book thus far has been on the ins and outs of coparental relationships. Children, who have also been featured players throughout these pages, have not yet received quite the same degree of scrutiny as we've given their parents' coparental alliance—until now. At 30 months, we undertook a variety of different assessments to establish how well toddlers were doing. We used a variety of different means for assessing toddler adjustment, as most studies to date have indicated that it is not possible to capture the diversity of adaptations that toddlers make with any single assessment tool. In this section, we provide an overview of how toddlers were doing on the key assessment measures we used. In the following section, we further summarize links between coparental and toddler adjustment.

The most widely used indicators of children's behavioral adjustment in both clinical and research settings have been Thomas Achenbach's age-graded Child Behavior Checklists (CBCLs). Their parameters are well understood by clinicians, and they afford the benefit of having clearly defined cutoff scores (as do the CES-D and the 1959 Locke–Wallace Marital Adjustment Test [MAT] for adults). Above these cutoffs, clinicians begin to worry about possible difficulties the child may be having. The CBCL yields overall summary scores indicating the notability of internalizing spectrum symptoms (on dimensions such as anxiety, depression, withdrawal, and the like) and the notability of externalizing acting-out symptoms (e.g., defiance and aggression). Because all toddlers exhibit fears and misbehavior, scores on the CBCL 1½–5 (Achenbach & Rescorla, 2000) as reported by mothers and fathers are contrasted with norms established for other children of a similar age. Scores of 60 or greater on either or both of these scales are typically taken as a point at which some concern may be warranted. In our sample, one third of the children had CBCL scores of 60 or above on either the internalizing or externalizing behavior problems scales or on both, according to one or both parents. This is important to establish at the outset, because the case we have been building is that coparental difficulties may create significant problems for young children. These data indicate that for a third of the youngsters we saw at 30 months, one or both parents were indeed already beginning to worry about difficulties exceeding the typical challenging behavior that toddlers manifest.

Besides behavioral problems, we were also interested, of course, in toddlers' adaptive capacities: their pre-academic and social competencies; their understanding of emotions; and their capacity for self-regulated, independent play during taxing and frustrating situations. Unlike the CBCL, no clinical cutoffs have been established for these various indicators. Just as with the CBCL indicators, however, we did find a rather wide range of adjustment on these different indicators. For example, on the Social Competence and Academic Competence scales of Cowan and colleagues' (1994) Child Adaptive Behavior Inventory (CABI), parents' ratings on the various constituting subscales ranged widely (maternal ratings of kindness ranged from 4 to 12, and paternal ratings ranged from 3 to 12; maternal ratings of social perceptiveness ranged from 4 to 12, and paternal ratings ranged from 5 to 12; maternal ratings of task orientation ranged from 5 to 12, and paternal ratings ranged from 7 to 20; etc.). On the lab-based measure of children's understanding of different emotions, scores ranged from 0 (*the minimum possible for the task*) to 12 (*the maximum possible for the task*). On the observational index of independent play, toddlers ranged from spending absolutely no time playing independently to playing independently for 100% of the time while they were waiting. As a result, we were comfortable that the different indicators we drew upon, each based on validated assessment paradigms introduced by leading scholars, distinguished among the various adaptive patterns of the toddlers in our study.

One question that is sometimes of interest to developmental researchers concerns the extent to which various indicators of child adjustment coalesce to form a unitary, universal indicator of adjustment or maladjustment. In 2005, Haskell, DeCourcey, and McHale undertook a detailed analysis of links between maternal and paternal ratings of toddler adjustment and toddlers' preferred adaptive strategies as they navigated the Grolnick, Bridges, and Connell (1996) waiting task we described in chapter 2. Recall that in the waiting tasks, conducted once with mothers and once with fathers, toddlers watched as attractive objects were placed out of reach. They then had to wait for 6 minutes before being given the object. Parents were kept occupied with questionnaires during the wait period. Haskell et al. were interested in determining whether the strategies toddlers engaged in to help regulate their emotions were consistent across parents and whether the strategies they used with each parent bore any relationship to how their fathers and mothers rated them on indicators of adjustment. Coders documented the strategies that the toddlers used (e.g., independent play, interactive bids, other caretaking requests and complaints, physical self-soothing, focus on the object, and passive engagement) in 5-second intervals. Strategy scores were determined by dividing the number of occurrences of each particular strategy by the number of intervals coded.

Correlational analyses of toddlers' strategy use while waiting with mothers and while waiting with fathers revealed that three of the emotion regulation strategies—passive engagement, physical self-soothing, and caretaking requests—were used consistently, regardless of the parent the child was waiting with, whereas the others—independent play, interactive bids, object focus, and complaining—were used differentially, depending on who it was the child was waiting with. When we examined how parents rated the adjustment of toddlers who showed different coping styles, we found that children high in strategies that were consistent across parental contexts tended to be rated as similarly adjusted by parents; toddlers who engaged in much passive engagement were rated as low in externalizing behavior by both mothers and fathers, whereas children who engaged in much physical self-soothing were rated as high in internalizing symptoms by both parents. An interesting exception, however, was with caretaking requests. Fathers rated children whom we saw make more frequent caretaking requests as being higher in externalizing symptomatology on the CBCL, whereas mothers saw these same children as unremarkable in terms of symptomatology.

What about the strategies used by toddlers that varied as a function of whether they were waiting with mothers or with fathers? Here the correlations with parent ratings did differ some. For example, the fathers of toddlers who showed a greater amount of independent play when waiting with fathers described their children as low in externalizing symptomatology. Mothers' ratings did not concur. However, the mothers of toddlers who showed more independent play with *them* rated their children as being more competent academically. Fathers' ratings did not concur. With respect to the making of interactive bids, fathers whose toddlers made more of such bids did not see their children as any more or less symptomatic or competent, whereas mothers whose toddlers made more of such bids portrayed their children as more competent socially, and with respect to the intensity of the child's object focus while the examiner was away, fathers described toddlers who were highly object focused with them as lower in internalizing symptoms while mothers rated highly object-focused toddlers as showing more externalizing symptomatology. Only for one variable—complaints—did parents concur. Both mothers and fathers whose children complained a lot while waiting with them rated their children as higher in externalizing symptomatology.

These findings are relevant in that they suggest that toddlers' developing emotion regulation skills include both a child component and a relational component. Understanding both the child's regulatory proclivities and the relational context in which they are striving to regulate emotions may be necessary in determining which set of strategies a toddler will use. Findings also suggest, however, that mothers and fathers may experience children who use certain regulatory behaviors differently in terms of adjustment. Consistent with a theme developed earlier in this book, one implication of these findings is that children may turn to different emotion regulation strategies to satisfy different caregivers' ideas about optimal regulation. In other words, effective emotion regulation during the toddler years may not just be what the child does to regulate emotions. It appears to also require that toddlers know in what relational contexts particular emotion regulation strategies are likely to work to promote their personal and relational goal attainment.

We find a similarly intriguing pattern in examining associations between parental ratings of child behavior problems and other indicators of child adjustment. Neringa Bruzgyte and Daniel Alongi (Bruzgyte, Alongi, & McHale, 2006) evaluated children's behavior during the family play interactions and examined their associations with parents' CBCL ratings. They found that children who were rated high in behavior problems by mothers showed a higher activity level, more anger, and less dependency during family interaction than did other children in the sample. Children rated high in behavior problems by fathers were likewise angrier and less dependent in the family. Bruzgyte et al. also found a very interesting set of associations between children's performance on Suzanne Denham's (1986) assessment of children's understanding of emotions (described in chapter 2) and parents' ratings of behavior problems. Toddlers who showed evidence of less advanced emotional knowledge on the task were described as having more behavior problems by their fathers, but not by their mothers. These data indicate how important it is to take stock of multiple informants' views of toddlers in studies of child adjustment. It seems unwise to dismiss the ratings of any given informant as being less relevant or more off the mark.

In the next section, we discuss links between coparenting solidarity and child adjustment. We spotlight what our data told us about associations between coparenting solidarity and parent and teacher ratings of toddler adjustment, toddlers' emotion understanding, and toddlers' manner of regulating emotions during the frustration task.

Links Between Coparenting and Toddler Adjustment

We have illustrated that we had a wide variety of child adjustment profiles at 30 months. Similarly, we had a wide variety of coparental adjustment profiles, but a key question remains: Was toddler adjustment associated with coparental solidarity in the ways we had imagined? Returning to our interview data for a moment, let's revisit why we had hypothesized in the first place that coparental solidarity (or lack of solidarity) would be associated with behavioral and socioemotional adjustment indicators.

In one of our interviews at 30 months, Rod was offering commentary on how he and his partner worked together as a couple. Relative to many other parents, Rod's view suggested more acute distress, as he shared his frustration over a recent incident:

> "It's like it happens 100 times a day. I'll hear her tell him, 'No chocolate before dinner.' Then he'll ask me and I'll say, 'What did your mommy say? No candy before dinner.' Then 2 minutes later I'll hear her in the kitchen saying, 'OK you can have just one piece.' It makes me crazy, and sometimes I just want to give up and say, 'I don't care. Do whatever you want with him.' But I know I can't. He needs rules and consistency and help figuring out what he should and shouldn't do. But it'd be so easy to just check out and not get involved."

Comments like this were actually fairly common throughout our 30-month interviews, although typically couched in less direct fashion. In this excerpt, we can see many of the themes developed so far in this book. Rod struck us as a parent who was clearly aware of the importance of coparenting solidarity and as someone actively striving to support his partner. At the same time, we heard from him the frustration that arises when mutually agreed-upon rules are subverted. He gives voice to the urge many parents feel to simply disengage after perceiving repeated invalidation or overturning of disciplinary activities, and he articulates the inner struggle of a resilient parent wrestling with the urge to forego active parenting efforts and to enable an "anything-goes" structure for his son. Less resilient parents, or Rod himself on a day when he was fatigued and when his defenses were low, could potentially respond by confronting and arguing with his partner in front of the child or by disengaging from the parenting episode for the moment, the rest of the day, or a much longer stretch of several days or more.

Our analyses did indicate that many parents had headed down this path by 30 months. Significant coherence was found among the various indicators of coparental cohesion and conflict at 30 months, as had been the case at both 3 and 12 months. As we did at the earlier time points, we created summary scores for both cohesion and conflict and used these indicators to form an overall index of coparental solidarity. The same sets of observational and self-report indicators as had been used at 12 months were again used at 30 months to assess coparenting cohesion. These included observational (CFRS) ratings of coparental warmth, coparental cooperation, maternal endorsement of fathers, paternal endorsement of mothers, and child-centeredness, and maternal and paternal reports of family harmony-promoting behavior on McHale's (1997) Coparenting Scale. The same sets of observational and self-report indicators used at 12 months were also used at 30 months to assess coparenting conflict. Pertinent CFRS indicators were: coparental competition, amount of verbal sparring, quality of verbal sparring, and degree of discrepancy in interparental warmth toward and involvement with the toddler. An updated version of the Coparenting Scale was used at 30 months, and both maternal and paternal ratings of child-related conflict on the relevant subscale were used. The final indicators were overall perceived difference scores on the Ideas About Parenting scale. The internal consistencies of the cohesion and conflict composites were each acceptable (.69 and .77, respectively).

As a final step in data reduction, we calculated an overall Coparental Solidarity score in a manner parallel to the one used for the 3- and 12-month data. First, we normalized the Cohesion and Conflict composite scores, and then we subtracted the Conflict score from the Cohesion score. In this way, high Solidarity families were those for whom the preponderance of measures at 30 months indicated that coparenting was high in cohesion and low in conflict. Mid-range scores characterized families for whom evidence of either low cohesion or high conflict were counterbalanced by more favorable scores on the other index. Low scores described families that were both low on cohesion and high on conflict. We then traced links between the coparenting solidarity scores and the different indicators of toddler adjustment.

Overall, findings supported the major thesis of our study; among children from families higher in coparental solidarity, there were multiple indications that the children were showing more positive social and emotional adjustment. For example, the toddlers whose parents had been evaluated as showing greater solidarity in their coparental alliance were rated by their fathers as more socially competent (on the CABI), and as having fewer behavior problems (on the CBCL). They were rated by their teachers and day-caregivers as showing stronger pre-academic skills (on the CABI). They demonstrated a more mature understanding of emotions on Denham's laboratory task, and they showed evidence of having gravitated toward being less reliant on their parents to help regulate their emotions, making statistically fewer caregiving requests and complaints to their mothers during the waiting task than other toddlers.

The only major assessment category that did not reflect the anticipated association with coparental solidarity was mothers' ratings of toddler adjustment; a curiosity, since maternal reports are most often used as proxies for child adjustment in the published research literature! Even here, we did find one important association. The overall coparenting *conflict* composite (one of the two composite scores that we used to construct the overall solidarity index) was significantly associated with mothers' ratings of toddlers' externalizing behavior problems on the CBCL. That is, in families in which we documented greater coparental conflict at 30 months, mothers saw their children as demonstrating more significant levels of acting out behavior. Also of note, a similar pattern was found in fathers' ratings of externalizing behavior problems, although for fathers the finding was at the trend level ($p < .10$).

What these data suggest to us is that coparental solidarity is indeed a critical force in helping young children to develop adaptive social and emotional competencies even as early as the toddler years. When parents had found ways to work constructively and supportively, toddlers showed multiple indications that they were developing positively in the realms of behavioral, social, emotional, and pre-academic competencies. We revisit and further discuss these critically important findings in chapter 10, but before concluding this chapter, we pose one final question of importance: What could we have predicted about 30-month coparenting and family process from what we had learned earlier about families?

What Could We Have Guessed From What We Knew Earlier?

How early could we have known that the families showing the greatest coparenting struggles at 30 months would be having such difficulties? This is a complicated question. For some families in the study, changing life circumstances intervened such that anticipated outcomes at 30 months simply couldn't have been predicted from what preceded. Job changes, moves, deaths in the family, addition of a temperamentally challenging baby brother or sister—all these were events chronicled among families in our study, and some swayed even the sturdiest of families. The real question for us was whether the information we had gathered at earlier time points about coparenting and family dynamics had any prognostic value.

What we learned is this: Coparenting solidarity at 30 months can indeed be forecast from coparental solidarity at 12 months. Despite the massive changes in infants' and toddlers' needs, adaptive patterns, challenges, and competencies, and despite a normative shift toward more active paternal engagement as greater disciplinary effort became warranted with the more active toddler, families that had been showing more cohesion, warmth, and affirmation and less oppositionality, antagonism, and disengagement in the coparenting process at 12 months continued on similar adaptive paths into the toddler years. Those who had been showing greater signs of difficulty earlier on continued to struggle to find an effective team spirit at 30 months. This statistically significant association between coparental solidarity across an 18-month span is among the most important findings from our study.

Could problems be traced back any farther than this? Here, the story gets interesting, we believe. Recall from chapter 5 that coparenting during infancy could be predicted from both prenatal assessments of pessimism and from early (3-month) coparenting solidarity. Hence, the tone for early family adjustment, right up through the end of the baby's first year, was indeed shaped by earlier adjustment between the parenting partners. In this manner, it might be argued that we can back things up to even before the baby arrives and forecast with some certainty which families are most likely to encounter difficulties. However, when we looked across the longer haul, the same associations tying prenatal and 3-month adaptive profiles to 12-month coparental solidarity were no longer in evidence by 30 months. The reach of prenatal adjustment, for the group as a whole, had largely washed away by the toddler years.

There was a small subgroup, however, for whom this was not so. In a recent analysis, McHale and Rotman (2007) used latent class analyses to identify subgroups of families within the larger sample and determined that for one group of families in the study there did appear to be cross-time links between pregnancy and 30 months. Among this group of families, early prenatal negativity on the part of fathers, combined with greater discrepancies in mothers' and fathers' prenatal descriptions of their ideas about parenting, did combine to predict more negative coparenting outcomes in toddlerhood. What was particularly interesting about this finding is the significance of discrepancies in parenting beliefs that had existed *before* the baby ever arrived on the scene. This difference score had not been meaningful in prenatal-to-3 month analyses or in prenatal-to-12-month analyses. Now suddenly, however, at the point in family development where fathers began stepping in to parent more actively in response to the shifting developmental competencies, challenges, and needs of the toddler-aged child, pre-baby differences in parenting beliefs appeared to exert predictive influence, but principally in the context of pre-baby negativity on the part of fathers.

Hence, there are at least two stories to tell in concluding this chapter. The first is that we see continuity through the evolution of the coparenting process by virtue of the impact that prenatal beliefs and outlooks have on the early emerging family process and the significant associations that link coparental solidarity at 3 months to solidarity at 12 months and solidarity at 12 months to solidarity at 30 months. Both maternal and paternal prenatal expectations, as well as prenatal marital quality, shape the early coparenting dynamic, with some evidence that maternal pessimism may be a particularly potent factor in the equation, but there is also some evidence, admittedly suggestive on the basis of the smaller sample size extending from pregnancy to 30 months, indicating that for a subgroup of families, paternal negativity and substantial differences in beliefs about parenting may become significant factors in forecasting coparental adjustment into the toddler years. We come back to these important findings again in chapter 8.

Summary

We covered much ground in this chapter and did our best to reflect the realities of life with a toddler and the strains that this developmental period can put on partners as they work to strengthen and build their coparental alliance. Emotions often run high, and even among families best weathering challenges, there are times that tax the most patient. In the end, we discovered two very important things. First, despite some noteworthy changes in family trajectories, owing to unanticipated or unavoidable life changes, those families who showed evidence of handling the ups and downs of toddlerhood most successfully were more likely to be those who had forged more supportive coparental alliances by the time of the baby's first birthday. Second, greater coparental solidarity during the toddler years was linked, in the expected ways, to toddlers' behavioral, social, and emotional adaptation in a variety of different realms. We have much more to say about the practical and clinical implications of these findings in the closing chapters. First, however, we turn our focus in chapter 7 to the comparison group of families in our study who were coparenting two young children. As we'll see, although there were many similarities, there were also a number of very interesting distinctions that characterized the lives and adaptations of these coparenting teams.

References

Achenbach, T. M., & Rescorla, L. A. (2000). *Manual for the ASEBA Preschool Forms & Profiles.* Burlington: University of Vermont, Department of Psychology.

Bruzgyte, N., Alongi, D., & McHale, J. (2006, March). *The family context of toddlers' behavioral and emotional adaptation.* Paper presented at the meetings of the Southeastern Psychological Association, Atlanta, GA.

Cowan, P. A., Cowan, C. P., Schulz, M. S., & Heming, G. (1994). Prebirth to preschool family factors in children's adaptation to kindergarten. In R. Parke & S. Kellam (Eds.), *Exploring family relationships with other social contexts: Advances in family research* (Vol. 4, pp. 75–114). Hillsdale, NJ: Erlbaum.

DeCourcey, W. M. (2005). *Parents' meta-emotion attitudes and toddlers' emotion competencies.* Unpublished doctoral dissertation, Clark University.

DeCourcey, W. M., Haskell, V., & McHale, J. P. (2005, April). *Concordance of coparents' meta-emotion strategies and toddler emotion expression.* Paper presented at the Society for Research in Child Development, Atlanta, GA.

Denham, S. A. (1986). Social cognition, prosocial behavior, and emotion in preschoolers: Contextual validation. *Child Development, 57*, 194–201.

Gottman, J. M., Katz, L. F., & Hooven, C. (1997). *Meta-emotion: How families communicate emotionally*. Hillsdale, NJ: Erlbaum.

Grolnick, W. S., Bridges, L. J., & Connell, J. P. (1996). Emotion regulation in two-year-olds: Strategies and emotional expression in four contexts. *Child Development, 67*, 928–941.

Haskell, V., DeCourcey, W., & McHale, J. (2005, April). *Cross-parent consistencies and differences in toddlers' emotion regulation strategies.* Paper presented at the Society for Research in Child Development, Atlanta, GA.

Katz, L. F., Wilson, B., & Gottman, J. M. (1999). Meta-emotion philosophy and family adjustment: Making an emotional connection. In M. J. Cox & J. Brooks-Gunn (Eds.), *Conflict and cohesion in families: Causes and consequences* (pp. 131–165). Mahwah, NJ: Erlbaum.

Katz, L. F., & Windecker-Nelson, B. (2004). Parental meta-emotion philosophy in families with conduct-problem children: Links with peer relations. *Journal of Abnormal Child Psychology, 32*, 385–398.

Kerllenevich, M. A., & DeCourcey, W. M. (2005, April). *Parental theories of emotion and emotion socialization: Teaching toddlers about the world of emotions.* Paper presented at the Society for Research in Child Development, Atlanta, GA.

Locke, H. J., & Wallace, K. M. (1959). Short marital-adjustment and prediction tests: Their reliability and validity. *Marriage and Family Living, 21*, 251–255.

McHale, J. P. (1997). Overt and covert coparenting processes in the family. *Family Process, 36*, 183–201.

McHale, J. P., & Rotman, T. (2007). Is seeing believing? Expectant parents' outlooks on coparenting and later coparenting solidarity. *Infant Behavior and Development, 30*, 63–81.

Radloff, L. S. (1977). The CES-D scale: A self-report depression scale for research in the general population. *Applied Psychological Measurement, 1*, 385–401.

How Things Change When a Sibling Joins the Picture

With Allison Lauretti and Melanie McConnell

Throughout this book, attempts have been made to integrate quantitative findings that capture salient trends across all the families we saw with qualitative data highlighting individual differences and individual family storylines through time. Toward this latter end, three Families Through Time researchers (James McHale, Donna Elliston, and Jessica Thompson) spent the better part of a year reviewing and discussing cross-time trajectories of each of the 46 families assessed at all four time points during weekly "case conferences." For these sessions, we began by reading the family's chart at Time 1, the prenatal evaluation. We reviewed carefully all they had shared with us about themselves, their families of origin, their marriages, and their expectancies for the future during the prenatal visits. We also reviewed video records of the interaction sessions and transcripts of interviews conducted. We then hazarded a collective guess based only on this information about the strengths and struggles we expected we might see at the following time point (3 months postpartum). We then did exactly the same thing after reviewing the 3-month data—on the basis of what we knew about the family's prenatal and 3-month strengths and risks, what might we anticipate at 12 months? Then again, with prenatal, 3-, and 12-month data in hand, we discussed patterns of adaptation or difficulty we expected to see at 30 months. Following this clinical case methodology, we were struck (perhaps not surprisingly) by the marked stability in coparental patterns and adjustment we saw in most families, but we did encounter some surprises as well. In these cases, we typically came to learn of factors beyond the family interior (a major family move, job loss, illness, or other major unanticipated stressor) that helped us to understand the seeming discontinuity in the pattern of coparental adjustment over time. Apropos to the topic of this chapter, however, there was another wild card that sometimes altered trajectories significantly for certain families.

A very potent revelation came as we reviewed all that the Simon family had shared with us over the course of their involvement with the project. After reviewing their charts from pregnancy, 3, and 12 months, we all believed we had a pretty good read on Todd and Sheila's coparenting alliance. Their family theme was in evidence even during the pregnancy, when both partners told us in their individual interviews that Sheila was going to be the primary parent and handle most child-related decisions and responsibilities. Sheila said that, although she wanted parenting to be a "joint adventure," she expected that she'd be doing most of the work because she would be staying home with the baby. She added that because she had a fair amount of experience with children, she had some concerns that she might intimidate Todd but hoped that wouldn't happen. Todd, for his part, was even more explicit in his expectation that Sheila would be handling the bulk of the work of child care, indicating that he expected her to "stay home and take care of the chores and the baby, so when I come home from work I can just play with her rather than having to do housework."

Were these prenatal expectancies a recipe for disaster? Although readers recalling some of the vignettes from the earlier chapters might imagine so, Todd and Sheila actually demonstrated very little distress at 3 months. In fact, our data indicated that the couple was faring at least as well as most other families in the sample. This is significant, because the couple's prenatal expectation that Sheila would run the show and Todd would contribute (albeit secondarily) was indeed in evidence when we visited the couple at 3 months. During the Lausanne Trilogue Play (LTP; Fivaz-Depeursinge & Corboz-Warnery, 1999), for example, Sheila was much more active than Todd and partially as a result, the coparenting process was evaluated as being in the moderate range on dimensions of both competition and verbal sparring. These ratings were based largely on Sheila's sporadic interference during Todd's play with their son Kyle, and on a joking remark she made (on behalf of Kyle), commenting on Todd's mistiming during a play interaction. During the same session, however, Sheila also coaxed Todd back into the play at one point when he drew back in response to Kyle's tendency to fixate largely on Sheila during the LTP's three-together episode. She even touched Todd gently at one point in an inclusive gesture that was relatively unusual during most family interactions. Furthermore, although the strong connection between mother and baby was featured during both the LTP and still-face task, Todd was nonetheless rated as high in warmth during the somewhat less frequent interactions he shared with Kyle. Also, both parents reported very high scores on Abidin and Brunner's (1995) Parenting Alliance Inventory and were rated by Susan Dickstein as showing high levels of affirmation during the birth narrative interview. In short, although Sheila was unquestionably the one taking the lead during family interactions, Todd had a comfortable and contributing role, and the couple seemed none the worse for wear at 3 months. To us, this supported the notion that what is particularly important in the transition to coparenthood is the extent to which both parents' wished-for expectancies about family dynamics come to be realized. In Todd and Sheila's case, both parents expected Sheila to call the parenting shots, and when this happened neither parent expressed substantive concerns, at least during the first 3 postpartum months.

We wondered, of course, whether this trend would continue to the 12th postpartum month. To help make this guess, we reexamined both the prenatal and the 3-month data and saw that both parents had reported contentment with the marriage at both the prenatal and postpartum assessments—a good sign. Todd's prenatal score on the Center for Epidemiological Studies Depression Scale (CES-D; Radloff, 1977) had been elevated, although readers may recall that we saw such elevations more as a sign of anxiety rather than depression per se in many families. Todd had been worrying about something, though not fatherhood (at least according to his prenatal interviews). Sheila, by contrast, reported very low depressive symptomatology both prenatally and at 3 months, which was also a good sign. Although Todd had pointed out some distinctions between his family's and Sheila's family's characteristic styles and tempos, he had convinced his interviewer (and those who rated his interview) that he and Sheila were aware of their different socialization experiences and had talked about such differences in discussions of their future family. Hence, there was no reason to believe that the coparental dynamic with Sheila leading the way (and occasionally critiquing Todd's involvement), Todd playing a secondary role but nonetheless engaging fully (as he could), and both partners being content with this arrangement would change substantially over the coming months. Indeed, it had not changed markedly by 12 months.

At 1 year postpartum, we saw a strikingly similar coparenting pattern in both self-report and observational data. For example, during the family interactions, we found evidence of both mild competitiveness and of coparental warmth and cooperation, as we had at 3 months. Sheila was again very engaged with Kyle throughout the session, much more so than Todd (who himself did engage meaningfully and with substantial warmth at various points during the session, just less often than did Sheila). Sheila set the tempo, introduced the games, and again interfered occasionally at times when Todd had the stage (e.g., introducing a different toy as Todd was trying to teach Kyle to fit blocks together). In contrast with the 3-month assessments, however, Todd now countered a wee bit, bouncing a large ball emphatically to attract Kyle's attention a few moments after Sheila had told Todd that "he [Kyle] doesn't like that ball."

These occasional, fleeting moments of dissonance during the session were consistent with Sheila's ratings of both conflict and disparagement on McHale's (1997) Coparenting Scale. Both scores were mildly elevated, her conflict rating placing in the 88th percentile among mothers in the study, and her disparagement rating in the 73rd percentile. However, just as had been the case at 3 months, these signs of dissonance were balanced by ample evidence that the couple remained comfortable with the pattern they had cocreated through that point in time. Warmth and cooperation ratings from the family interaction remained high. Ratings of child-centeredness (the extent to which the parents followed the lead of the baby rather than dictating the pace and tempo of the sessions themselves) were also high, as were observational ratings of the frequency with which Sheila provided endorsement for Todd's efforts and Todd for Sheila's efforts. These observational data were augmented further by both parents' reports of family-integrity promoting behavior on the Coparenting Scale. Items on this scale capture the frequency with which parents speak positively about one another with the child, include one another in family activities, and demonstrate affection openly (McHale, 1997). Sheila's family integrity score was in the 96th percentile among mothers in the study, and Todd's was in the 100th percentile. Hence, despite the fact that Todd was comparatively less engaged than other fathers in the study, both partners were clearly making efforts to coconstruct a climate that afforded the experience of respect and inclusion between and by both parents. Both parents' marital satisfaction scores actually peaked at the 12-month mark, and neither parent's depression scores raised any concerns.

Perhaps more than for any of the other families we had reviewed by then, we felt rather confident making our 30-month coparenting predictions, expecting the Simons to remain on the same coparenting trajectory they had begun charting before Kyle had ever arrived on the scene. And perhaps more than for any other family we reviewed, we were quite startled when we reviewed the family's 30-month data

The first thing that we found jarring was the way that the parents' scores on the Parenting Alliance Inventory (PAI; Abidin & Brunner, 1995) had plummeted from 3 to 30 months. At 3 months, both Todd's and Sheila's scores on the PAI (which assesses the degree of support and affirmation provided, felt, and received in the coparental alliance) topped out at the 100th percentile. By 30 months, they brought up the rear among couples in the study, Sheila's score placing in the 3rd percentile and Todd's in the 5th. Whereas Sheila's reports of conflict and disparagement did not stand out as prominently among mothers in the study as they had at 12 months (scores placing in the 74th and 49th percentiles, respectively), Todd's reports skyrocketed from the 48th percentile (conflict) at 12 months to the 100th percentile at 30 months, and from the 37th percentile (disparagement) at 12 months to the 77th percentile at 30 months. Perplexing as this was, we truly weren't prepared for what the observational data revealed.

We had fully expected to see a continuation of the 3- and 12-month coparenting dynamic—a very child-centered interaction with Sheila leading the way, Todd connecting periodically and warmly, and some mild nattering between the adults grounded by a very warm, cooperative, and mutually affirming interparental dynamic. Although some elements of this observed family dynamic remained in evidence during the interaction session (endorsement ratings remained high, and warmth and cooperation ratings placed at the middle of the pack), the topology of the interaction was exactly the opposite of what we had anticipated. As the tape began, there was Todd handing out assignments. He structured every task, was as engaged with Kyle as any father we had seen at 30 months, and gave Kyle relatively little latitude in charting the course of the interactions. He told Kyle when he could handle the puzzle pieces, who to distribute things to during the family picnic game, and where to stand during the horseshoe contest. Largely for this reason, the family process at 30 months, which had been rated as very child-centered at 12 months, now received the lowest rating possible. Raters assigned a score of 1, signifying that the session was thoroughly parent-centered, with the adults determining its pace and tempo. Sheila did participate in the activities, though far less actively, and challenged none of Todd's initiatives (as she had at 3 and 12 months). Indeed, our observational team was nearly 5 minutes into review of the tape before someone noticed the infant carrier tucked almost completely out of view near Sheila's feet.

As it turned out, baby Chelsea had joined the Simon family between our 12- and 30-month visits. Our assessment team had known this, of course, before they ever saw the Simons at 30 months, but working only from charts and tapes some 2 years later, our case conference group wasn't aware of this change. They had never actually met the Simons, and their process was to work systematically only from the summary scores that had been recorded for the key family variables in each family's chart at each of the study's time points (augmented by relevant interview-based and observationally based data from each of the first three time points). Only after spotting Chelsea did they attend to the major family transition that had reorganized the Simon family's coparenting alliance between Kyle's first birthday and the 30-month assessment. Clearly without having this knowledge of Chelsea's arrival in advance, our prediction that the Simons would continue on the same coparenting pathway that had been their family's dominant adaptation during Kyle's first year was as far off as it could possibly have been.

But what happened? What changed, and what stayed the same? Our data suggested that, just as Kurt Kreppner's research studies of the 1980s might have predicted, the birth of the second baby integrated Todd more thoroughly as an active parenting force in the family, but as this happened, Todd's stepping up necessitated a wholesale reorganization of the family group dynamic. It is conceivable that we simply caught the Simons at a really rough period of family disequilibrium, as they struggled to redefine the coparenting roles that had become comfortable ones for them through that point. Chelsea's arrival diverted much of Sheila's attention away from Kyle, and Todd—guided by the long-standing family ethic of support and cohesion—intensified his involvement so as to prevent Kyle from experiencing any void. As it turned out, however, Todd's style was substantially different from Sheila's. We had already seen ample evidence from the 3- and 12-month assessments that Sheila was not afraid to let Todd know when he wasn't doing things quite the way she would have done them, suggesting that Todd's increased involvement with Kyle at 30 months may have created a significant dilemma for Sheila. Did she continue to try to influence how Todd should be engaged with Kyle, or did she (in the service of maintaining and promoting coparental and family harmony) keep her reservations to herself and give Todd the room to do things his way?

Our data suggest that Sheila took the latter posture, holding back as Todd took greater responsibility for helping shape the family business of parenting. Todd's inclination toward provision of greater structuring and affording of less freedom to Kyle during the family interaction sessions went unchallenged by Sheila, who kept one watchful eye on Chelsea and the other on Todd and Kyle—but without interfering. Todd channeled most of his energies toward Kyle and paid relatively less attention to baby Chelsea (although admittedly she was not yet old enough to be a very engaged social partner at the time of our 30-month assessment with Kyle). During the times when Todd did attend to Chelsea during the visit, he was as always warm and attentive. Equally, however, the disparity between Todd's and Sheila's level of engagement with Chelsea was far greater than it had ever been with Kyle.

The effect of Chelsea's arrival on the broader family dynamic was equally interesting. On the one hand, neither Todd's nor Sheila's ongoing commitment to promoting family integrity changed markedly from earlier levels. In fact, on the Coparenting Scale, Sheila's score was the highest among all mothers in the sample, placing her in the 100th percentile, and Todd's score placed him in the 88th percentile; yet this was at precisely the same time as the degree of support that each of them felt for the coparenting burden they were assuming had bottomed out. Sheila, accustomed to calling the shots and having Todd as a willing partner in the parenting plan she had authored, now had abdicated much of the daily responsibility for overseeing Kyle's behavior to Todd, who on shouldering this role turned out to actually have a very different way of working with Kyle than Sheila. Furthermore, though perhaps not completely satisfied with Todd's way with Kyle, Sheila could not remain as engaged as she might have wished because she was feeling almost the total burden for Chelsea. Hence, her sentiments about coparenting support, never at issue with just the one child, changed dramatically once there were two.

From Todd's perspective, he too was feeling the strain. Quite content with the coparenting role he had played for 2 years with Kyle (the one he and Sheila had agreed upon before Kyle ever arrived on the scene), he found himself thrust into a position of parenting authority as Sheila turned her attentions to Chelsea. The fact that he stepped into a role of greater authority after having scoped out a different role in Kyle's life for 2 years—that of fun Dad, kibbitzer, and occasional backup for Mom's prerogatives, was a change not only for him but for Kyle as well. Kyle responded to the change, as do most children, by protesting more than a little bit. Many authors have written about the wholesale change in the firstborn's reality when the second-born arrives on the scene, and Kyle was no exception. A child who had been flexible, docile, and engaging for 2 years began responding with all the usual gusto of the terrible twos, and then some. Parent reports and interviews characterized his behavior as willful, obstinate, and contrary, and as marked by prolonged crying and yelling bouts. The change caught both parents by surprise, and Todd was the one who reluctantly stepped in to introduce and assert authority. Meanwhile, Sheila silently struggled with many of Todd's parenting decisions; hence, both parents reported feeling very low levels of support in the couple's coparental alliance at 30 months.

Despite this change, at the metafamily system level, many things had remained the same. We have mentioned the continuity in the couple's self-reported efforts to promote family harmony and the continuing high mother-to-father and father-to-mother ratings of affirmation based on the couple's behavior during the family interactions. Recall too that this had always been a couple with mild-to-moderate conflict ratings, even in the context of a supportive alliance. Although there were some interesting changes in the couple's conflict profile, their overall dissonance score was comparable at 30 months to the 3- and 12-month scores. One difference we saw at 30 months was Sheila's reduction in coaching and critique of Todd's efforts with Kyle during the family interaction, compared with 3 and 12 months. As we've suggested, this was likely due to both the attention she was devoting to Chelsea and to her partial letting go of her full-time "director's" role with Kyle. On the other hand, Todd was now reporting greater dissonance on his self-report of coparenting behavior. He indicated both that he and Sheila argued more often about Kyle in front of him and that he himself spoke disparagingly of Sheila to Kyle more frequently that he had in the past. Again, keep in mind that this is in the context of continuity in the couple's commitment to providing a consistent and unified front as parents. At 30 months, however, they were finding it more difficult to keep this seamless commitment than they had at 3 and 12 months.

Thus far, we have focused almost exclusively on Todd and Sheila's coparenting adjustment, but other information the couple shared with us at 30 months rounds out the family picture in important ways. First, it is important to note that, despite the decline in the levels of support Todd and Sheila felt from one another in their coparenting roles, neither parent was reporting clinically significant levels of marital distress or of depressive symptomatology. Although Todd's score on the Locke and Wallace (1959) Marital Satisfaction Test had slipped 18 points from where it stood at the time of Kyle's first birthday, it remained squarely in the middle of the pack for fathers in the sample and was virtually identical to his satisfaction rating at 3 months. Sheila's marital satisfaction score had slipped 9 points from the 12-month assessment but still remained among the higher scores for mothers in the sample. Although both parents showed small increases in their CES-D depression scores from 12 to 30 months, neither parent's score approached the clinical threshold. This seems important to say: The difficulties they were experiencing at 30 months seemed specifically concentrated in their struggles as coparents; there was not an "across-the-board" decline in the couple's mental health or marital adjustment. We return to this point again in chapter 8.

Second, and maybe of greatest interest to readers, the couple's current coparenting strains also coincided with their somewhat different impressions of Kyle's behavioral adjustment. Perhaps not unexpectedly, Sheila was less inclined to see Kyle as showing behavior problems on the Child Behavior Checklist (CBCL 1½–5; Achenbach & Rescorla, 2000) than was Todd, whose rating of the boy's behavior fell just 1 point short of the clinical range on total behavior problems. This is an interesting phenomenon that we also found at the group level in our study; coparental conflict was significantly associated with the magnitude of the difference between parents' CBCL ratings of total behavior problems. Couples showing more conflictual coparenting dynamics were more prone to see their child differently than were other couples. The fact that it was Todd rather than Sheila who provided the more extreme ratings of Kyle's adjustment is of further interest, given the group findings (reported in chapter 6) linking fathers', but not mothers', ratings of total behavior problems on the CBCL to our summary index of low coparental solidarity.

Sheila and Todd actually did concur that Kyle appeared to be having some difficulties with "internalizing" spectrum behavior problems (e.g., anxiety, withdrawal, sadness), as both parents rated him above the 90th percentile on this scale on the Child Adaptive Behavior Inventory (CABI; Cowan & Cowan, 1992). It was in the realm of externalizing behavior problems that the couple really saw Kyle differently. Todd rated his externalizing symptoms (e.g., oppositionality, defiance, aggression) in the 95th percentile on the CABI, whereas Sheila's score was at the opposite extreme, placing Kyle just within the 33nd percentile, or below the average toddler in our study. Given the circumstances we outlined regarding Todd's increasing parenting responsibilities and Sheila's begrudging relinquishing of her job as the primary socialization agent for Kyle, these discrepancies are certainly understandable, although worrisome in the longer run.

Had we been able to extend this project further in time, we would be in a better position to determine whether the coparenting challenges Todd and Sheila were facing at 30 months were transitory or whether they might worsen or crystallize into a dynamic of opposition and antagonism between the coparents. We saw the fact that the couple had a history of working collaboratively to promote family harmony (which they continued at 30 months) and of affirming one another as parents even in the face of philosophical differences as auspicious and possibly predictive that the couple would have found a way to right themselves by the time of a later assessment point. Much would hinge, of course, on factors beyond the family and on Chelsea's temperamental characteristics. An easy second-born might be seen as a family asset, whereas a temperamentally irritable baby would add another layer of strain and challenge.

We have spent as much time as we have on the Simons' story to drive home the point that the findings we have reported throughout the book are group findings, highlighting the importance of early coparental adjustment for later adjustment. In the end, however, every family's story is different, as the complex patterning of the data for the Simons at 30 months signifies. Through it all, however, we saw the earlier successful adaptation of the couple as a resource from which they could work to recalibrate their family's coparenting process.

We now turn to the more systematic assessments we completed of families with two young children. These data serve as the basis for findings reported through the remainder of this chapter.

Our Comparison Group Families

As chapter 2's co-authors set out to design the Families Through Time study, our colleague Allison Lauretti convinced us that it would be of tremendous importance to the coparenting literature to systematically study differences in families in which the baby was the first child and families in which the baby was a second child. On the basis of her suggestions, we included in our protocol plans to recruit at 12 months families in which the baby had a preschool-aged brother or sister 18–30 months older than the baby. Our rationale for doing so was that by 12 months, babies had at least begun to afford opportunities to their siblings for reciprocal social engagement; that is, when siblings sought to engage the baby socially, the baby was mobile, accustomed to making and responding to social bids behaviorally, and capable of sustaining interactions for extended periods.

Forty-two families with second-born infants contributed coparenting data at 12 months, and 39 of the 42 two-child families completed a full set of observational assessments. Of these 39 families, 22 had a second-born infant son and 17 a second-born infant daughter. All families also had a firstborn preschooler between the ages of 2 and 5 years (mean age = 39 months, *SD* = 9.05). In terms of the gender constellation of sibling dyads, 30.3% were brothers, 15.2% were sisters, 27.3% were older brother/younger sister pairs, and 27.3% were older sister/younger brother pairs. Median annual family income for this group of families was approximately $60,000, and couples had been married an average of 6.4 years. Mothers' mean age was 32.8 years, and fathers' mean age was 35.2 years. A total of 85.7% of mothers and fathers were Caucasian, and the remainder were of ethnic minority or undisclosed ethnic background. Comparisons of families of firstborn infants and families of second-born infants on these major demographic variables revealed only two differences between groups. Not surprisingly, fathers of second-born children were an average of 3 years older than fathers of firstborns, and parents of second-born children had been married an average of 1.5 years longer than parents of firstborns.

Two-child families completed all of the same evaluations as did one-child families, and there were no major deviations from the standard study protocol. The only major difference in the evaluations completed was that two-child families negotiated two, not one, family interaction sessions. In one session, all four family members were present; in the other, just the mother, father, and second-born were present while the older sibling completed some developmental assessments with other researchers. Sessions were counterbalanced to protect against carry-over effects. This design allowed us to compare coparenting during mother–father–baby triadic interactions in families with firstborns to coparenting during mother–father–baby triadic interactions in families with second-borns and to compare coparenting of firstborn and second-born children in the same family. We provide the details of these assessments and what we learned from them later in this chapter. First, however, we present findings detailing differences in how parents with one and two young children portrayed family life during our discussions with them about coparenting.

How Parents Talk About Life With One and Two Children

In chapter 5, we discussed the findings of Waterston, Babigian, and McHale (2002) concerning parents' discussions of the best and worst moments in their families. As part of their work, these researchers also examined differences in the stories told by parents with a firstborn 12-month-old, and parents with a second-born 12-month-old who had a preschool-aged brother or sister. We had anticipated finding some systematic differences in how parents represented family life, based in part on prior work by Kreppner and colleagues on how life changes for families when a second-born joins the picture. In some respects, our hunches were born out, although we were struck by the number of dimensions in which parents of one- and two-child families looked more similar than different.

Perhaps the most noteworthy difference between the two groups was in the degree of positive affective charge coloring parents' narratives. Both mothers and fathers of firstborn 1-year-olds were judged to exude higher levels of positive affect in their stories than did their counterparts with two children (these findings were statistically significant for fathers and approached significance, $p < .10$, for mothers). Mothers of firstborns also had an easier time than did mothers of second-borns in describing a typical time together for the family. Parents of second-borns had an easier time than parents of firstborns recalling the family's worst time together as a family. Mothers of second-borns were more likely than mothers of firstborns to say that best times of the kind they portrayed in their examples for us were actually relatively rare.

Although struck by these differences, we do not think that this pattern means that parents with two children cocreate less positive affective climates for their children; as we see below, our observational data did not support this interpretation. Rather, we believe that only children, as babies, simply command a greater amount of their parents' psychic energies. Parents follow more intensively their firstborn child's feats, are more prone to chronicle and celebrate their daily developmental advances more regularly and festively, and are also more accustomed to sharing news of special moments both with one another and with others outside of the immediate family triangle. When a second baby comes, parents are no less delighted by major developmental advances and priceless family moments, but having two children to coparent often means that babies' activities and advances are tracked a little less closely and intensively than is typical when there is just one child in the picture. In support of this perhaps inevitable shift in parents' realities, we do find interesting evidence in our observational data, described shortly.

Some readers with multiple children will interpret this set of findings simply as meaning that parents with two young children are in a more chronic state of exhaustion and that these differences in the narrative portrayals of family life by parents with one and two children simply mirror their energy levels. Before leaping to this conclusion, a few other findings from our analyses of families' best- and worst-moment stories will help to provide greater nuance to the picture. Although our data suggested that parents of firstborns do seem to paint a readier and more seamless picture of family cohesion, there was an interesting flipside to these findings. Both mothers and fathers in two-child families were less, rather than more, likely than parents with one child to indict a particular family member as the culprit when telling the story of their family's worst moment. Parents with one child frequently told stories in which a particular person (and in many cases, the baby) launched the family into its most negative moments, whereas parents in two-child families were much more likely to exteriorize blame outside the family. That is, parents in two-child families were more likely to indict no one in particular and to describe the worst times as a family affair with blame either not levied at all or distributed evenly within the system.

We viewed this finding as quite interesting. In many writings of family therapists who work with and write about families (usually with somewhat older children) in far greater distress than families in our study, there are allusions to families of multiple children selecting out a particular child as the family scapegoat, to whom many of the family difficulties are ascribed. We are reluctant to bring the term *scapegoat* into our analyses of families' worst-moment stories, although there did seem to be clear evidence that families with two young children are less, rather than more, inclined than families with one child to single out the baby (or preschooler) as having been the one to trigger family discord. Only children, in this regard, carried a somewhat heavier burden by virtue of their assigned role as instigator in many parents' stories. We find this phenomenon especially interesting in light of recent LTP case studies analyzed by Fivaz-Depeursinge and her colleagues (e.g., Fivaz-Depeursinge & Favez, 2006), which suggested that firstborn babies as young as 3 months are sometimes recruited to play detouring roles to waylay coparental conflict. We return to this point later; for now, we point out only that parents' family representations do seem to convey that firstborns occupy different emotional "life spaces" than do second-borns.

Narratives of parents with one and two children differed in a few other important respects. First, the narratives of fathers with one child were less likely to shift focus and splinter into stories of father–child or father–mother dyads than were the narratives of fathers with two children. Recall that we asked parents to describe the family's best time together as a family. Fathers with one child were able to come up with and maintain stories that featured all three family members (mother, father, and baby). By contrast, fathers with two children were more likely to begin with a family focus but switch into a story that focused only on a family subgroup, most often the father and one of the two children. We found this to be a very interesting finding as well, perhaps also speaking to the typical experience of children in two-child families. Although firstborn babies may derive the full acculturation experience of the family triad a great deal of the time, dyadic experiences within the broader family tetrad may be a much more common experience for children in two-child families.

Many parents with two children told us that the four-person family configuration seemed to prompt an adaptation of parallel twosomes, wherein one parent paired more often with the older child and the other parent more often with the baby. In fathers' stories at least, men with two children had a greater difficulty maintaining focus on the family foursome, so that the story of the family's best time frequently became a story with a dyadic focus. This raises some interesting issues. We could argue that for firstborn babies in nuclear families, even after a sibling arrives, there will always be a family triad, for this was the child's formative experience from the very beginning of life. For babies in nuclear families who have an older sibling, however, nondyadic family experiences with the coparents are almost always tetradic in nature. Indeed, parents confirm that the frequency of triadic experiences between second-born babies and the two coparents (without the sibling present) are very rare, but if fathers' stories provide any indication, experiences of particularly momentous enjoyment may come as often in dyadic settings as they do in family settings. This may tell us as much or more about fathers' life spaces than about babies, but we think it important to note that fathers with two children tended to be less inclusive of all family members in their stories that were ostensibly about the family's best moments.

The other difference between one- and two-child families that we found quite intriguing was that the stories of mothers with two children were more likely to characterize the family's best moment as having been during a time away from home, rather than a domestic moment. This bias was not seen in the stories of mothers with one child. There are several possible explanations for this finding. Perhaps the most simple is that because the two-child families had a preschool-aged child in addition to a baby, they were more prone to go out and, hence, more likely to have had opportunities to enjoy a best moment during one of these outings away from home. A second explanation, not necessarily antithetical to the first but admittedly more of an interpretive leap, is that the exponential shift in affective expression and intensity for families with multiple children is contained more effectively through structured family action than it is during the kinds of intimate, intensive, unstructured activities that are more common at home. There is an extensive scholarly literature on ways in which environmental structures evoke and support certain forms of activity and action more readily than other forms of action (Heller, Price, Reinharz, Riger, & Wandersman, 1984). That is, certain types of environmental space and structure more readily afford particular forms of action. Could it be that families with multiple young children come to make similar use of structured family activities as one strategy for helping to organize and contain affect in the family? Our confidence in the merits of this notion would be greater if two-child fathers had shown the same bias as two-child mothers in portraying their families' best times as having occurred on an outing rather than in the domestic sphere, but they did not. We raise this idea here principally as an alternate hypothesis for the seemingly paradoxical finding that in families that had more children, women as a group spoke of enjoying fewer, rather than more, best moments with the family in the home.

Beyond these group comparisons distinguishing the prototypical representations of parents with one and two young children, our team was struck by the sheer number of parents with two children who made mention of the depletion of their energies at each day's end, and we began to wonder whether there might be different reasons why parents with one and two young children come to feel overwhelmed in their parenting roles. Recall from chapter 5 that approximately a third of the mothers and 11% of the fathers in our sample told stories at 12 months that connoted a sense of feeling overburdened and overwhelmed. Waterston et al.'s (2002) analyses of linkages between the content of parents' family stories and other markers of family adjustment at the 12-month mark uncovered a very interesting pattern of correlations between these "overwhelmed" ratings and other indicators of parental and coparental adjustment. Specifically, when they averaged across the entire sample (without looking separately at one- and two-child families), women whose narratives conveyed a greater sense of feeling overwhelmed were more likely to report higher levels of depression, whereas men whose narratives indicated that they felt overwhelmed came from families lower in coparental solidarity (captured by the overall summary score reported and used in chapters 5 and 6). In other words, when mothers' stories hinted to researchers that they felt overwhelmed, they were more often depressed; when fathers' stories hinted that they felt overwhelmed, they were more often parenting in families in which we had documented low coparental solidarity.

What is of particular interest from the vantage of this chapter is that correlational patterns looked different in one- and two-child families. In families in which the baby was the parents' first, only the father's finding reported above emerged as significant; that is, it was only in one-child families that fathers' sense of feeling overwhelmed could be linked to low solidarity in the coparental alliance. There were no connections with men's feelings of being overwhelmed and low coparental solidarity in two-child families. By contrast, the finding linking maternal feelings of being overwhelmed and maternal depression surfaced in two-child families only. Said a different way, when mothers in one-child families reported feeling overwhelmed, this experience was not linked to concurrent levels of depression. In two-child families, on the other hand, feeling overwhelmed went hand in hand with feeling more depressed. Also of interest, feeling overwhelmed also went hand in hand with feeling unsupported in the work of parenting. Mothers in two-child families whose narratives were rated as conveying a greater sense of feeling overwhelmed reported greater discrepancies between "how it currently is" and "how I'd like it to be" on Carolyn and Philip Cowan's (1992) Who Does What survey. Here then was some of our most salient evidence that when fathers don't provide sought-after levels of child care support for mothers, mothers with two young children may be especially likely to feel the strain to the point that their representations of the family bear this out. The family representations of mothers with one child are not similarly tethered to real–ideal differences on the Who Does What survey.

What conclusions can be drawn from the results reported in this section? The interviews with parents helped bring several things into focus for us. First, there appears to be a level of positive energy in the narratives of parents of firstborn 12-month-olds, suggesting that the glow of new parenthood still burns brightly. Both mothers and fathers of firstborns spoke enthusiastically about their family's typical and best moments together as a family. One-child mothers in particular had a significantly easier time characterizing a typical time for the family and a harder time recollecting their family's worst moments than did their counterparts with two children, and were less likely to say that their families' best moments were relatively rare occurrences. Parents with two children, by contrast, were more temperate in their portrayals of the family but also more likely to talk of the family as a group when characterizing the family's rougher times, rather than levying blame at any particular family member. With greater seasoning appeared to come a more matter-of-fact processing of life's rough family moments, within the context of a more moderate affective posture on the family at its best. Second, fathers in two-child families were less inclined than fathers with one child to carry with them (or at least to communicate) coherent recollections of the entire family group at its finest; stories of shining moments for two-child fathers were more likely to morph into depictions of special moments for one family dyad or subsystem within the family. Fathers with just one child, by contrast, were more likely to communicate stories that maintained the involvement of all three members of the mother–father–baby triad.

Perhaps most relevant to this book on coparenting, the family representations of fathers of firstborns (but not fathers with two children) convey a sense that the father feels overwhelmed when there is evidence of low solidarity in the coparenting alliance at the time of the child's first birthday. Mothers' family representations at the time of their first baby's 1-year birthday are not similarly linked to coparental solidarity—but by the time the second child turns 1, mothers' family representations connote a sense of feeling overwhelmed when they feel fathers have not adequately stepped up to the plate to help with the work of parenting. By this point, the sense of feeling overwhelmed has also come to be linked closely with maternal depression.

In our view, these findings provide additional information and deeper shading to past findings that maternal depression is associated with violated expectancies concerning, and discontent over, the division of child care labor from the earliest months of new parenthood forward. Depression and discontent may go hand-in-hand for mothers, but neither has yet come to dampen mothers' public discourse about their families during their first baby's first year. The wear and tear of perceived inadequacies in parenting contributions by fathers becomes evident in women's family representations only by the time the second baby has attained the 1-year milestone. Interesting to note, the pattern for fathers seems to be the opposite. Men appear most vulnerable in the face of inadequate coparenting support and solidarity toward the end of their first baby's first year; by the time a second baby reaches the 1-year milestone, men's feelings of being overwhelmed are decoupled from the degree of solidarity in the coparenting alliance. Given the relatively smaller proportion of men in the sample for whom we were able to document convincing evidence of feeling overwhelmed, this latter conclusion is much more tentative. It does provide further hints, however, that the internal experiences of mothers and fathers coparenting young children may follow somewhat different trajectories.

The narrative-based data provided only one glimpse into the coparenting stories of families with one and two young children. In the next section, we describe lessons learned from our observational assessments of coparenting in family triads and tetrads.

Comparisons of Coparenting in One- and Two-Child Families

Reflecting on their first year as coparents for 1-year old Tiresa, Ellie told us:

> "We do a good job, but sometimes we're overly concerned—it's like we have a total focus on her. It'd be OK when we're all together to not be staring at her and watching what she's doing for 5 minutes."

This comment was not uncommon among parents with firstborns in our study. Although a number of the parents in our study were struggling to build a cohesive coparenting and family alliance, other parents of firstborns voiced a rather different concern. Ellie's comment mirrors those of numerous other parents who told us that they had been so concerned with whether they were doing a good enough job as parents that they were concerned that they might be overdoing it, or at least not giving their baby ample enough room to blossom independently of them. Try as we did, we simply couldn't locate any parallel comments of this nature that were made by parents of second-born babies! Indeed, when the second baby arrived on the scene, parents had to reorganize their daily lives and as a result had much less discretionary time to just relax and be alone together with the second-born baby. As we show later, this major difference between coparenting in one- and two-child families was also borne out in our observational data.

One benefit of our study's design in systematically including a comparison group of families who had two young children was that we were able to ask questions about whether the coparenting patterns parents showed when they were interacting together with their second-born children resembled, or differed in any important respects from, the coparenting patterns we observed among parents interacting together with firstborn children. One major thrust of our analyses was on whether there are systematic differences in parents' coparenting behavior with their children as a function of birth order.

As we thought about it, we realized that there are actually two very different ways of thinking about whether parents are more coordinated when coparenting their second-born than they are when coparenting their firstborn. If we take the position that family transitions are a stressor (contrary to the "honeymoon" myth, the parenthood transition had actually been portrayed as a crisis in the old sociological literature [e.g., LeMasters, 1957], probably also overstating matters), it could be argued that the birth of the first child is more profoundly disorganizing on couple relationships than is the birth of a second child. If so, we might expect to see more foundering in the coparenting dynamic of first-time parents than of seasoned parents. Following this line of reasoning, parents know what to expect by the time they welcome the second baby's arrival; hence, they may be less likely to attribute baby-related disruptions to problems with their partner or in the marriage. To the extent that this was so, it could be argued that coparenting of firstborn babies would normatively be expected to show less organization and coordination, compared with the more established coparenting patterns of experienced parents.

On the other hand, the key point that we endeavored to illustrate at the beginning of this chapter with our lengthy description of the Simon family's developmental trajectory through time is that the arrival of a second child also brings its own set of challenges and adjustments. Although the anxieties of new parenthood are typically less intense by the time of the second baby's arrival, the second child's socialization environment is fundamentally different than that of the first. It includes, of course, an older sibling, and the demands of caring for two young children induce different kinds of strain and anxieties for coparents. From a theoretical perspective, it is also interesting to ponder the metaphor of a "primary triangle" for later-born children. This concept has received much less attention from theorists and researchers, perhaps largely because mother–father–baby triads necessarily develop as a subsystem embedded within the broader family unit. Inevitably, as nearly every parent in our study told us, parent–parent–secondborn threesomes get much less opportunity to develop as well-organized, finely tuned units than parent–parent–firstborn units! For this reason, it might be anticipated that parents of later-born infants might actually be less well coordinated in coparenting the baby than parents of firstborn infants.

There is a smattering of prior research evidence consistent with this second possibility. For example, in Jay Belsky's Pennsylvania Infant and Family Development Project, individual parenting behavior was found to be susceptible to birth order effects. Belsky and his colleagues (Belsky, Gilstrap, & Rovine, 1984) noted that during dyadic (parent–baby) interactions, parents of firstborn infants typically displayed greater engagement, responsiveness, stimulation, and positive affect with their baby than did parents of later-born infants. In addition, when engaged together with their infant, couples with firstborns communicated more about their child and jointly showed more attention and more pleasure toward their baby than did parents of later-borns (Belsky, Spanier, & Rovine, 1983). We might legitimately wonder, then, whether firstborn babies experience coparenting that is more positive but also more intense and involved than that afforded later-born babies.

In addition to these cross-family differences in how parents might respond as a team to their first- and second-born infants, research studies have taught us surprisingly little thus far about whether coparenting behavior is different for siblings in the same family context. Kurt Kreppner's (1988; Kreppner, Paulsen, & Schuetze, 1982) groundbreaking research is one of the few exceptions, and his studies confirmed what most families know: As second-born children begin growing out of "babyhood" and become more active participants in families' dynamics at around 1 year of age, a major task for parents becomes management of sibling rivalry. But just how do coparents go about managing the task of parenting two children at once and of containing the rivalry typical among young sibling pairs? Some evidence from prior studies suggests that parents of young sibling pairs lean on their older child more heavily, providing greater structure and discipline with the firstborn than the younger child (e.g. Baydar, Greek, & Brooks-Gunn, 1997; Baydar, Hyle, & Brooks-Gunn, 1997; Volling & Elins, 1998). Our observational data provided the perfect opportunity to determine whether coparents did jointly structure and control the interactions of their older (preschool-age) siblings more intensively than they did the interactions of younger (infant) siblings during family interactions or whether any other aspects of coparenting differed depending on sibling status.

A refresher on our methodology may be helpful here. Recall that all families took part in triadic play sessions and that families with two children also took part in a tetradic play session (with the older sibling present). During the first 10 minutes of both the triadic and tetradic family play sessions, parents were instructed to help the infant learn to play with three developmentally challenging toys, including rubber stacking blocks, large beads that fit together to form a chain, and a shape puzzle from the Bayley Scales of Infant Development (Lipsitt, 1992). During the tetradic sessions, no instructions were given as to whether or how to involve the preschooler. Then during the final 5 minutes of all play sessions, families were told they were free to engage in unstructured play with a variety of developmentally appropriate toys. For families with two children, the same set of toys was available for both the triadic and tetradic interactions.

The videotaped family play episodes were then coded for coparenting of each child using the Coparenting and Family Rating System (CFRS; McHale, Kuersten-Hogan, & Lauretti, 2000). We were interested in indications of support and cohesion, indications of antagonism, and indications of joint involvement and oversight. With respect to support and cohesion, variables of particular interest were (a) cooperation, or the degree to which parents actively supported one another and collaborated in their parenting efforts; (b) warmth, or positive affect and humor between parents during family interactions; and (c) endorsement of the partner, or the degree to which each parent conveys approval of and appreciation for the other's parenting efforts and actions. Because our focus was the family-level dynamic, a composite variable indexing total coparental endorsement was constructed by summing maternal and paternal endorsement ratings.

Two CFRS indicators estimated the presence of coparenting antagonism and dissonance. Competition assessed the degree to which parents rivaled one another for the child's attention and affection. Verbal sparring indexed the degree to which parents showed signs of disapproval, disagreement, or conflict with one another. Finally, to measure coparental involvement and oversight, we called upon some measures constructed from CFRS ratings of each coparenting partner's individual engagement with each child. Unlike the previous rating scales, each of which clearly sampled a facet of the interactive process between adults, the CFRS measures we used to construct these indicators (warmth and investment) are themselves parent–child measures. By combining them, however, we had a way to index the tandem parenting children received when the coparenting partners engaged together with them in family context. Parent–child warmth, rated separately for mothers and fathers, assessed the degree of positive affect and affection between each parent and the target child. A composite variable indexing total parent–child warmth was constructed by summing ratings of mother–child and father–child warmth. Parent–child investment assessed the extent of each parent's engagement with, and availability and attentiveness to, the child. A composite variable indexing total parent–child investment was constructed by summing ratings of mother–child and father–child investment.

Finally, a third CFRS measure was included to index coparental structuring. Child- versus parent-centeredness ratings assessed the degree to which the coparents' interactions with the child were driven more by the child than by the parents. This feature of the coparenting process is reflected in a summary score that is most aptly considered a family-level variable. Low scores on this index indicate that the coparents, rather than the child, are the ones directing and structuring the session, often choosing not only which toys the child is allowed to play with but also how the child is to play with them. Conversely, high scores on this variable indicate that activities during family interactions are largely focused around the child's expressed interests and initiations, with minimal parental structure or control imposed on the child's exploration. Midrange scores signify a balance between parental control and the child's autonomy.

Triadic interactions were coded once for coparenting of the infant, and tetradic interactions were coded twice—once for coparenting organized around the infant and once for coparenting organized around the preschooler. To ensure consistency across raters, Melanie McConnell coded together with both infant and sibling coding teams. To guard against carry-over effects based on familiarity, we devised the coding schedule so as to maximize the amount of elapsed time in weeks and months between the necessary two viewings of two-child families in the two different contexts. CFRS interrater reliabilities, estimated by intraclass correlations (ICCs; as outlined by Shrout & Fleiss, 1979) were calculated separately for coparenting of infants in the triad, coparenting of infants in the tetrad, and coparenting of preschoolers in the tetrad. For all variables, reliabilities were well within acceptable scientific bounds. Only one measure, the variable indexing paternal endorsement, showed a substantial restriction of range, rendering ICC an inappropriate estimate of reliability. As an alternative, percent agreement was calculated for this variable. Analyses indicated that coders achieved exact agreement in 79% and 70% of cases for coparenting of the infant and preschooler, respectively.

So what did our data tell us? For ease of interpretation, we report results in two sections, summarizing how coparenting processes varied as a function of infant birth order (i.e., first- vs. second-born) and sibling status (i.e., older vs. younger).

Birth Order Effects on Coparenting

To determine whether the birth order of infants affected quality of coparenting during triadic (mother–father–infant) interactions, observed coparenting of firstborn and second-born infants was compared. A between-subjects multivariate analysis of variance (MANOVA) was conducted, examining the eight coparenting indicators (competition, cooperation, verbal sparring, coparental warmth, child-centeredness, total parent–child warmth, total parent–child investment, and overall interparental endorsement) as a function of birth order. The analysis came out significant, indicating that parents' coparenting behavior during triadic interactions with their firstborn infants was significantly different than parents' coparenting behavior during triadic interactions with their second-born infants. We then completed follow-up univariate analyses of variance (ANOVAs) to establish exactly how they were different. These analyses showed that during triadic family interactions the coparenting pair was more intensively invested in engaging with and attending to their baby when the child was a firstborn than when he or she was a second-born.

Therefore, second-born babies draw less of a concerted, coordinated parenting effort from mothers and fathers when the family is together than do firstborn babies. This is a really interesting finding to us, because both the first- and second-born infants were studied in the family triad (without siblings present). Because there were no differences in the setting in which families were assessed, we feel rather confident in our conclusion that the difference we saw for first- and second-born infants reflected a difference in the parenting stance of the adults. The coparents did indeed show less intensive joint oversight with their second-born infants than they did with their firstborn infants! However, they were no more or less supportive and no more or less antagonistic; the finding was limited to differences in joint structuring, involvement, and oversight.

But does this "mellowing" that comes from seasoning as a parent spill over to how parents jointly oversee their firstborn as well? To answer this question, we compared parents' coparenting behavior with their second-born infants to their coparenting behavior with their older, preschool-age children. On the basis of past research, we had reason to believe that joint coparental monitoring of the older siblings would be more prominent—that is, more parent-centered (and less child-centered) and marked by greater overall levels of coparental investment with the children than that of younger siblings. Potential differences in other aspects of coparenting of siblings in the same family were also examined.

Sibling Effects on Coparenting

For this second set of analyses, we focused only on the tetradic play interaction and on how the adults dealt with each of the two siblings during that play interaction. McConnell and the coders working with her had rated parents' parenting and coparenting behavior with respect to each child separately; that is, how well they cooperated when engaging together with the baby and how well they cooperated together when engaging with the preschooler; how competitive they were when engaging together with the baby and how competitive when engaging with the preschooler; and so forth. These data were then used to compare coparenting of the older and younger child. A repeated-measures MANOVA was used to determine whether any overall effect could be detected. For this set of analyses, the variables indexing coparental warmth and verbal sparring were excluded. This is because these variables were conceptualized as family-level variables in the CFRS. It is not usually possible, for example, to specify that a tiff has blossomed in front of one child but not the other.

The set of six remaining coparenting scores were examined, with sibling status (i.e., older vs. younger) included as a repeated-measures factor. The resulting MANOVA indicated that coparenting of older and younger siblings did indeed differ. Follow-up univariate tests indicated that three of six comparisons were significant. Specifically, the parenting partners cooperated more effectively, showed more intensive joint investment in the interaction, and engaged in a way that was more parent-centered (and less child-centered), when they coparented the older siblings compared with when they attended to the younger siblings—in the same interaction context.

Immediately we thought of the Simons: Recall that Todd and Sheila had adopted a strategy identified in some of Kreppner's studies (e.g., Kreppner et al., 1982), wherein the father assumed more responsibility for parenting the older sibling while the mother took on primary responsibility for parenting the infant. However, Todd spent relatively little time engaging with baby Chelsea during the family interaction session, whereas Sheila, for her part, did not divest entirely from engaging with Kyle, participating in the family play but dividing her attention between both younger child and older child. As a result, the joint parental attention devoted to Kyle was indeed more than that devoted to Chelsea, although the reason for this difference could be attributed to Todd's differential involvement more than Sheila's.

We thought it important to explore whether this specific dynamic was widespread among two-child families in this study. In the Simon family's case, there was less of an imminent need for Todd to tend to Chelsea because she was still just a few months old and often nestled contentedly in an infant carrier at the time we completed our 30-month assessment with Kyle, but what about in our larger sample of comparison group families, in which both the 12-month-old baby and his or her preschool sibling were each mobile, engaging, and compelling interactive partners in their own right? Our systematic look at these families did not suggest that the pattern of findings we described above could simply be attributed to differential father investment. We approached this issue by conducting two post hoc paired t tests to compare (a) mothers' and fathers' individual investment with the older sibling and (b) mothers' and fathers' individual investment with the younger sibling. Results of these analyses indicated that parents did not differ in their levels of investment with older siblings—or with younger siblings, for that matter. In other words, coparents' more intensive investment with their older children was not simply a function of higher paternal or maternal investment alone. It was truly a coconstructed dynamic.

In summary, our findings reveal that observed coparenting processes may differ on the basis of infants' ordinal position in the family. Analyses comparing coparenting of firstborn 12-month-olds (in triadic context) with coparenting of second-born 12-month-olds (in triadic context) showed that higher levels of joint investment are observed in the triadic interactions of families where the infants were firstborn. This pattern was not explained by differential maternal or paternal investment alone but indicates differential coparental investment with infants as a function of their birth order. These analyses are consistent with findings reported by Jay Belsky over 20 years ago (e.g., Belsky et al., 1984), indicating that parents together show more attention and more stimulating behavior toward first-born infants than they do toward later-born infants. It may be that insights gained from coparenting a first child allow parents of second-borns to be less anxious or concerned and more laid back in coparenting their second infants, compared with parents of first-borns who jointly tend to be more intensely involved and invested.

At the same time, we want to underscore that our analyses did not suggest that the coparenting of first- and second-born infants in triadic context differed along dimensions of either harmony (i.e., interparental warmth, cooperation, interparental endorsement) or dissonance (i.e., competition, verbal sparring). This is an important finding, indicating that first-time parents in our study did not systematically show more miscoordination or conflict during coparenting interactions with their baby than did more experienced parents of second-borns. The difference we found was in the quantity and intensity of joint investment, not the quality of coparenting coordination.

Researchers and Theorists Take Note: Coparenting Is Child-Specific

We close this chapter by underscoring an important insight gleaned from our systematic study of two-child families that until now has largely been absent from studies of coparenting in the published literature: Parents do not coparent each of their children the same way. First, our study indicated that couples are more cooperative when coparenting older siblings than younger siblings; that is, parents more actively supported and reinforced one another and built upon one another's ideas and efforts more often and more effectively when interacting with their preschooler than with their infant. Moreover, coparenting interactions organized around older siblings were more parent-centered than were interactions organized around younger siblings. In other words, with older children, coparenting practices tended to be more directive, more controlling, and more structuring. Perhaps not surprisingly, then, parents together also showed higher levels of investment with older siblings than they did with younger siblings.

Similar findings have sometimes been found in studies of young sibling dyads that have examined individual parenting practices. Such studies suggest that parents emphasize discipline, structure, and control more with older than with younger siblings (Baydar, Greek, & Brooks-Gunn, 1997; Volling & Elins, 1998). Volling and Elins (1998) suggest that parents may respond to developmental differences in children by increasing parental control with older siblings whose greater physical and cognitive capabilities necessitate more parental involvement, attention, limit-setting, and discipline than infants. Our study indicates that parents may also be more apt to actively work together to provide such structure for older siblings. Most important however, these findings suggest that parents show substantial flexibility in tailoring coparenting activities to the developmental needs and demands of the particular child with whom they are interacting.

Still not entirely clear from our study is whether age effects, birth order effects, or a combination of both are behind our findings. Readers will note that we found both that parents showed greater joint levels of investment with firstborn preschoolers (compared with second-born infants) and with firstborn infants (relative to second-born infants). It may be that parents show more intensive joint involvement with firstborns from infancy onward, whereas second-borns do not get integrated into a primary triangle in the same way.

It is important to say that the sample in our study was not large enough to allow us to meaningfully study the gender and age constellation of sibling pairs. We think this is a limitation of our work, because previous studies of differential parenting of siblings suggests that child gender may matter for some families in how parents respond to siblings (e.g., Baydar, Hyle, & Brooks-Gunn, 1997; McHale, Updegraff, Jackson-Newsom, Tucker, & Crouter, 2000). Another large-scale study the scope of ours, focusing specifically on girl–girl, boy–boy, boy–girl, and girl–boy constellations would be needed to convincingly establish whether there are any meaningful differences in how coparenting unfolds in these different kinds of families.

Finally, this is an apropos point to remind readers that our sample was rather homogeneous with respect to race, class, and culture. In some cultural groups, roles for first- and later-born siblings are more clearly circumscribed by cultural expectancies, which undoubtedly also play a major role in organizing parenting and coparenting activities. There are also cultural and subcultural differences concerning the extent to which older siblings, even as young as preschool age, are expected to assume a caregiving role of their own. We hence caution that the findings reported both in this chapter and in this book may have limited generalizability in cultural and socioeconomic groups where norms and interactions diverge markedly from the group we studied. Equally, however, we also know that within-group differences on the kinds of coparenting dimensions we have been studying can often be as substantial or more substantial than between-group differences (Kurrien & Vo, 2004; see also Cowan, Cowan, Cohen, Pruett, & Pruett, in press), and so we advocate that studies of coparenting in diverse groups be guided by emic rather than etic perspectives (McHale, Kuersten-Hogan, & Rao, 2004).

This concludes the data-driven portion of the book. In the concluding chapters, we review what we think we have learned and discuss what we see as the most important implications of this work for families and clinicians.

References

Abidin, R. R., & Brunner, J. F. (1995). Development of a parenting alliance inventory. *Journal of Clinical Child Psychology, 24*, 31–40.

Achenbach, T. M., & Rescorla, L. A. (2000). *Manual for ASEBA Preschool Forms & Profiles*. Burlington: University of Vermont, Research Center for Children, Youth, & Families.

Baydar, N., Greek, A., & Brooks-Gunn, J. (1997). A longitudinal study of the effects of the birth of a sibling during the first 6 years of life. *Journal of Marriage & the Family, 59*, 939–956.

Baydar, N., Hyle, P., & Brooks-Gunn, J. (1997). A longitudinal study of the effects of the birth of a sibling during preschool and early grade school years. *Journal of Marriage and the Family, 59*, 957–965.

Belsky, J., Gilstrap, B., & Rovine, M. (1984). The Pennsylvania infant and family development project: I. Stability and change in mother–infant and father–infant interaction in a family setting at one, three, and nine months. *Child Development, 55*, 692–705.

Belsky, J., Spanier, G. B., & Rovine, M. (1983). Stability and change in marriage across the transition to parenthood. *Journal of Marriage and the Family, 45*, 567–577.

Cowan, C. P., & Cowan, P. A. (1992). *When partners become parents: The big life change for couples*. New York: Basic Books.

Cowan, C., Cowan, P., Cohen, N., Pruett, M., & Pruett, K. (in press). Supporting fathers' involvement with kids. In J. Berrick & N. Gilbert (Eds.), *Raising children: Emerging needs, modern risks, and social responses*. New York: Oxford University press.

Fivaz-Depeursinge, E., & Corboz-Warnery, A. (1999). *The primary triangle: A developmental systems view of mothers, fathers, and infants*. New York: Basic Books.

Fivaz-Depeursinge, E., & Favez, N. (2006). Exploring triangulation in infancy: Two contrasted cases. *Family Process, 45*, 3–18.

Heller, K., Price, R., Reinharz, S., Riger, S., & Wandersman, A. (1984). *Psychology and community change: Challenges of the future* (2nd ed.). Homewood, IL: Dorsey.

Kreppner, K. (1988). Changes in parent–child relationships with the birth of the second child. *Marriage & Family Review, 12*, 157–181.

Kreppner, K., Paulsen, S., & Schuetze, Y. (1982). Infant and family development: From triads to tetrads. *Human Development, 25*, 373–391.

Kurrien, R., & Vo, E. A. (2004). Who's in charge?: Coparenting in south and southeast asian families. *Journal of Adult Development, 11*, 207–219.

LeMasters, E. E. (1957). *Modern courtship and marriage*. Oxford, England: Macmillan.

Lipsitt, L. P. (1992). Discussion: The Bayley scales of infant development: Issues of prediction and outcome revisited. *Advances in Infancy Research, 7*, 239–245.

Locke, H. J., & Wallace, K. M. (1959). Short marital-adjustment and prediction tests: Their reliability and validity. *Marriage and Family Living, 21*, 251–255.

McHale, J. (1997). Overt and covert coparenting processes in the family. *Family Process, 36*, 183–201.

McHale, J., Kuersten-Hogan, R., & Lauretti, A. (2000). Evaluating coparenting and family-level dynamics during infancy and early childhood: The Coparenting and Family Rating System. In P. Kerig & K. Lindahl (Eds.), *Family observational coding systems: Resources for systemic research* (pp. 151–170). Hillsdale, NJ: Erlbaum.

McHale, J. P., Kuersten-Hogan, R., & Rao, N. (2004). Growing points for coparenting theory and research. *Journal of Adult Development, 11*, 221–234.

McHale, S. M., Updegraff, K. A., Jackson-Newsom, J., Tucker, C. J., & Crouter, A. C. (2000). When does parents' differential treatment have negative implications for siblings? *Social Development, 9*, 149–172.

Radloff, L. S. (1977). The CES-D scale: A self-report depression scale for research in the general population. *Applied Psychological Measurement, 1*, 385–401.

Shrout, P. E., & Fleiss, J. L. (1979). Intraclass correlations: Uses in assessing rater reliability. *Psychological Bulletin, 86*, 420–428.

Volling, B. L., & Elins, J. L. (1998). Family relationships and children's emotional adjustment as correlates of maternal and parternal differential treatment: A replication with toddler and preschool siblings. *Child Development, 69*, 1640–1656.

Waterston, L., Babigian, R., & McHale, J. (2002, July). *Parents' stories about their families reflect individual and family functioning at infant age 12 months*. Paper presented at the Meetings of the Eighth World Congress of the World Association for Infant Mental Health, Amsterdam, the Netherlands.

CHAPTER 8

What We Learned and What Families Ought to Know

As we began our study, many of the beginning outlines of what we later came to learn in this project had already been sketched by family scholars and researchers. We reviewed much of this work in chapters 1 and 2 in mounting a case for why the particular study we conducted was needed. The Families Through Time project confirmed much of the conventional clinical wisdom about families and family development and added a number of new insights about how men and women get into and get out of (or in more unusual cases, find a way to avoid altogether) coparenting difficulties in their new families. In this chapter, we summarize the main lessons learned from this study and highlight the findings we believe to be of greatest interest and importance to parents planning or starting out families together.

In many ways, the findings deserving of the greatest emphasis are those that supported the major hypotheses outlined in chapter 2: Early difficulties in coparenting adjustment can be anticipated with some degree of confidence even before the baby arrives; early coparenting difficulties do tend to foreshadow later coparenting difficulties; and problems in coparenting during the toddler years can be linked to problems in adjustment, even as early as 30 months of age. These are important findings indeed and underscore the need for expectant couples to be better prepared to meet the coparenting challenges likely to confront them as they become new parents. We deal with the issue of primary prevention and skill-building more explicitly in chapter 9. Here, we systematically review some of the major take-home points for parents and professionals.

1. Prenatal Family Expectations and Couple Relationship Patterns Are Prognostic

All things being equal, if you want to know how well couples will adapt to their new family roles as coparents, talk to them individually during the pregnancy. Although this suggestion probably sounds like a no-brainer, it is more complicated than it may seem. What kinds of things matter? Is the parent's family of origin experience formative in any meaningful way, or is the manner in which the parent is thinking and talking about the future family as, or more, significant? How important is the couple's marital relationship in predicting their postbaby adjustment as coparents? Will the kind of baby who joins the family alter, in any meaningful ways, the relationship between prenatal adjustment and postpartum coparental functioning?

These are all critical questions for parents and clinicians alike, so let's start with the first one first: In talking with expectant couples about their future families, what would we most want to know? Before our study began, we thought it very important to ask systematically about how coparenting dynamics had operated in each partner's family of origin. We knew, from Mary Main's exquisite theorizing and attention to detail in developing the Adult Attachment Interview (Main & Goldwyn, in press), that men's and women's own experiences of having been parented in the families they grew up in affected the quality of relationship they developed with their own babies, by virtue of the parents' states of mind with respect to attachment. What was daunting, however, was that Main's work indicated that it was not so much what parents said about the quality of parenting in their origin family but how they spoke about it. Parents who discounted the importance of attachment-related experiences, idealized their parents, or showed an ongoing preoccupation with the parenting they had received with no evidence of having let go were the ones more likely to have insecurely attached children, even when their narratives contained fewer memories of out-and-out conflict and distress than in other families. In fact, the inability to remember was one of the best predictors of negative outcomes in the new generation.

Unfortunately, because the Adult Attachment Interview focuses primarily on the respondent's dyadic (mother–child and father–child) relationships, but not in detail on the nature of the origin family's coparenting or group-level dynamics, we could not rely on this interview to help learn about coparenting in the families in which our study participants grew up. We did, however, administer the AAI to our families anyway, in part because we suspected that a lack of coherence in the representation of relationships would adversely affect parents' capacity to work collaboratively with their partner to co-construct a supportive coparenting alliance. Indeed this is what we found: Parents whose states of mind with respect to attachment were less coherent (and thereby less likely to be secure or autonomous) were less likely to attain high levels of coparental solidarity during the early postpartum months (Talbot et al., 2006).

But what is the significance of recalled coparental conflict? How prominent are such recollections, and do they also affect coparental functioning in any directly meaningful way? Both systematic study and lay wisdom ("Oh no, I sound exactly like my parents!!") suggest that we often repeat what we know best. Reasoning that parents in our study would carry memories of their parents' coparenting behavior every bit as salient as their recollections of other family dynamics, we sought to establish what it was that parents "knew" about coparenting by asking them how their parents had worked together as a team during their childhoods (chapters 2 and 3). Recall that the Coparenting Interview then moved from questions about coparenting dynamics in the families in which the men and women had grown up to questions about their expectations of coparenting and family dynamics in their future families. Parents' narratives were then judged on a 7-point negativity scale ranging from 1 (*no recollections whatsoever of coparenting difficulties in the family of origin*) to 7 (*multiple characterizations of coparents as having been actively and intentionally nonsupportive, competitive, or undermining of one another, or, alternatively, overly disinterested, disengaged, or quietly hostile*). These ratings were assigned to both the segment of the interview in which parents spoke about their origin families and then again to segments of the narrative in which interviewees mused about what the future would bring. McHale and colleagues' (2004) analysis of coparenting interviews from this study revealed that recollections of interparental animosity were actually quite commonplace. Forty-six percent of mothers examined and 42% of fathers received the most extreme negativity scores of 5, 6, or 7, indicating that a very sizeable percentage of adults recall that their parents experienced significant problems in their coparenting partnership during their formative years.

Are parents who report problems in their parents' coparenting alliance back when they were children at greater risk for encountering similar problems in their new family? Surprisingly, our data indicated that as a group, they are not. However, parents did encounter coparenting problems in their new family when the segments of the coparenting interview pertinent to the future family were rated as high in negativity. In this case, negativity predicted not only early adjustment difficulties, as reported by McHale and colleagues (2004), but also difficulties much further down the road (see chapter 6; McHale & Rotman, 2007). This seems rather important to take note of; recollections of problematic coparenting as a child may be less prognostic than concerns about problems lying ahead in the future family. This is certainly not to say that coparenting problems in the family of origin are irrelevant. Quite the contrary, they serve as a very important basis for parents' views of family life and, unexamined, may in fact come to affect parents' ways of doing things in the new family. A major revelation to us, however, was the openness with which expectant parents in our study spoke about difficulties their parents had had in working together, how they themselves had been affected by their parents' problems, and how they planned to make conscious efforts not to repeat negative coparenting patterns in their new families. Perhaps for this reason, coparenting negativity in the origin family was not as closely connected with postbaby family functioning as we might have imagined. What did seem clear, however, was that parents who feared that they and their partners may not be able to work effectively together as a coparenting team were frequently right and, hence, are at risk.

The significance of current life circumstances was amplified further by the McHale et al. (2004) finding that marital quality too predicted postpartum coparental adaptation. Specifically, couples who were observed to work less well together when trying to negotiate conflict showed less cooperative, supportive parenting at 3 months postpartum. Combined, prenatal representations and marital quality explain a statistically significant 31% of the variance in coparenting cohesion at 3 months, indicating that it isn't where you come from, but where you currently are, that matters most. Parents and partners who grew up in challenging circumstances but who have found ways to talk together about their differences—be they differences about finances, relatives, friends, free-time activities, their sex life, or other contentious topics—are likely to also commiserate together about their dreams and wishes for the family. They may also be better positioned to broach fears and worries they harbor about origin-family influences or about their own or their partner's parenting. Initiating and sustaining such discussions about difference may initially heighten anxiety but may ultimately allow true differences to get talked about and accommodated, with the result being that partners will feel connected and supported rather than underappreciated, disconnected, or devalued. Concerns about parenting and coparenting, spoken or unspoken, may be an endemic part of new parenthood, but ***when grounded in a relationship in which disagreements and differences can be aired openly and dealt with sensitively, coparenting concerns may be less likely to play out***. When such a supportive context doesn't exist or materialize, early coparenting problems appear much more likely.

2. Parents and Professionals Should Address, and Not Downplay, the Harboring of Discontent Experienced During the Earliest Postpartum Months

"It's just a phase." "It will pass." "He'll grow out of it." Conventional wisdom shared every day by concerned family members or friends trying to be of help when loved ones are struggling through some rough times in their family. All things being equal, perhaps the best advice to give someone experiencing family difficulties, especially if he or she is considering doing something rash is to "stay the course." Challenges and stresses arise in virtually everyone's lives from time to time, and they can feel overwhelming when at their peak. Moreover, matters can get worse when someone tries a hasty, ill-conceived solution rather than giving things time to settle down and reflecting on what went wrong.

The problem, however, is that once a crisis has passed, things often don't get talked about. Family members breathe a sigh of relief and try to get back to business as usual without making the effort to talk through fears, anger, and hurt feelings. For others, when a crisis lifts, there really isn't a return to feelings of contentment, energy, and enjoyment. The feeling that something isn't quite right remains, but parents simply suffer in silence, feeling disconnected and unhappy, and sometimes even disrespected and unloved. Discontent can feel doubly distressing in the early months after a baby arrives. This is because parents wonder how it can be that this momentous life event, which has brought some unparalleled moments of meaning and happiness, has also introduced new feelings of resentment, jealousy, and frustration. What we learned in this study replicates and expands upon some of what we already knew: By 3 months postpartum, parents have many priceless moments of pride and joy to share but also many stories of stress, strain, and exasperation. For many families, there is a balance between these very diverse sets of experiences, with parents feeling that they are plotting a good course and finding ways to work through difficulties and differences. For other families, however, things just haven't clicked, and one or both parents have become aware of a growing gap that has felt difficult to bridge.

The million dollar question is: Is coparenting distress at 3 months just an expectable phase, something parents will "grow out of," something that will pass, given enough time? Or is it the harbinger of more troubles to come later on down the road? This is a difficult question to answer definitively, because a sizeable number of parents report elevated signs of depression such as sleeping and eating irregularities, periodic dysphoria, and/or increases in marital dissatisfaction during the early months after a baby's arrival. This said, however, data from this study do indicate that parents who aren't working well together as coparenting partners at 3 months are indeed more likely to still be experiencing coparenting problems 9 months later, as the baby turns 1 year of age. Also, families struggling as coparents at 12 months are more likely to be experiencing coparenting difficulties at 30 months. So when parents get off to a rocky start, it is important to take notice, because for many families this is not just a phase, nor something that will resolve spontaneously.

Let's think about why this might be. As reviewed above, our study indicated that for some families, problems at 3 months can be forecast from marital difficulties or a pessimistic outlook evident during the pregnancy. Our Adult Attachment Interview data also indicated that early coparenting problems are more likely when parents have not adequately come to terms with relationship struggles they experienced in their own families of origin. These findings, collectively, make good sense. Men and women who grew up in families in which their parents had difficulties expressing affection, stifled the expression of children's emotions, triangulated children in as confidantes or as mediators of adult conflicts, and created an atmosphere of insecurity because of ongoing tensions between the adults or between adults and children have much to overcome themselves as they reach adulthood. Some parents successfully reckon with and work through the emotional vestiges of negative childhood experiences. Some dismiss such experiences as having been unimportant, and some struggle to move beyond distressing childhoods, unable to fully come to terms because the emotional challenges remain for them. In the latter cases, parents faced with the normal challenges of working together with a partner to co-create a satisfying emotional environment in their new family may have a particularly difficult time, especially when their marital partnership was already on somewhat shaky ground and/or when the parent-to-be was already anticipating problems before the baby even arrived on the scene. When early coparenting challenges arise (Why isn't he helping me? Why doesn't she see how much I'm doing? Why is the baby in our bed? How do we stop this endless crying? Why can't we discuss this without ending up in a fight?), couples with fewer resources to bring to bear end up feeling less supported and connected as a coparenting team, and their internal distress begins to creep into their day-to-day interactions as well.

Our analyses detected several different patterns that begin emerging very early. In some families, the dynamic was one in which there was evidence of disconnection between parents. Although both parents were connected with the baby, mothers' connection was especially strong and fathers sometimes felt like a third wheel. In our analyses of these families, fathers were less vocal than were mothers during the birth narratives, withdrew from Who Does What discussions when disagreements arose, and were less engaged during the Lausanne Trilogue Play (LTP; Fivaz-Depeursinge & Corboz-Warnery, 1999) interactions than were other fathers. Compared with other fathers, they also indicated on the Parenting Alliance Inventory (Abidin & Brunner, 1995) that they felt less supported and that their efforts as parents were not as valued by their partners. Our impression of these family systems was that fathers did not feel that they were truly and fully coparents, and so they deferred to mothers, but were unhappy about this state of affairs. Mothers in such families often felt the void and wanted their partners to be more involved but dealt with this by increasing their energies in the baby. So a self-perpetuating cycle evolved; fathers began to feel like outsiders but did not know how to act to change things, whereas mothers worked harder and ever harder to care for the baby, wishing that fathers would be more involved but unwittingly reinforcing fathers' sense of disconnection through their own intensive engagement with the baby.

In other families, fathers seemed quite content to play a secondary role. They enjoyed the time they spent with the baby, and did not feel especially left out. Their partners sometimes were quite content with the role father was playing (recall, e.g., Todd and Sheila from chapter 7), but in other families, mothers were quite resentful. Indeed, many mothers in our study voiced frustrations that their partners enjoyed all the benefits of parenthood but paid none of the dues. Some mothers were vocal about fathers' lack of involvement in the work of parenting, whereas others kept their unhappiness to themselves. Indeed, for many mothers in our study, the 3-month assessments represented the first time they had vocalized their frustrations, often to the shock of their partners who had somehow remained unaware that their partners were as unsettled and overwhelmed as they were.

Then there were families in which both partners were quite aware of the friction between them but felt unable to do much about it. These were families in which we saw a lot of jawing back and forth between partners during the family interaction sessions—criticisms of too much involvement or of inattention to baby's signals during the LTP or still-face interactions, failure to support one another's views and even questioning of one another's recollections of what transpired the day the baby was born, insults traded during discussions of Who Does What—in short, evidence of substantial dissonance that had already begun to show up during, and sometimes impede the sensitivity of, transactions with the baby. Our impression of some of these families was that lively bickering was an enduring trademark of their relationship; when they didn't see eye to eye, they said what they felt and sometimes did so in a way that felt a bit harsh and disconfirming. In other families, however, the disagreements were more subtle and indirectly expressed (as when a parent criticized the other by giving voice to the baby "I really don't like it when you do that, Dad—it's a comfort thing for me"). In such families, we wondered whether the stresses of new parenthood introduced a new level of complexity into their relationship that they were not well prepared for and didn't know how to process effectively.

For all of these families—those in which parents struggled with feelings of disconnection, lack of support, and unhappiness; those in which one or both parents were silently smoldering with as-yet unexpressed or only infrequently expressed anger; and those in which contentiousness was already a daily feature of family life—the common denominator seemed to be frustrations felt over the inability to have created family patterns that felt satisfying to all. It is important to remember that many to most parents took issue, on occasion, with how their partner handled the baby or with decisions that seemed to be made unilaterally and without the desired degree of consultation. However, such feelings did not invariably come to affect family interactions; they did so primarily when parents' discontent became a predominant focus in the relationship. This bears repeating. Occasional annoyance with, or periodic feelings of distance from, one's partner appear to be normal during the early months of new parenthood. Daily and intense discontent that brews over child-related issues is not.

Keep in mind that our summary index of coparental solidarity (the index that showed stability through time) was based both on parents' beliefs and views about the coparenting partnership and on the observations we made of how well they were working together. Families in our study who were in the most distress were, hence, those who not only felt but also showed signs of strain during the assessments. We think this is a very important point. Although parents may not be aware of it, feelings of discontent at 3 months have already begun to color how they interact with their babies. As new work from Fivaz-Depeursinge and colleagues (Fivaz-Depeursinge & Favez, 2006; Fivaz-Depeursinge & Lavanchy, 2006) has shown, babies themselves may already be attuned to family distress, as evinced by the remarkable patterns of engagement and avoidance 3-month-olds show during triadic interactions with their mothers and fathers. The fact that we were able to reliably detect coparenting strain, on the basis of a relatively brief but comprehensive assessment of families during our home visits, suggests that there are firmly established coparenting and family dynamics even just 100 days after babies have joined their family.

The take-home message for both parents and professionals is never to simply assume that difficulties during the early postpartum months are simply just a phase. For some parents, the acute adjustments they find themselves having to make during the early days and weeks after the baby comes along—adjustments that can feel stressful, exhausting, and sometimes downright exasperating—will indeed subside with time. But when one or both parents is feeling undersupported, devalued, or at wit's end, this should not be ignored. Evidence from our study indicates that when there is individual distress, there is frequently also some sign of disturbance in family interaction patterns. Such disturbance, unchecked, continues on throughout the baby's infancy and often into the toddler years as well.

3. Although Rare, Some Couples Do Find Ways to Counteract Marital Difficulties to Forge a Positive Coparental Alliance

In one of the most authoritative treatises on marital relationships to date, John Gottman (1994) outlined several of the most important ingredients of marriages that succeed and fail. Gottman argued that couples must attend to the everyday, sometimes mindless exchanges that often go ignored, because such exchanges truly are the foundation of successful relationships. He advised that couple conflict is inevitable, and so the ways that partners negotiate conflicts when they do emerge are what will make or break relationships. Couples whose relationships deteriorate through time are those who fall into patterns that thwart successful communication and resolution. Particularly damaging in relationships, Gottman's work revealed, is the presence of criticism, contempt, defensiveness, and stonewalling.

Although Gottman did not go the route of other academic (e.g., Lakoff, 1975; Tannen, 1994) and popular writers (Gray, 1992) to spotlight the importance of differences in men's and women's communication patterns, his research did illustrate how gender differences in emotional arousal contribute to communication impasses and breakdowns. In particular, flooding (which occurs when one is overwhelmed by an onslaught of negative physiological arousal during an argument) can be linked to particular patterns of behavior both before and after the aversive physiological shift, and although both men and women become aroused during conflict discussions, men are much more likely to fall victim to flooding. Hence men, Gottman contended, must learn to manage their arousal. Developing strategies as simple as taking deep breaths during contentious arguments when conversations threaten to spiral out of control can help. Women, for their part, help matters when they manage not to frame complaints as criticisms, as criticisms often spark the overwhelming and noxious arousal men experience.

Although Gottman's work does not focus on coparenting per se, it does emphasize the importance of partners' making mental maps of one another's worlds. Unfortunately many (and in some cultural and subcultural groups, most) men, Gottman points out, were not raised to notice domestic concerns. Herein lies a challenge, as such men are learning on the fly to recognize all that their partners do as partners and as parents. Men who help make marriages work endeavor to learn what matters most to their partners, what they worry about, and what they most wish for themselves and for their lives.

Women also do not inevitably gain access into men's presumptive world of interests and concerns. Many perspectives have been offered on why this might be. One reason is that men often do not openly share their frustrations and worries, sometimes, as it turns out, because they are trying to shoulder burdens themselves and protect partners from worry (Wile, 1988). Men are also reluctant to open up thorny issues because they want to protect themselves from the unpleasant, arousing effects of conflict. But much less often discussed is that men simply feel more at peace when not contemplating concerns and focusing instead on simpler things in life. On their own time, left to their own devices, many men elect not to delve into deep introspection. When such men do reach out and initiate or take turns in conversations about matters important to their partners (and by extension, to the marriage), they are often making a gesture to forego their preferred manner of navigating the day. These preferences for simplicity are not descriptive of all men, or of men all of the time, but they are nonetheless important features in mapping men's worlds, features often critiqued, disparaged, devalued, and even written off as selfish, adolescent, or asocial. However, to understand men's phenomenological worlds and preferences is to understand the importance of quietude, living for the moment, and just "being with"—features every bit as important to men's core identity as providing for, protecting, and sexually expressing themselves.

Although these behavioral patterns and preferences are typically cast as male–female differences, data indicate that men's negativity and women's withdrawal can be every bit as detrimental in marriages as women's criticism and men's withdrawal, as Roberts (2000) documents in an article discussing "fire and ice" in relationships. The point here is not to pathologize either the raising of conflict or the avoidance of conflict but only to underscore for readers that couples need to be conscious of how their own preferred styles might not jive with those of the partner. Bottom line, it is simply not possible to know how heartfelt comments shared with one's partner about personal discomfort or about relationship worries get processed by the partner unless such disclosures are then discussed. Equally, it is really not possible to know how one's well-deserved quest for periods of solitude affects the partner without some discussion together. This is where lessons learned from Wile, Gottman, Roberts, and others comes most in handy, because couples are not inclined to check in regularly with one another about how things are going. This is unfortunate, because checking in can make a world of difference.

With respect to coparenting discussions, we hope that it has become abundantly clear in this book that couples with infants and toddlers do routinely disagree on all manner of things when it comes to how their partner is going about parenting. Many of these disputes have been featured in past chapters, but the list is truly endless. He doesn't like it that she teases their son because he thinks it will erode the boy's sense of masculinity and dampen his self-confidence. She doesn't like it that he spoils their daughter by indulging her because she is going to stop listening to Mother and attend only to Dad. He doesn't like it that she doesn't take a turn at disciplining when he's at home and comforts their crying children after he chastises them, because the children are coming to see him as the heavy. She feels frustrated that he has been devoting most of his attention to their younger son and that their older daughter, for 2 years the apple of both their eyes, is now feeling left out. There are as many concerns as there are families, and readers can undoubtedly add their own personal concerns to this list; yet surprisingly few of the parents in our study told us that they had ever spoken as frankly about their worries to their partner as they did to us. Why?

We think this is where the interplay between marital adjustment and coparenting dynamics may be uniquely important. We have emphasized that strong coparenting relationships are built on the backs of strong couple relationships and that couples that were having difficulty communicating effectively before the baby's arrival did not suddenly develop such propensities after the baby's arrival. So communication is critical—no surprise there—and data from our study verified that couples who experienced greater difficulties during prenatal marital discussions showed less cohesive coparenting at 3 months (McHale et al., 2004). Beyond this general finding, however, matters get interesting and complex. Some writers have talked about marital and coparenting relationships interchangeably, as though coparenting dynamics are nothing more than marital dynamics played out in front of and with children. Our data indicate that matters are a bit more complex than this.

It is certainly true that couples who bicker more in their marriage also bicker more when children are on the scene (McHale, 1995), and data from our study reveal that disengagement from family interactions at 3 months postpartum is more likely in families where men also withdraw from Who Does What problem-solving conversations with their partners (Elliston & McHale, 2006). However, these very same data indicate that among women who withdraw during Who Does What conversations, competitive coparenting dynamics and not disengaged ones are most commonly seen during the family's coparenting interactions (Elliston & McHale, 2006). In other words, although tendencies toward disengagement and withdrawal may be one common outcome for maritally distressed first-time fathers, maritally distressed first-time mothers seldom follow that same course (McHale & Fivaz-Depeursinge, 1999). Rather, women have a somewhat greater tendency to become mildly contentious and critical, and when their contentiousness is matched by their husbands, a noncollaborative and even antagonistic coparenting dynamic can come into being.

For these reasons, our research team believes strongly that there is value in thinking about marital and coparenting dynamics separately, even as we acknowledge their unquestionable interplay and occasional overlap. Doing so can allow parents and professionals to think creatively about how to facilitate coparenting communication even when the couple has not enjoyed a long history of effective marital communication. We develop this point further in chapter 9, but here we note a few of the lessons we learned in this study most pertinent to parents. ***Couples from distressed marriages who felt they had been more successful in preventing marital difficulties from affecting their coparenting told us that they regularly found times to talk with one another about their children, even when they were not communicating about other matters.*** In such parents' minds, perhaps because the routine conversations we had with them about coparenting relationships from the very outset had a consciousness-raising effect, how they were coparenting their children was something they both valued and wanted to get right. By no means did they always agree or succeed in altering some of the things they did that they felt were detrimental, but they were aware of and made efforts to talk through major points of difference.

We think this is one of the most valuable points that parents and professionals should take home from this work. In 1992, discussing the failures of mediation in dampening the destructive coparenting processes that predominate in families after divorce, Eleanor Maccoby and her colleagues pointed out the futility of trying to cultivate a workable coparenting alliance postdivorce in families where none had ever existed predivorce. As family therapists have known for more than 50 years now, marital distress usually comes to spill over into family-level dynamics. Empirical studies of marital–coparenting relationships have confirmed this, but some couples in our study, conscious that they were allowing their frustrations with one another to adversely affect the protection, comfort, and security that they as a team wanted to provide for their children, made efforts to right themselves in their coparenting efforts, even as they continued to struggle in their marriages. Other similarly struggling couples were not aware of how marital difficulties were affecting (and being affected by) coparenting difficulties, or they recognized this but found themselves unable to effectively stem the tide of spillover from the one family domain into the other. Although we were not in the business, as was Gottman in his research studies, of forecasting which of the couples in our study would stay together and which would eventually divorce, we would be hopeful that divorcing couples who had found ways to communicate about coparenting even as their marriage took a turn for the worse would be more effective, more cooperative, and better coordinated coparents postdivorce than those who had not.

What all this tells us is that couples can find ways to work in the best interests of children, even in the face of marital distress—but that it is exceptionally hard to do so. Who among our couples are most able to do so? Here, we uncovered some findings that reminded us of another important finding from Gottman's research studies. One of Gottman's most important conclusions, that successful marriages are those in which men allow their partners to influence them, stirred some controversy several years ago when the press misinterpreted his finding as meaning that marriages succeeded only when husbands let their partners tell them what to do (Maugh, 1998). This flawed interpretation of Gottman's important finding fed into many of the worst nightmares that men are said to have about surrendering their own autonomy and voice. Finding ways for both partners to maintain a separate and independent self and to feel effectively in control of their own lives is important and challenging, following the transition to new parenthood (Cowan & Cowan, 1992), but Gottman's finding was never intended to suggest that the solution was for men to surrender their voice. It was, however, a wake-up call to many men who for acculturation and other reasons may not be as acclimated as are women to following leads rather than charting courses.

Our data indicate that men who reported greater ego resilience—tolerance for ambiguity, capacity to take a hit, and to go with the flow—helped promote effectively functioning coparenting relationships, even in the face of marital distress. This finding surfaced at various points in our data. For example, men who reported greater ego resilience during the pregnancy were less likely to withdraw during disputatious discussions about Who Does What at 3 months postpartum than were less resilient men (Elliston & McHale, 2006), and in families with more resilient fathers, marital distress was less likely to "spill over" and affect the coparenting relationship than it was in families with less resilient fathers (Talbot & McHale, 2004). These findings were specific to fathers; more ego-resilient women show many strengths, and many of them undoubtedly muster enough fortitude to keep marital distress from influencing coparenting dynamics, but Talbot and McHale's study suggested that ego-resilient women may actually be just as, or even more, likely to simply turn away from fathers and take on more of the parenting burden themselves, rather than trying to egg fathers on. These were complex findings and more difficult to interpret clearly, but the findings in which men were concerned were much more unambiguous; ***fathers who rolled with the punches and remained engaged without withdrawing or retaliating helped prevent marital distress from compromising coparenting***.

In certain respects, this finding could create some alarm. Ego resilience is a trait, after all, isn't it? Something cultivated over a lifetime, based on temperamental dispositions, on the quality of parenting received, and on the ability to incorporate and learn from life's hard lessons. Men come into marriages more or less ego resilient, so are men who are less resilient (and their partners) simply out of luck? Perhaps, at some of the nether extremes of personality, this may be so, but we don't believe we had very many men from these nether regions in our study. Most were hard-working, effective, and caring partners, fathers, workers, and citizens. They cared enough to reveal their vulnerabilities to us, at least grudgingly, and to let us know what they saw as flaws in their own coping styles, marital dynamics, and coparenting relationships. The very act of doing so indicates that they possessed all the requisite capacities to work to bolster their flexibility and resilience. If personal growth is conceived as most likely to occur within the confines of a supportive relationship, then supportive relationships between coparents can help to enhance resilience among men, especially when men are aware that they are trying to work on enhancing their resilience and take responsibility for doing so. For their part, women (knowing of their husbands' efforts) can agree to offer feedback less critically and to affirm positives. In families in which both partners were attentive to the importance of their own roles in communication processes, couples found a way to make productive conversations about coparenting a part of their weekly routines.

And when things go astray? There remains a world of hope. Men and women care about their children. They want to be good parents. They are willing to collaborate to do what's best for their children, even when they don't see eye to eye on other things, and they do so best when they are able to honestly and openly talk with one another about things that are not sitting well with them, staying engaged while doing so. However, many things prevent parents from being able to do so. "If I criticize my partner, he or she will take it personally. Nobody wants to be accused of being a bad parent." "What if I reveal the concern I have that my partner is not pulling adequate weight, is yelling too much, is unnecessarily inculcating fear in our child, or is allying too closely with our toddler and creating a bigger chasm between us—and it prompts a fight or an icy reaction? Or worse, what if he or she doesn't even care, and keeps right on doing things the same way? Wouldn't it just be best to bite my tongue and wait to parent our child the 'right' way when I'm alone with him or her?"

Note that all of these "fear" responses have their roots in a belief that the partner will not be able to benefit from discussion and that discussion will erode (rather than strengthen) the coparenting alliance. Such fears may be irrational, on the basis of carryover concerns from how things went in the parent's own family of origin, or they may be well-founded in the history of the couple's marital dynamics. They may also reflect an investment by the parent in the family's status quo. Paradoxical though it often seems at first to parents and others unfamiliar with systems theory, there is a powerful homeostasis in families that often militates against major systemic change. If a parent who had been more distant or more critical with a child were to effectively become warmer, more connected, and more patient, the child may gravitate more frequently to that parent and spend less time with the parent with whom she previously shared a more positive connection. Parenting is an interesting balancing act; too many demands by the child can feel overwhelming and emotionally exhausting, too few can leave parents feeling oddly empty and disconnected. In families in which parents are communicating, it is possible to share such sentiments, but again only if there is no fear of disqualification or hostile reaction by the other.

What lessons can parents take from the families in our study? Coparenting is above all a partnership and an alliance between two people. An effectively functioning alliance is one in which both partners mutually agree upon a plan of action and support that plan, both when they are parenting alone and when they are parenting together. As with any effectively functioning structure, both partners need to have input into the plan, take into consideration their partner's wishes and preferences, and evaluate the effectiveness of the plan over time. This will inevitably mean bringing a critical eye to bear, evaluating progress, discussing problems, and revising previously agreed-upon plans as needed. No progress can be made if parents do not share their perspectives, because the team is then working without all the necessary information to chart an effective course. If one partner feels he or she cannot share, this needs to be discussed. Resolutions will not always come easily or quickly, but knowing what is important to one's partner is crucial. Fathers need to know when mothers are feeling overwhelmed, disqualified, and at the end of their rope. They need to take responsibility to help change things without feeling that they are the root of the family's problems. Mothers can help fathers get and stay involved in coparenting conversations by raising concerns gently and not taking personally fathers' concerns about what they would like to see mothers do differently. Above all, both partners need to provide affirmation to one another for the things they do well and that their children love. When couples follow these ground rules and recognize when they are stalling a conversation because they are feeling defensive, misunderstood, unappreciated, or simply exerting some payback for other non-child-related squabbles they have hanging over their heads, they are in a better position to look each other in the eye and say "Let's get back to coparenting."

4. Certain Themes Can Be Expected to Stir Contentiousness Among Coparenting Teams

In chapter 6, we provided a rather exhaustive list of what parents would most like to change about their partners, and we have provided many other examples throughout the book of things that most get parents' goats. In this section, we provide a brief summary so that readers might see that they are not alone! Some of what we learned will come as no surprise, but other things may be a bit surprising.

During the earliest postpartum months, parents are doing their best to form an effectively functioning coparenting and family process. As we've indicated, most parents overestimate the extent to which fathers will share the caregiving load; hence, one area of contention in many families is the sheer division of responsibilities between parents (see also Cowan & Cowan, 1992). Who Does What discussions were among the more eye-opening exercises for many families in our study. Many mothers could not believe that fathers gave themselves as much credit as they did for duties they rarely shouldered. Many fathers could not believe that mothers trivialized their contributions and did not appreciate that so much of their nonwork time was subsumed with family chores rather than with activities that fathers would much rather be doing for self-sustenance. Parents were clearly bringing a different metric to bear, and in many families, the burden seemed very weighty; yet we discovered that many dissatisfied mothers had rarely shared their frustrations with their husbands and that even fewer husbands had shared their concerns with their wives. Both partners suffered in silence, although we saw frustrations leaking out in many of the triadic play interactions, in which partners would take jabs at one another or show their discontent in other ways.

Among the more commonly mentioned dilemmas of new parents were disputes about whether to let the baby sleep with them, whether to respond to the baby when she was crying or just let her cry it out, whether to consider using pacifiers, whether to leave the baby with someone for a brief spell so the couple could have some time alone, and how to allocate shared time together. In many couples, neither fathers nor mothers felt they had any regular time for recharging, and in some of these families, this had taken a toll. In other families, one or both parents had found ways to carve out alone time but often without calibrating such excursions with the partner, creating an uncomfortable silence and unspoken tension. Although this latter issue reveals as much about marital dynamics as about coparenting, it became a coparenting issue when one parent (most often the mother) responded by becoming even more intensely reliant on the baby while the other grew to be, or at least to feel, increasingly more disengaged. In some families, mothers' greater involvement and growing expertise with babies left fathers feeling excluded, so much so that they entertained concerns that their wives didn't trust them with the baby and micromanaged every interaction they had with the child. Mothers did not couch things in these terms but did acknowledge that it made them feel uncomfortable when they saw their partners engaging the baby in a way that they felt was making the baby uncomfortable. Couples struggling with this issue seldom found a quick solution to their dilemma, frequently couched as "If you want me to spend more time taking care of her, you have to let me do things my way." In many ways, this was a coparenting mantra for fathers at both 3 and 12 months. Gottman's finding about the importance of fathers allowing themselves to be influenced by mothers comes to mind again here.

By 12 months, we were hard pressed to find any families in which the partner's discontent over "who does what" came as any surprise. In fact, by this time such discontent was a well-recognized feature of the family dynamic. In the more distressed families, disputes over fathers' participation in the work of child care had reached crisis points. According to one father:

> "We were at the mall, and I had him. When we met up, she saw that he had gone in his diaper and I hadn't changed him. Honestly, I don't know when he went, because I hadn't noticed it. But then all of a sudden she starts screaming in this crowded mall about how I never change diapers, and making me feel like the Antichrist."

This comment was indicative of how many fathers felt at 12 months, although relatively few went as far in characterizing themselves in such an extreme manner. Fathers spoke about how their partners tended to get frustrated easily, blow up over little things, make mountains out of molehills, and needed everything done just so. They couldn't always understand why mothers insisted that babies (and fathers) needed to do things a certain way and wished their partners could let their hair down a little about parenting issues. As discussed in chapter 5, some fathers also believed that they played an important regulatory role in the family, keeping calm when their partners became flustered and stepping in with the baby to relieve some of the stress.

Mothers, on the other hand, saw matters differently. They felt that they would not get as worked up as they did if their partners would step in without being asked and pull their fair share of the weight. Fathers' positive relationships with babies as playmates were viewed with mixed emotion; mothers valued the closeness that fathers and babies felt but sometimes resented that the closeness came at no cost to fathers, who did little of the drudge work. Other mothers worried that fathers were not spending enough time with babies. Some commented that fathers tended to spend most of their time in the evenings watching television or at the computer rather than spending quality time in enriching activities with the baby. They worried that babies would come to believe that they were of secondary importance to fathers and wanted to change this situation. Fathers' perspectives, not surprisingly, were once again somewhat different. A fair number of the men in our sample (like all of the working women in our study and the working mothers chronicled in Hochschild's 1989 *The Second Shift*; see also Hochschild & Machung, 2001) invoked the metaphor of having "two jobs" (at their place of employment during the day and at home with the baby at night). Some commented that they were being made to feel guilty for trying to sneak 30 minutes on the computer or watch a TV program all the way through without being called to duty. In one form or another, such issues were articulated by a great many of the families we saw at 12 months.

By 30 months, our list of things that partners would want to change about one another's parenting had grown quite exponentially. We described these themes in great detail in chapter 6 (see Table 6.1), but a few bear repeating here. One of the most striking comments of parents with toddlers, expressed in one form or another by the majority of parents in our study, was that they wanted both themselves and their partners to work on controlling their temper. Different families said this in different ways, some using very gentle terms and saying that outbursts with their toddlers were relatively rare but always upsetting to them, whereas others described them as regular daily occurrences, but the extent to which expressions of negative emotion had become a feature of family life during the toddler years in a manner seldom seen during infancy was quite striking.

With the infusion of more potent and pointed emotions into the family system came an accompanying imperative for parents to develop strategies to encourage, manage, and consequate different expressions of emotion. Families routinely struggled with how best to handle toddlers' angry outbursts, and sometimes also bouts of personal (biting, hitting) or object (throwing things, sweeping things off tables) aggression. Parental perspectives on how to handle such behavior ran the gamut, including zero-tolerance time outs, ignoring, voice raising, guilt induction, spankings, and conversations about anger, and it was not unusual for parents to tell us that they and their partner lacked consistency in responding, both as individuals and as a coordinated team. Parents also told us of a variety of other worries they had and about disagreements between them as to whether certain toddler behaviors (e.g., hair twirling, self-stimulation, and occasional bonking of heads on walls when fatigued) were normal and transitory or whether they were cause for clinical concern. Parents continued to disagree on longer standing issues such as co-sleeping, thumb sucking, and noncompliance at mealtimes and bedtimes.

Of all these daily issues that challenged the solidarity of the coparental alliance, parents were most disturbed when they felt their partner was consciously or unwittingly engaging in parenting strategies that were creating problematic habits or belief systems in the child. Some of these concerns have been mentioned elsewhere in the book. Some parents were certain that that their partners were teaching their children to be afraid of bugs, snakes, dogs, monsters, the dark, or all people outside the immediate family. Others feared the opposite, that their partners were not teaching their children sufficient caution about climbing onto furniture, running off in crowded places, talking to strangers, or walking to the car without holding hands. Parents disagreed with their partners permitting toddlers to develop interests in television programming and toys (e.g., pretend make-up) created for "tweens" (the 8-to-12 preteen set), or children's programming that contained any form of aggression or weaponry. Many worried that their partners were teaching children values that conflicted with those they were trying to inculcate in the child. One parent expressed concern about a flip and insensitive comment the partner had made when their child asked why a woman taking tolls at a booth sported short-cropped hair. Another had grown upset when the partner made a denigrating comment about a garment worn by a television character of a different race whom the child liked.

In short, parents had very clear ideas about habits, traits, and beliefs they didn't want their child developing, and quite frequently these were habits, traits, and beliefs that parents believed had been maladaptively foisted upon or inculcated in them by their own origin families. They did not want their children to be precociously mature, tentative, prejudiced, haughty, or in one father's terms, a "weenie." Given these strong and unwavering sentiments, it is no wonder then that parents had such strong reactions when they believed their partners were working at cross-purposes and not acculturating the child to grow into the kind of individual they felt would be the most well-adjusted.

Although disagreements about how best to raise the child to become a strong, secure, potent, and well-adjusted person created significant distress for parents, discussions about these issues were among the most difficult for parents to have, and so many parents never had them. Here, then, was one enduring area where parents worked at cross-purposes but had trouble calibrating with one another. Why they had difficulty is not clear. According to one father, conversations often took the form of accusations: "Don't tell him that, you're scaring him," or "Why do you keep buying (lip gloss, bangles) for her? She's only 2!" Conversations were not conversations at all but unresolved, child-related disputes, and as Grych and Fincham (1990) have pointed out, these kinds of disputes are especially disturbing to children. Also in many families, parents sought to remedy perceived damage done by partners by talking to the child in private so as to communicate the exact opposite message as that sent by the partner. Some did so unflinchingly. Others did so with great regret, recognizing that they were deconstructing in private the solidarity of the unified front the parents sought to present to their toddler publicly. Again, we emphasize that an alliance is only an alliance to the extent that it remains intact across settings, situations, and stressors. Private undoing or discounting of the partner's parenting stances is sometimes necessary and even wise, but when it becomes a fundamental thread in the fabric of the family's everyday emotional experience, it ultimately comes to undermine the coparenting alliance.

What we learned, then, is that differences of opinion about child rearing are not at all uncommon; in fact, they come to be almost everyday occurrences by the time children have reached the toddler years. Parents find it easy to talk about, though not always agree upon, children's misbehavior. They find it much harder to talk about concerns they have over how their partner is acculturating or helping to "form" the child, and when they do say something, they often do so in accusatory ways that upset themselves, their partners, and the child. However, ***without confronting and discussing major differences in perspective and the reasons behind their strongly held beliefs, parents are in danger of continuing to work at cross-purposes, with negative ramifications for children***. Some of the ways this can play out are discussed in the next section.

5. Coparental Difficulties and Dynamics Cause Problems for Children

In 1990, Lawrence Hirshberg published a very interesting article in which he introduced 1-year-olds to a potentially anxiety-provoking stimulus and asked parents (mothers and fathers) to offer two different sets of signals to the baby. The stimulus was a contraption called a "visual cliff," a Plexiglas screen covering what appeared to be a "drop" or fall. To the baby, it might appear on first glance that venturing onto the screen so as to crawl across and reach the parents could lead to a tumble, even though the journey was, of course, completely safe. Years of experience with the visual cliff taught that babies would cross when beckoned warmly by parents who assured them it was safe and stay back when parents sent the opposite message that it may not be safe. However, Hirshberg wondered what would happen when babies were given conflicting sets of messages by parents, so he instructed one parent to look fearful and the other to look calm, happy, and to be encouraging. His results were quite striking. Faced with the dilemma of conflicting messages from parents, babies frequently grew quite distressed and, most interesting of all, exhibited behavior that attachment researchers have come to describe as "disorganized" (without a clear adaptive aim or goal). Such behaviors included such unusual reactions as "freezing," remaining still and not moving at all. In other words, babies were placed into an impossible dilemma that they couldn't resolve, and it disrupted their capacity to act confidently and decisively. Independently, either parent's messages to the baby would have enabled the baby to make an informed decision and act accordingly. It was the conflicting emotional messages that left babies without recourse.

Hirshberg's was only an experimental paradigm, of course, and one might well wonder whether his findings have any farther reaching effects or generalizability, but the genius of his investigation was that it found a way to inculcate focused stress and placed babies in a situation where they sought aid from the parenting team about how to proceed. When the parents behaved in accordance, as some did (different sets of parents in Hirshberg's study were instructed to give concordant, rather than discordant, signals), babies were able to deal effectively with the stress. It was when the parents were inconsistent that the babies behaved maladaptively. The link between coparenting dissonance and infant disorganization was one that stayed with us over the years. What if longer term dissonance in parenting signals and expectancies have similarly disruptive and disorganizing effects on infants and toddlers? Isn't it hard enough for babies to learn to internalize rules and standards even when parents are being consistent? How much more difficult is it when messages are regularly inconsistent?

Furthermore, what if the coparenting climate, in addition to being inconsistent, is also negative and hostile? Developmental theorists have spent the past 30 years demonstrating convincingly that babies' ability to explore the environment is affected by the security of attachment they share with mothers or other primary caregivers. Secure attachments stem from relationships that are sensitive and responsive and in which the babies develop a sense of trust, predictability, and security. Such security is what allows babies to invest fully in the object world, exploring, creating, pursuing possibilities. In contrast, insecure babies do not explore as creatively and deeply. Some insecure babies appear, on the surface, to become absorbed in the object world, but closer looks indicate that such babies play only on a surface level and do not lose themselves in play. Their exploration appears to serve more as a defensive avoidance of interpersonal relations rather than a lighthearted frolic in the world of objects enabled by secure interpersonal relations. John Bowlby wrote about this "attachment–exploration" balance many decades ago (e.g., Bowlby, 1969), and attachment research has borne out his insights.

Security, however, has almost always been conceived as something "given" to babies by primary caregivers. This dyadic caregiver–baby model, as we have contended throughout this book, has continued to be the dominant force in infant mental health theory and practice, but as Patricia Minuchin emphasized in her 1985 clarion call to developmental researchers, it is the family unit—whoever might comprise that family unit—that constitutes the child's experiential reality, especially from later infancy forward. As important as it is to know about secure attachment bonds with primary caregivers (and such bonds are unquestionably critical for babies' mental health and development), we miss out on a hugely important facet of the child's socialization experience when we fail to ask whether babies feel security at the level of the family (Cummings & Davies, 1996; Davies & Cummings, 1994; McHale, 1997; McHale & Cowan, 1996). Negativity—conflict, undermining, disparagement, disqualification—between coparents threatens the child's trust in the family's integrity and perpetuity as a bastion of security.

Over the years, when we have submitted articles from our study for publication in scientific journals, reviewers have sometimes asked "So what's the difference between parenting and coparenting?" We already know, after all, that parenting practices unquestionably influence children's development, and there is a temptation simply to say "The more dominant parent's style will be the one that wins out and that will have the most profound influence on the child's personality." But this is a very interesting choice of terminology. The term *winning out* suggests a contest, a competition, in which there is one clear winner and one clear loser. By extension of this logic, to the extent that the winner possesses a parenting style that is effective in promoting competence and confidence, this would undoubtedly be a fine and acceptable outcome. To the extent that the winner's parenting style is one that inculcates uncertainty, insecurity, mistrust, despondence, or aggression, the outcome would be a bad one.

The metaphor of "greater muscle" is an unpleasant one. Stances such as "I know better, and I'm stronger, so I win" can lead to the same substantial damage in families as they do in two-party political systems that do not work to find common ground. When battles for ascendancy, rather than discussion and compromise, take over in families, children are placed in an impossible dilemma. There is no good decision for a child who is regularly presented with two very different positions by his or her parents. During infancy, insecurity and disorganization may occur. During the toddler years, fear and anxiety—or alternatively, recklessness and lawlessness—may dominate. Over time, moral development may even be disrupted, as children learn that rules are arbitrary and it is permissible to follow one set of rules in one circumstance but to ignore them in another.

We are talking about extremes here, of course. As we've stressed, coparenting disagreements are ubiquitous, and what matters most is how parents handle disagreements between them and whether they use their discussions productively to fortify their alliance and increase their consistency with their children. Take, for example, a situation in which a toddler plays for the umpteenth time with her parents' DVD collection and litters them throughout the apartment. One parent chides her, and she begins to cry. The scolding parent tells the child to follow the rules and to stop crying and buck up. The other parent picks the child up and strokes her hair. Sound familiar? These kinds of occurrences are not uncommon in families, and when they happen only infrequently they probably have very little impact, but when such routines become regularized (parent A chastises and parent B comforts the reprimanded child, publicly or privately), problems can get set in motion. Over time, parent A's authority can be undermined. Or just as possibly, parent B's authority can be undermined. The child may eventually become fearful and constrained in one parent's presence, or disrespectful and noncompliant in the other's. As suggested above, she may learn that rules are arbitrary and that they need to be followed only when certain people are present. Such learning may lead the child to become secretive, engaging in certain behaviors permitted by one parent but hiding them from the other, stricter parent.

Toddlers, of course, love and respect both parents, and the reality for most families is seldom that one parent is always the heavy and the other always the rescuer. In fact, parents who spoke with us were as concerned with their own inconsistency as with that of their partners or of the inconsistency between them and spoke about their own tempers, lack of patience, and ineffective follow-throughs with their children every bit as much as their concerns about how their styles differed from those of their partners. Our point here is certainly not to minimize the importance of individual parents' behavior with their children but rather to emphasize that the true value of coparenting comes when parents can step in interchangeably for one another when one's defenses are down and work with the child in a manner that does not undercut the other. When the coparenting partner reliably fails to step in, however, or steps in but works at cross-purposes (recall the lament of Suzanne, in chapter 6, who had worked mightily to get their baby to sleep alone only to have her husband Tom bring him back into their bed one afternoon and reverse all progress made), problems begin brewing.

Until the time of this study, the field had marshaled relatively little evidence that coparenting solidarity (or lack of solidarity) has an impact as early as the toddler years. That situation has now changed. We provided some of the big-picture findings in chapter 6: In families with greater coparental solidarity, toddlers demonstrated greater emotional literacy and self-reliance when regulating emotions during frustration tasks. They were described by fathers as more socially competent and as plagued by fewer behavior problems, and teachers and day-caregivers saw them as possessing stronger pre-academic skills. In contrast, toddlers in families in which parents were experiencing greater coparenting conflict were described by mothers as plagued by more acting out and defiant behavior, and there was a trend approaching significance for fathers in these families to describe their children the same way. These are just some of the major big-picture findings, emanating from analyses that relied upon the molar summary constructs we formed.

Other analyses we conducted to test specific hypotheses consistent with the theoretical framework we have developed provided additional findings that are worthy of note. For example, our colleague Chris Scull and several of his collaborators (2006) were interested in learning whether coparenting discord during the infancy period specifically foreshadowed toddler inattention, inattentiveness, and hyperactivity at 30 months. Although there is no question that inattention and inattentiveness, inability to concentrate or sit still, intolerance with waiting, frustrating easily, getting into everything, quickly shifting activities, and being unusually loud are descriptors endemic to the toddler years, they can nonetheless be worrisome when they are pervasive and cross-situational. Hence, Scull created a single composite index in which he included relevant reports from mothers, fathers, and teachers and observational measures of the toddler from laboratory visits. He then examined indicators of coparenting dissonance that had been documented at 12 months and asked whether they foreshadowed the 30-month symptom composite. His analysis indicated that both infants' 12-month activity level as reported by parents on the Infant Behavior Questionnaire (IBQ) and mothers' ratings of coparenting conflict at 12 months were harbingers of later symptoms during toddlerhood and that the child and family indicators each explained unique variance in the outcome, suggesting that the family's coparenting dynamics played a contributory role beyond child factors.

Consistent with the "family-level security" notions developed above, we also found evidence that toddlers appear less likely to delve into the world of family emotions when there are strains in the coparental relationship. In chapter 2, we mentioned an earlier pilot study for this project in which Allison Lauretti and colleagues (1999) discovered that 30-month-olds from families low in coparenting cohesion were more reluctant to engage in lab tasks that evoked negative imagery about families. Lauretti et al. adapted a version of McHale, Neugebauer, Asch, and Schwartz's (1999) family doll story methodology and asked 72 toddlers to use a set of bear dolls to tell stories about happy, sad, and mad families. The dolls sported facial expressions that mirrored the emotions (sad mother, father, and child dolls had sad faces with a tear running down the cheek; mad dolls had grumpy expressions and furrowed eyebrows). Fewer than half of the toddlers (about 40% in all) were actually able to tell any kind of meaningful story or to enact the bears interacting with one another, but most children handled the dolls and participated in the assessment. However, toddlers from families low in coparenting cohesion were significantly less likely to engage with the mad and sad family dolls than were children who came from families that had exhibited higher levels of cohesion.

We sought to replicate Lauretti et al.'s finding in our study and did find suggestive evidence—less dramatic but nonetheless consistent with the earlier set of findings—that toddlers from families experiencing coparenting difficulties likewise shied away from the same lab task asking them to think and talk about negative emotions in the family. Our colleagues Eric Nemic and Spiro Kotsios (Nemic, Kotsios, & McHale, 2007) rated toddlers' propensity to participate actively in the telling of sad and mad stories and then examined associations between these ratings and concurrently measured indicators of coparenting. Their data indicated that in families in which mothers reported more conflict in the coparenting relationship and in which the coparents showed less of a positive connection during family interactions, toddlers were less likely to engage in telling sad stories. They were also less likely to engage in telling mad stories, just as in the Lauretti study, but they were no less likely to engage in the happy family task. So we now have evidence that in two separate studies, toddlers from families showing signs of coparenting strain at 30 months were less comfortable engaging in conversations and storytelling about negative family emotions. Although we did not have a tried-and-true measure of toddler insecurity to rely upon, these findings are wholly consistent with the notion that young children explore ideas and emotions less freely and deeply when they are less secure emotionally.

In all, the story told by the data from the Families Through Time study indicated rather convincingly that when the parents' coparenting alliance was suffering, toddlers were also struggling on a wide range of cognitive, social, and emotional indicators. In chapter 9, we explore some of the implications of our study and its findings for couples, and for the professionals who work with them. In a concluding chapter, we offer a final take-home message and some words of wisdom to families, from families.

References

Abidin, R. R., & Brunner, J. F. (1995). Development of a parenting alliance inventory. *Journal of Clinical Child Psychology, 24,* 31–40.

Bowlby, J. (1969). *Attachment and loss. Volume I: Attachment*. New York: Basic Books.

Cowan, P., & Cowan, C. (1992). *When partners become parents: The big life change for couples.* New York: Basic Books.

Cummings, E. M., & Davies, P. (1996). Emotional security as a regulatory process in normal development and the development of psychopathology. *Development and Psychopathology, 8*, 123–139.

Davies, P. T., & Cummings, E. M. (1994). Marital conflict and child adjustment: An emotional security hypothesis. *Psychological Bulletin, 116*, 387–411.

Elliston, D., & McHale, J. (2006, March). *The family context of coparenting withdrawal at three months post-partum.* Paper presented at the Southeastern Psychological Association, Atlanta, GA.

Fivaz-Depeursinge, E., & Corboz-Warnery, A. (1999). *The primary triangle: A developmental systems view of mothers, fathers, and infants.* New York: Basic Books.

Fivaz-Depeursinge, E., & Favez, N. (2006). Exploring triangulation in infancy: Two contrasted cases. *Family Process, 45*, 3–8.

Fivaz-Depeursinge, E., & Lavanchy, C. (2006). *A trial intervention in a family therapeutic assessment based on the Lausanne Trilogue Play paradigm.* Paper presented at the 10th World Congress of the World Association for Infant Mental Health, Paris.

Gottman, J. M. (1994). *What predicts divorce? The relationship between marital processes and marital outcomes.* Hillsdale, NJ: Erlbaum.

Gray, J. (1992). *Men are from Mars, women are from Venus: A practical guide for improving your communication and getting what you want from your relationships.* New York: Guilford Press.

Grych, J., & Fincham, F. (1990). Marital conflict and children's adjustment: A cognitive–contextual framework. *Psychological Bulletin, 108*, 267–290.

Hirshberg, L. (1990). When infants look to their parents II: Twelve-month-olds' response to conflicting parental emotional signals. *Child Development, 61*, 1187–1191.

Hochschild, A., & Machung, A. (1989). *The second shift: Working parents and the revolution at home.* New York: Viking–Penguin.

Hochschild, A., & Machung, A. (2001). Men who share "the second shift." In J. M. Henslin (Ed.), *Down to earth sociology: Introductory readings* (11th ed., pp. 395–409). New York: Free Press.

Lakoff, R. (1975). *Language and woman's place.* New York: Harper & Row.

Lauretti, A., Hill, A., Connell, A., & McHale, J. (1999, April). *Links between toddlers' nonverbal responses during doll play and family relationships.* Paper presented at Society for Research in Child Development, Albuquerque, NM.

Maccoby, E. E., Mnookin, R. H., Depner, C. E., & Peters, H. E. (1992). *Dividing the child: Social and legal dilemmas of custody.* Cambridge, MA: Harvard University Press.

Main, M., & Goldwyn, R. (in press). Adult attachment rating and classification systems. In M. Main (Ed.), *A typology of human attachment organization assessed in discourse, drawing and interviews* (working title). New York: Cambridge University Press.

Maugh, T. (1998, February 21). Study's advice to husbands: Accept wives' influence. *Los Angeles Times,* p. A1.

McHale, J. P. (1995). Coparenting and triadic interactions during infancy: The roles of marital distress and child gender. *Developmental Psychology, 31*, 985–996.

McHale, J. P. (1997). Overt and covert coparenting processes in the family. *Family Process, 36*, 183–201.

McHale, J. P., & Cowan, P. A. (1996). *Understanding how family-level dynamics affect children's development: Studies of two-parent families*. San Francisco: Jossey-Bass.

McHale, J. P., & Fivaz-Depeursinge, E. (1999). Understanding triadic and family group interactions during infancy and toddlerhood. *Clinical Child and Family Psychology Review, 2*, 107–127.

McHale, J. P., Kazali, C., Rotman, T., Talbot, J., Carleton, M., & Lieberson, R. (2004). The transition to coparenthood: Parents' prebirth expectations and early coparental adjustment at 3 months postpartum. *Development and Psychopathology, 16*, 711–733.

McHale, J. P., Neugebauer, A., Asch, A. R., & Schwartz, A. (1999). Preschoolers' characterizations of multiple family relationships during family doll play. *Journal of Clinical Child Psychology, 28*, 256–268.

McHale, J. P., & Rotman, T. (2007). Is seeing believing? Expectant parents' outlooks on coparenting and later coparenting solidarity. *Infant Behavior & Development, 30*, 63–81.

Minuchin, P. (1985). Families and individual development: Provocations from the field of family therapy. *Child Development, 56*, 289–302.

Nemic, E., Kotsios, S., & McHale, J. (2007, April). *Are toddlers in low coparenting solidarity families more reluctant to engage in family story tasks?* Paper presented at the Society for Research in Child Development, Boston.

Roberts, L. J. (2000). Fire and ice in marital communication: Hostile and distancing behaviors as predictors of marital distress. *Journal of Marriage and the Family, 62*, 693–712.

Scull, C., Alongi, D., Bruzgyte, N., & McHale, J. (2006, May). *Infant and family process predictors of ADHD symptoms at 30 months.* Paper presented at the meetings of the Association for Psychological Science, New York.

Talbot, J., Elliston, D., Thompson, J., Scull, C., Lieberson, R., & McHale, J. (2006, July). *Do early coparenting dynamics benefit from coherent states of mind with respect to attachment?* Paper presented at the 10th World Congress of the World Association for Infant Mental Health, Paris.

Talbot, J. A., & McHale, J. P. (2004). Individual parental adjustment moderates the relationship between marital and coparenting quality. *Journal of Adult Development, 11*, 191–205.

Tannen, D. (1994). *Gender and discourse.* New York: Oxford University Press.

Wile, D. B. (1988). In search of the curative principle in couples therapy. *Journal of Family Psychology, 2*, 24–27.

CHAPTER 9

Expanding Beyond Dyadic to Family Group Formulations in Mental Health Practice

In chapter 2, we commented that the first impulse of parents (and helping professionals) who find that something is amiss with the infant is to ask "What (or who) is behind this?" This is, of course, so that they can channel the necessary energies into addressing the root of the problem. In infant mental health practice, clinical contacts with families of young infants involve evaluations of the babies' development and of possible cognitive, motor, language, affective, and regulation difficulties. This is both to establish whether important delays or impairments are present and to estimate the extent to which any such problems are affecting child and family functioning (Egger, Fenichel, Guedeney, Wise, & Wright, 2006; ZERO TO THREE, 2005). Current standards of practice also call upon clinicians to evaluate strengths and weaknesses in family functioning (Egger et al., 2005), but to many clinicians, *family* ends up translating into *caregiver–child* or *maternal*, for reasons of time, resources, or theoretical bias. As a result, clinical formulations and intervention plans in families with infants most often single out mother–infant dyadic relationships. In this sense, there is an implicit assumption that it is mothers who are responsible, if not for contributing to the infant problem in the first place then at least for helping to perpetuate its maintenance and proliferation.

Chapter 2 also considered the long history of this focus on mothers as instigators and culprits and hinted at some of the conclusions and therapeutic choices that such a focus can lead to. One such conclusion is that mothers themselves are in need of some direct therapeutic attention. When this is a guiding assumption, work with the mother–infant subsystem necessarily calls for some form of psychodynamic or cognitive–behavioral intervention with the mother herself. Extending the metaphor further, preventive interventions would be expected to center on the expectant mother, her phenomenology, and perhaps also her supports during the pregnancy. The aims of such interventions would be to boost mother's capacity for adapting to the stresses of the early postpartum period so that she and her infant do not get off on the wrong foot.

Fathers or father–infant dyads are very rarely a focus of therapeutic intervention in contemporary infant mental health practice, despite the increasing popularity of interventions designed to foster early father–infant bonding and highlight the role fathers can come to play in infants' lives. Fathering initiatives that appeal to men's sensibilities, such as "boot camps for new dads," are a growing phenomenon and presence within North American health care systems. Such initiatives have been guided by both theory and research concluding that babies profit in a great many ways from men's active involvement as parents (Phares, 1996; Pleck, 1997); yet despite the growing popularity of such interventions, fathers are not held as responsible for infants' and toddlers' early adjustment problems as mothers are. Perhaps for this reason, men's psychodynamics and internal working models of relationships are rarely a focus of fathering interventions. Indeed, for the most part, fathers simply disappear from view when early infant adjustment problems come to the attention of mental health professionals.

Men's fathering roles are not alone in taking a back seat. The predominant mother–baby dyadic focus of early interventionists stands in stark contrast to the predominant focus of prenatal preventive efforts, which prioritize husband–wife dyadic relationships. Such prenatal efforts are guided by a premise that strong communication and more positivity than negativity in the marital partnership will benefit infant mental health. More specifically, parents in less discordant marriages are expected to enjoy greater emotional support from each other and, hence, experience less strain as parents. Relatively few conceptualizations of infant mental health problems view marital discord as a direct instigator of such problems, however—in contrast with case conceptualizations in families of older children, in which marital conflict is often viewed as being responsible for, or at least contributing to, the child's symptomatology. The point highlighted here, however, is the curious disconnect between the prenatal emphasis on marital adjustment and the postnatal neglect of the relationship between the parents to focus on mother–baby dyads.

The family process spotlighted in this book, of course, has been neither that of parent–child relationship disturbances nor that of marital adjustment and deterioration; nor has the focus even been on infant and toddler mental health, though as we reported in chapter 8, a significant number of parents in our study were concerned about toddlers' anxiety, overactivity, impulsivity, noncompliance, and aggression (common reasons, all, for clinical referral). Our focus, rather, has been on the underpinnings and development of the family-level dynamics that in most cases preceded such child difficulties and in other cases developed in tandem with them. From the very beginning, parents are acutely aware of relationship dynamics from their origin families that they do not want to reproduce, and they also have a sense of relationship dynamics from their partners' families that they do not want to see carried forward. However, despite these good intentions, and despite their explicit focus on and attunement to coparenting issues by virtue of their participation in our study, a large subgroup of our study families did ultimately find themselves in nonsupportive, disconnected, and sometimes even contentious coparenting partnerships. How did this happen, and how can the lessons we learned in this study inform future preventive efforts for families anticipating the journey into coparenthood?

This chapter was conceived as a "thought chapter." Its aim is to reflect on current thrusts of early interventions with families and urge that coparenting and family-level processes be systematically integrated into case formulations and planned interventions from pregnancies forward. We begin by selectively reviewing influential parent–child and marital interventions, highlighting the kinds of choices available to families and to those who work with emergent family systems. As we examine how interventions aim to effect change within the system, it will become apparent that few directly target the coparental system in any comprehensive way (if they attend to it at all—and most do not). After this look at parent–child and marital interventions, we examine some small-*N* and pilot projects that are newly underway and that are seeking to influence early coparenting and/or family group dynamics, to provide readers with a beginning sense of how the thinking behind such efforts has proceeded to date. This chapter concludes with points about coparenting and triadic interventions that all infant–family interventionists should take to heart and into practice, even if their work continues to remain principally focused on one or more of the dyadic subsystems within the emergent family system.

What's Available Now: Major Thrusts of Current Preventive and Early Interventions

Efforts to Strengthen and Promote Early Parenting

There was a time not so long ago when the most that parents could expect from routine prenatal care was a focus on mothers' physical health and symptomatology. Fathers were ignored, even when they attended prenatal check-ups with mothers, and the couple received only limited preparation for labor and delivery. No more. Most hospitals now offer prenatal childbirth classes, and the majority of first-time parents take advantage of these offerings. Because most classes request that mothers bring a partner or support person with them, fathers have attained some visibility (though not always during routine check-ups; one father told us, "The doctor asked 'How are you?' and I said I was doing OK. He told me, 'I wasn't talking to you—I was talking to your wife'"). The curriculum for most contemporary childbirth classes, however, usually takes parents only through the initial hours following the delivery. More progressive programs do offer some education to parents about what to expect during the early days and weeks of new parenthood, but very few go beyond this to offer any substantive parenting or skills training.

Several historically important demonstration projects did incorporate parenting education into their preventive interventions. Among the best known of these early prevention studies was an effort designed for lower socioeconomic, unmarried, urban-dwelling teen mothers who were at risk for parenting disturbances because of myriad stressors they confronted (Olds, Henderson, Phelps, Kitzman, & Hanks, 1993; Olds, Henderson, Tatelbaum, & Chamberlin, 1986; Olds & Kitzman, 1993). Education about infant development and about effective parenting practices was an important component of Olds's program, which proved remarkably successful in reducing the prevalence of severe negative outcomes. Current-day programs for at-risk parents, such as state and federal Healthy Start initiatives, often include some variant of these educational efforts, although few offer the comprehensive, high-quality wraparound services afforded to mothers in the seminal Olds project. Curiously, anticipatory parenting classes for mothers who are not at the extremes of risk have never been part of the fabric of North American obstetric practice, and so new mothers typically come to the attention of clinicians only when mothers or babies, or both, struggle with clinical symptomatology following the baby's arrival.

Disruptions in mother–infant relationships are not uncommon, however (Brockington, 1996), and maternal depression is an especially common presenting complaint (Brockington, 2004; O'Hara, 1997; Weissman & Olfson, 1995). This is significant, because postpartum depression contributes both to impairments in parenting (Cohn, Campbell, Matias, & Hopkins, 1990) and to a high incidence of insecure attachment in babies and young children (Lyons-Ruth, Zoll, Connell, & Grunebaum, 1986). More broadly, mother–infant relationship disturbances constitute a very large number of cases presenting at child guidance clinics (Robert-Tissot, Cramer, Stern, & Serpa, 1996). Techniques of intervention with mother–infant relationship problems vary, but in general they either involve work with mothers in dynamically based or cognitive therapy; work with mother–infant interactions through counseling, educational support, or interaction guidance to foster mothers' accurate reading of the infant's signals; or work with both. The rationale for these approaches is that maternal symptoms interfere with mothers' capacity to accurately and sensitively read infant signals. Over time, the mismatch begins to have a debilitating effect on the baby, furthering the mother's distress and feelings of incompetence. Infant–parent psychotherapy models first gained prominence following Fraiberg, Adelson, and Shapiro's (1975) seminal paper, "Ghosts in the Nursery," and owe their current toehold in infant mental health practice to the efforts of Daniel Stern (2004). Empirical evidence for the effectiveness of early dyadic interventions has been mounting and will be summarized here shortly.

Not all postpartum interventions with mothers get to the point of working with maternal representations or mother–infant interactions, however. For example, many interventions target postpartum depression symptoms, anticipating that maternal improvement will translate into relationship improvements. But does it? The jury remains out, as evidence has been decidedly mixed. One challenge in determining what works and what doesn't is the sheer variety of different interventions with depressed mothers that reportedly provide symptom relief. Improvements have been reported for psychoeducational interventions (Honey, Bennett, & Morgan, 2002); home visits by nurses (Wickberg & Hwang, 1996), health care visitors (Holden, Sagovsky, & Cox, 1989), and social workers (Armstrong, Fraser, Dadds, & Morris, 1999); interpersonal psychotherapy (Clark, Tluczek, & Wenzel, 2003; O'Hara, Stuart, Gorman, & Wenzel, 2000); cognitive–behavioral therapy (Appelby, Warner, Whitton, & Faragher, 1997); support groups (Chen, Tseng, Chou, & Wang, 2000); and even telephone-based peer support (Dennis,

2003). Terrific as it may sound to have an almost infinite array of choices from which to select, not all the studies that documented maternal symptom improvement have also reported attendant effects on mother–infant relationships. In some cases, this was because researchers did not assess them, whereas in others, it was because such effects did not materialize (see, e.g., Clark et al., 2003; O'Hara et al., 2000; for important exceptions, see Armstrong et al., 1999; Cooper et al., 2002; Murray, Cooper, Wilson, & Romaniuk, 2003). Moreover, very few interventions involved fathers—unfortunate, because evidence from a few studies that did indicated that involvement by the babies' fathers had salutory effects (e.g., Gordon & Gordon, 1960; Misri, Kostaras, Fox, & Kostaras, 2000).

In contrast to these studies, published evidence from dyadically based therapies indicates that such interventions often do effect positive change in mother–infant relationships. Field's (1997) review of interventions designed to enhance maternal mood and improve interactions between depressed mothers and babies identified several coaching strategies and imitation techniques that decreased intrusive mothers' overstimulation and helped mothers read and respond more sensitively to infant cues. She also concluded that attention-getting techniques promote the social responsiveness of withdrawn mothers. In a more recent study, Clark et al. (2003) compared interpersonal therapy (in which babies accompanied mothers to their sessions) with a mother–infant psychotherapy intervention. The latter intervention combined a mothers' group for therapeutic intervention and peer support and an infant therapy group that helped babies become more regulated and socially engaged. It also included a mother–infant dyadic group designed to promote sensitive responsiveness of mothers to babies. Improvements in both maternal perceptions and in relational variables materialized for both the interpersonal therapy and the mother–infant intervention groups, with the latter proving especially helpful for more severely depressed women. Infant–parent therapies have also proven effective with other high-risk samples (e.g., Cicchetti, Rogosch, & Toth, 2000; Heinicke et al., 1999; Lieberman, Weston, & Pawl, 1991).

Remembering the "Who's responsible?" question invoked at the start of the chapter, we find it worthy of note that mothers, at least initially, were the ostensible referred patient in many of these studies.

However, infant–parent therapies have also proven effective when babies have been the referred patients. For example, Cohen, Lojkasek, Muir, Muir, and Parker (2002) compared an infant-led psychotherapy, Watch, Wait, and Wonder (WWW; based on principles introduced by Wesner, Dowling, & Johnson, 1962) with a psychodynamic therapy for mothers in which the infant was present. Cohen and her colleagues found that both interventions led to improvements in mother–infant interactions that continued to be apparent at 6 months follow-up. Of interest, infant–mother attachment security, which had shown immediate improvement in the WWW group, witnessed similar improvement by the 6-month follow-up for the psychodynamic intervention group as well. This gain in attachment security for the latter group of infants materialized even though the WWW group mothers continued reporting greater comfort dealing with infant behaviors and less parenting stress at the time of that follow-up.

Also working with clinically referred infants, Robert-Tissot and colleagues (1996) compared the effectiveness of two brief mother–infant intervention models (offered for a maximum of 10 sessions only) in changing maternal representations, behavioral interactions between mother and infant, and infant symptoms. The two models they compared were a traditional psychodynamic psychotherapy model, following Fraiberg (1980) and Cramer (1995), and an interactional guidance model, following McDonough (1995). The psychodynamic treatment focused on a core-conflictual relationship and on mothers' attributions about the baby (and on links to similar conflicts that mothers had experienced in their past). The main goal was to adjust mothers' distortions about the baby and the relationship. An innovation of the approach, however, was that actual interactions between mothers and babies were sometimes used to accentuate mismatches between the infants' signals and the mothers' reactions to them. The interaction guidance model, by contrast, remained squarely in the "here and now." Maternal misperceptions of children's signals were tackled directly by calling upon video-assisted feedback and coaching. Portions of video recordings of mother–infant interactions were selected by therapists to review with mothers. Positive caregiving behaviors during the flow of interaction were selectively attended to and reinforced, to build mothers' sense of competency. Mothers were also guided to select infant cues and characteristics and to attend and respond to the cues. Therapists intervened to provide alternative explanations of misperceived infant behavior as such reframes were needed. A more thorough description of this approach is provided in McDonough (1995).

Robert-Tissot and colleagues found that both forms of treatment improved "biologically based" difficulties (e.g., their sleeping and feeding habits and rhythms) and that improvements were still maintained at the 6-month follow-up. Mothers from both groups also showed more sensitivity and less intrusiveness during interactions with babies immediately after treatment, with further improvement still in these realms at the 6-month follow-up. Both groups of mothers also perceived both their own competence and the baby's adaptability more positively, showed increases in self-esteem, and demonstrated less negative affect at both follow-ups. In fact, the only differences in outcome between the two interventions were differences in degree, and these were related in expectable ways to emphases of the treatments. The psychodynamic group showed a greater improvement in self-esteem than did the interaction guidance group, and the interaction guidance group showed greater gains in sensitivity during play with objects.

Taken together, these findings are very impressive. They indicate that significant infant and relationship difficulties can often be arrested by sensitively targeted early interventions with mothers and babies, but where exactly *should* practitioners direct their efforts? Stern (2004), writing on the therapist's choice of focus in working with mother–infant dyads, contended that it actually does not matter much which "port of entry" (mother, infant, or dyad) the interventionist chooses and privileges. His point was that although the technique used to affect change in the mother–infant relational system will be different depending on the approach, the end results are likely to be similarly positive because meaningfully changing one aspect of the mother–infant relationship system will then have reverberating effects and change all other parts.

So where have fathers been in all this work? As indicated earlier, they are often only on the periphery in the early mother–infant intervention literature, if there at all. Clinicians prioritize the mother–infant dyad because it is almost universally seen as constituting the baby's most salient early "holding environment." The metaphor of a holding environment was, of course, that of D. W. Winnicott (author of the famed adage, "there is no such thing as an infant; there is always an infant and someone"). Curiously, in Winnicott's (1957) *Maturational Process and the Facilitating Environment,* he actually portrayed the holding environment as "father, mother, and infant, all three living together." However, early preventive interventions that actually take the family triad as their focus of intervention have been rather uncommon (Fivaz-Depeursinge and colleagues' [2004; 2006] work using the Lausanne Trilogue Play and the recent handful of intervention experiments it has inspired, stands as the notable exception and will be discussed later in this chapter). By and large, when fathers have been attended to, the thrust of clinical efforts has been to promote their level of engagement with their new babies.

Although fathering initiatives and programming targeting new fathers have proliferated over the past decade, intervention research evaluating such initiatives lags behind parallel work evaluating mother–infant therapies. Research efforts have been complicated by confusions about how best to measure and understand father involvement (for some of the discussion and debate on this topic, see Hawkins & Dollahite, 1997; Lamb, 2004; Lamb, Pleck, Charnov, & Levine, 1987; Palkovitz, 1997; Tamis-Lemonda & Cabrera, 2002). With mothers, the aim of most interventions is to promote maternal sensitivity to infant cues and to decrease intrusiveness. With fathers, the focus has often been less on parenting quality and more on parenting involvement—and herein lies part of the problem. Lamb et al.'s (1987) tripartite conceptualization (engagement, including routine play and caregiving interactions; accessibility, or the father's actual physical presence and psychological availability to the child when needed; and responsibility, or the extent to which father takes care of arranging doctors' appointments, child care, and the like) has guided many studies of fathering but has also been criticized by some fatherhood researchers (e.g., Hawkins, Bradford, et al., 2002; Palkovitz, 1997, 2002). Questions have been raised about the model's emphasis on quantity over quality of early fathering and about its underestimation of important affective and cognitive dimensions that distinguish among fathers (e.g., the presence of children in their fathers' thoughts). Schoppe-Sullivan, McBride, and Ho (2004), after they analyzed father involvement data from the Child Development Supplement of the

Panel Study of Income Dynamics (PSID-CDS; Hofferth, 1998), surmised that father involvement does look to be a multidimensional construct, but that assessments of father involvement are really only of practical use to clinicians to the extent that they validly reflect particular dimensions of clinical concern.

Despite persistent questions about how best to evaluate productive early fathering, researchers have forged ahead. Some early intervention studies with families conducted during the newborn period provided conflicting evidence of the promise of brief interventions (Belsky, 1985; Myers, 1982). Subsequently, Brent McBride's (1990, 1991; McBride & Mills, 1993) studies examining the effectiveness of early education programs with new fathers indicated that such programming promoted fathers' comfort, competence, and responsibility as parents. At the same time, however, McBride found that early father engagement still remained much below mother engagement. In McBride's 1991 study, intervention-group fathers did not show gains in amounts of interaction time or in their accessibility on workdays. These findings underscore Schoppe-Sullivan and colleagues' point that the success of clinical interventions may depend on the particular facets of fathering that have been targeted.

But if that is the case, then what should the focus of fathering interventions ideally be? Should their main aim be to promote men's early emotional engagement with their babies? Should it be to enhance their sensitivity to mother's workload and take on more child care and domestic responsibilities (Hawkins & Roberts, 1992)? To be more knowledgeable about infants (Matthey & Barnett, 1999) and/or more resilient when they are chided by their partners or by other family members for tending to the baby "improperly"? To take the initiative to reach out to and talk with their wives when they sense that strain in the marriage is leading mothers to focus their energies even more intensively on the infant and away from the couple (e.g., Belsky & Volling, 1987)? And are brief modules that promote the value of father engagement (appended as they often have been to existing childbirth classes) really sufficient to achieve such aims? Or are more intensive and comprehensive interventions necessary to trigger meaningful effects?

Important questions all, but questions still awaiting answers. At present, there is little consensus in the empirical literature concerning best practices for promoting early fathering. To date, very few major studies have undertaken randomized clinical control trials of efforts to promote early father engagement, although some have been sponsored and are in the works. For example, Doherty, whose 1998 position paper on "responsible fathering" (Doherty, Kouneski, & Erickson, 1998) stimulated some rather pointed scholarly exchange (see Doherty, Kouneski, & Erickson, 2000; Walker & McGraw, 2000), recently conducted one such major project for the Maternal and Child Health Bureau of the Department of Health and Human Services. The project, which Doherty implemented within a health maintenance organization, sought to determine whether an educational intervention helped promote greater father involvement (time and assumed responsibility) with babies, better father–child interaction quality, reductions in parenting stress, and enhanced support felt in the coparenting alliance. Working with 165 middle-class families, most of whom were European American and well educated (94% reporting at least some college, with 74% having attained college degrees), Doherty and colleagues offered an eight-session program that ran from the second trimester of the pregnancy through the fifth postpartum month.

Doherty's curriculum was designed to enhance fathers' knowledge, skills, and commitment to the fatherhood role; to foster coparental teamwork in the couple (including maternal support for and expectations of father involvement); and to help the couple deal more constructively with contextual issues such as work and cultural expectations. The intervention, which included mini-lectures, group discussion, videos, skill demonstrations, role plays, and use of "parent role models," was delivered by a team of male–female licensed parent educators. Doherty and colleagues found that the 70 fathers in their intervention condition showed more positive interactions with their babies (including less intrusiveness, higher warmth, and better synchrony) than did the 67 control-group fathers and spent an average of 42 more minutes per day with babies on workdays than did control-group fathers. It is interesting, however, that the intervention did not show similarly positive effects on coparenting, which was assessed with a self-report index, Frank,

Olmstead, Wagner, and Laub's (1991) Parenting Alliance Scale (which measures the respondent's perception of support received from the coparent and their respect for that person's parenting abilities).

This is a very revealing and important set of findings, one that highlights a point that our research team has made elsewhere (e.g., McHale, 2007, in press; McHale & Alberts, 2003). In contrast with Stern's (2004) contention that the port of entry into a mother–infant dyad matters little because changes in one part of the system will have a reverberating effect, clinicians should be more cautious in assuming that interventions designed to strengthen dyadic, parent–child relationships within the family will have the same desired positive ripple effects in bolstering the coparenting alliance. When we have made this point in the past, our focus has usually been on the infant mental health field's bias in attending principally or only to mothers in early clinical interventions—enhancing mother–infant bonds without integrating fathers has the potential to hamper, rather than promote, the parallel development of a strong coparental partnership and alliance. Precisely the same point can be made about interventions aiming to strengthen engagement by fathers, however. In chapter 2, we called attention to some of the counterintuitive negative effects that have occasionally been documented when fathers violated mothers' prenatal expectancies by being more involved with the baby than the mothers had imagined they might be (e.g., Hackel & Ruble, 1992). Positive father engagement, although empowering for fathers and beneficial for babies, may or may not enhance coparental solidarity, depending on whether the two active parenting partners work together to coordinate and cooperate as allies. According to Doherty's data, among the only preventive interventions to systematically look in on the issue thus far, enhancing fathering engagement did not have salutary effects on coparenting in families.

In summary, there is accumulating evidence that relatively extensive (8–10 sessions) contacts with families around mothering or fathering do promote parent–child relationship quality. Mothering and fathering interventions may not show the same salutary effects on coparenting, particularly if they fail to explicitly attend to changes for the couple. In the next section, we turn our attention to the couple, examining what is currently known about the efficacy of marital interventions before babies arrive on the scene.

Strengthening Couple Relationships Through Marital Education

Perhaps the most fundamental lesson learned from family development studies completed during the 1980s and 1990s was that positive family relationships emanate from strong marital partnerships. This much, we believe we know. So much so, in fact, that the current United States Department of Health and Human Services Administration for Children and Families has endorsed marital education programs as a valuable approach for strengthening families. How did this movement take root? Much is owed to the pioneering efforts of Philip and Carolyn Cowan (1992), whose seminal study of couples' groups led by mental health professionals during the transition to new parenthood set a standard and opened the doors for the flood of marital education programs that have stormed the scene over the past decade. Based on converging evidence revealing declines in marital satisfaction and increases in marital conflict following the birth of a first child, the Cowans created a program they believed would help expectant couples approach and address marital conflict more productively. The curricula for these programs, and those that have been developed in the years since (see Hawkins, Gililand, Christiansens, & Carroll, 2002), share several key commonalities along with a few important differences in emphasis. However, the aims of all, in one form or other, have been consistent in their quest to teach expectant parents how to attend to their relationship as a couple before they begin experiencing distress.

Why marital *education* programs? What are they, and what do they seek to accomplish? Halford and Simons (2005) reviewed three major approaches to such interventions: the provision of *information* to heighten awareness, the individualized assessment of and *feedback* to couples using standard inventories, and the provision of more formal *skills training*. Information and awareness programs, by far the most common, provide couples with didactic materials. They are also sometimes accompanied by group discussions of expectations and/or of relationship processes. Beyond this, programs occasionally incorporate some demonstrations of key relationship skills, but few actually provide explicit skills training. Whereas information and awareness programs typically aim their pitch at small- to moderate-sized groups, assessment and feedback programs are a bit more individualized. They give feedback to partners after they complete standard inventories, and sometimes they also set relationship goals with the couple. Yet very few such programs go the extra step of then teaching skills. Skills training programs, of course, do afford structured training in key skills such as communication and conflict management.

Do information and awareness programs, and assessment and feedback programs (i.e., those that don't provide explicit skills training) foster couple relationship skills? We aren't entirely sure, because with few exceptions, such programs have not been systematically evaluated within controlled clinical trials (Halford & Simons, 2005). That hasn't dampened their popularity, however. Information and awareness programs are in wide use. Couples like them (Halford, Markman, Kline, & Stanley, 2003) and they evaluate them positively. Only skills training approaches, however, can be said for sure to reliably exert medium-range effects lasting as much as 4–5 years of marriage (Halford & Simons, 2005). Unfortunately, even the effects of skills training approaches do attenuate over longer periods. It also remains unclear whether such programs are helpful to higher risk couples; indeed, many couples at risk for marital difficulties never avail themselves of such education at all (Halford, O'Donnell, Lizzio, & Wilson, 2006). To date, there has been a dearth of systematic research on relationship education programs as supports during the transition to parenthood, though explicit focus on the particular knowledge and skills that will be needed to navigate the transition is likely to be necessary.

Exemplars of the movement to strengthen marriages include the work of the Cowans, Gottman, and Markman and associates, all of whom have also been important influences on the recent federal Healthy Marriage Initiative. The Cowans were the field's true pioneers in the implementation of systematic support strategies for couples making the transition to new parenthood (chronicled in Cowan & Cowan, 1992). Their work examined the value and aftereffects of a couples' group that met weekly for 6 months both before and after the baby's arrival. The Cowans sought to design groups that would provide a supportive context for spouses to learn from other couples also expecting a first child and provide a safe place to air and discuss concerns about family issues under the watchful guidance of a mental health professional couple. Group agendas for sessions highlighted risk and protective factors known to affect children's development (e.g., parents' personal adjustment, past and present relationships in their family of origin, developing relationships with the child, bond with one another, and access to social supports outside the family). Agendas were established and introduced by group leaders, although couples did collaborate in the process of setting these agendas. Most sessions began broadly by focusing on the topic or survey of the week but frequently turned to focus intensively on one or more couples' current, ongoing struggles. The Cowans found that the groups exerted a protective effect over time. Intervention participants experienced significantly less of a decline in marital adjustment than did comparison participants over the first 5½ years of parenthood (Schulz, Cowan, & Cowan, 2006), providing support for the efficacy of the intervention.

Because the intervention effects did not extend to the couples' children when they were followed up in kindergarten, the Cowans recommended that future couple-focused prevention programs build in periodic "booster" sessions after the baby's arrival. They then gave their recommendation some teeth by completing a new study that intervened with a fresh sample of parents with children of preschool age (see Cowan, Cowan, & Heming, 2005). In this demonstration project, the Cowans contrasted two intervention conditions: (a) a set of groups focusing primarily on strengthening parent–child relationships and promoting parenting competencies and (b) a set of groups focusing primarily on marital and coparenting issues. Although both sets of groups did ultimately touch upon both parenting and coparenting issues, they did so in very different doses. The Cowans found that, although the parenting-focused condition did promote greater parenting effectiveness (as observed 1 year later), it had no effect on coparenting quality. By contrast, the condition with the marital–coparenting focus led not only to improvements in parent–child relationship quality but also to improvements in coparental functioning (as documented during interactions of parents teaching and playing together with their child). Also of note, both interventions promoted children's academic achievement and muted their externalizing and internalizing behaviors in kindergarten and in first grade (Cowan et al., 2005).

Guided by the Cowans' efforts, Markman, Stanley, and colleagues, and John Gottman entered the fray. Each expanded their own career work on the long-term efficacy of marriage-strengthening interventions to create new transition to parenthood programs. The approach developed by Stanley and Markman is the Prevention and Relationship Enhancement Program (nicknamed "PREP"; Stanley, Blumberg, & Martin, 1999). PREP is appropriate for couples at many different points in relationship development, though it is an adaptation of the core PREP program (dubbed "Becoming Parents") that is relevant to this review (see Silliman, Stanley, Coffin, Markman, & Jordan, 2002). The Becoming Parents intervention consists of 27 classroom hours. It includes brief lectures, video clips, couple and group discussions and exercises, and homework assignments created to help couples learn and practice relationship-strengthening skills. One major curricular focus is on active listening skills as a means of avoiding escalation of negative emotion, withdrawal, and invalidation of the partner. Markman's prior PREP studies suggested that couples with PREP training showed more positive and fewer negative communication behaviors at later follow-ups than did control couples. They also showed lower levels of marital violence and significantly reduced rates of separation and divorce (Jordan, Stanley, & Markman, 1999; Markman, Renick, Floyd, & Stanley, 1993; Markman, Stanley, & Blumberg, 2001). Beyond the basic PREP curriculum, the Becoming Parents adaptation added a focus on the management of fatigue, stress, and anger; the division of household labor; and lessons in infant care, and the program does include a 3-hour "booster" session when infants are 6–8 weeks old and 6 months old. Outcome data on the program's efficacy are not yet available.

Gottman's expansion of his research program to involve couples transitioning to new parenthood is also relatively recent. Gottman's far-reaching, intricate, and intensive research studies of couples are legend, and he and the PREP group have engaged in some lively and occasionally charged scholarly debates about what works and what does not for couples seeking to strengthen their marriages (e.g., Gottman, Carrère, Swanson, & Coan, 2000; Hafen & Crane, 2003; Stanley, Bradbury, & Markman, 2000). More specifically, Gottman's position has been that "active listening" is actually not an effective strategy for couples and that it should be abandoned by clinicians wishing to strengthen marriages and relationships (Gottman et al., 2000). Gottman and colleagues also take issue with the notion that anger and its reciprocity are dysfunctional in marriages. They cite Gottman, Coan, Carrère, and Swanson's work indicating that divorce is predicted not by anger per se but rather by highly negative emotions—specifically, by the constellation of contempt, belligerence, and defensiveness (which, along with withdrawal, Gottman dubbed the "Four Horsemen of the Apocalypse" in 1994).

Disagreements between leading marital researchers about what is effective and what is not can be perplexing for mental health professionals (and for couples!). Recognizing this, Gottman has worked hard to draw connections between his own empirical studies and his preventive interventions and marital work with couples. Some key Gottman recommendations have been that husbands accept influence from their wives and that wives raise concerns gently, as discussed in chapter 8. Gottman's parenthood transition program, an initiative he calls "Bringing Baby Home," is, like Markman's, actively in progress. It is built upon work he completed with Alyson Shapiro and Sybil Carrère (Shapiro, Gottman, & Carrére, 2000) and is one of several current hospital-based projects. Gottman's aim is to learn more about couple changes across the parenthood transition so he can help them navigate the transition more successfully. His project is of special interest because it aspires to create an intervention that can be administered by hospital personnel. Because issues pertinent to the training and qualifications of interventionists are often omitted in published reports and articles, Gottman's effort to devise a clinically relevant curriculum that is nonetheless accessible for delivery by nonclinicians represents a bold step for the field. The Bringing Baby Home program starts with standard birth preparation curricula but then augments the curriculum with an additional 2-day couples workshop and/or support group.

The prenatal add-on program is 2 days long; both couples' workshop and 6-month support group formats are being tried out. Several themes, including strengthening the marriage, regulating conflict, getting to know the baby, and building strong family interactions, are featured in the intervention. Detailed written materials have been developed and are given to couples. Gottman's aims are quite ambitious—he seeks to help couples better understand early child development and to normalize stress during the postpartum period and to help them find ways to deal with such stress. He also seeks to promote father engagement in infant care and to improve quality of parent–infant interaction, to prevent relationship deterioration and escalation of hostility, and to help couples coparent effectively. In other words, his aims are to strengthen functioning not just within different family dyads but also within the triadic mother–father–baby system. Early reports on this effort, available both on the project's Web site and in a preliminary report by Shapiro and Gottman (2005), indicate that the 2-day add-on to standard birth preparation classes has a positive effect on dampening postpartum depression and limiting the escalation of hostile affect.

Although work on the Bringing Baby Home project had not been fully completed at the time of this writing, John and Julie Gottman had already begun adapting and expanding their intervention methods (e.g., incorporating innovative "Oprah"-like video segments as triggers for opening discussions) in new groups with unmarried couples having children together. Theirs is one of a new series of efforts concerned with strengthening family relationships for unwed new parents. Robin Dion has provided several informative summaries of this work, with useful overviews of such programming available in Dion (2005) and in Dion, Devaney, and Hershey (2003). In the 2003 report from Dion et al., the authors outline several relevant program development strategies for these target families. More broadly, however, the kinds of programming recommendations they outline impress as not only viable but actually rather progressive strategies that would stand to benefit new families of all kinds in all communities. Among the initiatives and innovations they call attention to are programming in prenatal clinics, in community-based family resource centers, and in one-stop centers for new parents that provide comprehensive arrays of family programs under one roof.

These are only a few of the great many approaches currently utilizing couples' group strategies. Other initiatives have experimented with extensive self-help programs that sometimes augment and sometimes stand in for the professionally led interventions detailed above. For example, Halford has developed one of the more creative means for getting educational information to couples via something he calls a "Couple Care" package. Halford's program shares much in common with other packaged programs (such as "Marriage Moments," a supplement to childbirth classes currently being piloted in Utah hospitals and based on the ideas of Fowers, 2000). For example, it makes use of both activity guidebooks and instructional DVDs. However, the Couple Care package goes beyond such programs by also scheduling 30- to 40-minute telephone calls with professional relationship educators. These individuals review with couples the content of each unit in the workbook, help the couples clarify any ideas that they are struggling with, and assist them in identifying and implementing self-change processes.

Individually tailored approaches are exemplified by James Cordova's marital "check-up" (Cordova et al., 2005). The check-up is a brief two-session assessment and feedback intervention. Clinicians first identify concrete indicators of deterioration in the couple relationship and then set out to motivate couples to start actively attending to these concerns. In the assessment phase, each partner completes the Marital Satisfaction Inventory, the Conflict Tactics Scale, and the short version of Gottman's Oral History Interview. Couples also engage in a videotaped problem-solving discussion. After the session, clinicians review the survey, interview, and interaction data (as we reviewed "Families through Time" couples' charts and data during the case conference sessions described earlier in this book). They identify concrete warning signs (e.g., contempt or stonewalling), and present their findings to couples in a follow-up session scheduled a week or two later. Interventionists begin by summarizing the couple's relationship history and strengths, relying upon data that couples provided in the Oral History interview. They then propose two to three possible areas for improvement based on their assessment, explaining how each dovetails with research on predictors of deterioration. Couples are asked whether this feedback reconciles with their own experience; if it does, they are asked to generate ideas about how they might prevent their problem from eating away at their marriage. Clinicians follow up on positive suggestions to help the couple build their ideas into action plans. They also share their own ideas and support spontaneous requests for help-seeking if these are raised by couples. The marital check-up has not yet been used with couples making the transition to new parenthood, although the researchers have marshaled evidence that its efficacy rates rival those of interventions discussed above (e.g., Gee, Scott, Castellano, & Cordova, 2002).

Clearly, there has been no shortage of ideas about how best to deliver programs to enhance marital functioning. Field leaders have designed workshops, classes, ongoing support groups, and check-ups. They have created ancillary DVDs, CDs, Web sites, pamphlets, and other written materials. They have innovated with the use of lectures, demonstrations, role-plays, and discussions. Interventions have been delivered by male–female psychologist couples, by solo mental health professionals, by nurses, by paraprofessionals and clergy, and even by relationship educators who do their connecting with couples over the telephone—and this is truly just the tip of the iceberg. Interested readers should consult Doherty and Anderson (2004), for example, for a review and discussion of community-based marriage initiatives. The common thread is that all these initiatives aim to help couples focus on the importance of tending their relationship and improving their skill in engaging and negotiating differences between them.

The marriage education movement has truly borne fruit in recent years. Somewhat surprisingly, though, despite the widespread and extensive efforts to strengthen marriages, few professionals have trained their eyes specifically on strengthening and preventing problems in coparental relationships. Indeed, many in the field, including Doherty's group, occasionally talk about marital and coparental relationships interchangeably. This relative neglect of coparenting alliances in marital education programs is perplexing, given the seminal Cowan and Cowan finding that division of child care labor concerns, disagreements about what's best for baby, and other coparenting issues surface soon after the baby's arrival. It is even more perplexing given mounting evidence that marital distress may exert its influence on parenting (Floyd, Gilliom, & Costigan, 1998; Margolin, Gordis, & John, 2001) and on child development (Katz & Low, 2004; McHale & Rasmussen, 1998) through the impact it has on coparenting relationships. As a rule, the marital education field has been principally concerned with changing partners' perspectives and teaching them communication and negotiation skills. Improvements are then expected in men's and women's efforts as parents and as coparents, although studies have seldom systematically examined whether such improvements indeed materialize. This situation is just now beginning to change, as we discuss in the next section.

Efforts to Promote Positive Coparenting and Family Group Dynamics

The guiding thesis of this book has been that coparenting dynamics represent a unique, powerful force in families related to, but also distinct from, parenting or marital processes. The newly emerging tendencies to cooperate, support, accommodate, override, undo, undermine, rectify, and disconnect often have precipitants in parents' individual psychologies or in their relationship histories before the baby's arrival. However, their adaptation as coparents can never be fully anticipated because this adaptation is fundamentally influenced by the as-yet-unknown contributions of a third party, the baby. For this reason, relevant prevention and intervention efforts stand their greatest chance for success if they include ways to work directly with men's and women's mutual support of and coordination with one another in their new parenting roles.

Parents actually begin experimenting with these roles as coparents during the pregnancy, as revealed by our interview-based data and by those of von Klitzing, Simoni, Amsler, and Bürgin (1999), as well as the prenatal LTP enactments chronicled by Carneiro, Corboz-Warnery, and Fivaz-Depeursinge (2006). Couples, however, do not truly become coparents until they are actually engaging with their newborn in the postpartum months. The real genius of the Cowans' seminal efforts was that they recognized the importance of continuing to work preventively with couples after they had delivered the baby. Unlike childbirth education efforts, which had helped couples prepare up through (but not beyond) the moment of delivery, or more recent efforts that give parents a prenatal heads-up about early infant temperament and development, postpartum blues, and relationship change (but then leave couples to their own devices after the baby's arrival), the Cowans stayed connected with couples to help guide and support their efforts during the initial postpartum months. Other interventionists, at least those who have received funded support from grant agencies, have followed suit in recent years, and the postpartum connections seem to be critical components of preventive efforts seeking to instantiate enduring effects in new families. Even so, very few of these efforts have sought to understand the coparental dynamics brewing in the family—the very dynamics our studies find to be critically important through time.

However, there are some important exceptions, and not surprisingly, Fivaz-Depeursinge and her colleagues have been at the forefront of these efforts. Fivaz-Depeursinge, Corboz-Warney, and Keren (2004) proposed the clinical value of structured therapeutic assessments of early family relationships, and they (e.g., Fivaz-Depeursinge & Lavanchy, 2006; Keren, 2006; Ron-Miara, Sherf, & Keren, 2006), with a handful of others (Harrison, 2006; Mazzoni, Micci, Vismara, & Castellina, 2006; Philipp, 2006; Rabain & Aidane, 2006; Togliatti & Lavadera, 2006; Vizziello, Simonelli, Bighin, & Pasquato, 2006), have recently begun evaluating the LTP paradigm's utility in clinical settings. From Fivaz-Depeursinge's vantage, the point of entry for intervention in work with preverbal infants in their family must be through bodily communication and interaction occurring between the infant and her parents. Having families enact interactions, she argues cogently, makes far more sense than assigning them to talk about interactions. We ascribed to this principle in our central use of the LTP to evaluate coparenting in our study. But from an interventionist perspective, the LTP is perhaps of greatest value because it can help heighten parents' attunement to their three-way relationship. Heightened attunement can be achieved through judicious use of video feedback to promote parents' conscious awareness of parenting and coparenting behavior, in the manner described by McDonough (2004; see also Hedenbro, 1997). It can also sometimes be achieved through direct interventions with problematic patterns of interactions themselves, either as they are occurring during the session in real time (see, e.g., Fivaz-Depeursinge et al., 2004), or by prescribed take-home assignments for the period between sessions. Although they stay squarely focused on observable behaviors within the triad, Fivaz-Depeursinge and colleagues do regularly talk with parents about their own accompanying "triangular" experiences and feelings.

As discussed in chapter 4, Fivaz-Depeursinge's model also goes beyond the coparenting framework emphasized in this book. The Lausanne group's analyses touch not only on how coparenting dynamics frame the baby's development but also on how babies exert their own influence to affect ongoing family dynamics, patterns, and interactions. LTP evaluations determine whether all family members stay included in (participating) in the triadic interaction, whether everyone keeps to their roles (not interfering from their third-party role during the 2 + 1, not abstaining from engagement, not interrupting one another during the 3-together), whether the family is able to co-construct a joint focus of attention, and whether the partners are emotionally in touch with one another, or out of tune with one another. As long as all partners are participating, interventions can be focused on observed behavior. The interventionist can help to promote engagement or to draw boundaries. She can also work with parents to persist for longer periods, follow babies' leads more closely, or up- or down-regulate babies' affect. Video replays can be used to facilitate discussion of miscoordination and serve as a launching point for more detailed discussions of subjective experience. Families in which coparenting dynamics are exceptionally competitive or miscoordinated can be especially challenging. Fivaz-Depeursinge provides detailed case examples and discusses some of these challenges in several thoughtful publications (e.g., Fivaz-Depeursinge et al., 2004).

Although not yet evaluated in controlled clinical trials, Fivaz-Depeursinge's innovative contributions in charting tangible directions for systems consultations can be expected to play a major formative role in future preventive and intervention work with young families. The practice of systems consultations using the LTP has already begun to have such influence in Israel, where such consultations are being taught to professionals in a nationwide early childhood psychiatry program (Keren, Fivaz-Depeursinge, & Tyano, 2001) Although formal analysis of LTP interactions is an intricate, intensive enterprise, the kinds of coparenting and family process information elicited by the LTP and the interactions it evokes afford an important and concrete starting point for family interventionists.

Beyond Fivaz-Depeursinge's efforts, two other preventive intervention projects designed specifically to promote the early development of positive coparenting alliances are being pilot tested. Mark Feinberg, who published a thoughtful treatise on coparenting and preventive intervention in 2002, is applying the perspective he developed in his paper in a "Family Foundations" program focusing on the transition to new parenthood. As are many of the other efforts detailed in this chapter, Feinberg's intervention study is delivered in collaboration with childbirth education departments in local hospitals. It is an eight-session series of classes with half delivered before birth and half after birth. Feinberg worked to translate findings on coparenting and triadic family relations into a practical, skill-building educational experience for new parents. He is seeking to establish whether efforts to improve supportiveness and decrease conflict in coparenting relationships will foster more positive triadic interactions and warmer, more sensitive parenting behavior.

Design of the curriculum was a challenge, given that little had gone before. For example, Feinberg's intervention tries to teach couples the fine distinction between active coping tactics (e.g., avoiding a bout of hostile conflict in the presence of children, a good thing) and more prolonged withdrawal after encountering dissonance (a bad thing). Couples discuss research findings indicating that protection of infants and children from hostile interparental conflict translates into positive outcomes but that withdrawal from the couple relationship (often a signal of relationship deterioration) harkens negative outcomes for children and marriages (Cox, Paley, Payne, & Burchinal, 1999; Katz & Gottman, 1993). They also discuss how not all conflict is harmful and how constructive management of conflict can be beneficial (or at least not detrimental; Cummings & Wilson, 1999; Easterbrooks, Cummings, & Emde, 1994). Classes involve some of the couple communication and problem-solving skill training that Markman, Gottman, and other couple interventionists utilize, but the focus of discussion remains on the coparenting enterprise. Materials distributed likewise focus principally on the unique challenges of new coparenthood (e.g., issues around the division of labor). Although the focus is not on enhancing parental sensitivity or competence per se, the curriculum does attend to babies and parenting. However, even in such modules as how to foster a secure attachment, Feinberg's curriculum focuses on how parents cooperate in working to promote these goals.

This is an interesting conceptual approach, and one that much more closely approximates the goal of engaging partners around the importance and impact of coparenting solidarity. The approach is unquestionably a psychoeducational one, although Family Foundations classes interweave a combination of didactic presentation by group leaders, discussion, communication and written exercises, and videotapes of other couples discussing and sometimes dealing with problems of early coparenthood. Classes are structured by a preset curriculum, and group leaders are trained to maintain fidelity to the curriculum but also to be sensitive to participants' needs and concerns. In Feinberg's current randomized trial of Family Foundations, couples in the intervention will be compared with couples randomly assigned to a control condition and receiving services as usual. Preliminary analyses examining data from the first two cohorts of 51 intervention and control families, available at the time of this writing, suggest that the program appears to be having a positive impact on maternal symptoms of depression, on father–child relationship quality, and on the coparenting relationship (Feinberg, Kan, & Puddy, 2005).

A second study newly underway is one being conducted by Brian Doss at Texas A&M University. Doss set out to determine whether a more streamlined intervention (four sessions—two 90-minute sessions prebaby and two 90-minute sessions 3½ months after the baby has arrived) can have a meaningful impact on the emerging coparenting dynamic in families. Doss's study shares several commonalities with Feinberg's but also differs in some important respects. For example, postbirth contacts with families strive to provide some individually tailored feedback for families. Doss is also attempting to tackle the issue of whether coparenting-focused intervention is as effective or more effective in promoting coparenting solidarity than a marital education intervention. To address this latter question, he is randomly assigning couples to participate either in a coparenting-focused intervention, a marriage-focused intervention, or an information-only (control) group. The two active intervention groups will each complete the four 90-minute sessions, whereas the information-only control group will take part in just one 90-minute session before birth. All couples will also take part in evaluations during the third trimester (before the intervention) and at 1, 3, 6, and 12 months postpartum.

As Doss has conceptualized it, the information-only condition involves one individual prebirth appointment during which the couple is taught about and given a chance to discuss early infant development with a project staff member, raising any questions they may have. Couples are also given a copy of Eisenberg, Murkoff, and Hathaway's (2003) *What to Expect the First Year*, a book that focuses largely on physical, cognitive, and social development of infants but not on either marital or coparenting dynamics. Doss's marriage relationship intervention was designed to adhere to principles of integrative behavioral couple therapy (IBCT; Jacobson & Christensen, 1996). In the two sessions before the child's birth, the intervention aims to develop a relationship theme and help the couple identify ways to retain positive and restrict negative interactions after birth. In the two sessions after birth, the intervention focuses on problems surrounding the relationship theme (e.g., lack of positives or an increase in negatives) and helping the couple reconnect with each other. The clinicians delivering the intervention are instructed to remain focused on the marital relationship and issues without directly intervening in the coparenting relationship or directly modifying coparenting behavior.

By contrast, Doss's coparenting interventionists are instructed to stay focused on the anticipated and actual coparenting relationship, without venturing into territory ordinarily the province of marriage education or interventions. His protocol calls for two sessions before birth to focus on an exploration of each partner's expectations and on the completion of a mutual coparenting plan. Then in the two sessions after birth, clinicians will use the couples' responses to the coparenting measures administered during the 3-month evaluation as a basis to discuss and problem-solve any difficulties the couple experienced with their plan. They will then work with the couple to develop a revised coparenting plan for the remainder of the baby's first year. Although Doss will be gathering coparenting data as part of his outcomes assessment, he does not plan to make use of interaction data in the individualized feedback he provides to parents; parents' survey reports form the basis of the coparenting plan evaluations and updates.

There is much to admire in Doss's innovative plan, although one might reasonably wonder whether it will prove feasible to offer "marital-only" or "coparenting-only" interventions. The Cowans, for example, found that discussions of marital issues regularly crept into their parenting intervention groups, and discussions of parenting crept into their marital groups. It is even more likely that long-standing marital dynamics will enter into play during discussions of coparenting, given the regular and ongoing dialectic between the two, discussed in some detail in chapter 6. That said, however, Doss's study is a bold one that will make an interesting contribution to the literature and help pave the way for subsequent studies looking to crystallize interventions that target early coparental functioning.

Before concluding this section, we want to make the point that future studies will need to carefully assess how interventions with families exert their effects. In a small pilot project completed in one of the Worcester-area hospitals from which a number of our Families Through Time participants had been recruited, our colleague Inna Khazan (2005) offered a one-session educational module to expecting first-time parents as an add-on to their standard childbirth class curriculum. Khazan focused in her session on helping parents think ahead to changes that would be introduced to their lives by babies. She imagined that such information would help couples to adjust what may have been overly romanticized prenatal expectations and hoped that this would render them better prepared for postpartum challenges. Specifically, she predicted that less significant contrasts between imagined and actual postpartum circumstances would help parents adjust more quickly and perhaps thereby also reduce postpartum depressive symptomatology. She also wondered whether sharing this information as issues for the couple would help to promote a more cohesive early coparental alliance, although she did not offer a coparenting intervention of the sort that has been described previously in this section.

Khazan (2005) actually did detect some positive effects of her brief intervention. However, one of its unintended outcomes was that parents left her session underestimating how positive their babies would be (but estimating, more realistically than control group parents, how much they would cry and fuss). Khazan found that among women for whom there were substantial preintervention-to-postpartum expectancy violations about infant behavior, postpartum depressive symptomatology was higher only for those who had been part of a control condition (completing prenatal surveys but not completing the one-session addendum). Among mothers in the intervention condition, bigger expectancy violations did not beget increases in depressive symptomatology. Also of note, more pronounced symptoms of postpartum depression were associated with poorer 3-month coparenting quality—but again, only among families in the control group. For the intervention group, more pronounced depressive symptomatology was actually met by greater solidarity in the coparenting relationship. One interpretation of this finding is that fathers, sensitized to the early strains of new parenthood, rallied in support of their distressed partners in a manner not seen among control-group families.

We mention this study in this section both because it is one of the rare brief intervention projects that have examined or shown meaningful effects on coparental adjustment and because it highlights the value of assessing parents' prenatal expectancies. Although the expectancies that Khazan (2005) chose to emphasize in her time with parents were those about the baby and his or her anticipated impact on the family, it is conceivable that helping parents discuss and examine their expectations together may have helped model a useful process. We will know much more about the value of helping parents think and talk explicitly together about coparenting dynamics once the results are in from Doss's and Feinberg's studies. Their projects will undoubtedly help sharpen future preventive intervention efforts. In the following concluding section, we speculate on what an ideal coparenting intervention might seek to target, based both on the current state of the prevention field and on lessons we learned from parents in the study that has been the focus of this book.

Knowing What We Now Know—Where to From Here?

The Families Through Time study affirmed our working supposition that strong coparenting alliances rely both on the relationship dynamics that had characterized the couple's partnership before the baby's arrival, and on the beliefs, worldviews, and coping skills of each partner. Because both predict early coparental functioning, the most effective interventions are likely to be those that speak both to the couple's relationship and to each partner's own sensibilities, fears, and aspirations. Although it is not yet certain whether marital education per se can be expected to encourage positive coparental dynamics (for when two becomes three, relationships are a whole new ballgame), coparenting alliances should be strengthened by helping couples address blind spots in their marital relationship. For this reason, consultations with couples about the ways in which they have historically run into troubles in their relationship, and about how they get unstuck after communication has broken down for them, certainly would seem to require a place in prenatal interventions. Skill-building interventions seem especially valuable. Our own research team plans to keep its eyes continually focused on developments in the marital education literature. Debates about what works best can often be contentious, but in general couples benefit from a mutual understanding of how and when they have worked themselves into a corner and from a mutual appreciation of ways in which they can reconnect with each other when things have taken an ugly turn.

Our study also taught us that even strong marriages can founder once babies arrive on the scene. The big reason for such changes is that the emotional life of the family has itself changed dramatically. Most parents will say they were not fully prepared for the scope of the changes to their lives; not only the drop in sexual intimacy and the increase in exhaustion, worry, and ambivalence, but also the occasionally intense feelings of anger, sadness, jealousy, possessiveness, and disqualification. Many families experience an initial flood of activity and support from well-wishers followed by a sharp falling off so that the coparents find themselves largely alone as they try to balance the creation of their own individual bonds with the baby, the retention of an intimate connection with one another, and the establishment of mutually satisfying new coparenting and family routines. Just as the high moments with a new baby can be without parallel, the strains that parents often feel can seem very foreign and formidable. The individual coping skills of parents come strongly into play during these early months (and long beyond them, as well). For this reason, we believe that prenatal and postbirth interventions also need to help parents build individual self-awareness and fortify their coping capacities.

Virtually every single one of the individual parent measures we examined in this study played some role in explaining variability in concurrent and later coparental functioning. Parents who had insecure states of mind with respect to attachment had a more difficult time coconstructing a mutually supportive coparenting alliance (Talbot et al., 2006). We suspect that the difficulties that insecure parents have historically had in placing their trust in others, rooted deeply in their relationship histories, make it particularly difficult to accede responsibility for the child to the coparent, and this is precisely because sharing requires trust. Lest it seem that we are talking only about mother's unwillingness to "let father in," we point out that both mothers' and fathers' insecurity predicted coparenting difficulties, and coparenting solidarity was most adversely affected in families in which both partners were insecure. Moreover, insecure states of mind with respect to attachment interacted with marital quality, so that insecurity in combination with significant marital problems amplified coparenting risk further still (Talbot et al., 2006).

Early coparenting problems in our sample were also more pronounced in families in which mothers and fathers had expressed negative outlooks about the future family during prenatal assessments. For fathers, most telling were expressions of concern during the prenatal coparenting interviews (see chapter 3). For mothers, prenatal negativity radiated across many different measures: more significant concerns expressed during our coparenting interview, a greater discrepancy between how they imagined they would share child-care responsibilities with their partner and how they hoped it would be, and a greater perceived discrepancy between their own ideas about parenting and those of their husband. In short, many mothers (and fathers) were imagining before the baby ever arrived that they would encounter some difficulties finding their way to a mutually satisfying coparenting relationship—and they were frequently right.

Whether these concerns were borne of fear that they couldn't truly trust anyone except themselves with their baby to be, of their past experiences of being misunderstood or let down by their partner, of conscious or unconscious fears that they would replicate contentious or otherwise problematic coparenting dynamics they had lived through as children in the families they grew up in, or from a combination of these factors, the expectancy really seemed important. However, we must underscore that core expectancies are not always readily obtained from parents. We found no particularly magic question that a clinician or researcher could ask that would trigger parents' expressions of concern. Even the most distressed parents would often initially insist that they had no concerns about their partner's promise as a parent or about the couple's ability to chart a course together for their child, and relatively few parents shared concerns outright without much probing or prompting.

Most parents we interviewed required sufficient opportunity to warm up before sharing their concerns, and we were fortunate to have some skilled interviewers who afforded parents the needed space to reflect on their fears and concerns. Hence, creative thought needs to be given to the best ways to engage expectant couples in discussions of coparenting concerns. It is not clear, for example, whether group discussions would foster or hamper such explorations. Much there would ride on the safety of the group dynamic and the skill of the facilitator, and even with both conditions met, many guarded individuals may never let loose.

Besides insecure states of mind with respect to attachment and a negative outlook about the future family, a third individual trait that was especially important in predicting later coparenting successes or struggles was the parent's own ego resilience. Ego resilience, a very important construct studied by Jack and Jean Block (1980), concerns the person's ability to be flexible and tolerant, to break set and try different ideas when one fails, and to "take a hit" and bounce back without retreating or retaliating. Sounds terrific, but who among us can truly boast being such a resilient individual? Few, of course, but men and women do differ in their propensity to muster resolve and reserve under stress. Also, our data were clear that resilient fathers-to-be in particular were less likely to withdraw and more likely to stay collaboratively involved in working to consensus in coparenting discussions observed at 3 months postpartum (Elliston & McHale, 2006). Further, in families with more resilient fathers, marital distress was less likely to spill over and negatively affect the couple's coparenting relationship at 12 months postpartum (Talbot & McHale, 2004). Hence, fathers' resources appear to be particularly important assets for the developing coparental partnership.

This is important for clinicians, especially those who do not routinely work with fathers, to recognize. Ego resilience, like states of mind with respect to attachment, is a quality seeded and cultivated over the long course of a person's life. So what does it mean to say that a family with a less resilient father is one more likely to run into coparenting difficulties? As we discussed in chapter 8, this sounds rather defeatist; how can one create resilience where little has heretofore existed? Our own perspective is that the skills of the resilient person—recognizing the need for restraint, self-talk and self-soothing, evaluation of alternative options when a roadblock has been hit—are actually all imminently teachable traits. Indeed, many marital therapies informed by the Gottman and Levenson (1992) finding that men quickly lose their capacity for effective problem-solving once they have reached the boiling point (i.e., once they have become overrun by physiological arousal during heated arguments) do just such teaching. Maintaining composure during critical moments appears, in fact, to be one common denominator in much of the work we have reviewed.

Most clinicians (and parents) would agree that finding ways not to have knee-jerk reactions, become overly harsh or critical, hold a grudge, or act out in anger when slighted or wronged by the partner is what enables productive communication to continue or resume. Giving in to impulses to criticize the partner, or to shut him or her out by stonewalling or withdrawing, makes repair more difficult. A person cannot be taught, even in a time-intensive preventive intervention, to not have the cognitive and physiological reactions that they do, but they can learn to identify their own triggers and response tendencies, and such knowledge is the first step in gaining some leverage to not act out by denigrating, belittling, or stonewalling. Preventive interventions hence need to help parents become attuned to the intense, often unspoken, emotional reactions they have as marital partners and as new parents. They need to help them develop a common language for owning and talking about affronts for those times when impulses haven't been successfully arrested (because there will continue to be such times!). Also, they need to help couples devise a routinized pattern of getting together to discuss recent high and low points, as often every week as is feasible for them.

Of the points developed above, the most challenging issue to tackle will be working with couples to recognize how their own desires to do what is right for their baby may unwittingly lead them into a path of coparenting conflict. All parents, men and women, want to create a climate for their baby that optimizes the child's development. For many parents, this means fixing the things that went wrong in their own childhoods. He wants his son to be more assertive than he was. She wants their son to be a peaceful person and not to act out anger as it was acted out in her family. She wants her daughter to develop the strong social grace that somehow eluded her. He wants his daughter to excel academically so that her happiness as an adult can derive from her own career successes and not those of a partner who may fail her. As we outlined in chapter 5, even teenagers look to their future children to help resolve developmental issues with which they have struggled, often naming their future children and deciding how many sons and daughters they plan to have years before ever entering into serious romantic relationships (McHale, Loding, Blaisdell, & Lovell, 1996). The wish to do right by one's future children is so extraordinarily powerful and universal that when family life begins taking a turn in a direction different than the one wished for or planned, very strong emotions are evoked. When this happens, parents often end up working at cross-purposes, even when they both individually are striving to do what they believe best for their baby. For this reason, we do not believe that preventive interventions, even having done an exquisite job helping couples build a mutual awareness of one another's hopes and aspirations prenatally, will be able to exert meaningful long-term effects unless they also include a postbaby intervention component.

This is a supposition that needs to be tested, of course, but our sense is that even with the Cadillac of all prenatal intervention approaches, nothing readies the two-person marital subsystem for the three-person family system (and as we tried to convey in chapter 7, the same can be said for the transition from three to four!). Future research efforts may prove this notion to be wrong, of course. A hearty diet of prenatal education and skills training may equip new parents with the essential tools they need to navigate early family life with minimal follow-up. This would certainly be an ideal, cost-saving outcome and one that would enhance the likelihood of accessibility to the majority of new families through existing institutional systems and infrastructures. If postnatal interventions are needed, after all, we could potentially need an entire new skilled army of early interventionists trained to recognize and work with triadic family patterns, just at the moment when we are beginning to gain a toehold in the training of professionals to work with mother–baby dyads! In families' best interests, however, we believe it is time to call the question.

In so doing, we want to sound another note of caution. Just as we advised that there is as yet no quick and easy inroad to accessing expectant parents' concerns (founded or not) about their partner and the future coparenting relationship, we also do not yet believe we can advocate one "best," most expedient means of responsibly evaluating the family's early coparenting dynamic. The LTP, to the skilled clinician, currently stands as the most useful and relevant tool, but even here we found in our study that our ratings of coparenting during LTP interactions were not as broadly connected with other indices of coparenting as were our evaluations of coparenting following the emotionally evocative still-face challenge (see chapter 4). We found our most useful assessment for identifying father withdrawal to be the "Who Does What" discussion (Elliston & McHale, 2006), and also we uncovered, in reviewing mothers' and fathers' responses on the self-report Parenting Alliance Inventory, many unhappy parents who were not otherwise identified by any remarkable patterns during observations. Hence, early follow-ups with families ought to rely not on a single index or assessment, but on a multifaceted look at the early coparental partnership privileging both interactions and intersubjective experience. The former can be a lead-in to the latter, as Fivaz-Depeursinge's work suggests, but we would advocate for the metaphor of a "full physical" rather than the quicker "check-up" or "booster" notions popular in the current literature. Coparenting partnerships that get off on the wrong foot often continue to founder over time. For this reason, we advocate for thoughtful, multifaceted preventive interventions that maximize their pop by strengthening parents' already existing resolve to work well together to do what's right in the best interests of their baby.

Summary and Conclusions

We have covered a fair amount of ground in this chapter and attempted to sketch the broad outlines of how effective prevention and early intervention efforts with families might be composed. To summarize key points developed:

1. Prenatal interventions would benefit by targeting both interpersonal relationship dynamics and intersubjective, individually held beliefs and perspectives.
2. While marital education programs may have positive radiating effects in promoting positive coparental relationships, it may

also be necessary to target coparenting more focally (in addition to, rather than in lieu of, communication skill training).

3. Although marital interventions may ultimately be found to affect positive outcomes in the coparenting alliance, interventions that focus principally on either mother–child or father–child relationships but short-shrift coparental coordination are unlikely to have the same positive ripple effects. Coparenting interventions, however, might be expected to enhance parenting.
4. While it is important to learn about concerns parents hold about their partner or the future coparenting alliance prenatally, accessing such concerns requires careful clinical skill, and there is as yet no single fail-safe means for eliciting them, especially in the context of a blanket psychoeducational intervention.
5. Interventions should follow up with parents after the baby's arrival to continue to work preventively with the coparenting dynamic that has actually materialized.
6. As was true with prenatal interventions, postnatal interventions should target both interpersonal relationship dynamics and intrapsychic experiences and perspectives.
7. As much as possible, postnatal coparenting evaluations need to look across multiple contexts and rely upon observations, interviews, and self-reports.
8. Interventionists should thoroughly review all such data obtained during initial postpartum visits in structuring follow-through consultations. Cordova's marital check-up and Doss's evaluation and revision of a coparenting plan are examples of this model. Fivaz-Depeursinge's important writings on interaction guidance provide useful insights concerning the use of observation in such efforts.
9. With respect to timing, we can state unequivocally that a crystallized pattern of coparenting adjustment already exists by 3 months postpartum. Three months would hence be a time when interventionists could access this underlying

organization through observation, interview, and self-report (and we do recommend relying upon all three). Earlier evaluations and interventions may also be of value, though it is unclear whether core triadic patterns can reliably be accessed through observation prior to 3 months.

10. Coparenting assessments do not trump other important evaluations, such as problems in the mother–infant relationship, infant colic, feeding or sleep problems, or significant parental psychopathology or depression. All clinical contacts need necessarily continue to be sensitive to these clinical issues.

Nothing is more crucial than creating a positive early family environment for infants and toddlers. The early course of family life sets the stage for later developments, and so it is imperative that helping professionals stand ready to help parents cocreate mutually supportive alliances. Returning to the question that kicked off this chapter—who's responsible?—we question the wisdom of holding either mothers or fathers (or even both parents) individually culpable when coparenting relationships go astray. We should start with the assumption that, in every family, parents have at least somewhat different ideas about how they'd ideally wish to raise their children and aim to help both partners become aware of and help actualize one another's most dearly held aspirations. Both men and women are able to help their partners when they know their views and their sensitivities; when they broach conversations about coparenting concerns gently (but *broach* them rather than stifle them); and when they allow one another to find their own ways of working with the child, accepting, and accommodating their stylistic differences. Both men and women can also help each other by listening to one another and validating their standpoints, by appreciating both the expanse of family work and the need for alone time to replenish, by taking responsibility for shouldering work without being prodded, and by listening nondefensively when the partner has been courageous enough to share his or her sentiments that change is needed. What we learned, above all, from our couples was that regular communication was key, even when such communications made matters worse for a spell rather than better.

We learned a number of other lessons too. In the last chapter, we provide a final recounting of important themes and conclusions culled from our multiyear tour down the bumpy road of coparenthood.

References

Appleby, L., Warner, R., Whitton, A., & Faragher, B. (1997). A controlled study of fluoextine and cognitive–behavioural counseling in the treatment of postnatal depression. *British Medical Journal, 314*, 932–936.

Armstrong, K. L., Fraser, J. A., Dadds, M. R., & Morris, J. (1999). A randomized controlled trial of nurse home visiting to vulnerable families with newborns. *Journal of Pediatrics and Child Health, 35*, 237–244.

Belsky, J. (1985). Experimenting with the family in the newborn period. *Child Development, 56*, 407–414.

Belsky, J., & Volling, B. L. (1987). Mothering, fathering, and marital interaction in the family triad during infancy: Exploring family system's processes. In P W. Berman, & F. A. Pedersen (Eds.), *Men's transitions to parenthood: Longitudinal studies of early family experience* (pp. 37–63). Mahwah, NJ: Erlbaum.

Block, J. H., & Block, J. (1980). The role of ego-control and ego-resiliency in the organization of behavior. In W. A. Collins (Ed.), *Minnesota Symposium on Child Psychology* (Vol. 13, pp. 39–109). Hillsdale, NJ: Erlbaum.

Brockington, I. (1996). *Motherhood and mental health*. New York: Oxford University Press.

Brockington, I. (2004). Postpartum psychiatric disorders. *Lancet, 363*, 303–310.

Carneiro, C., Corboz-Warnery, A., & Fivaz-Depeursinge, E. (2006). The prenatal Lausanne Trilogue Play: A new observational assessment tool of the prenatal coparenting alliance. *Infant Mental Health Journal, 27*, 207–228.

Chen, C., Tseng, Y., Chou, F., & Wang, S. (2000). Effects of support group intervention in postnatally distressed women: A controlled study in Taiwan. *Journal of Psychosomatic Research, 49*(6), 395–399.

Cicchetti, D., Rogosch, F. A., & Toth, S. L. (2000). The efficacy of toddler–parent psychotherapy for fostering cognitive development in offspring. *Journal of Abnormal Child Psychology, 28*, 135–148.

Clark, R., Tluczek, A., & Wenzel, A. (2003). Psychotherapy for postpartum depression: A preliminary report. *American Journal of Orthopsychiatry, 73*, 441–454.

Cohen, N. J., Lojkasek, M., Muir, E., Muir, R., & Parker, C. J. (2002). Six-month follow-up of two mother–infant psychotherapies: Convergence of therapeutic outcomes. *Infant Mental Health Journal, 23*, 361–380.

Cohn, J. F., Campbell, S. B., Matias, R., & Hopkins, J. (1990). Face-to-face interactions of postpartum depressed and nondepressed mother–infant pairs at 2 months. *Developmental Psychology, 26*, 15–23.

Cooper, P. J., Landman, M., Tomlinson, M., Molteno, C., Swartz, L., & Murray, L. (2002). Impact of a mother–infant intervention in an indigent peri-urban South African context: Pilot study. *British Journal of Psychiatry, 180*(1), 76–81.

Cordova, J. V., Scott, R. L., Dorian, M., Mirgain, S., Yaeger, D., & Groot, A. (2005). The marriage checkup: An indicated preventive intervention for treatment-avoidant couples at risk for marital deterioration. *Behavior Therapy, 36*(4), 301–309.

Cowan, C. P., & Cowan, P. A. (1992). *When partners become parents: The big life change for couples*. New York: Basic Books.

Cowan, C. P., Cowan, P. A., & Heming, G. (2005). Two variations of a preventive intervention for couples: Effects on parents and children during the transition to school. In P. A. Cowan, C. P. Cowan, J. C. Ablow, V. K. Johnson, & J. R. Measelle (Eds.), *The family context of parenting in children's adaptation to elementary school* (pp. 277–312). Mahwah, NJ: Erlbaum.

Cox, M. J., Paley, B., Payne, C. C., & Burchinal, M. (1999). The transition to parenthood: Marital conflict and withdrawal and parent–infant interactions. In M. J. Cox & J. Brooks-Gunn (Eds.), *Conflict and cohesion in families: Causes and consequences* (pp. 87–104). Mahwah, NJ: Erlbaum.

Cramer, B. (1995). Short-term dynamic psychotherapy for infants and their parents. *Child and Adolescent Psychiatric Clinics of North America, 4*, 649–660.

Cummings, E. M., & Wilson, A. (1999). Contexts of marital conflict and children's emotional security: Exploring the distinction between constructive and destructive conflicts from the children's perspective. In M. J. Cox & J. Brooks-Gunn (Eds.), *Conflict and cohesion in families: Causes and consequences*. (pp. 105–129). Mahwah, NJ: Erlbaum.

Dennis, C. (2003). The effect of peer support on postpartum depression: A pilot randomized controlled trial. *Canadian Journal of Psychiatry, 48*(2), 115–124.

Dion, R. (2005) Healthy marriage programs: Learning what works. *The Future of Children, 15*, 139–156.

Dion, R., Devaney, B., & Hershey, A. (2003, November). *Toward interventions to strengthen relationships and support healthy marriage among unwed parents.* Manuscript prepared for *Vision 2004: What is the Future of Marriage?* and presented at the 65th Annual Conference of the National Council on Family Relations, Washington, DC.

Doherty, W. J., & Anderson, J. R. (2004). Community marriage initiatives. *Family Relations: 53*, 425–432.

Doherty, W. J., Kouneski, E. F., & Erickson, M. F. (1998). Responsible fathering: An overview and conceptual framework. *Journal of Marriage and Family, 60*, 277–292.

Doherty, W. J., Kouneski, E. F., & Erickson, M. F. (2000). We are all responsible for responsible fathering: A response to Walker and McGraw. *Journal of Marriage & the Family, 62*, 570–574.

Easterbrooks, M. A., Cummings, E. M., & Emde, R. N. (1994). Young children's responses to constructive marital disputes. *Journal of Family Psychology, 8*, 160–169.

Egger, H., Fenichel, E., Guedeney, A., Wise, B. K., & Wright, H. H. (2006). Introducing DC: 0-3R. *Zero To Three, 26*, 35–41.

Eisenberg, A., Murkoff, H., & Hathaway, S. (2003). *What to expect the first year.* New York: Workman.

Elliston, D., & McHale, J. (2006, March). *The family context of coparenting withdrawal at three months post-partum.* Paper presented at the Southeastern Psychological Association, Atlanta, GA.

Feinberg, M. (2002). Coparenting and the transition to parenthood: A framework for prevention. *Clinical Child and Family Psychology Review*, 5, 173–195.

Feinberg, M., Kan, M., & Puddy, R. (2005, May). *An intervention for new families targeting coparenting: Preliminary evidence.* Poster presented at the meeting of the Society for Prevention Research, Washington, DC.

Field, T. (1997). The treatment of depressed mothers and their infants. In L. Murray & P. J. Cooper (Eds.), *Postpartum depression and child development* (pp. 221–236). New York: Guilford Press.

Fivaz-Depeursinge, E., Corboz-Warnery, A., & Keren, M. (2004). The primary triangle: Treating infants in their families. In A. J. Sameroff, S. C. McDonough, & K. L. Rosenblum (Eds.), *Treating parent–infant relationship problems: Strategies for intervention* (pp. 123–151). New York: Guilford Press.

Fivaz-Depeursinge, E., & Lavanchy, C. (2006, July). *A trial intervention in a family therapeutic assessment based on the Lausanne Trilogue Play paradigm.* Paper presented at the 10th World Congress of the World Association for Infant Mental Health, Paris.

Floyd, F. J., Gilliom, L. A., & Costigan, C. L. (1998). Marriage and the parenting alliance: Longitudinal prediction of change in parenting perceptions and behaviors. *Child Development, 69*, 1461–1479.

Fowers, B. J. (2000). *Beyond the myth of marital happiness: How embracing the virtues of loyalty, generosity, justice, and courage can strengthen your relationship*. San Francisco: Jossey-Bass.

Fraiberg, S. (1980). Clinical assessment of the infant and his family. *Clinical studies in infant mental health* (pp. 23–48). New York: Basic Books.

Fraiberg, S., Adelson, E., & Shapiro, V. (1975). Ghosts in the nursery. *Journal of the Academy of Child Psychiatry, 14*, 387–421.

Frank, S. J., Olmstead, C. L., Wagner, A. E., & Laub, C. C. (1991). Child illness, the parenting alliance, and parenting stress. *Journal of Pediatric Psychology, 16*, 361–371.

Gee, C. B., Scott, R. L., Castellano, A. M., & Cordova, J. V. (2002). Predicting 2-year marital satisfaction from partners' discussion of their marriage checkup. *Journal of Marital & Family Therapy, 28*(4), 399–407.

Gordon, R. E., & Gordon, K. K. (1960). Social factors in prevention of postpartum emotional problems. *Obstetrics and Gynecology, 15*, 433–437.

Gottman, J. (1994). *Why marriages succeed or fail*. New York: Simon & Schuster.

Gottman, J., Carrère, S., Swanson, C., & Coan, J. A. (2000). Reply to "From Basic Research to Interventions." *Journal of Marriage and Family, 62*(1), 265–273.

Gottman, J. M., & Levenson, R. W. (1992). Marital processes predictive of later dissolution: Behavior, physiology, and health. *Journal of Personality and Social Psychology, 63*, 221–233.

Hackel, L. S., & Ruble, D. N. (1992, June). Changes in the marital relationship after the first baby is born: Predicting the impact of expectancy disconfirmation. *Journal of Personality and Social Psychology, 62*, 944–957.

Hafen, M. J., & Crane, D. R. (2003). When marital interaction and intervention researchers arrive at different points of view: The active listening controversy. *Journal of Family Therapy, 25*(1), 4–14.

Halford, W. K., Markman, H. J., Kline, G. H., & Stanley, S. M. (2003). Best practice in couple relationship education. *Journal of Marital & Family Therapy, 29*(3), 385–406.

Halford, W. K., O'Donnell, C., Lizzio, A., & Wilson, K. L. (2006). Do couples at high risk of relationship problems attend premarriage education? *Journal of Family Psychology, 20*, 160–163.

Halford, W. K., & Simons, M. (2005). Couple relationship education in Australia. *Family Process, 44*(2), 147–159.

Harrison, A. (2006, July). Use *of the LTP in a parent consulation model*. Paper presented at the 10th World Congress of the World Association for Infant Mental Health, Paris.

Hawkins, A., Bradford, K., Palkovitz, R., Christiansen, S., Day, R., & Call, V. (2002). The Inventory of Father Involvement: A pilot study of a new measure of father involvement. *The Journal of Men's studies, 10*, 183–196.

Hawkins, A. J., & Dollahite, D. C. (Eds.). (1997). Beyond the role-inadequacy perspective of fathering. *Generative fathering: Beyond deficit perspectives* (pp. 3–16). New York: Sage.

Hawkins, A. J., Gilliland, T., Christiansens, G., & Carroll, J. S. (2002). Integrating marriage and education into perinatal education. *Journal of Perinatal Education, 11*(4), 1–10.

Hawkins, A. J., & Roberts, T. (1992). Designing a primary intervention to help dual-earner couples share housework and child care. *Family Relations, 41*, 169–177.

Hedenbro, M. (1997). Interaction, the key to life: Seeing possibilities of children through video pictures. *The Signal, 5*, 9–15.

Heinicke, C. M., Fineman, N. R., Ruth, G., Recchia, S.L., Guthrie, D., & Rodning, C. (1999). Relationship-based intervention with at-risk mothers: Outcome in the first year of life. *Infant Mental Health Journal, 20*, 349–374.

Hofferth, S. L. (1998). *Report on 1997 data collection for the PSID child development supplement*. Retrieved April 25, 1999, from www.isr.umich.edu.src/child-development/home.html

Holden, J. M., Sagovsky, R., & Cox, J. L. (1989). Counseling in a general practice setting: Controlled study of health visitor intervention in treatment of postnatal depression. *British Medical Journal, 298*, 223–226.

Honey, K. L., Bennett, P., & Morgan, M. (2002). A brief psycho-educational group intervention for postnatal depression. *British Journal of Clinical Psychology, 41*, 405–409.

Jacobson, N., & Christensen, A. (1996). *Integrative Couple Therapy: Promoting acceptance and change*. New York: Norton.

Jordan, P., Stanley, S., & Markman, H. (1999). *Becoming parents*. San Francisco: Jossey-Bass.

Katz, L. F., & Gottman, J. (1993). Patterns of marital conflict predict children's internalizing and externalizing behaviors. *Developmental Psychology*, 29, 940–950.

Katz, L. F., & Gottman, J. M. (1996). Spillover effects of marital conflict: In search of parenting and coparenting mechanisms. *New Directions for Child Development, 74*, 57–76.

Katz, L. F., & Low, S. M. (2004). Marital violence, co-parenting, and family-level processes in relation to children's adjustment. *Journal of Family Psychology, 18*, 372–382.

Keren, M. (2006, July). *Using the Lausanne Trilogue play paradigm in an infant mental health clinic*. Paper presented at the 10th World Congress of the World Association for Infant Mental Health, Paris.

Keren, M., Fivaz-Depeursinge, E., & Tyano, S. (2001). Using the Lausanne family model in training: An Israeli experience. *The Signal, 93*, 1–7.

Khazan, I. (2005). *Expectations-based intervention as a tool to reduce severity of postpartum depression and improve coparenting*. Unpublished doctoral dissertation, Clark University.

Lamb, M. E. (2004). Fathering in America: New challenges and champions. Retrieved June 24, 2006, from *PsycCRITIQUES*.

Lamb, M. E., Pleck, J. H., Charnov, E. L., & Levine, J. A. (1987). A biosocial perspective on paternal behavior and involvement. In J. B. Lancaster, J. Altmann, A. S. Rossi, & L. R. Sherrod (Eds.), *Parenting across the life span: Biosocial dimensions* (pp. 111–142). New York: Aldine de Gruyter.

Lieberman, A. F., Weston, D. R., & Pawl, J. H. (1991). Preventive intervention and outcome with anxiously attached dyads. *Child Development, 62*, 199–209.

Lyons-Ruth, K., Zoll, D., Connell, D., & Grunebaum, H. U. (1986). The depressed mother and her one-year-old infant: Environment, interaction, attachment, and infant development. *New Directions for Child Development, 34*, 61–82.

Margolin, G., Gordis, E. B., & John, R. S. (2001). Coparenting: A link between marital conflict and parenting in two-parent families. *Journal of Family Psychology, 15*, 3–21.

Markman, H., Stanley, S., & Blumberg, S. (2001). *Fighting for your marriage (revised and updated edition)*. San Francisco: Jossey-Bass.

Markman, H. J., Renick, M. J., Floyd, F. J., & Stanley, S. M. (1993). Preventing marital distress through communication and conflict management training: A 4- and 5-year follow-up. *Journal of Consulting and Clinical Psychology, 61*, 70–77.

Matthey, S., & Barnett, B. (1999). Parent–infant classes in the early postpartum period: Need and participation by fathers and mothers. *Infant Mental Health Journal, 20*, 278–290.

Mazzoni, S., Micci, A., Vismara, L., & Castellina, I. (2006, July). *Clinical LTP: From assessment to planning parents–children psychotherapy*. Paper presented at the 10th World Congress of the World Association for Infant Mental Health, Paris.

McBride, B. A. (1990). The effect of a parent education/play group program on father involvement in child rearing. *Family Relations, 39*, 250–256.

McBride, B. A. (1991). Parent education and support programs for fathers: Outcome effects on paternal involvement. *Early Child Development and Care, 67*, 73–85.

McBride, B. A., & Mills, G. (1993). A comparison of mother and father involvement with their preschool age children. *Early Childhood Research Quarterly, 8*, 457–477.

McDonough, S. C. (1995). Promoting positive early parent–infant relationships through interaction guidance. *Child and Adolescent Psychiatric Clinics of North America, 4*, 661–672.

McDonough, S. C. (2004). Interaction guidance: Promoting and nurturing the caregiving relationship. In A. J. Sameroff, S. C. McDonough, & K. L. Rosenblum (Eds.), *Treating parent–infant relationship problems: Strategies for intervention.* (pp. 79–96). New York: Guilford Press.

McHale, J. (2007). When infants grow up in multiparent relationship systems. *Infant Mental Health Journal, 28*(4).

McHale, J. P., & Alberts, A. E. (2003). Thinking three: Coparenting and family level considerations for infant mental health professionals. *The Signal, 11*, 1–11.

McHale, J. P., Loding, B., Blaisdell, B., & Lovell, S. (1996, August). *Conceptions of parenting and coparenting among college-aged students*. Paper presented at a meeting of the American Psychological Association, Toronto, Ontario, Canada.

McHale, J. P., & Rasmussen, J. L. (1998). Coparental and family group-level dynamics during infancy: Early family precursors of child and family functioning during preschool. *Development and Psychopathology, 10*(1), 39–59.

Misri, S., Kostaras, X., Fox, D., & Kostaras, D. (2000). The impact of partner support in the treatment of postpartum depression. *Canadian Journal of Psychiatry, 45*, 554–558.

Murray, L., Cooper, P. J., Wilson, A., & Romaniuk, H. (2003). Controlled trial of the short- and long-term effects of psychological treatment of postpartum depression: 2. Impact on the mother–child relationship and child outcome. *British Journal of Psychiatry, 182*, 420–427.

Myers, B. J. (1982). Early intervention using Brazelton training with middle-class mothers and fathers of newborns. *Child Development, 53*, 462–471.

O'Hara, M. (1997). The nature of postpartum depressive disorders. In L. Murray & P. J. Cooper (Eds.), *In postpartum depression and child development* (pp. 3–31). London: Guilford Press.

O'Hara, M. W., Stuart, S., Gorman, L. L., & Wenzel, A. (2000). Efficacy of interpersonal therapy for postpartum depression. *Archives of General Psychiatry, 57*, 1039–1045.

Olds, D. L., Henderson, C. R., Phelps, C., Kitzman, H., & Hanks, C. (1993). Effect of prenatal and infancy nurse home visitation on government spending. *Medical Care, 31*, 155–174.

Olds, D. L., Henderson, C. R., Tatelbaum, R., & Chamberlin, R. (1986). Improving the delivery of prenatal care and outcomes of pregnancy: A randomized trial of nurse home visitation. *Pediatrics, 77*(1), 16–28.

Olds, D. L., & Kitzman, H. (1993). Review of research on home visiting for pregnant women and parents of young children. *Future of Children, 3*(3), 53–92.

Palkovitz, R. (1997). Reconstructing "involvement": Expanding conceptualizations of men's caring in contemporary families. In A. J. Hawkins & D. C. Dollahite (Eds.), *Generative fathering: Beyond deficit perspectives* (pp. 200–216). New York: Sage.

Palkovitz, R. (2002). *Involved fathering and men's adult development: Provisional balances*. Mahwah, NJ: Erlbaum.

Phares, V. (1996). *Fathers and developmental psychopathology*. Oxford, England: Wiley.

Philipp, D. (2006, July). *Brief family therapy with very young children*. Paper presented at the 10th World Congress of the World Association for Infant Mental Health, Paris.

Pleck, J. H. (1997). Paternal involvement: Levels, sources, and consequences. In M. E. Lamb (Ed.), *The role of the father in child development* (3rd ed., pp. 66–103). Hoboken, NJ: Wiley.

Rabain, D., & Aidane, E. (2006, July). *Using the Lausanne trilogue play as a clinical assessment procedure*. Paper presented at the 10th World Congress of the World Association for Infant Mental Health, Paris.

Robert-Tissot, C., Cramer, B., Stern, D. N., & Serpa, S. R. (1996). Outcome evaluation in brief mother–infant psychotherapies: Report on 75 cases. *Infant Mental Health Journal, 17*(2), 97–114.

Ron-Miara, A., Sherf, R., & Keren, M. (2006, July). *The links between infant's symptoms and diagnoses and the family alliance.* Paper presented at the 10th World Congress of the World Association for Infant Mental Health, Paris.

Schoppe-Sullivan, S. J., McBride, B. A., & Ho, M. R. (2004). Unidimensional versus multidimensional perspectives on father involvement. *Fathering, 2*, 147–163.

Schulz, M. S., Cowan, C. P., & Cowan, P. A. (2006). Promoting healthy beginnings: A randomized controlled trial of a preventive intervention to preserve marital quality during the transition to parenthood. *Journal of Consulting and Clinical Psychology, 74*, 20–31.

Shapiro, A. F., & Gottman, J. M. (2005). Effects on marriage of a psycho-communicative-educational intervention with couples undergoing the transition to parenthood, evaluation at 1-year postintervention. *Journal of Family Communication, 5*, 1–24.

Shapiro, A., Gottman, J., & Carrére, S. (2000). The baby and the marriage: Identifying factors that buffer against decline in marital satisfaction after the first baby arrives. *Journal of Family Psychology, 14*, 59–70.

Silliman, B., Stanley, S. M., Coffin, W., Markman, H. J., & Jordan, P. L. (2002). Preventive interventions for couples. In H. A. Liddle, D. A. Santisteban, R. F. Levant, & J. H. Bray (Eds.), *Family psychology: Science-based interventions* (pp. 123–146). Washington, DC: American Psychological Association.

Stanley, S. M., Blumberg, S. L., & Markman, H. J. (1999). Helping couples fight for their marriages: The PREP approach. In R. Berger & M. T. Hannah (Eds.), *Preventive approaches in couples therapy* (pp. 279–303). New York: Brunner/Mazel.

Stanley, S. M., Bradbury, T. N., & Markman, H. J. (2000). Structural flaws in the bridge from basic research on marriage to interventions for couples. *Journal of Marriage & the Family, 62*(1), 256–264.

Stern, D. N. (2004). The motherhood constellation: Therapeutic approaches to early relational problems. In A. J. Sameroff, S. C. McDonough, & K. L. Rosenblum (Eds.), *Treating parent–infant relationship problems: Strategies for intervention* (pp. 29–42). New York: Guilford Press.

Talbot, J., Elliston, D., Thompson, J., Scull, C., Lieberson, R., & McHale, J. (2006, July). *Do early coparenting dynamics benefit from coherent states of mind with respect to attachment?* Paper presented at the 10th World Congress of the World Association for Infant Mental Health, Paris.

Talbot, J. A., & McHale, J. P. (2004). Individual parental adjustment moderates the relationship between marital and coparenting quality. *Journal of Adult Development, 11*(3), 191–205.

Tamis-Lemonda, C. S., & Cabrera, N. (2002). Handbook of father involvement: Multidisciplinary perspectives. *Family Therapy, 29*, 193–193.

Togliatti, M., & Lavadera, L. (2006, July). *The evaluation of family alliances with conflictual families*. Paper presented at the 10th World Congress of the World Association for Infant Mental Health, Paris, France.

Vizziello, G., Simonelli, A., Bighin, M., & Pasquato, S. (2006, July). *The use of the LTP in parental difficulties: When, why, where by whom?* Paper presented at the 10th World Congress of the World Association for Infant Mental Health, Paris.

von Klitzing, K., Simoni, H., Amsler, F., & Bürgin, D. (1999). The role of the father in early family interactions. *Infant Mental Health Journal, 20*(3), 222–237.

Walker, A. J., & McGraw, L. A. (2000). Who is responsible for responsible fathering? *Journal of Marriage and Family, 62*, 563–569.

Weissman, M. M., & Olfson, M. (1995). Depression in women: Implications for health care research. *Science, 269*(5225), 799–801.

Wesner, D., Dowling, J., & Johnson, F. (1962). What is maternal-infant intervention? The role of infant psychotherapy. *Psychiatry, 45*, 307–315.

Wickberg, B., & Hwang, C. P. (1996). Counselling of postnatal depression: A controlled study on a population-based Swedish sample. *Journal of Affective Disorders, 39*, 209–216.

Winnicott, D. W. (1957). The capacity to be alone. *In The maturational process and the facilitating environment.* New York: International Universities Press.

ZERO TO THREE. (2005). Diagnostic classification of mental health and developmental disorders of infancy and early childhood: Revised edition (DC:0–3R). Washington, DC: ZERO TO THREE.

Our Families Through Time

There are countless books available to families concerning "best practices" for raising children. There are as many or more guidebooks, handbooks, and encyclopedias available for helping professionals, and there is the conventional wisdom passed down within families that is often the most sage advice of all. With all of this information readily accessible to parents and practitioners, it is difficult to sum up concisely how or why a book of this nature was needed on the scene at all. If we had to sum it all up in just one essential soundbyte, the bottom-line message from this multiyear, intensive, and extensive undertaking would be just this: Children profited when their mothers and fathers were working together as parents, and they struggled when they were not. The clinicians and family scholars who had introduced and promulgated family systems theories long before the "Families Through Time" study had ever been conceived had advised us that this might be the case, of course. Also, the parents who contributed to our study themselves told us of ways in which they believed coparental divisiveness in their own families of origin had affected them as they were growing up. Not surprisingly, then, the prospective longitudinal data from our study confirmed that toddlers faring the best at 30 months were indeed those whose parents had come upon ways to navigate and accommodate their differences in parenting views, ideologies, and styles.

None of this may come as much of a surprise to readers. Still, even we were impressed by just how early coherent coparenting adjustment patterns had begun taking shape, by how stable coparenting adjustment proved to be over time, and by how many different realms of child adjustment were ultimately linked to coparental functioning. Something else struck us as well. Although we had fully expected to find that coparenting solidarity would be an important force, resource, and bastion within families, we underestimated how hard-won such solidarity would actually be in so many families and how elusive it would prove to be for others even despite their best intentions. Indeed, disequilibrium was common even among a number of the families in which couples had been working quite well as a team before babies came along. As it turned out, making room for children in the emotional world of couples was never without some challenge. Jerry Lewis, Martha Cox, and their associates (e.g., Lewis, 1989; Lewis, Owen, & Cox, 1988) had hinted that this would be so back in the 1980s; something inevitably has to give, and couples find themselves drifting farther and farther from their familiar patterns as new family routines begin to take firm hold in the early days, weeks, and months of new parenthood.

Furthermore, with their new baby at home, the annoyance and frustration that parents found themselves experiencing (and recognizing in their partners) surprised them and at times felt quite childish to them. The ambivalent feelings they identified sometimes frightened them. The established patterns of arguing out relationship issues that they knew quite intimately suddenly took new turns with a baby on the scene to provide diversions, often preventing them from reconciling as regularly as they used to before the baby's arrival. And . . . these were occurrences that were common in well adjusting families! In couples already struggling, babies frequently provided welcome short-term respite from couple tensions and reason not to embark on difficult discussions together. In the short run, this diversion often provided a stabilizing force in families. Over the longer term, however, many babies in detouring family systems became party to more problematic family patterns and dynamics, and significant difficulties for the child and the family were often not far off. Indeed, of perhaps the greatest pertinence both to parents and to professionals, our data indicated that early coparenting problems were sustained and often intensified over the course of the study. They did not simply typically wane and ultimately disappear with the passage of time, as health care professionals are wont to promise parents. Instead, our data revealed that, as children aged, coparenting difficulties frequently became more pervasive and more complex. And ultimately, we found, such problems came to impress upon children in one or more developmentally relevant ways.

From the very beginning of this book, we have emphasized that what our study sought to provide was a characterization of the early coparenting landscape in families but that our results do not put us in any direct position to provide a foolproof set of directions for navigating this landscape. As we note at the conclusion of this chapter, even couples themselves did not concur that there was any one best route. As they told us, many of the choice points that they approached turned out to have been fraught with potential for wrong turns. For example, parents sometimes discussed their regret over mothers having decided to stay home rather than return to work as planned, in response to the baby having proven to be more demanding than they had anticipated. The reverse was also true; other parents wanted to take back decisions they had made to work swing shifts or to embark on new business ventures that kept them away from the baby and the family during formative periods. As babies grew and began making new demands, parents also routinely faced decisions about whether and how to accommodate their partner's inclinations or whether to insist that things be done their own way. As we discovered, the parents in our study—almost to a person—did in fact have clear ideas about the type of environment they most wanted to create for their children and the methods of intervention they thought would be most likely to help mold the kind of child they most wished to have. This was rather fascinating; during the pregnancy, such expectations were seldom yet in full (or even partial) voice. Indeed, a number of fathers had little to say beyond that they expected their partners to be excellent parents. Once they were actively parenting, however, it was far easier to solicit clearly articulated opinions. Among the subset of parents who did express clear-cut views during the pregnancy about what they believed would be best for their children, their stances often stemmed directly from positive life experiences, family, or cultural prescriptions. Just as frequently, though, they were borne of the parent's tenacious determination about what not to do, from negative experiences they had had in their own families of origin.

The main point is that parents inevitably had notions about what they thought would be best for their children, and why they believed this to be so. As our study progressed, we saw some parents adhere to these beliefs unwaveringly long after the baby's arrival, defending their perspectives with grim determination. Anti-spanking stances were an example of such an unwavering belief among some parents. Insistence on not "parentifying" the child was another; determination not to force the child to grow up too quickly, yet another. Other parents maintained more of a "play it by ear" attitude both during the pregnancy and after the baby's arrival and were willing to try new things when old approaches didn't work well. However, it's important to make a critical distinction here. Periodically throughout this book, we (following suit with many seasoned scholars in our field) have made reference to parenting as a set of practices, guided by a set of beliefs. Conceptualizing parenting in this way badly obscures the reality that other very powerful forces underlie and drive what mothers and fathers ultimately find themselves doing with their children. Beneath those parenting beliefs and behaviors lies a powerful emotional system prompting parents to act as they do to satisfy thirsts for closeness and intimacy. It impells them to act in accordance with lessons learned about relationships from their own attachment histories and experiences and fuels their quest to conquer and master their own childhood experiences of hurt and exclusion through sought-after successes of children (Cassidy, Woodhouse, & Hoffman, 2006). Also, it drives their oft-unacknowledged desires to attain a measure of immortality by creating children who will carry forward important legacies and succeed in creating even better ones. This emotional underworld of fears, wishes, and dreams is rarely spoken about by parents, but it is every bit as much a source of parenting activities as is the more readily accessible belief set that it fuels. We believe that it is this emotional system that parents need to get in touch with and ultimately process with one another if they are to work most successfully and collaboratively as coparents.

The big question for most parents is the same as it is for all adults: What would happen if you were to share your wishes, dreams, and fears and not have them validated by your partner? For example, parents may worry that if they were to reveal their strong negative reactions when their partners tease their son or daughter and confess their own upsetting childhood experiences of having been teased, their partners might respond in a disqualifying or derisive manner, pouring further salt into the wound. When parents maintain this concern, their response, instead of confiding in their partners to try to alter the dynamic that disturbs them, may be to work on their own to fortify the child's sense of potency and self-worth immediately after each teasing episode. Thus, the pattern that develops becomes one of one parent goading, the other soothing, and the child becoming an unwitting party in this coparenting shuffle. Even when the wellspring for parenting decisions is not as emotionally charged, the choice to stand by a partner's intervention with the child when it stands at odds with one's own requires a powerful leap of trust and confidence. Such trust and confidence may be a prime reason why we uncovered several meaningful associations between coparenting and men's ego resilience; more resilient fathers may have been more apt to accept the mother's lead and to let her establish parenting routines and ground rules without casting aspersions on her decision-making abilities, even when things weren't working well. They may also have been better able to introduce their own perspectives and ideas in a manner that respected, rather than challenged, mothers' efforts. Dienhart and Daly (1997) have described similarly tolerant and giving attitudes among mothers who find ways to support fathers' early parenting efforts with children.

Parents, of course, seldom think or talk about coparenting collaboration in quite this way during the earliest days and weeks of new parenthood. From their perspectives, mothers and fathers are simply working night and day to develop routines that keep the baby happy and that allow the two of them at least some down time. Even during the first postpartum months, important decisions about discontinuing efforts to breast feed and going to the bottle, ditching the bassinette at night and bringing baby to bed to sleep between mother and father, or reconsidering a once firm decision on the mother's return to work can evoke intense emotional reactions. As we learned, in many families these reactions may never get discussed at any length by parents, leading to their intensification over time. If parents do not begin early on to voice their views about important parenting matters on which they hold opposing views, then down the road their disputes over such seemingly trivial issues as how to manage a centipede's surprise appearance in the baby's play area or how long to prolong a battle over getting dressed can trigger disquietingly intense negative reactions in one or both parents. It is such intensification of unvoiced negative feelings that, unless discussed sensitively and respectfully by the parents, can come to fuel one or both parent's disengagement from active parenting collaboration and/or disparate socialization and disciplinary strivings by the two parents.

It is important to emphasize once again that family life is replete with many small moments of disagreement and resolution or impasse every day. Every reader is likely to see themselves and their partnership represented somewhere in the issues described in these pages. No single event individually reveals all that much of what we ultimately need to know about the coparenting alliance developing within the family. Collectively, however, such moments do come to coalesce into an overall experience of working in tandem or working at odds. It is this core sense and spirit that professionals need to access and reckon with if they are to help families regain their footing once it has been lost. Our experience in this study suggested that professionals have different inroads to tap into the solidarity of the coparenting alliance. They might rely upon semistructured observations of the parents simultaneously playing, teaching, comforting, and parenting together; upon interviews with parents that ask directly about their alliance; or upon questionnaires that can be used to open discussions with parents about the degree of support they experience from their parenting partner or about the divergence in their parenting ideologies. However, our experience also taught us that no specific index is ever able to capture or reveal all that is important, and therefore multiple assessments of coparenting adjustment would undoubtedly be the most responsible approach.

In one regard, it is probably sufficient just to know whether one parent is experiencing distress or feeling devalued or not supported. That person's unhappiness is likely to ultimately fuel problems at other levels as well. Having said this, it is equally important to remind interventionists that eliciting such feelings takes considerable sensitivity, tact, and patience. A great many of the parents in our study worked very hard to place and to maintain a positive spin on family matters in their lives. Such individuals were typically quite reticent to openly criticize their partner, even when our observations of the family process convinced us that the couple and their coparenting alliance were indeed struggling. In working with such individuals and families, we concur with Fivaz-Depeursinge et al. (2004) that video feedback can be an unparalleled tool to help couples visualize their process and gain access to accompanying feelings of being excluded, ignored, interfered with, or disqualified.

We've written this book with professionals in mind, but without question our main intended audience has been parents themselves. Branching out from the big-picture conclusions drawn in chapter 8, what final nuggets would we offer to parents from what we learned, as suggestions for putting into practice themselves?

We have a few ideas and encouragements with which we'd like to close this book.

During the Pregnancy: Thinking and Planning Ahead

First, one of the more startling discoveries of our study was that parents rarely spend time thinking and talking about coparenting their child before the baby's arrival. In our study, it was very common for parents to tell us, even a few weeks before their baby was due, that they had really never spoken with their partner at all about parenting perspectives and ideologies, let alone how they might coparent together and resolve differences between them once the baby arrived. Most had discussed a few big-picture issues such as decorating and setting up the baby's room, the mother's planned return to work, and even setting up college trusts. Many had also agreed, at least implicitly, that fathers would take active responsibility for feedings and changings (although others had never had such discussions—recall the very disparate views of Ron and Candice from the beginning of chapter 3). But even when parents had discussed generalities, few had spoken in much detail about how they envisioned actually raising the baby. In fact, many expectant parents told us how challenging they found the completion of the Ideas About Parenting survey, which asked them to provide their own ideas about parenting and then what they believed their partner's ideas to be. Our data indicated that they were indeed wrong as often or more often than they were right in making these estimations about their partners' views. So predominant was this pattern, in fact, that we came to wonder why it might be that expectant couples do not share with one another their personally held hopes and aspirations for the baby, beyond the general goal of providing a loving and secure home environment.

One reason might be that people often think of and talk about parenting in terms of actions—feeding, changing, playing—and in terms of guiding philosophies. For example, many parents pondering how they'd wish to raise their child may say only that they simply want their child to be happy and that they'll support whatever paths she chooses. Who could find fault with such a perspective?

The issue, however, is that parents rarely look ahead to why they might be likely to endorse certain choices and to reject others, faced with important decision points. To take a very common example that we've raised at various times throughout this book, couples rarely pondered, "If she has a hard time adjusting to sleeping in the crib in her room, what will we do? Will we bring her into our room and make a place for her next to our bed? Will we put her in our bed and let her sleep next to us? What if we decide to let her sleep with us, but then one of us begins feeling that it isn't a good idea? Will we be able to talk about this and reverse our field if need be?" It's really quite difficult, if not impossible, to anticipate such scenarios or to know how one will respond in the heat of the moment. Nonetheless, our sense after completing this study is that it would be beneficial and instructive for expectant parents to have an idea about whether they and their partner are entering into parenthood with radically dissonant views on such topics as how long to let babies fuss while settling, co-sleeping, equal turns in addressing the baby's middle-of-the-night needs, use of babysitters during the early months, and so forth.

How to broach topics of parenting and coparenting difference? One possibility is that parents could get engaging conversations started simply by sharing their views about the kinds of items sampled by instruments such as the Ideas About Parenting survey. The Cowans used such instruments as triggers for discussion in their work with couples during the transition to parenthood (Schulz, Cowan, & Cowan, 2006), and the kinds of topics raised (e.g., "fathers have a special knack for raising sons," "babies should be left to cry it out when they are fussy") can lead to more meaningful discussions about the source and depth of belief systems. Among all our findings, we were particularly struck by the long-term connection between more substantial differences in men's and women's ideas about parenting during the pregnancy and lower levels of coparenting solidarity assessed far down the road, when children were 30 months old. Parents' prebaby notions about how they would ideally wish to raise their child had staying power and prognostic value, so parenting views actually were accessible even before the baby arrived. When such views were quite different than those maintained by their partner, difficulties often arose down the road. This may seem less surprising when considering the kinds of items contributing to prediction of coparenting problems during the terrible twos—items such as "I like to see a child have opinions and express them, even to adults," and "Although it's not always easy to do, the best way of handling a temper tantrum is to ignore it."

Students taking undergraduate classes in clinical psychology often ask their instructors whether it's wise to probe about sensitive issues during initial assessment sessions, for fear that doors may get opened that would be better left closed. In other words, if someone's struggling already, why touch off some potentially new problem area by broaching something negative that the person hadn't yet even contemplated? The answer to that question, of course, is that if a negative escalation began simply by asking about something, then it was a good thing to have asked so that the interventionist can know the depths of the problem and help provide the kind of support the person needs to deal with the deeper issues. What happens, however, if a couple begins discussing similarities and differences in parenting philosophies before the baby's arrival? In contrast to the clinical situation, no interventionist is on call if the couple comes to realize that they do differ but cannot reconcile their deeply rooted beliefs about what would and wouldn't be in baby's best interests. In this situation, we would imagine that parents could find benefit in either the shorter term marital workshops now proliferating in communities or in referrals that might follow from such workshops. Many communities also boast infant mental health professionals versed in family work, though many other communities suffer without. It is our belief that this research study solidifies the case that such infant–family mental health professionals are not only essential but critical players in comprehensive systems of care universally available to all family systems in all communities. In the meantime, parents must not fear and avoid discussions of parenting beliefs and values because of worries that their views may turn out to be in conflict. Just getting a dialogue started will help launch a critically important coparenting conversation that will need to continue for at least the next 2 decades.

Before moving ahead, it is worthy of mention that several of the parents in our study did divulge some of the interesting prebaby conversations that they had gotten into, often triggered by their just kidding around. Jeremy, for example, told us of a productive conversation that he and Kim had had after his surprisingly strong reaction to Kim's comment that "With all this classical music he's been listening to in the womb, he'll probably grow up to be a concert pianist." Jeremy said his first gut reaction was, "If he becomes a piano-playing boy, he's going to get beaten up all the time by the other boys." Kim had been surprised to find out that Jeremy equated piano playing with being feminine, and the two parents got started on some prolonged conversations concerning their views about gender roles and how strongly Jeremy felt about their role in steering their son away from what he considered to be feminine activities. Jeremy recognized his bias and even apologized for it. He also said that philosophically, he believed that all kids should be treated the same and afforded the same opportunities; he couldn't imagine standing for the couple's daughter (if they were ever to have one) being the victim of gender bias. With that said, however, when it came down to it, he saw it as the couple's job as parents to help equip their son with an unambiguously masculine self-identity, and he believed that the route he and Kim should follow in doing so was promoting "boy" activities and steering their son away from "girl" activities.

Jeremy was courageous in voicing a belief set that many fathers hold but never verbalize. Gender role socialization is just one of the many issues about which parents feel strongly, whatever their views: proper ways of handling peer conflict, the value and importance of becoming a good rule-follower, the value and importance of being a free spirit, the timing and permissibility of access to toys such as pretend guns and fashion model dolls, perspectives on sleepovers, views about dating—the list goes on and on. Parents' views about all of these issues, and many more, have very deep and strong roots. We rather doubt that discussing belief differences during the pregnancy will probably do much to dampen the tenacity of the parents' personally held views several years down the road. Rather, they are likely to resurface with renewed vigor just as soon as the child encounters such evocative life experiences as teasing, encouragement from agemates to engage in play that is more mature than parents themselves have allowed, and so forth. However, if the couple has become aware that they actually hold disparate views on handling such issues (which would not be at all unusual), they will have begun the process of moving toward a shared, mutually accommodated parenting stance.

We emphasize again here that such conversations rarely come naturally or easily. Indeed, in a subgroup of our expectant couples, they had been avoided altogether. In extreme cases, the perspectives of the two parents were so different and/or fraught with pessimism that it was hard to imagine that the couple would make an easy transition to new parenthood. The problem was not just that the parents were in very different places; as we've indicated, very few of the "Families Through Time" parents held fully symmetrical views about parenting. Rather, it was that the parents were in very different places and they didn't seem to know how to begin the process of reconciling. Communication about parenting has its roots in communication about other important relationship issues, and it was undoubtedly for this reason that prenatal marital adjustment was itself strongly prognostic of early coparental adjustment.

After the Baby Arrives: Building a Coparenting Alliance During the Early Months

From all we've just said, it might reasonably be inferred that parents who had enjoyed super marriages before the baby's arrival made super adjustments to new parenthood—but this conclusion would be misguided. Although a few families in our study did appear to have exceptionally strong marriages and make relatively smooth adjustments to the baby's arrival, this was far from the norm. Rather, even some of the best prepared parents found themselves quite surprised by how challenging the early months of new parenthood actually were. Most parents had been prewarned by friends, family, and occasionally by medical professionals that their sleep and sex lives were going to feel the strain, and so they had at least some forewarning when these changes materialized. Many, however, found the fatigue much more depleting than they had imagined, and this was doubly so when their babies struggled with colic or sleep difficulties, as many did. Furthermore, all the kinds of early adjustment difficulties that have been documented in the literature were present among families in our study as well: postpartum blues and depression, seen not only among mothers but also among fathers; frustrations over loss of independence and relationship intimacy; ambivalence about returning to work; anger about well-meaning advice from parents and in-laws that played into worries about parenting competencies.

What our study has added to this collective wisdom is that parents had also begun developing prototypical adjustment patterns and signature family dynamics as a coparenting team by 3 months postpartum. This was apparent in how they engaged the baby during the Lausanne Trilogue Play (LTP; Fivaz-Depeursinge & Corboz-Warnery, 1999) interactions, in how they collaborated to comfort their baby following the still-face challenges, in how they worked with one another in presenting their family to an outsider as they related the story of the day their baby was born, and in how they negotiated a stressful discussion of differences in perspective on who had done what since their baby arrived. Some couples showed difficulties in just one or two of these assessments (e.g., fathers may have revealed tendencies toward withdrawal only during who does what discussions, mothers may have revealed tendencies to ignore and override father's input only during the still-face soothing segment), whereas other couples showed some impairments and struggles across most or all of them. On the basis of encounters such as these, together with the thousands of other unassessed coparenting moments that had preceded our visit, parents had also developed a general sense of being supported (or less well supported) by their coparenting partner.

What did our assessments teach us about early coparenting, and what is the take-home message for parents and professionals? Most clearly, we would say that parents have already entered into a very powerful and self-sustaining set of dynamics, patterns, or habits by 3 months postpartum, even when such patterns are not readily evident to them. Baby cries and Mom is always the one to respond first. Father doesn't empty as much of the bottle during feedings as does Mother, and she reliably comments on this, making Father feel that she sees him as a second-rate caregiver. Father mentions to his mother that the baby has been having trouble going down at night, prompting Grandma to gently offer a tidbit of advice from her years of accumulated wisdom and causing Mother to feel inadequate herself and agitated with Father. Mother and Father disagree about putting baby down in the crib because she protests—so she avoids the crib altogether when Father isn't home, he uses it unfailingly when mother isn't home, and he accedes to her taking baby out of the crib after he has put her down when Mother is home (while inwardly fuming). Father somehow manages to avoid changing a single diaper for 10 days running, and Mother's frustration mounts until she lets loose one evening, causing Father to feel utterly unappreciated for having given away all his usual evening discretionary hours to attending to and playing with their baby. Frustrations mount and don't get discussed but prompt couples to turn in to bed at different times and find ways not to talk, cuddle, or be intimate for days and weeks at a time. When such patterns have become habit by 3 months, they tend not to fade and disappear with time. Relationship issues continue to suffer, coparenting dynamics move toward antagonism or disconnection, and the baby becomes the family's focal point for relating. In extreme cases, the baby is actually recruited into the three-person dynamic as a stabilizing force, enabling positive affect between mothers and fathers around baby-related issues but also serving as a diversion that prevents couples from working with one another and righting their own flagging relationship.

As this dynamic continues over time, mothers and fathers face substantial risk for abandoning their own relationship almost entirely to focus all their family energies on the child. Having different ideas about how best to socialize the baby and about what works best with her invariably takes root, parents do not coordinate their efforts and babies find themselves in very different worlds with mother and with father. Moreover, it isn't long before babies themselves come to recognize and react to these tensions between the parents: Some of Fivaz-Depeursinge's most recent work indicates that certain babies may already even show a traumatic-like sensitization and hypervigilance during triadic play during the earliest postpartum months (e.g., Fivaz-Depeursinge & Favez, 2006)! The result is a variety of untoward consequences that include anxiety, uncertainty about the trustworthiness of the family's foundation as a secure home base (even when secure attachments have developed with each parent individually), emotional and behavioral dysregulation when the child is together with both parents and forced to negotiate conflicting sets of emotional rules and behavioral standards, and an overreliance on social context rather than on the self when exploring and navigating social relations outside the family.

How do parents and professionals recognize when a negative trajectory is afoot? The fact that there was a fair degree of overlap among our different measures of coparenting distress at 3 months suggests that parents themselves may be pointedly aware of when they have reached a point of frustration, even when they have yet to articulate this to their partners. It also suggests that helping professionals should be able to uncover trails to these frustrations by talking to parents about their disparate perspectives and experiences or by capitalizing on observations of behavioral patterns present in the three-person interaction dynamic as points of entry for discussions with the family about their modus operandi. Parents, who are the first to know that they are frustrated, but who fear rocking the boat by airing discontent with their partner, might agree to set aside times to talk with one another about frustrations each is feeling so they can make some overtures toward change, and then talk again to see if changes they personally have tried to make have been detected by partners. Parents may also benefit from talking with knowledgeable infant–family professionals about ways to alter the patterns that have begun to develop at 3 months, for changing these patterns at 3 months, difficult though it can be, is infinitely easier than changing more ingrained patterns when the child is 1 year old or 2—or 15, for that matter.

The Coparenting Alliance at the Time of the Baby's First Birthday

By the child's first year of age, we found parents only too eager to talk about the stresses they were experiencing. Indeed, there seemed something almost therapeutic for parents just in talking to our staff about the many balls they were juggling and the different strains they were feeling. Both fathers and mothers had no problem regaling interviewers with stories of their families' worst moments but had to search longer and harder for examples of their family's golden moments. Their babies by this point had become very active partners in and elicitors of their family's relational dynamics, and their mobility allowed them to preferentially seek out specific experiences with one or the other parent and to trigger or alter family routines. Their more active participation in family life made experiences much more enriching, but also much less under parents' reliable control!

How were families adjusting? Our data substantiated findings from earlier studies (e.g., McHale, 1995; McHale, Lauretti, Talbot, & Pouquette, 2002) in documenting that families differed greatly in their tempo and rhythms. Some families' rhythms were distinctively child-centered, prompted by the leads and initiatives of the children. Others were just as unmistakably parent-centered, guided by the structure and preferences of the parenting adults. Parents too had coconstructed well-established rhythms and patterns between the two of them and had clear views about how and how well they did things. Although a rather small subgroup of fathers professed to hold nothing but admiration for their wives' parenting efforts and their family's adroitness in navigating the week, the remainder of the fathers and all of the mothers had rather different things to say. Indeed, we were impressed by how little difficulty parents had articulating things they'd like to change, including aspects of their partner's way with the baby.

Mothers' most common complaint at 12 months was that fathers were not as actively engaged in caring for their babies as the mothers needed them to be. Although a few mothers commented that they also felt that fathers needed to pay greater attention to the babies, this concern was actually relatively uncommon. The most widespread issue was mothers' belief that fathers were not pulling their weight in caregiving the baby—diapering, bathing, dealing with both routine and middle-of-the-night distress. At 3 months, a great number of mothers in our study had likewise been unhappy about the "Who Does What" of child care, but many of these women had been keeping their dissatisfaction largely to themselves. Not so at 12 months, when virtually all mothers who raised such concerns with us made it clear that their partners were quite aware of how they felt. Even so, many of their partners actually didn't let on that they were fully aware of how their wives had portrayed them. This was despite the fathers' having discussed their own wishes that mothers would lighten up a bit and not be as concerned with how things got done, as long as they got done.

This was by far the most common family presentation at 12 months: mothers expressing general discontent with fathers' level of caregiving involvement (and occasionally, with their general level of involvement with the family) and fathers simultaneously expressing sentiments that they were dedicating substantial time to the family at the expense of other things and not being valued for so doing. Mothers wanted fathers to step up without being asked to shoulder a more meaningful share of caregiving responsibility, to spend less time just "hanging out" with the baby and more time tending to the child's regular caregiving requirements. Fathers' focus, by contrast, was on the discrepancy between their own style and tempo and that of their partners. Many men couldn't understand why mothers insisted that care be given just so and on such a tight schedule. About one in four fathers also expressed concern with how mothers structured the baby's day, disciplined, or stimulated children. There were individual differences, of course, including a handful of families in which these general roles were reversed (such that fathers felt they were handling an inordinate share of the burden and mothers criticized the quality, not quantity, of father involvement). However, these were the exceptions.

Our own sense is that coparenting solidarity suffered in most families because parents were not as attuned to their partners' world views, concerns, and complaints as their partners needed them to be. Although parents felt their partners ought to realize how they felt and act supportively, and some insisted that they'd complained until they were blue in the face, most still believed that their partners just didn't quite get it. To be fair to mothers, many fathers who shared their perspectives with us told us that they had not actually confided in their partner about how they felt. Some of these men kept silent because they believed their wives would have felt personally attacked and wounded if they knew their concerns. Others kept mum because they fully expected mothers to simply discount their feedback as unjustified whining by someone who was as much a part of the problem as a part of the solution. As a result, many fathers with something to say simply ate their concerns. Compounding matters, relatively few fathers actually had fully accurate reads on their partner's sensibilities about the amount of work they were shouldering or about their wish that husbands become fuller partners in caring for their child. Recall Gottman's (1994) stress on the importance of attunement by men to their partners' presumptive worlds. Our study concurred that the more unaware fathers were, the more alienated mothers felt.

A take-home message for fathers of infants would seem to be that they should make efforts to cultivate greater awareness and appreciation for just how much family work their partners do and of how much their lack of proactive engagement in the work of parenting burdens their partners. Women do not appreciate men stepping in to help when they have reached the end of their ropes; they want fathers stepping in, unasked, long before the ends of their ropes even appear on the horizon. Many women even blanche at mention of the word *help*. They wonder how it was that someone appointed them family taskmaster and how they can get out from under this unsavory and exhausting role. This is certainly not true of all mothers, but it was a pervasive theme among the families in our study.

What are the perspectives of men? As summarized in chapter 8, although fathers do recognize that they do much less than their wives, they also see themselves as thoroughly engaged with their family. They worry not just about making significant enough financial contributions to their families but about many other things. They are just as concerned as mothers about day care quality and take stock of goings-on at day care centers when dropping babies off or picking them up. Not only do they think about their families while at work, but just like mothers, they often handle business on the child and family's behalf from the workplace, and just like employed mothers, they then assume parenting duties almost immediately upon returning home from work, upping their involvement further still on weekends. They crave sedate, slow-paced evenings with their families and admittedly become upset when they find absolutely no unimpeded time for themselves, and like women, they do not believe their partners understand or appreciate their felt burdens.

However, despite the fact that neither men nor women felt thoroughly validated by their coparenting partners, observational data from our study revealed something rather interesting. Mutual support between partners as they parented children together was greater in dual-income families than in families in which fathers were the sole source of family income. Notwithstanding the current rhetoric and opining about optimal family structures extolling the virtues of two-parent families, coparental functioning was most cooperative at 12 months when others besides the parents were shouldering part of the baby's care during the day. When mothers handle responsibilities for children all day and look to fathers to carry or at least lighten their burden during the evenings, fathers who work all day frequently find (from their perspective) little or no respite upon returning home. Under such conditions, the coparental system reveals the strain.

Although there are no sure-fire salvos for this circumstance, we advocate that both mothers and fathers make the time to ask about, consider, and validate one another's perspectives. Partner empathy can go a long way toward enabling positive and productive conversations about parenting differences. It also appears that sharing child-care responsibilities with relatives or others outside the family may help solidify coparental partnerships in some families. Much rests, of course, on the caliber of care provided by the nonparental caregivers, but there may be something to the "it takes a village," or collective caregiving, perspective after all, despite some of the heat that metaphor has taken.

The Toddler Years

Let's revisit points of interest relevant to coparenting through the rough-and-tumble toddler years. Thirty months actually turned out to be a rather interesting and challenging time for parents. Their children hadn't just begun toying with the word *no*; they had mastered its expression in thought, word, and deed. If there is a time when coparents need to be better attuned than when parenting 2-year-olds, it's hard to know when; only certain phases of early to mid-adolescence would seem to be a rival. As parents in our study told us loud and clear, they themselves often felt every bit as frustrated and exasperated as did their toddler. Of all the data in our study, we were probably most struck by the sheer number of families who told us that they, their partner, or both of them needed to work on their patience with the child and to try to cut down on their own mini-eruptions when their defenses were down and good judgment went by the wayside. We've seen the periodic Internet-based surveys claiming that the overwhelming majority of North American parents "fess up" to having a great many things they need to work on as parents. Even so, we were not quite prepared for just how ubiquitous parental frustration and short temperedness were during the toddler years.

Parents, of course, would probably say this doesn't surprise them in the least. To their credit, in fact, many parents were already actively working on managing their frustrations better when we saw them at 30 months. Some even felt they had turned the corner and that they were much more even tempered at the time we saw them than they had been a few months earlier. However, as many told us they had significant work to do, and a number felt really stymied when it was their partner's behavior that they most wanted to change, but didn't know how. Consider the following from Mark:

> "It's really hard to be supportive when I completely disagree with what she's doing. The worst are the hour-long battles over drinking a glass of milk. After Signe gave up the bottle, she became pretty indifferent to drinking milk. The doctor said 'Try yogurt,' but she's not a big fan of yogurt either. So I do realize that she has to get calcium. But I figure, if she drinks half a glass of milk, that's fine. We'll just give her more later. But for Francine, it has to be every single drop every time. So there ends up being screaming, crying, and threats every night. And I often get pulled into it, which I hate. Sometimes it takes all my energy not to yell 'She's done already. Just let her be!' But I know all that would do is prolong the agony further. So I'll usually just try to avoid the drama and zone out in front of the TV while they work it out. It's not going to change. I really wish Francine would lighten up on the milk thing, but she won't budge no matter how many times I tell her how I feel about it."

Mark's lament was far from unusual. Most parents had some version of this scenario. Mom didn't like Dad's making empty promises (e.g., promising a trip to the zoo, a favorite fast food restaurant, or an amusement park) that he had no intention of keeping—which Dad used as a bargaining tool to get their son to take baths, eat when he refused, get ready for bed, and the like. Dad couldn't abide all the empty threats Mom made daily, which he believed were not only making their daughter fearful but also teaching her that adults couldn't be relied upon to follow through. Mom was upset at how differently Dad handled their son's angst when she left on a business trip than she did when he was away: She wanted him to do as she did, reassuring their son and helping him mark off days on the calendar until she returned, whereas he felt that the boy was better off not being inundated by reminders of her temporary absence, insisting that their son was actually just fine as soon as Mom had been gone for a half hour or so. Such differences are probably present at times in every family, but the difference is that some parents make time to talk together when they differ, whereas others keep silent and simply vow to do the opposite of their partner when the next opportunity presents itself, hoping that somehow, magically, the partner will take notice and model after them. As our observational, interview, and self-report data revealed, however, this latter eventuality is rather unlikely in low-solidarity families, in which the modus operandi is often two distinctly different parenting stances that do not mesh well. Over time, as we learned, low levels of solidarity begin to affect children.

Extrapolating from the example Mark provides about his coparenting with Francine, we can see another potential problem that surfaces in many low-solidarity families. Note Mark's posture that, when things spiral out of control between Francine and Signe, his stance is to retreat into the woodwork rather than stepping up to help, thus depriving Signe of a potential resource during a time of emotional distress. Throughout this book, we have emphasized the importance of a unified front between parents and intimated that children are not well served when parents allow themselves to be played one against the other by the toddler. Not sufficiently emphasized, however, has been the valuable role that sympathetic parents can play in helping their young children regulate intense feelings and emotions toward the other. Back in Chapter 1, we made brief reference to the ideas of Stanley Greenspan (1998), who maintained that third-party parents play a fundamentally important role during their child's "Oedipal years" in helping children to manage ambivalent feelings toward the active parent. In low coparenting solidarity families, however, fathers or mothers who regularly "check out" during parenting episodes in which they disagree with the partner are robbing children of this resource of relying on the second parent to help them regulate intense emotions. This pattern of emotional unavailability by coparents in distressed family alliances is not just unique to and important during the ostensible Oedipal phase. It can be observed even during earliest infancy in the LTP enactments of some distressed families. For example, while in the LTP's third-party role, parents in distressed alliances as early as 3–4 months are sometimes observed to ignore babies even when the babies have explicitly sought to reference them during highly stimulating play with the other (active) parent. Fivaz-Depeursinge and colleagues have (2007) posited that such micro-interactions may be clinically significant, signaling a parent's propensity to retreat from the family triad and to withdraw emotional support when the partner and child are engaged. When the child cannot rely on that parent to help coregulate her precarious affective state in a moment of need, the child is much more likely to become *dys*regulated.

By contrast, in families where couples have coconstructed a supportive system and come to provide regularly consistent communications to children, parents are far less likely to ignore partners or children during moments of emotional need. Indeed, it is by virtue of the solidarity of the couple's alliance that a parent is able to step away from his or her usual no-nonsense stance to make reparations with a child who has managed to get into a precarious state with the other parent. Such conflict situations are part of every family's experience, and the way they are typically resolved may make an important difference in shaping toddlers' regulatory capacities through time. It is important that parents and clinicians understand the difference between parents who sabotage their partners' efforts with children because they distrust the partner's parenting and parents who feel comfortable intervening as needed to help correct a deteriorating situation between the partner and child without jeopardizing the frame of a historically supportive coparenting alliance. Among families who have managed to attain this latter sense of mutual support and solidarity, the coparenting alliance can truly be a resource for supporting mothers' and fathers' individual parenting efforts (cf. Floyd, Gilliom, & Costigan, 1998; Margolin, Gordis, & John, 2001). Consequently, children from such families are doing well, often exceptionally well. In our study, toddlers from families for whom observational, interview, and self-report data signaled high levels of support and solidarity were rated by adults as showing fewer behavior problems and better pre-academic skills, were more knowledgeable about different emotions, and were less, not more, dependent on adults when attempting to regulate their behavior and emotions while frustrated. More generally, when adults provide an environment that communicates clear messages about adherence to family rules and limits, about the permissibility and value of emotional expression, and about expectations for age-appropriate strivings toward independence and self-reliance, children can feel grounded, supported, and encouraged.

Contrast these experiences with those of toddlers whose parents work at cross-purposes. Such children learn that rules are capricious and arbitrary. They find their expression of emotions to be oddly potent in certain situations but discounted or punished in others. Many find that gauging different adults' emotions provides more valuable survival value about acceptable action than does moving from their own internal experience, and children discover that adults can be goaded into altering environmental contingencies or played one against the other. Although toddlers enjoy immediate gratification from manipulating parents into ignoring bedtime or mealtime rules when the other parent is absent, indulging them at the shopping mall, or acquiescing in one of a dozen other ways, they also begin owing dues to the beneficent parent and learning that the absent parent's authority is suspect. As discussed in chapters 6 and 8, learning that one set of adaptations is appropriate when one parent is present whereas a different set of rules reigns when the parent is absent can have a singularly disruptive effect on moral development. Children are taught to be secretive, to scan the environment for cues concerning things acceptable in certain situations that are taboo in others, and to recognize opportunities to bend and break rules.

It is important once again here to assure readers that our study was not populated by "super coparents," who never stumbled and who always stuck up for one another. It is doubtful that any of the participants in our study, even those who had the highest solidarity evaluations in the sample, would characterize themselves as such. Coparenting disputes were regular, everyday occurrences. Every parent had times when they found themselves correcting a partner's intervention with the child or comforting the child when a fatigued partner had intervened a bit too harshly. Parents sometimes granted their children special privileges, and most found themselves saying something critical about their partner to the child, at least on rare occasions when their defenses were down. The difference, the key difference, is that in some families, these kinds of activities became the fabric of everyday experience, whereas in others, they were occasional blips against a background of support, solidarity, and open communication. Jason provided some insights into some adjustments their family had made over time:

> "Not long ago, I would say things like 'What did your Mommy tell you?' and 'You know Mommy doesn't like it when you do that.' I thought I was being supportive, but Mary told me that when I said things like that, I sent Josalyn the message that *Mommy* didn't like what she was doing but Daddy could care less. And she was right, of course. Often when I said that, I did really disagree with her, and I was biting my tongue. So now, when we discipline her, I make it a point to say 'You know Mommy and Daddy don't like you doing that,' to signal that we're together about it. I still don't always agree with Mary, but the difference now is that I'll wait and talk to her about it later to explain my view and see if we can lighten up a little or do things differently. I don't like putting Josalyn into a position where she ends up escalating or behaving defiantly because she's just too tired and worn down, and neither of us is listening to her."

This is one example of the kinds of tangible adaptations that couples made. Most important, in this case, was Jason and Mary's willingness to discuss openly their discontent with what the other was doing, in a manner that encouraged change rather than one or both of them digging in their heels. Throughout this closing chapter, we have emphasized the importance of such communication and regular conversations between parents, but we've also tried to be realistic in pointing out that, for many couples, initiating such conversations in the hopes of beginning an ongoing dialogue about coparenting would truly be treading new ground. Readers may remember that many of the parents we spoke with confided that they were honestly not certain what would happen if they were to share their perspectives with their partners. The most commonly expressed fears were either that (a) sharing their views of what they thought the partner was doing that was creating problems for the child would unnecessarily upset their husband or wife or that (b) opening up and explaining why they thought things needed to be different was a bad idea because they would only end up getting discounted and blamed.

To the extent that these fears exist in families, gearing up for such conversations can be difficult. As we've emphasized, productive conversations about parenting are most likely to occur in families when:

- Parents establish a habit of talking openly and honestly about their differences.
- Parents trust that their partner will be sensitive to and listen to their views.
- Parents come to value, rather than feel negatively about, different roles they play with their children and how their children relate differently to them and to their partners at different times.

The couple's history of sharing their fears and vulnerabilities with one another will hence be an important predictor of whether couples will be able to launch parenting dialogues before, or soon after, the baby is born. However, even having regular parenting conversations, although perhaps the best inroad to creating an effective coparenting alliance, will not always be enough. For parents must inevitably sometimes overrule one another, have a discussion about handling the child's behavior in front of the child despite best intentions to keep such discussions private, or deal honestly with a child's puzzlement about why the parent behaved in a manner that was at odds with the parent's usual stance about how things should be handled. Having established a habit of talking regularly about parenting rules and decisions does give mothers and fathers opportunities to review what has been working and what has not, and it also affords an outlet for parents to air their emotional reactions to how the other parent intervened when the intervention rubbed them the wrong way, and to advocate for different approaches the parent believes would be in the child's and family's best interests. But talk alone is not always enough to spark an accord, and impasses may be reached nonetheless.

For these reasons, couples often find value in professional assistance when they have been unable to engage with one another in such dialogues or need help getting unstuck when impasses have been reached. Skills fostered in communication workshops such as those discussed in chapter 9 (e.g., the importance of soft start-ups) can often prove helpful in gearing up for parenting conversations when fear is holding parents back. However, couples can and should also turn to infant–family mental health professionals when they are experiencing coparenting problems. This can be an appealing option in families in which at least one of the partners is not ready to self-identify as needing a marital tune-up, but in which the parents have begun to realize, and concur, that they need some help developing an effective working alliance as coparents.

Infant mental health professionals themselves have recently begun cultivating an increasing comfort and familiarity with triadic and family models and interventions, a trend that seems certain to continue. At the same time, however, a number of other practitioners in the field who were dyadically trained will not be as accustomed to thinking outside the bounds of mother–baby relationships. Hence, many agency professionals and private practitioners who already work with infants, toddlers, and their families may themselves feel some hesitancy in prompting couples' discussions of parenting beliefs. Such hesitancies can be particularly acute when clinicians are parents themselves. However, as most interventionists know, growth and development derive from struggles with moderate levels of emotional tension, and meaningful alteration of accustomed patterns and habits are possible only in the context of both emotional support and emotional challenge (Minuchin & Fishman, 1981). Well-meaning couples often fall into the trap of avoiding dissonance to protect one another from feared impacts of negative emotions, rendering straight talk about individual experience difficult, if not impossible (Jones & Lindblad-Goldberg, 2002). For this reason, consultations and brief therapies can provide couples with a safe place to air differing perspectives and to question their old methods and experiment with new strategies. In the ideal, such interventions would assist couples in formulating more elaborate and mutually agreed understandings of both their child and the central roles they themselves play in supporting the child's social and emotional development.

Of course, interventions only succeed when both parties really wish to build something together. If either parent is truly not open to change or is inflexible about accommodating, even the best professional's hands are tied. Fortunately, most parents—including a great many in high conflict separating couples (e.g., Togliatti & Lavadera, 2006)—are able to agree that they do wish to do what's best by their child, even though they don't always know what that is. This is the reason why we have advocated working directly with couples on strengthening their coparental alliance rather than relying exclusively on "trickle-down" effects from marital education or intervention. Addressing coparenting challenges directly and building consensus stands a very good chance to affect positive family change, particularly when both partners can be helped to understand how greater organization, accommodation, and emotional connection with one another in their coparenting efforts will enable them to support their children's drive toward and capacities for self-regulation and social–emotional competence.

We have one final note for helping professionals. This is rewarding work, but it is also very demanding. Couples do not need advice on which of them is "right" as much as they need help developing mutual insight and reflection about how each of them responds emotionally to their child and aid in helping to connect with, validate, and support one another. The exception, of course, is when neither parent is accurately reading and responding to the child's signals. In such cases, more intensive effort in promoting parenting capacities and fostering intuitive parenting behaviors is called for. Also, although parents of toddlers and young children can and do often profit from learning explicit strategies such as those advocated and taught by proponents of positive behavior management (e.g., Fox, Dunlap, & Cushing, 2002), the points developed in this book remain the same: If one parent is not on board, the most faithful adherence to any "behavior change" regimen by the other parent is doomed to failure. The key is building the alliance first, and the first step for doing so will be diagnosing where major differences lie and what's not being talked about effectively.

Summary and Conclusions

During the final months of our project, we got in touch one final time with nearly all of the 46 families who had contributed to the Families Through Time study at each of its four major assessment phases. We shared with both mothers and fathers what we thought we had learned about their family, explained what we had seen as their family's high and low points, and asked whether our assessments coincided with their own experience, now in retrospect. We also asked each parent separately what, from his or her perspective, had been the rockiest time for the couple's alliance as coparents and what had helped them make it through. The answers we received were almost as diverse as were the parents themselves. This, to us, underscored the point that there *is* no one best path and that each family finds its own way within their own unique life experiences and contexts.

As to what helped, many parents cited their own relationship as having been a critical asset, distinguishing between their affinity for one another as partners and their work together as coparents. Some discussed the importance of friends and family members as confidantes, whereas others said that they had found counseling to help them make it through difficult patches. Five couples discussed how difficult the transition had been after the child's baby brother or sister was born, because the second baby's temperament was much more difficult than the first and the couple had been ill prepared to manage things. Two of these couples felt that as the second child developed better self-regulatory skills, their family got back on an even keel, whereas the other three indicated that they were still struggling with the second child's impact on their family. Two parents spoke explicitly about how their faith had helped them overcome difficult periods. Two others told us that it had been an accurate diagnosis of a toddler's disabilities or mental health issues that had proven to be a turning point for them. Two parents described how the coparenting relationship had improved as they came to better understand more about parenting in their partner's own cultural group. Over a dozen parents told us that the regularity of their Families Through Time study contact visits and the periodic invitations to revisit their relationship as partners had been valuable to them.

These latter reports suggest one unintended consequence of this longitudinal study: Heightening parents' awareness of their coparental alliance prompted certain parents to think more focally about how they were coparenting than they otherwise might have, had they never met us. We want to reiterate that we provided no therapeutic services to families of any kind, although we did help parents with referrals to coordinated child care services, mental health professionals, or other community resources on those occasions when they asked for help. We would like to think that, for at least some families, the Families Through Time project served as an informal auxiliary resource that helped them refocus when they experienced some strains. For others, we probably did not play such a role, although we were heartened by the ongoing willingness of over 90% of the couples that we approached about continuing through all assessments to stay with us. This valuing of connection indicates to us that family consultation services would be a valuable asset to families of infants and young children. As proposed in chapter 9, Robin Dion (2005; Dion, Devaney, & Hershey, 2003) has offered several creative ideas about ways to develop and institutionalize such programming within existing infrastructures and systems of community care.

We also want to comment on the insight of parents who felt their coparenting alliance strengthened as they learned more about their partner's native culture. The number of North American children in biracial and multicultural families is skyrocketing, and we know precious little about what makes for the most effective coparenting alliances in such families. Until such a time as research can inform us about the unique shadings of culture in the transition to coparenthood, practitioners should be sensitive to the unique and heightened coparenting challenges faced by many multicultural families. Although we are already making some headway toward understanding and appreciating paths to coparenting solidarity in adoptive, gay and lesbian, step-, multigenerational, and foster family systems (McHale, Khazan et al., 2002), much remains to be learned about coparenting dynamics in the multitude of adaptive family structures into which infants and young children bring love, joy, and challenge.

In the end, our study taught us that creating supportive, trusting and consistent coparenting alliances is far from easy, but it also confirmed that when parents succeed in doing so, their children unquestionably profit. Over time, children's realization that they can count on a predictable, stable, and supportive family context headed by parents or cocaregivers who stand behind one another comes to reap benefits. Perhaps most important, it helps them to navigate later challenges with greater ease, thanks both to their confidence in their family's cohesiveness and to the skills they have learned along the way. The road is indeed a bumpy one, but we hope that reading the stories, challenges, and adaptations of the families who contributed to this project have the wished-for impact of heightening readers' own sensitivities to the vital importance of this alliance in their own families. Few aspects of family adaptation are as important.

References

Cassidy, J., Woodhouse, S., & Hoffman, K. (2006, July). *Remembering the pain of the past: Adult representations of childhood experiences and related caregiving behaviors*. Paper presented at the 10th World Congress of the World Association for Infant Mental Health, Paris.

Dienhart, A., & Daly, K. (1997). Men and women cocreating father involvement in a nongenerative culture. In A. Hawkins & D. Dollahite (Eds.), *Generative fathering: Beyond deficit perspectives* (pp. 147–164). Thousand Oaks, CA: Sage.

Dion, R. (2005). Healthy marriage programs: Learning what works. *The Future of Children, 15*, 139–156.

Dion, R., Devaney, B., & Hershey, A. (2003, November). Toward interventions to strengthen relationships and support healthy marriage among unwed parents. Manuscript prepared for *Vision 2004: What is the future of marriage?* and presented at the 65th Annual Conference of the National Council on Family Relations, Washington, DC.

Fivaz-Depeursinge, E., & Corboz-Warnery, A. (1999). *The primary triangle: A developmental systems view of mothers, fathers, and infants*. New York: Basic Books.

Fivaz-Depeursinge, E., Corboz-Warnery, A., & Keren, M. (2004). The primary triangle: Treating infants in their families. In A. Sameroff, S. McDonough, & K. Rosenblum (Eds.), *Treating parent–infant problems: Strategies for intervention* (pp. 123–151). New York: Guilford Press.

Fivaz-Depeursinge, E., & Favez, N. (2006). Exploring triangulation in infancy: Two contrasted cases. *Family Process*, *45*, 3–18.

Fivaz-Depeursinge, E., Frascarolo, F., Lopes, F., Dimitrova, N., & Favez, N. (2007). Parent–child role-reversal in trilogue play: Case studies of trajectories from pregnancy to toddlerhood. *Attachment and Human Development*, *9*, 17–31.

Floyd, F. J., Gilliom, L. A., & Costigan, C. L. (1998). Marriage and the parenting alliance: Longitudinal prediction of change in parenting perceptions and behaviors. *Child Development, 69*(5), 1461–1479.

Fox, L., Dunlap, G., & Cushing, L. (2002). Early intervention, positive behavior support, and transition to school. *Journal of Emotional and Behavioral Disorders, 10*(3), 149–157.

Gottman, J. (1994). *Why marriages succeed or fail*. New York: Simon & Schuster.

Greenspan, S. (1988). The second other: The role of the father in early personality formation and the dyadic–phallic phase of development. In S. Cath, A. Gurwitt, & J. Ross (Eds.), *Father and child: Developmental and clinical perspectives* (pp. 123–138). Cambridge, MA: Blackwell.

Jones, C. W., & Lindblad-Goldberg, M. (2002). Ecosystemic structural family therapy. In F. W. Kaslow (Ed.), *Comprehensive handbook of psychotherapy: Vol. 3. Interpersonal/humanistic/existential* (pp. 3–33). New York: Wiley.

Lewis, J. (1989). *The birth of the family: An empirical inquiry*. Philadelphia: Brunner/Mazel.

Lewis, J., Owen, M., & Cox, M. (1988). The transition to parenthood III: Incorporation of the child into the family. *Family Process*, *27*, 411–421.

Margolin, G., Gordis, E. B., & John, R. S. (2001). Coparenting: A link between marital conflict and parenting in two-parent families. *Journal of Family Psychology, 15*, 3–21.

McHale, J. P. (1995). Coparenting and triadic interactions during infancy: The roles of marital distress and child gender. *Developmental Psychology, 31*, 985–996.

McHale, J., Khazan, I., Erera, P., Rotman, T., DeCourcey, W., & McConnell, M. (2002). Coparenting in diverse family systems. In M. Bornstein (Ed.), *Handbook of parenting* (2nd ed.; pp. 75–107). Mahwah, NJ: Erlbaum.

Minuchin, S., & Fishman, H. C. (1981). *Family therapy techniques*. Cambridge, MA: Harvard University Press.

Schulz, M. S., Cowan, C. P., & Cowan, P. A. (2006). Promoting healthy beginnings: A randomized controlled trial of a preventive intervention to preserve marital quality during the transition to parenthood. *Journal of Consulting and Clinical Psychology, 74*, 20–31.

Togliatti, M., & Lavadera, L. (2006, July). *The evaluation of family alliances with conflictual families*. Paper presented at the 10th World Congress of the World Association for Infant Mental Health, Paris.

About the Authors

Amy Alberts (MS/ABD, Tufts University, 2006, Applied Child Development) is currently a doctoral candidate and research assistant at the Institute for Applied Research in Youth Development, Medford, MA. She works with the 4-H Study of Positive Youth Development and collaborates at the Brazelton Institute, Children's Hospital Boston.

Valerie M. Bellas (MA, Hunter College, 1996; ABD, Clark University, 2006, Clinical Psychology) is currently a doctoral candidate at Clark University, Worcester, MA.

Julia M. Berkman (BA, Brown University, 1997; PhD, Clark University, 2005, Clinical Psychology) is currently in private practice at Child and Family Psychological Services, Inc., Norwood, MA.

Meagan Carleton Parmley (PhD, Drexel University, 2006, Clinical Psychology) is currently a postdoctoral fellow at the Cognitive Behavioral Institute of Albuquerque, NM.

Wendy Marian DeCourcey (MS, Portland State University, 1999; PhD, Clark University, 2004, Clinical Psychology) is currently a research analyst at the Office of Planning Research and Evaluation of the Administration for Children and Families at the Department of Health and Human Services in Washington, DC.

Christina Kazali (PhD, Clark University, 2002, Clinical Psychology) completed her postdoctoral training at the University of California, San Francisco, with specialty training in child trauma. She currently works fulltime in the private sector in Ballard, CA.

Inna Khazan (MA, Clark University, 2000; PhD, Clark University, 2005, Clinical Psychology) is currently a clinical psychologist in private practice.

Regina Kuersten-Hogan (PhD, Clark University, 1998, Clinical Psychology) is currently a visiting assistant professor of Psychology at Assumption College, Worcester, MA.

Allison Lauretti (PhD, Clark University, 2002, Clinical Psychology) is currently an instructor in psychology at Harvard Medical School, and a staff psychologist at

Children's Hospital Boston. Dr. Lauretti maintains a private practice specializing in the treatment of children and families in the metro Boston area.

Melanie McConnell (PhD, University of Vermont, 2006, Psychology) is currently a psychologist at British Columbia Children's Hospital in Vancouver, BC, Canada.

James P. McHale (MS, Tulane University, 1985, Developmental Psychology; PhD, University of California at Berkeley, 1992, Clinical Psychology) is past director of clinical training at Clark University (2000–2003). He trained as a family therapist at both the Palo Alto Veteran's Administration Medical Center and the Philadelphia Child and Family Therapy Training Center and is now a professor of psychology and program coordinator of the University of South Florida St. Petersburg Division of Psychology, Social Work, and Philosophy, and director of the Family Study Center, at the University of South Florida St. Petersburg.

Jean A. Talbot (MA, Mount Holyoke College, 1995; PhD, Clark University, 2001, Clinical Psychology) is in full-time practice as a clinical psychologist in the primary care clinics of Rochester General Hospital. She is a clinical senior instructor in psychiatry at the University of Rochester Medical Center.